FROM RAJ TO REPUBLIC

SOUTH ASIA IN MOTION

EDITOR
  Thomas Blom Hansen

EDITORIAL BOARD
  Sanjib Baruah
  Anne Blackburn
  Satish Despande
  Faisal Devji
  Christophe Jaffrelot
  Naveeda Khan
  Stacey Leigh Pigg
  Mrinalini Sinha
  Ravi Vasudevan

FROM RAJ TO REPUBLIC

Sovereignty, Violence, and Democracy in India

SUNIL PURUSHOTHAM

STANFORD UNIVERSITY PRESS
STANFORD, CALIFORNIA

STANFORD UNIVERSITY PRESS
Stanford, California

©2021 by the Board of Trustees of the Leland Stanford Junior University. All rights reserved.

No part of this book may be reproduced or transmitted in any form or by any means, electronic or mechanical, including photocopying and recording, or in any information storage or retrieval system without the prior written permission of Stanford University Press.

Printed in the United States of America on acid-free, archival-quality paper

Library of Congress Cataloging-in-Publication Data

Names: Purushotham, Sunil, author.

Title: From raj to republic : sovereignty, violence, and democracy in India / Sunil Purushotham.

Other titles: South Asia in motion.

Description: Stanford, California : Stanford University Press, 2021. | Series: South Asia in motion | Includes bibliographical references and index.

Identifiers: LCCN 2020021114 (print) | LCCN 2020021115 (ebook) | ISBN 9781503613256 (cloth) | ISBN 9781503614543 (paperback) | ISBN 9781503614550 (ebook)

Subjects: LCSH: Political violence—India—History—20th century. | Democracy—India—History—20th century. | Constitutional history—India. | India—Politics and government—1947-

Classification: LCC DS480.84 .P895 2021 (print) | LCC DS480.84 (ebook) | DDC 954.04/2—dc23

LC record available at https://lccn.loc.gov/2020021114

LC ebook record available at https://lccn.loc.gov/2020021115

Cover map: 1947 map of Partition of India and Pakistan, Phyllis Newman Antique Prints. Paper with burnt edge, iStockPhoto.

Cover design: Rob Ehle

Typeset by Kevin Barrett Kane in 10.75/15 Adobe Caslon Pro

CONTENTS

INTRODUCTION
Sovereignty, Violence, and Democracy, 1946–52   1

1   Azad Hyderabad in the Age of Empire and Nationalism   10

2   The Battle for Hyderabad   76

3   Foundational Violence: State and Society in Partitioned Punjab   127

4   Nation and Narration: Testimony, Citizenship, and Sovereignty   159

5   An Indian Yan'an: Telangana, 1946–52   182

6   The Camp and the Citizen   225

EPILOGUE
From Raj to Republic, 1946–52   247

Abbreviations Used in Notes   253
Notes   255
Bibliography   311
Index   333

FROM RAJ TO REPUBLIC

INTRODUCTION
Sovereignty, Violence, and Democracy, 1946–52

BETWEEN 1946 AND 1952, the British Raj, the world's largest colony, was transformed into the Republic of India, the world's largest democracy. Independence, the Constituent Assembly Debates, the founding of the Republic, and India's first universal franchise general election took place amid the violence and displacement of the Partition, the uncertain and contested integration of the princely states, and the forceful quelling of internal dissent and revolutionary challenges to the Indian state. This book tells the story of these transformations as a history of sovereignty and democracy in India. It investigates the ways in which violence constituted a postcolonial regime of sovereignty and shaped the historical development of democracy in India at the foundational moment of decolonization and national independence.

The book's three case studies—the princely state of Hyderabad, the partitioned Punjab, and revolutionary Telangana—were key sites of a multicentric subcontinental event of violent transformation. In emphasizing the eventfulness of this period, the book attends to ruptures, departures, and structural changes. Historical events are not single moments in time but have internal temporalities: sequences marked by opening ruptures or breaks, periods of uncertainty and dislocation, and, ultimately, closure.[1]

This event and the processes of its suturing were foundational of a new regime of sovereignty in India between 1946 and 1952. A regime of sovereignty conceptualizes the legal, territorial, and institutional dimensions of sovereignty as arising out of historically contingent power relations between state and society. Violence and coercive force were constitutive of the contractual and negotiated dimensions of sovereign power at the founding moment of the Indian Republic.[2] *From Raj to Republic* takes the linking of sovereign power to state structures as resulting from "practices dispersed throughout, and across, societies."[3] Sovereignty is understood here as dynamic and relational, emerging out of an "unstable blend of law and violence."[4] The book connects elite and subaltern activities and links top-down processes of historical change to bottom-up ones: constitutional and institutional transformations were constitutively linked to the domain of popular politics and the violent mediation of relations between state and society.

The partition of Britain's Indian empire into the two new nation-states of India and Pakistan is now widely recognized as a world historical event of cataclysmic violence. Understandably, scholarly accounts have focused largely on the divided provinces of Punjab and Bengal. This has obscured significant developments that occurred elsewhere in the subcontinent. In recent years, moreover, the story of Partition's violence and its lasting trauma has come to eclipse that of freedom in various forms of collective memory. By approaching violence and freedom as mutually constitutive, as Shruti Kapila has suggested, this book examines instead the ways in which violence generated and conditioned the historical development of democracy and democratic structures in India.[5] Violence provided the context for, and gave meaning to, India's founding moment.[6] I attend to the creation of new power relations and social hierarchies in the course of the making of a national, territorial, republican, and liberal polity in India.

From Raj to Republic consists of six chapters in three sections, beginning with the princely state of Hyderabad, followed by the partitioned Punjab, and ending with the peasant revolution in Telangana. Eight days after the Partition Plan was adopted in June 1947, the Nizam of Hyderabad declared that he would "resume the status of an independent sovereign."

Under the British Raj's system of paramountcy, Hyderabad was considered the "premier" state among the nearly six hundred Indian states, commonly referred to as the princely states. The Nizam was a sovereign monarch not only within his territories but within the wider British imperial system.[7] The Raj's imperial regime of sovereignty—parceled, layered, and uncodified—was archetypal of the global order of modern empires.[8] India was thus exemplary of the way in which new regimes of national sovereignty were created and consolidated at the end of empire in the middle decades of the twentieth century.[9]

Sovereign kingship, from the British Crown to the hundreds of Indian monarchs, was a key pillar of the Raj's imperial regime of sovereignty. In the decades prior to 1947, Mir Osman Ali Khan, the seventh and last Nizam of Hyderabad, took efforts to assert his sovereign prerogatives, secure his territorial claims, shore up the legitimacy of his dynasty, and modernize his state through administrative and constitutional reforms, economic initiatives, industrial projects, and institution-building efforts like Osmania University. He sought to secure the legal standing of his state within the domain of imperial constitutionalism and cultivated an international reputation as a leader of Muslims. Hyderabad came to be seen, despite its demography, as a Muslim state. Hyderabad and the princely states were central to interwar constitutional developments, to the failure of a federal solution for a united India, and, ultimately, to the postwar sprint toward Partition.

The case of Hyderabad highlights the multiplicity of non-national conceptions of sovereignty in late colonial India.[10] The 1935 Government of India Act envisioned a Federation of India that would unite British India and princely India by codifying and affirming the sovereignty of the princely states within a written constitution. The Indian National Congress responded by making opposition to the federation a central plank of their platform, by launching *satyagraha* in Hyderabad and other princely states throughout India, and by demanding a sovereign constituent assembly. Hyderabad and the princely states were thus central to the republican turn of the Indian National Congress in the later 1930s and, ultimately, to the communal settlement of 1947. Claims to popular sovereignty and constituent power developed out of highly consequential interwar debates over federation and the future of dynastic kingship and monarchical authority. When Jawaharlal Nehru declared to the Constituent Assembly in December 1946 that "a free India can be nothing but a republic," he referred directly to the princely states.[11]

Hyderabad would, in 1947–48, become the third front of Partition, where the Hindu-Muslim question and the question of sovereign kingship in a democratic India came together in an acute and consequential fashion. As a Hindu-majority state ruled by a Muslim dynasty and completely landlocked in the heart of peninsular India, an independent Hyderabad posed a territorial and ideological challenge to the national project at the moment of decolonization and independence. India's nationalist leadership, especially following the Partition, came to see the consolidation of the nation-state's territory as a matter of paramount importance. Between August 1947 and September 1948, Hyderabad became a site of violent contestation, and the Nizam took his case all the way to the United Nations Security Council. The battle for Hyderabad was fought by a wide array of actors across the Deccan and culminated with the annexation of the state by the Indian Army via the "Police Action" of September 1948. The Congress commandeered and redeployed the coercive institutions of the colonial state in service of the national project. In the year leading up to the Police Action, the government of India instituted an economic blockade of Hyderabad, and provincial governments raised tens of thousands of "home guards" and stationed police along the borders of the Nizam's dominions.

Yet in transitioning from an anticolonial mass movement into a ruling party, the Congress sought to consolidate state power, not by arrogating and monopolizing violence, but by dispersing violence into the body politic. Partisan cadres from the Congress, the Hyderabad State Congress, the Socialist Party, the Arya Samaj, and the Hindu Mahasabha joined the Andhra Mahasabha and the Communist Party of India (CPI) in an armed struggle against the Nizam. In this effort they were aided by provincial ministries controlled by the Congress, as well as local police forces. The Indian nation-state thus achieved a sovereign presence in the Deccan through ambivalent efforts to incite, control, and subdue violence. Feeding off the anxieties and pathologies arising out of the Partition, nationalist leaders and the nationalist press framed Hyderabad's bid for independence as an existential threat to the nation. In doing so, they conflated the Nizam's rule with the domination of a Hindu majority by a Muslim minority. The Police Action precipitated an event of violence directed at Hyderabad's Muslims, which was viewed by India's nationalist leaders as a legitimate articulation of popular sovereignty, a foundational coming together of the people and the state. The Police Action was an important event in the making of the territorial nation-state and worked to constitute national majorities and minorities at a foundational moment of the Republic. Hyderabad, like the other princely states, was provisionally absorbed into the Indian Union, and was dissolved at a later date.

In light of these developments in peninsular India—the internalizing of Hyderabad within a new national formation—the book turns to the Punjab, where an event of civil war and ethnic cleansing transformed an imperial space into an international border and gave rise to a new national regime of sovereignty and citizenship. The two chapters on Punjab are based primarily on the archive of the East Punjab Liaison Agency (EPLA). The EPLA was established in September 1947, at the peak of violence and dislocation, to work with the Military Evacuation Organization on the exchange of population between India and Pakistan. The EPLA was tasked with identifying, protecting, and transporting Indian subjects in Pakistan's territory. The sovereignty of the new Indian nation-state was staked on the creation and maintenance of the new international border, a process that was grounded in sovereign claims over populations and individual bodies, including, and perhaps especially, those located in Pakistani territory.[12] These claims were contested and ambivalent. *From Raj to Republic* examines the experiences of Punjab's subaltern groups—lower castes, tribals, Christians, converts, prisoners, abducted women—to illuminate how social hierarchies were reanimated by new ideological frameworks as they were inscribed and internalized within a new national regime of sovereignty and citizenship. Violence provided the pretext and context for originary invocations not only of state sovereignty but of citizenship. Partition and its aftermath were crucial elements in the forging of a new social contract after August 1947.[13] Displaced peoples and other victims made claims upon the state as a matter of right: claims to security, restitution, and welfare.[14]

In the decades after 1947, the Indian state sought to convert the violence, horror, and betrayal of Partition into tragic yet heroic narratives of national struggle and freedom.[15] The EPLA archive contains a number of first-personal testimonial narratives—"statements"—that were created through the encounter between vulnerable subjects (including "recovered women") and state officials in the context of the refugee camp. This speech of Partition survivors—its provocation, appropriation, and concealment—constitutes a domain of ambivalent mediation between histories of individual experience and those of sovereignty and democracy.[16] By making explicit claims upon state resources and tasking the state with rectifying wrongs, these testimonial narratives provide a glimpse into practices of citizenship, the grammar of sovereignty, and fraught relations of power at a foundational moment of Indian democracy. Narratives of victimization and vulnerability invited the state to undo harm, giving rise to a new regime of state sovereignty premised on the protection of and care for life and the restoration of a normative social order. Through processes of translation and bureaucratic mediation, the original speech acts became constituent strands of a national master narrative in which refugee "relief and rehabilitation" served as a key marker of state legitimacy. In this way, the regime of sovereignty that arose out of Partition was cast as peace, rather than betrayal, and the suffering of survivors as a call for collective action and discipline.

From 1946 until 1951, peasant revolutionaries in the Telangana districts of Hyderabad State, led by the Andhra Mahasabha and the CPI, battled landlords, the Nizam, and the Indian Union. They fought for *praja rajyam*, people's rule. This entailed a complete remaking of rural social relations: the exile of landlords and state officials, social dignity for lower castes, and a redistribution of land based on the ideal of "land to the tiller." Telangana was at the center of the wider subaltern upsurge that swept India after the Second World War.[17] "In its character and political objectives," Hamza Alavi noted in 1965, "it was the most revolutionary peasant movement that has yet arisen in India."[18] At the very moment of independence, peasant revolutionaries in princely Hyderabad put forth a radical vision of a just and democratic society in thousands of villages across Telangana. In doing so, they made popular claims on the exercise of violence and raised fundamental questions about the nature of decolonization, popular sovereignty, and Indian democracy.

At the same time, the Congress-led government of India was refashioning the Raj into a sovereign nation-state, and the Constituent Assembly was developing the juridical and institutional basis of postcolonial India's liberal democracy.[19] In the days after the Police Action in Hyderabad, Indian Union forces turned their attention to Telangana, initiating a counterinsurgency that would continue until the end of 1951. India's "passive revolution" was thus a highly contested and violent process.[20] In Telangana, what Ranajit Guha called the "*historic failure of the nation to come to its own*" can be grasped most acutely.[21] One common theme that runs throughout the book is an examination of Vallabhbhai Patel and Jawaharlal Nehru as key thinkers and practitioners of sovereignty and democracy, and of the roles played by other nationalist leaders, civil servants, and state functionaries in the violent transformation of the Raj into the Republic.[22]

Telangana was also central to the development of communist theory and practice at the moment of independence, to the domestication of Indian communism within the institutional confines of India's liberal democracy, and to the first articulations of Indian Maoism. For the communist leadership, Telangana was an embryonic revolutionary state. The CPI denounced August 1947 as a "false independence" and embarked on an insurrectionary path that envisioned Telangana as the spark in a prairie fire that would set India ablaze. The party's Andhra Provincial Committee adopted a program of people's war and agrarian revolution inspired by Mao and the example of China. Telangana was hailed as India's Yan'an.[23] Although rarely acknowledged, in the three years after the Police Action the revolution in Telangana expanded into new areas, the armed struggle developed into guerrilla warfare, and more people joined the fight, most significantly the Adivasi communities who inhabited the hills and forests of northern Telangana.

The counterrevolution in Telangana was a constituent event in the making of the postcolonial state's security architecture. The government of India declared Telangana a "Special Area" (a juridical state of exception), military and police forces exercised arbitrary and excessive violence, and home guards and other vigilante forces were raised. Adivasis living in the hill and forest regions of Telangana were, by the thousands, forcibly relocated to roadside camps. The implementation of such "ameliorative measures" illuminates how colonial traditions of bureaucratic authoritarianism were reanimated by an ideology of national development that linked progress to the sovereignty of the state. Telangana was emblematic, moreover, of the struggles of India's Adivasis for rights and autonomy vis-à-vis a nascent postcolonial state formation making sovereign claims and fostering development at its internal frontiers. In late 1951, after years of revolution and counterrevolution, of insurgency and counterinsurgency, the CPI unilaterally withdrew the armed struggle.

Months later, the people of Telangana went to the polls in India's first general election. A vision of a revolutionary future, one among the many forged in the crucible of late colonial India, was violently tamed within the institutional framework of liberal democracy and state-led economic development that sought to bring about social transformation through a progressive and managed process.[24] The Telangana insurrection nevertheless inaugurated the postcolonial trajectory of Maoism in India, which has, since its resurrection in the "Spring Thunder" of 1967, existed as both shadow and mirror of India's liberal democracy. Revolutionary politics may have been pushed to India's geographical and social margins—its internal frontiers—but it was not extinguished. The persistence of the dream of an Indian Yan'an within and alongside India's liberal democracy and authoritarian state serves as a reminder that the vitality of democracy in India lies, not merely in the ideals of its constitution or the robustness of its institutions, but in the resilience of Indians in their fights, against each other and against all odds, for their rights.

The events under consideration here were both transformative of an extant order and foundational of a new one. This alchemical transformation of the Raj into the Republic was no conjurer's trick, nor merely a benevolent gift from an enlightened elite. It took place during a time of tremendous turmoil, movement, frenetic action, and, above all, violence. Even as it advances arguments for India as a whole, *From Raj to Republic* aims to pluralize the stories we tell about this highly consequential period in Indian history.[25] The conjunctures of the late 1940s were "exceptionally complex and contradictory."[26] There is no single story to tell, but many stories that should be understood as both distinctive and interconnected. The chapters address the book's themes of sovereignty, violence, and democracy from different locations and by asking different questions.

CHAPTER ONE

AZAD HYDERABAD IN THE AGE OF EMPIRE AND NATIONALISM

ON JUNE 11, 1947, eight days after the announcement of the Partition, the Nizam of Hyderabad, Mir Osman Ali Khan, issued a *firman* declaring that Hyderabad State would not accede to either of the newly announced dominions. "The result in law of the departure of the Paramount Power in the near future," the Nizam asserted, "will be that I shall become entitled to resume the status of an independent sovereign."[1] At 82,698 square miles, Hyderabad State was larger than the provinces of Bengal (77,442) and Bombay (76,443) and, indeed, larger than England and Scotland put together (80,752).[2] The Nizam's landlocked dominions occupied the lion's share of the Deccan Plateau, sharing a border more than 2,600 miles long with Bombay, Central Provinces and Berar, Bastar, Madras, Mysore, and the Deccan States. With a population of around seventeen million, Hyderabad was larger than any dominion of the British Commonwealth as well as a good number of United Nations member states. The Asaf Jah dynasty had ruled Hyderabad for more than two centuries and laid claim to the legacy of both the Mughal Empire and an even longer history of Muslim rule in the Deccan.

The response to the Nizam's declaration of independence among Indian nationalists was apoplectic. With a civil war threatening to engulf northern India and with Partition looming, the prospect of further threats to the territorial integrity of the nation-state was alarming. For B. R. Ambedkar, law minister in the Union Cabinet, Hyderabad was "a new problem which may turn out to be worse than the Hindu-Muslim problem as it is sure to result in the further Balkanisation of India" and challenge India's claim to sovereignty internationally.[3] Jawaharlal Nehru observed that "Hyderabad is full of dangerous possibilities."[4] Vallabhbhai Patel explicitly linked his acceptance of Partition to the prevention of Hyderabad's bid for independence: "When we accepted division, it was like our agreeing to have a diseased limb amputated so that the remaining may live in a sound condition."[5] Hyderabad, the Sardar argued, was "situated in India's belly. How can the belly breathe if it is cut off from the main body?"[6] Patel's corporeal metaphor was rather well worn, tapping into a deep discursive reservoir regarding a national geography as embodied in the figure of Bharat Mata.[7] Yet it was also an inheritance from interwar constitutional debates that grappled with the intractable problem of the Indian states. "India could live if its Moslem limbs in the North-West and North-East were amputated," the Oxford doyen of imperial history Reginald Coupland noted in 1943, "but could it live without its heart?"[8] The Nizam's *firman* put this question to the test, ushering in the decisive phase in the struggle over sovereignty in the Deccan that would come to a swift, violent resolution fourteen months later with the Police Action of September 1948.

While the Nizam's bid for independence was a contingent response to the June 3 Partition Plan, it was also decades in the making. At the time of the Nizam's *firman*, Hyderabad was not the only Indian state openly contemplating independence. Bhopal and Travancore also made public intimations to that effect. Jammu and Kashmir, shortly to become a site of violent contestation and an enduring reminder of the fraught legacies of the Raj, had no intention of acceding to either India or Pakistan. The intractable conflict over Kashmir has ever since been internationalized as the territorial locus of enmity between the nation-states of India and Pakistan. Indeed, India referred the Kashmir issue to the United Nations. In contrast, India's nationalist leaders were anxious to keep Hyderabad a "purely domestic issue," and they denied that Hyderabad had "any right in international law."[9] It was not coincidental that the Police Action took place as the United Nation's Security Council began discussions on whether to hear Hyderabad's appeal.[10] Hyderabad was "no longer an international affair," Patel remarked as Indian forces entered the state on September 13, 1948, but "a States Ministry function."[11]

I. The Imperial Constitution: Hyderabad and the Raj to 1935

In his June 11, 1947, *firman*, the Nizam prefaced his claim to "resume the status of an independent sovereign" on the "result in law of the departure of the Paramount Power."[12] From a legal perspective, the Nizam's claim was in line with a centuries-long history of imperial constitutionalism. Hyderabad had historically played a preeminent role as a sovereign yet subordinate state within the Raj's imperial constitution. The Indian Independence Act, given royal assent on July 18, was quite clear that the territories of the new dominions of Pakistan and India would, at least initially, be formed out of British India alone.[13] The act, moreover, held that the "suzerainty of His Majesty over the Indian States lapses" and with it all "functions," "obligations," and "powers, rights, authority or jurisdiction" exercised by the British Crown vis-à-vis the Indian states.[14] The act was a unilateral revocation of all treaties and other relations between the British Crown and the Indian states. On the one hand, this represented the fulfillment of a long-cherished goal of the princes: paramountcy was not transferred to, or inherited by, the successor governments of the Raj. On the other hand, by breaking with the frameworks and conventions of imperial constitutionalism, the British betrayal of the Indian states gave Indian nationalists the opportunity to consolidate India into a unitary territorial nation-state. They would be, as V. P. Menon informed a receptive Sardar Patel, "writing on a clean slate, unhampered by treaties" or other legal rights of the states that had confounded interwar constitution-making efforts.[15]

The Nizam's *firman*, then, brought to the fore the fundamental tension of the Raj's imperial regime of sovereignty: the elaborate jurisdictional edifice of the Raj, on the one hand, and, on the other, the inability of paramountcy to be satisfactorily codified. Treaties, *sanads*, and other legal documents had, since at least 1857, coexisted with what imperial

MAP 1. India before Partition in 1947.

administrators referred to as "usage" or "political practice." Paramountcy was ultimately a political fact unconstrained by the law. This constitutive tension between legal and political domains did not simply come to an end in mid-1947. Indeed, it was precisely through such indeterminacy that the Raj was dismantled and the Republic built up. The distinction between the provinces of British India and the Indian states was even maintained in the republican Constitution of 1950. India's claim to Jammu and Kashmir—and all the other states aside from Hyderabad—rested on the legal standing of the Instruments of Accession signed by the Maharaja and his counterparts from other states. In the case of Hyderabad, nationalist leaders discarded legal arguments in favor of those based on demography, popular sovereignty, and the de facto supremacy of the government of India.

There was general consensus that the Nizam and his state possessed and exercised sovereignty before August 1947. What was disputed, however, was the character and quality of that sovereignty and whether, as the Nizam asserted, it "entitled" him to "resume"—after nearly two centuries—the "status of an independent sovereign" within the emergent postwar international order. The Nizam's bid for independence was the culmination of long-standing efforts to affirm and consolidate his sovereignty, both within his territories and in Britain's Indian empire more broadly. The ultimate triumph of republicanism over dynastic kingship in India was not preordained, nor was its history merely a staid legalistic narrative. It was, rather, a highly contested, multifaceted, and violent process. Indeed, in parts of Africa, the Middle East, and Southeast Asia, monarchs not only survived decolonization but were able to expand and consolidate their claims to sovereignty. South Asia was hardly unique in the tensions between nationalist projects of self-determination and the legal ambiguities of imperial regimes of sovereignty.

In their September 1948 appeal to the United Nations, Hyderabad's representatives argued that, from the date of the Indian Independence Act, Hyderabad, "already a sovereign State, became also independent for international purposes."[16] India's representative to the Security Council responded that Hyderabad "is not competent to bring any question before the Security Council; that it is not a State; that it is not independent; that never in all its history did it have the status of independence; that neither in the remote past nor before August 1947, nor under any declaration made by the United Kingdom, nor under any act passed by the British Parliament, has it acquired the status of independence."[17] The government of India argued that Hyderabad and other Indian states were not international entities under the system of paramountcy and did not simply earn international status by virtue of paramountcy's cessation. Hyderabad's delegates conceded that the Indian states had "no international life" under paramountcy.[18] But, they argued, by virtue of the lapsing of paramountcy, Hyderabad had become sovereign *as well as* independent.

As Eric Beverley has observed, Hyderabad's case was exemplary of the transition from a world in which sovereignty was often ambiguous and fragmented, where "minor states—sovereign but subordinated—occupied a vast legal gray area," to a postwar international order premised on "monistic" notions of territorial sovereignty.[19] The British united all of India under one imperial system, but the Raj was not a coherent or codified entity. It was marked instead by territorial fragmentation, legal plurality, and layered and dispersed forms of sovereignty. It was a complex institutional matrix, a messy aggregate of legal orders and administrative jurisdictions. This arrangement was an outcome of the contingencies of colonial conquest between 1757 and 1857 and was further elaborated in the decades after the insurrection.[20] The British conquest was piecemeal, taking place over the course of a hundred years, during which time the East India Company signed treaties with or otherwise subordinated hundreds of Indian sovereigns and magnates, who would later form the bulk of the Indian "princes." Following the British reconquest in the wake of 1857–58, these contingent arrangements of conquest were molded into a permanent institutional structure and constitutional order.

The post-1857 imperial constitution consisted, broadly, of "two Indias," each internally differentiated: the directly ruled British Indian provinces and the indirectly ruled Indian states. Coexisting and codependent, these two Indias were juxtaposed across the subcontinent, giving the sovereign landscape of the Raj an extraordinary spatial character, one marked by the proliferation of territorial anomalies. The Indian states collectively occupied approximately two-fifths of the total area of the subcontinent. There was a staggering diversity among the states themselves, ranging from small units no larger than a few villages to large polities replete with the trappings of modern administration. All were autocracies, as was the Raj more broadly. They exercised varying degrees of internal autonomy; the vast majority were petty "semijurisdictional" or "nonjurisdictional" rather than "full-powered" states.[21] All states ceded rights of external affairs and of the ability to wage war to the British.

Despite their enormous differences, the states were lumped together into the single category of "princely," "native," or "Indian" states—a "uniformity of

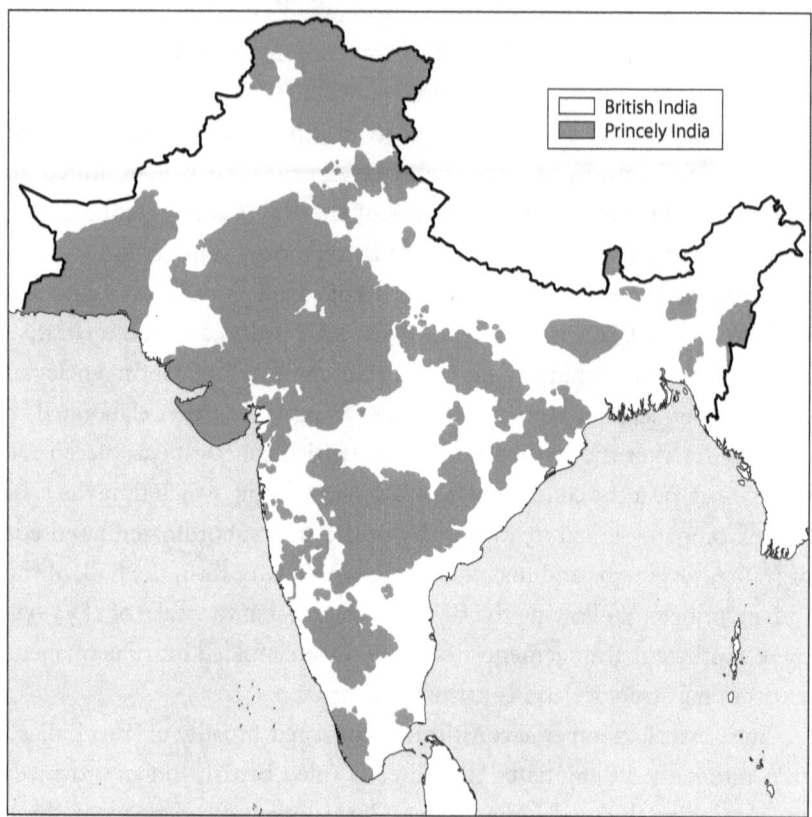

MAP 2. British India and Indian Princely States.

terminology" that posed significant challenges to late colonial constitution-making efforts.[22] Indeed, their legal, constitutional, and institutional qualities differed wildly. Only around forty major states had formal treaty relations with the British. The government of India did, however, issue *sanads* (certificates of protection and recognition) and letters of understanding to many states lacking formal treaty rights.[23] The British never systematized their relations with the princes, adopting instead an ad hoc approach that dealt separately with each state or groups of smaller states through the Political Department, which was under the direct control of the viceroy as the Crown representative. The underlying principle of this system was the concept of the "paramountcy" of the British Crown. Although treaties, *sanads*, and other legal documents suggest that paramountcy was a legal, contractual, and consensual relationship, ultimately it was founded on British military supremacy and the right of conquest. "The paramount supremacy of the British Government," the government of India proclaimed in 1877, "is a thing of gradual growth; it has been established partly by conquest; partly by treaty; partly by usage."[24] The right of the government of India to intervene in the internal affairs of states (regardless of treaty status) in the event of perceived misrule or disorder was an essential, if infrequently exercised, dimension of paramountcy. Despite the routinization of paramountcy after 1857, however, the Raj was never codified into a unified legal architecture. This "indefinite suzerainty" left "largely unresolved certain fundamental questions of conquest, sovereignty and subjecthood."[25] The imperial constitution of the Raj relied instead on administrative practice and convention, what imperial administrators referred to as "usage" or "political practice." Henry Maine observed that "no general rules" could apply to the division of sovereign powers between the British and the Indian states. These would be deduced instead "from *de facto* relations" between the paramount power and individual states.[26]

Beginning in 1759, the Nizams of Hyderabad signed more than a dozen treaties with the British. Hyderabad's position within the Raj was characterized by "hierarchical relations in the political domain" and "the language of reciprocity in the legal sphere."[27] The initial treaties of the late eighteenth century were primarily military in nature, as the expansionist East India Company moved to vanquish first its European rivals and then Mysore and the Marathas. The alliance with Hyderabad was a crucial factor in British victories over Tipu Sultan and the Marathas, ensuring British dominance in peninsular India and, perhaps, the subcontinent as a whole. In 1766, a treaty of "honor, alliance and friendship ... and mutual assistance" distinguished Hyderabad's sovereignty from that of the Mughals.[28] The Treaty of Perpetual and General Defensive Alliance signed in 1800 aimed at the "reciprocal protection of their respective territories" and held the Nizam to be an "equal partner with the Company."[29] An 1803 treaty guaranteed British recognition of Hyderabad "until the end of time."[30]

Hyderabad was, as Kavita Datla argued, "absolutely central to the forging of the British imperial order, and generative of the very practices that came to characterize colonial expansion and governance."[31] The idea of paramountcy as a historical partnership of sovereignty—of empire as collaboration—persisted even as the hierarchical relationship between the British and the Indian states was affirmed within the post-1858 imperial constitution.[32] The Nizam's loyalty in 1857 was a crucial factor in the ability of the British to hold on to their Indian empire. After the fall of Delhi, the governor of Bombay telegraphed the resident at Hyderabad that "if the Nizam goes, all is lost."[33] When Hyderabad's prime minister Sir Salar Jung later visited England he was hailed as the "saviour of Indian empire."[34] It was after the Mutiny that the Nizam became referred to as "Our Faithful Ally," a title officially bestowed to Mir Osman Ali Khan after the First World War.[35] The "Native Chief," for Lord Curzon, was a "colleague and partner"; on another occasion he described "the Princes" as not simply "appendages of Empire, but its participators and instruments."[36] For Lord Hardinge they were "colleagues in the great task of imperial rule."[37] Indeed, Mir Osman Ali considered Hyderabad's contributions to both World Wars a continuation of his state's historically central and constitutive position within the Raj's imperial regime of sovereignty.[38]

All the same, Hyderabad was not immune to the power dynamics of the military and financial relationships that developed out of the East India Company's subsidiary alliance system.[39] Hyderabad's "friendship" with the British was, in practice, not a relationship among equals. From as early as the 1790s, Hyderabad was sovereign but not independent. Certainly, from the end of the Third Anglo-Maratha War in 1818, at the latest, the British were a class apart from any other sovereign state in India.[40] After 1858, Lord Canning wrote, "The distinction between independent and dependent States lost its significance."[41] Like other subordinate sovereigns, the Nizam of Hyderabad was forbidden to establish formal relations or go to war with any other state, either outside or within the Indian Empire. The British arrogated the right to intervene in Hyderabad's internal administration, although the influence of the resident over the Nizam tended to wax and wane over time. Over the latter half of the nineteenth century, Hyderabad established itself as the "premier state" within the Raj's imperial regime of sovereignty, the first among unequals. Mir Osman Ali Khan, who became Nizam in 1911, sought to further distinguish Hyderabad from other Indian states, positioning himself for his eventual bid to "resume the status of an independent sovereign."

Over the first half of the nineteenth century, Hyderabad's subsidiary alliance with the British consistently eroded the financial stability of the state, which in turn allowed the British to demand concessions. As a result, the territorial contours of Hyderabad State were almost constantly changing. The Nizams ceded territories to the British, and, on occasion, territories were restored to them. As a result, the border between the Nizam's dominions and British India was a sprawling frontier zone, marked by juxtaposed jurisdictions and territorial enclaves.[42] It was this frontier that would become a site of contestation between competing projects of sovereignty as Indian nationalists and revolutionaries challenged Hyderabad's commanding position in peninsular India from 1938 onwards. After the First World War, Mir Osman Ali Khan sought the restoration of territories ceded to the British as part of his efforts to affirm and consolidate the sovereignty of his state and his dynasty. Indeed, he used each phase of constitutional negotiations between 1919 and 1947 to push territorial claims, most notably with respect to Berar.

Hyderabad became landlocked after ceding claims to areas on the Coromandel coast, including the port town of Masulipatnam, in 1759, and the Northern Circars through treaties in 1766 and 1788.[43] The Nizam abandoned his claim to *peshkash* in the latter areas in 1823. In 1800, the Nizam lost the Ceded Districts (Anantapur, Kadapa, Karnool, Ballari, and parts of Tumakuru and Davanagere) that he had gained in 1792 from the Treaty of Seringapatam. But it was the fertile cotton-growing districts of Berar, the richest part of the Nizam's dominions, that became a point of long-standing dispute. Berar exemplified the ambiguities, tensions, and contradictions of the Raj's imperial regime of sovereignty. According to an 1853 agreement, Berar was put under British administration in exchange for relief from the crushing debt placed on Hyderabad by the maintenance costs of the Hyderabad Contingent as per the terms of the subsidiary

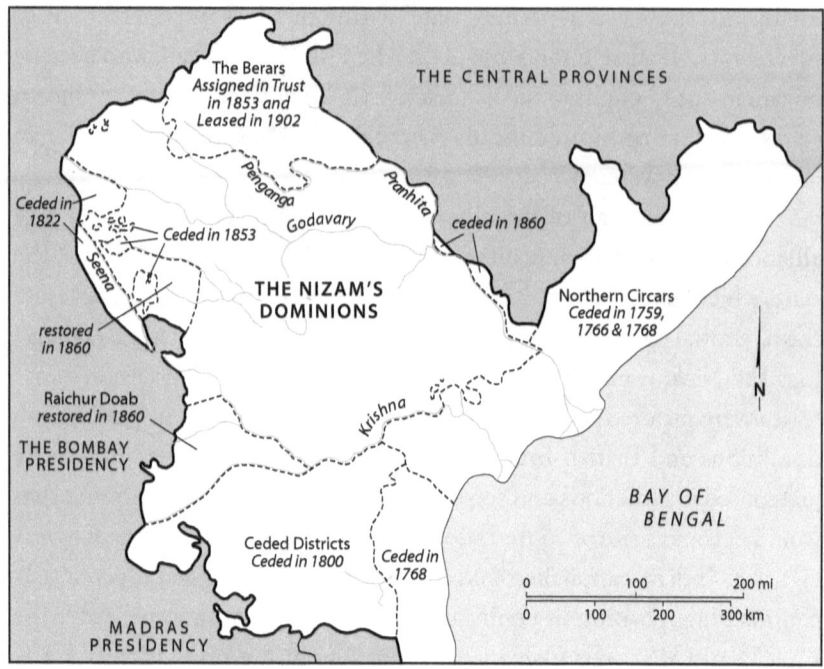

MAP 3. The Nizam's Dominions.

alliance. Berar was to be "held in trust" by the British, yet the Nizam maintained his claim to sovereignty over the "Assigned Districts," as well as to their surplus revenue.[44]

In that same 1853 agreement, the Nizam ceded the districts of Osmanabad and Raichur, only to have them returned in 1860 as a reward for his loyalty in 1857–58. Yet the British refused to return Berar. In 1866 and again in 1873, the Nizam's *diwan*, Salar Jung, officially requested the restoration of Berar, but he was repeatedly rebuffed.[45] Salar Jung reminded his British counterparts that Berar was "the garden of our sovereign's country, which was taken from him, under circumstances of humiliation to him and to us which are still vividly imprinted on the memory of the Hyderabad people." He vowed never to "cease from sorrowing or relax our anxious efforts" to have Berar returned to Hyderabad.[46] True to his word, Salar Jung again requested restoration in 1876. The government of India responded that "in the life of states as well as of individuals, documentary claims may be set aside by overt acts" and that "great political changes not only introduce new rights and new duties, but may ever modify the interpretation of treaties or render them altogether void."[47] Here we have an enunciation of paramountcy as an evolving political fact existing beyond and not beholden to treaties or, indeed, the law more generally. Viceroy Reading would, famously, strike a similar chord when Mir Osman Ali Khan raised the Berar issue again in the early 1920s.

Nizam Mahboob Ali Khan, Osman's predecessor, intended in 1901 to ask the viceroy for the restoration of Berar as a favor to Hyderabad on the occasion of the coronation of Edward VII. The viceroy, Lord Curzon, repeatedly informed the Nizam that Berar was not going to be restored, despite Hyderabad's generous support for the British effort in the Boer War. The Nizam was instead induced to lease the districts to the British in perpetuity. A 1902 treaty reaffirmed the Nizam's "sovereignty" over the "Assigned Districts" while at the same time recognizing the "exclusive jurisdiction" of the British.[48] The British agreed to pay the Nizam a fixed sum of Rs. 25 *lakhs* (2.5 million) per year from Berar's revenues.[49] Although the British administered Berar as part of the Central Provinces, its inhabitants remained subjects of the Nizam. This parceling of sovereignty and jurisdictional authority was exemplary of the fragmented and contingent nature of the Raj's imperial regime of sovereignty and its territorial order.

The First World War marked a watershed moment for political life in India and, indeed, the colonial world more broadly.[50] Millions of Indians were mobilized for the war and suffered more than a hundred thousand casualties. The Indian princes, and the Nizam of Hyderabad most prominently of all, vigorously supported the British effort. It was in this context that the secretary of state for India, Edwin Montagu, committed in August 1917 to the "progressive realisation of responsible government in India as an integral part of the British Empire."[51] This announcement inaugurated a sustained phase of constitutional contestation in late colonial India, one that would conclude in 1947 or, in the case of the Indian states, with the Police Action against Hyderabad in 1948. The 1919 Government of India

Act applied only to British India, yet Montagu and Viceroy Chelmsford noted that the reforms "cannot leave the States untouched."[52] Montagu and Chelmsford reiterated the Indian states' "immense value as part of the polity of India" and assured the princes that "no constitutional changes which may take place will impair the rights, dignities and privileges secured to them by treaties, *sanads*, and engagements or by established practice."[53] Taking note of the "ambiguity and misunderstanding" concerning the "exact position" of the states, they suggested efforts to "simplify, standardize and codify existing practice for the future."[54]

This task of codifying the Raj's imperial constitution became the dominant imperative of, and would ultimately confound, interwar constitution-making efforts. The basic framework for reforms aimed to unite British India and the Indian states under a federal constitution. The idea of an Indian federation was central to interwar political imaginaries, lending itself to divergent, innovative, and radical visions of India's future. In many of these visions, not least the official British one, the Indian states took on a new and integral role. For Montagu and Chelmsford, the only practicable model for codifying the Raj was "some form of federation."[55] Over the course of the 1920s, the idea of federating the Raj became something of an elite consensus. Indeed, federalism provided for Indians and the British alike a common language for elaborating questions of rights, democracy, and sovereignty. The 1919 Constitution was a transitional one; it was a step toward a "progressive realization." As such, it opened up both a wide range of possibilities and a good amount of uncertainty. Federation pointed to a likely scenario in which the provinces of British India would be democratized at the same time as the sovereignty and autonomy of the Indian states would be put on sounder legal footing. Indeed, reconciling the distinct theories of political legitimacy and territorial authority of the "two Indias" within a heterogeneous constitutional structure was precisely the intent behind the "Federation of India," the centerpiece of the 1935 Government of India Act.

The pressure for constitutional reform placed on the British by Indian nationalists at once enabled and posed risks for a dependent sovereign, like Mir Osman Ali Khan, who aspired to be an independent sovereign. The newfound all-India relevance of the Indian states spurred, for the first time, collective action among the princes. The Chamber of Princes was established by royal proclamation in 1921 as a consultative body to the viceroy. The king-emperor reiterated his "determination ever to maintain unimpaired the privileges, rights and dignities of the Princes of India." This pledge was to remain "inviolate and inviolable."[56] The Chamber had 108 member states and another twelve seats reserved for the representation of an additional 127 smaller states. Excluded from the Chamber entirely, but still considered Indian states, were 327 estates, *jagirs*, and other petty entities, of which 287 were located in Gujarat and Kathiawar.[57] The Nizam, seeking to distinguish himself from his princely counterparts, stood aloof from the Chamber.

The Nizam saw the end of the First World War and the inauguration of constitutional reforms as an opportunity to consolidate and even expand his claims to sovereignty. He chose to pursue two objectives: to secure territory and to shore up the legitimacy of his dynasty. He emerged from the war with two new official titles: "Faithful Ally of the British Government" and "His Exalted Highness." The latter title especially worked to confirm Hyderabad's status as the "premier" state of the Raj and to distinguish the Nizam from other subordinate sovereigns. His gun salute was raised from fourteen to twenty-one, the most of any of the princes. In 1922, as Gandhi's first India-wide mobilization and boycott was roiling the country, the Nizam hosted the Prince of Wales, the future king-emperor, in an elaborate ceremony. The Nizam aspired, without much success, over the course of the 1920s and 1930s, to acquire the title of king.[58] Beginning in 1918, a series of constitutional, institutional, and economic reforms sought to further equip Hyderabad with the trappings of a modern state.

The Nizam also sought the restoration of territories ceded by his ancestors. In 1923, he wrote to Viceroy Reading asking for the restoration of Berar as a gesture of goodwill in light of his support for British war efforts.[59] The Nizam contended that excepting "matters related to foreign powers," the "Nizams of Hyderabad have been independent in the internal affairs of their State just as much as the British Government in British India." Hyderabad and the government of India were partners in the Raj: the two governments "stand on the same plane without any limitations of subordination of one to the other." In addition to petitioning the viceroy, the Nizam reached out to other princes and even to nationalist leaders, including Gandhi. He promised to "grant autonomy to the inhabitants of Berar" if it became "an integral part of the Hyderabad State." The Mahatma, however, declined to engage with the Nizam.[60]

In 1926, Reading responded to the Nizam's letter regarding Berar with a classic statement on paramountcy: "The Sovereignty of the British Crown is supreme in India, and therefore no Ruler of an Indian State can justifiably claim to negotiate with the British Government on an equal footing. Its supremacy is not based only upon Treaties and Engagements but exists independently of them."[61] To add insult to injury, Reading lumped the illustrious head of India's most populous state, a dynasty that had origins in the Mughal Empire, in the same category with petty estate holders and *jagirdars*: "The title of Faithful Ally, which Your Exalted Highness enjoys, has not the effect of putting your Government in a category separate from that of other States under the Paramountcy of the British Crown."[62] As a further humiliation, Reading undermined the Nizam's internal autonomy by imposing personnel on his state's administration, thus restricting the Nizam's field of action even within his own state. The key posts of director-general of revenue and director-general of police were to be filled by British officers officially deputed by the government of India. The government of India also installed a representative as a member of the Nizam's executive council and, further, reserved the right to approve all future appointments to the council.[63] The message was clear: the Nizam and the British did not "stand on the same plane."

The public humiliation of the Nizam alarmed the Chamber of Princes, who pressed the government of India to establish "permanent political machinery" for "regulating the relations of the States to the Crown and to the Government of British India, with a view permanently to protecting the rights of the States."[64] The Chamber argued that their sovereign prerogatives as delineated in treaties, engagements, *sanads*, and other legal documents had been undermined over time by usage and political practice. Most important of all, they wanted assurances that paramountcy could not, and would not, be transferred from the British to a federal government run by Indians or indeed any other successor government. They argued, crucially, that their constitutional relationship was with the British Crown and *not* with the Government of India. Thus they could not be compelled to join a potential Indian federation without their explicit consent.[65]

Reading's successor, Lord Irwin, appointed the Indian States Committee in 1928 to evaluate the constitutional standing of the Indian states. Known as the Butler Committee, its report, submitted to Parliament in 1929, made a number of interventions that would prove consequential to constitution-making efforts in the following years. The report insisted that paramountcy was "impossible to define." Their tautology—"Paramountcy must remain paramount"—offered little clarity.[66] Paramountcy was a historical and thus essentially political fact "based upon treaties, engagements and sanads supplemented by usage and sufferance and by decisions of the Government of India and the Secretary of State embodied in political practice."[67] The report emphatically supported the virtually unlimited conception of paramountcy in Reading's 1926 letter to the Nizam, adding further that usage "lights up the dark places of the treaties."[68] Paramountcy was not "a merely contractual relationship, resting on treaties made more than a century ago," but rather a "living, growing relationship shaped by circumstances and policy, resting ... on a mixture of history, theory and modern fact."[69] Paramountcy, as a theory of imperial sovereignty, exceeded the limits of the law.

The Indian states, seeking a firmer legal basis for their constitutional claims to sovereignty, were largely disheartened by the Butler Committee's conclusions. Yet, significantly, the committee supported the Chamber's claim that the constitutional standing of the Indian states arose out of their relationship with the British Crown rather than the government of India.[70] As a result, the Indian states could "not be handed over without their agreement" to any new government brought into being in British India. Paramountcy could not be transferred to "a new government resting on a new and written constitution."[71] Thus was born the princely veto.[72] The formation of an all-India polity required the consent of the Indian states. The Butler Committee determined, moreover, that in the event of "widespread popular demand for change, the Paramount Power would be bound to maintain the rights, privileges and dignity of the Prince." This commitment was affirmed with the Indian States (Protection) Act of 1934, which intended to assuage princely concerns regarding federation by guaranteeing the states protection from activities organized in British India and by imposing penalties on press statements exciting hatred, contempt, or disaffection for state administrations.[73]

The 1919 Constitution was intended as a transitional one. As the next step in India's "progressive realisation" of responsible government, the Indian Statutory Commission chaired by John Simon was established in 1927. Their report, submitted to Parliament in 1930, concluded that "the ultimate constitution of India must be federal, for it is only in a federal constitution that units differing so widely in constitution as the provinces and the States can be brought together while retaining internal autonomy."[74] The Simon Commission recommended another transitional constitution, one that would establish a legal-institutional framework for the federation-to-be: "It's accomplishment must remain a distant ideal."[75] The princely veto was maintained: "The States cannot be compelled to come into any closer relationship with British India." The new constitution, instead, should provide "an open door whereby, when it seems good to them, the Ruling Princes may enter on just and reasonable terms."[76] They endorsed the Butler Committee's conception of paramountcy and recommended, moreover, that it be vested in the individual of the viceroy as Crown representative rather than the government of India. The states, moreover, would not be required to make any internal reforms. In the official British imagination, then, federation would be a codification and shoring up of the extant imperial regime of sovereignty.

In November 1930, the idea of an all-India federation moved quite rapidly and unexpectedly from a "distant ideal" to an immediate matter of practical concern. At the opening session of the first of three Round Table Conferences convened to develop India's next constitution, the Indian States Delegation announced an agreement with moderate British Indian leaders to support an all-India federation as a dominion within the British Commonwealth of Nations. Crucially, not only the Chamber representatives but also those from the major states of Baroda, Kashmir,

Hyderabad, and Mysore threw their weight behind the idea of federation.[77] This development was contingent on a number of factors, most notably the absence of the Congress, who boycotted the conference. Nevertheless, federation was established as the consensus framework for India's constitutional advance, even if princely support would fracture by 1935. The Indian states, as the princely delegate K. N. Haksar noted, "held the future of India ... in the hollow of their hand."[78]

The 1935 Act maintained the anomalous position of Berar while confirming both British jurisdiction and the "continuance of the sovereignty of His Exalted Highness over Berar."[79] In order to corral the Indian states into the proposed federation, the British offered a number of concessions. In 1936, the Nizam was given the right to be consulted about the appointment of the governor of the Central Provinces, the right to fly the Asaf Jah flag on public buildings in Berar, the right to hold *darbars* there, an annual payment of twenty-five *lakh* from Berar's revenues, and the title of "His Highness the Prince of Berar" for his heir apparent.[80] In a visit to Hyderabad, Viceroy Willingdon made it clear that the agreement reaffirmed the Nizam's sovereignty over Berar, giving "some real as well as ceremonial effect to the sovereignty of the Nizam." In exchange, the Nizam should "be prepared to accede to federation in respect to his territories known as the Berars."[81] The Nizam also waived his claim for "a free corridor to the sea at Musulipatnam and a permit to develop a port" as per the Hyderabad Commercial Treaty of 1802.[82] In a personal letter from "Your sincere friend and Emperor," Edward VIII wrote to the Nizam in October 1936 that he was "glad to avail myself of this occasion further to recognise the sovereignty of Your Exalted Highness in the territory of Berar."[83] With the 1935 Act and the proposed federation, it seemed as if Hyderabad and other Indian states had succeeded in affirming and securing their sovereignty amid late colonial India's constitutional transformations. It was in light of this fact that calls for "responsible government" in British India rapidly gave way to a fierce, multifaceted contestation over sovereignty in India over the course of the latter half of the 1930s. New battle lines were drawn as the Congress pitted a republican program of popular sovereignty against the legitimacy of dynastic kingship.

II. The Failure of Federation, 1935–39

The Federation of India envisioned by the 1935 Constitution offered the Indian states a distinct set of advantages. While provincial autonomy in British India began immediately, the federation was prospective. The federation would come into existence only if and when the requisite number of Indian states had signed Instruments of Accession. The Instruments of Accession explicitly confirmed the "sovereignty" of the rulers and were customizable, allowing individual states to enter the federation on different terms. The states retained control over internal administration and were exempt from federal powers of legislation, except in areas specified by the act and further limited by the terms of accession.[84] The act gave the states 104 out of 260 seats in the upper house of the central legislature and 125 out of 375 in the lower house. Delegates from the states were to be nominated by the rulers rather than elected. By joining the federation, the states would exchange a vague paramountcy for a definitive delineation of powers between a federal government and its constituent units. Both their supporters and their detractors expected the autocratic states to serve as conservative bulwarks against British Indian nationalists.

In sum, federation offered the Indian states the opportunity to secure their dynastic rights and their territorial integrity within a written constitution. The 1935 Constitution guaranteed princely representation in an all-India federal government, which would have allowed the states to play a role in governing British India, while setting limits on the extent to which the federal government could intervene in the states. If the Indian states had moved collectively and swiftly to establish the Federation of India before the outbreak of war in 1939, their subsequent position in all-India politics would have be considerably strengthened. Instead, the failure of federation left the Indian states facing a radically altered context when constitutional negotiations resumed after the war. The success of the Indian states in affirming their sovereign status and their role in all-India affairs in 1935 put them on a collision course with political forces in British India, a process hastened by the 1937 provincial elections. The late 1930s was a key moment of departure for Indian political life, and Hyderabad and the Indian states were right in the middle of it all. After the war, it became increasingly clear that the competing programs of the Muslim League, the Congress, and the Indian states could no longer be adequately triangulated. Something had to give. Ultimately, the princes paid the price for a communal settlement among the nationalists of British India.

Despite the numerous advantages of federation, the Indian states largely prevaricated and, ultimately, failed to seize the moment.[85] Despite his success with regard to the legal standing of his claim to Berar, the Nizam resisted joining the federation, ultimately refusing to convert his treaty relationship with the British Crown into a constitutional relationship with the government of India. Hyderabad, like other states, sought to push its advantage by placing additional conditions on accession and by raising technical issues relating to finance and railways, among other things. Not wanting to alienate the princes, Linlithgow, who became viceroy in 1936, took a slow and cautious approach to bringing the Indian states into the federation. A finalized Instrument of Accession was not sent out until January 1939, and war broke out months later.

The factor that most steeled princely opposition to federation leading up to 1939 was the open hostility from the nationalists of British India. Indeed, the 1935 Act and the 1937 provincial elections were major turning points in Indian history. The Indian states played a central role in these developments. For the Muslim League, the fact that the vast majority of princes were Hindus meant that federation, as Iqbal noted in his 1930 presidential address, served the "double purpose" of entrenching British power and giving an "over-whelming majority to the Hindus in an all-India Federal Assembly." Iqbal argued that federation represented "a kind of understanding between Hindu India and British Imperialism—you perpetuate me in India and I, in return, give you a Hindu oligarchy to keep all other Indian communities in perpetual subjection."[86] This was precisely the position taken by the League after the passing of the 1935 Act. While they grudgingly accepted the Communal Award and provincial autonomy, the League rejected the act's federal provisions as "most reactionary, retrograde, injurious and fatal to the vital interest of British India *vis-à-vis* the Indian States."[87] There were indications that Jinnah's advice played a part in the Nizam's refusal of the government's "final offer" on federation in 1939. The League congratulated the Nizam for his "brave stand" that "saved India from a grave political crisis."[88]

The Muslim League was not alone in rejecting the 1935 Act and its Federation of India on the basis of the Indian states. For B. R. Ambedkar, the proposed federation would place "the strings of India's political evolution in the hands of the Princes," who would then control the "destiny of India."[89] Federation would "hinder British India from setting up in motion processes which would result in the democratization of the Indian States" and, at the same time, would "help the Indian States to destroy democracy in British India."[90] The very act of federating amounted to an affirmation of the sovereign status of an Indian state, which "means the recognition of its indestructibility which means its right to the integrity of its territory and to guaranteeing of its powers of internal administration." Codifying the imperial regime of sovereignty, and thus institutionalizing the ad hoc jurisdictional structures of the Raj, for example, would have made reorganizing India into linguistic states impossible. It would have also foreclosed the possibility of a universal regime of citizenship rights in India. "What," Ambedkar concluded, "is the use of housing British India and the Indian States under one edifice if the result is to make them quarrel with each other?"[91]

What most worried the princes, however, were the dramatic shifts in the rhetoric, policy, and strategy of the Indian National Congress vis-à-vis the Indian states. As an organization, the Congress had long mirrored the divide between British India and the Indian states. Under Gandhi's influence, the Congress had since 1919 largely followed a policy of "noninterference" in states' affairs.[92] They generally did not organize in the states and accepted the sovereignty of the rulers. They asked instead that the Indian states establish constitutional monarchies providing for responsible government. At the 1920 Nagpur session, for example, the Congress asked "all the sovereign princes of India to establish full responsible government in their states."[93] This demand was reiterated at the 1928 Calcutta Congress: "This Congress assures the people of the Indian States of its sympathy with and support in their legitimate and peaceful struggle for the attainment of full responsible government in the States."[94] Attitudes toward the states within the Congress shifted dramatically over the course of the 1930s. In bringing the Indian states to the center of national politics, the 1935 Act and the Federation of India were, of course, integral to this shift. Yet a new generation of leaders, many of whom were socialists, also developed a critique of colonial feudalism and pushed the Congress to take a more aggressive approach toward the states.

Jawaharlal Nehru played a key role in pushing the Congress into a confrontation with the Indian states. "I must frankly confess," Nehru declared in his presidential address at the Lahore Congress in 1929, "that I am a socialist and a republican, and am no believer in kings or princes."[95] He asserted that the "the only people who have the right to determine the future of the States must be the people of these States. This Congress which claims self-determination cannot deny it to the people of the states."[96] That year the Congress adopted the *purna swaraj* resolution demanding complete independence. In the 1931 Karachi Resolution, the Congress adopted a Resolution on Fundamental Rights and Economic Policy, which called for democratic control of key industries and services, mineral resources, railways and, crucially, land reform. The Congress Socialist Party, formed in 1934 with Nehru's support, called for the "elimination of princes and landlords and all other classes of exploiters without compensation" and for the "redistribution of land to peasants."[97]

The policy of noninterference in the Indian states was abandoned during Nehru's next stint as Congress president from 1936 to 1937.[98] It became the stated policy of the Congress to "break" the federation. In his presidential address to the Faizpur Congress in December 1936, Nehru declared, "We go to the legislatures to combat the Act and seek to end it."[99] The objective was to prevent the establishment of the federation: "The present federation that is being thrust upon us is a federation in bondage and under the control, politically and socially, of the most backward elements in the country."[100] Nehru painted the states as anachronisms and argued that treaties, "held up to us so often now as sacred documents which may not be touched," should be discarded. The states, having gained "extraordinary power under the federal scheme," remained "wholly outside the control of the rest of India." Opposition to the federal part of the constitution, then, was "the central pivot of our struggle.... We have got to break this federation." In order to have a "clean slate to write afresh," Nehru insisted that the "constitution cannot be wrecked by action inside the legislatures only. For that, mass action outside is necessary, and that is why we must always remember that the essence of our freedom lies in mass organisation and mass action."[101]

Mass action against the Indian states began shortly after the Congress's electoral triumph and its formation of ministries in eight of the eleven provinces of British India in 1937. The Congress aimed to "democratize the constitution by a *tour de force*."[102] Protests, some violent, and *satyagrahas* against states throughout India were aided and abetted by the new Congress's ministries. This political storm extended across the country, from Travancore in the South to Dhami in the Himalayas, from Gujarat to the principalities of Orissa, to the princely heartland of Rajputana and even to major states like Mysore and Hyderabad.[103] Gandhi fasted in Rajkot, demanded "full responsible government," and asserted that "the people" were "the real rulers of Rajkot under the paramountcy of the Congress." The Mahatma framed the struggle in Rajkot not merely as a struggle for constitutional government in the states but as a struggle against British imperialism or, as he put it, "the disciplined hordes of the British empire."[104] More concerning to the rulers of the states, however, was Gandhi's claim that the Congress, now governing multiple provinces throughout India, was in "alliance with the British Government" and thus had every right to intervene in the affairs of "the States which are vassals of the British."[105]

For Nehru, the struggle against the states was the central battleground against British imperialism and the biggest obstacle to the unity and independence of a modern, democratic India. The stakes were high; these were not simply local struggles for civil liberties or representative institutions. "Today," he argued in 1939, "the problem of problems is that of the Indian States."[106] He challenged the very existence of the states themselves: "The states in modern India are anachronistic and do not deserve to exist."[107] Pushing for a more aggressive platform at the 1938 Haripura Congress, he observed that the Indian states "exemplified two things—the feudal order and British imperialism—both of which I dislike intensely."[108] So central had the states become to all-India politics that Nehru took over as president of the All India States Peoples Conference (AISPC) in early 1939.

In his presidential address to the AISPC, Nehru took note of the "mighty awakening among the people of the states" and prophesied that when "the history of India comes to be written, the year 1938 will stand out as the year of this awakening."[109] The majority of states, he remarked, "are sinks of reaction and incompetence and unrestrained autocratic power, sometimes exercised by vicious and degraded individuals."[110] He rejected the entire legal basis of the Raj's imperial constitution, referring to treaties as "monstrous impositions" that would not be recognized or accepted by the Congress: "The only final authority and paramount power that we recognise is the will of the people."[111] He singled out Hyderabad as "exceedingly backward politically and socially," with the "lowest level of civil liberty in India."[112] He defended the *satyagraha* initiated by the Hyderabad State Congress in 1938 and joined by the Hindu Mahasabha and the Arya Samaj, although he lamented that the "political issue" was getting "mixed up with communal and religious ones."[113] The 1938–39 *satyagraha*, conducted by British Indian forces, made Hyderabad a focal point of all-India political contestations, as discussed in chapter 2.

The Congress's opposition to federation was part of a radical and often unacknowledged departure prompted by the 1935 Constitution. This was the demand for a sovereign constituent assembly. This demand, the origin of India's Constituent Assembly that would meet in between 1946 and 1949, arose directly out of debates over federation and the sovereignty of the Indian states. The Congress first raised the issue in 1934, in response to the constitutional proposals contained in the White Paper of 1933. "The only satisfactory alternative," resolved the Working Committee, "is a Constitution drawn up by a Constituent Assembly elected on the basis of adult suffrage."[114] The Congress framed the 1937 elections as a plebiscite on the 1935 Constitution and a referendum on their demand for a constituent assembly. That assembly, Nehru insisted, "must not be conceived as something emanating from the British Government"; if "it is to have any reality, it must have the will of the people behind it and the organised strength of the masses to support it."[115] The demand for a constituent assembly was a demand for a break from the extant frameworks of imperial constitutionalism, a break necessitated by the sovereignty of the Indian states. The monarchical Indian states were, in this respect, the raison d'être of Indian republicanism.

The 1935 Act inaugurated the decisive phase in late colonial India's political and constitutional development, which laid the groundwork for the sweeping changes to the subcontinent's sovereign landscape that occurred after the Second World War. The act and the subsequent 1937 provincial elections precipitated a decisive shift away from the politics of community and special interest representation, constitutional safeguards for minorities, and the technical and enormously complicated allocation of sovereignty through federation—that is, some of the core features of imperial constitutionalism. The Congress's antimonarchical republicanism, insistence on popular sovereignty, and demand for a constituent assembly had a significant impact on India's multidimensional political arena.[116] For many Indian Muslim elites, the electoral power of the Congress raised the specter of majoritarianism more acutely than ever before. Between 1937 and 1939, Muslim thinkers and leaders produced an array of alternative federal schemes (examined below), leading up to and following the adoption of the Lahore Resolution in 1940. The turn to Pakistan, the shift from minority to nation, emerged out of a context of competing claims to sovereignty in late colonial India, a context in which the Indian states played a crucial role. After the passing of the 1935 Act, the Aga Khan, for example, suggested that Muslims should strive to establish a "United States of Southern Asia": "In all-India affairs we should be out-and-out federalists, using all our influence so that our provinces get at least such autonomy as the great Indian Princes will enjoy under the Federation."[117] For C. A. Bayly, the Aga Khan's vision represented an ethnic nationalism "gestating within the husk of an imperial federation."[118] Hyderabad, where a Muslim dynasty ruled over a Hindu majority, became a convergence point of important all-India political developments. As a result of the Congress's antimonarchical majoritarian and republican turn, the states hesitated to join the federation and, in so doing, missed their best, and ultimately last, opportunity to secure themselves in India's future constitution. States throughout India also undertook "reform" measures aimed at mollifying political discontent and strengthening their standing for the next round of constitutional negotiations. This chapter now turns to a discussion of those reforms in Hyderabad, situated within wider efforts to modernize Hyderabad in the decades after 1919.

III. Hyderabad as a Modern State

From the end of the First World War, the Nizam, his administration, and an embryonic civil society endeavored to develop Hyderabad into a modern state.[119] While the Nizam sought to further his claims to sovereignty in the domain of imperial constitutionalism, these efforts were complemented by a project to "modernize" Hyderabad.[120] After 1919, the Nizam pursued two objectives: to secure territory and to shore up the legitimacy of his dynasty (and the principle of sovereign kingship more broadly). Political, economic, and educational reform efforts aimed to transform Hyderabad while simultaneously shoring up the patrimonial system centered on the authority of the Nizam.

These efforts to forge a unique modernity in Hyderabad have been explored at length in recent works. Kavita Datla argued that Osmania University, founded in Hyderabad in 1918 as India's first vernacular university, constituted an important alternative to hegemonic colonial and nationalist notions of modernity, secularism, progress, and futurity.[121] Osmania sought to systematize Urdu into a "worldly vernacular" that could "rival English as a language of business, science, and learned conversation and that could also therefore potentially *democratize* the effects of Western education."[122] The university also enhanced Hyderabad's status as an important center of a transregional "Urdusphere" that connected Muslim intellectuals in India with those as far away as Kabul, Durban, Istanbul, and Cairo.[123] In a similar vein, Eric Beverley has shown how Hyderabad's autonomy as a minor sovereign in the Raj facilitated state-led urban development and industrial expansion, first in the capital city and then statewide. Indeed, personnel who led this modernizing effort in Hyderabad would later go on to influence the postcolonial Indian nation-state's planning efforts. Beverley observes that an ethical patrimonialism legitimized and shaped modernist visions and that such efforts, in turn, legitimized the patrimonial system in Hyderabad.[124] Patrimonialism and modernity in Hyderabad, Beverley concludes, were mutually constitutive.[125]

The Nizam's government touted industrial development, infrastructural improvements, public welfare programs, and institutional reforms after 1919 as evidence of its modernizing agenda.[126] Indeed, Hyderabad developed all the standard trappings of a modern bureaucratic state, made efforts to improve public health, education, and agriculture, and had its own currency and army. Without getting into the extensive details of these developments, I want to highlight how they were deployed as part of a discourse and rhetoric of progressive and ethical government. The Nizam, for example, was fond of giving visiting dignitaries and his critics alike copies of the paean to Hyderabad's historical uniqueness and reformist zeal written by the roving journalist St. Nihal Singh in 1923.[127]

After the Nizam's declaration of independence in 1947, his government deployed this modernization discourse in its effort to further its claims to sovereignty and an international personality. For example, the pamphlet compiled by Hyderabad's Labour Ministry for the International Labour Organization's Asian Regional Labour Conference held in New Delhi in October 1947 portrayed Hyderabad to an international audience as a distinctly modern state. The pamphlet began with a map of the subcontinent showing Hyderabad as distinct from India and Pakistan and noted the state's size relative to the population and territory of other independent nations. "Under his [the Nizam's] beneficent and progressive regime," the pamphlet announced, "Hyderabad has discarded much of the old-fashioned, out-worn methods and policies of past ages and has emerged into a new era, full of promise for the future."[128] Countering Indian nationalist portrayals of Hyderabad as anachronistic and medieval, the pamphlet argued that "the administration of Hyderabad is carried on by a regular system of departments on lines very much similar to those followed in India, due allowance being made to local conditions and traditions."[129] This argument about Hyderabad's modernity was coupled with one regarding the dynastic legitimacy of the Nizam's sovereignty: "The Nizam is known even to this date as Shah-e-Deccan (King of Deccan) and is the visible heir to the Moghul Empire's glory."¹³⁰ Hyderabad's modernity was due, almost exclusively, to the efforts of its "enlightened monarch." In light of Hyderabad's magnitude and modernity, the pamphlet called August 14, 1947, a "Red Letter Day," when paramountcy lapsed and the Nizam "resumed his independent status and assumed full sovereignty in his own right."¹³¹

Political reforms within Hyderabad also sought to "modernize" the state while shoring up the legitimacy and authority of the Asaf Jah dynasty. Hyderabad was a unitary state, where the Nizam, as head of the state, was the sovereign source of the law as well as the supreme executive. "This," noted a 1938 report on constitutional reforms in Hyderabad put out by a collection of moderate notables calling themselves the Hyderabad People's Convention, "is the basic factor of the constitution in its internal aspect."¹³² Yet Hyderabad was in many respects also a version of the Raj in miniature. It too was a composite of territorial, jurisdictional, and, one could argue, sovereign domains. The patrimonial state of Hyderabad centered on the personage of the Nizam, but beneath him was a wide spectrum of landholding elites with jurisdictional rights, including the Hindu *samasthan* rajas, whose authority dated to the Kakatiya and Vijayanagar empires; the *Paigah* nobles, whose ancestors were given land by the first Nizam; *ilaqadars* and *jagirdars*, who were granted land for their service to the state or other contributions to Hyderabad; and *zamindars, watandars*, and *deshmukhs*, all of whom exercised considerable administrative and judicial prerogatives, including the exercise of violence.¹³³ Indeed, the *samasthan* rajas even signed Instruments of Accession with the Indian Union in 1949.¹³⁴ Hyderabad State was a multitiered and decentralized political system centered on the Asaf Jah dynasty and a landholding elite.

In the two decades preceding the 1938 *satyagraha*, political developments and constitutional reforms within Hyderabad generally adhered to principles that legitimized and reaffirmed the Nizam's sovereignty and patrimonial authority. Beginning in the 1920s, there were various efforts to reconcile and reconfigure popular politics, democracy, and sovereign kingship. Karen Leonard has traced the development of a "Deccani nationalism" premised on a "Deccani synthesis" that brought together elements of Hindu and Muslim culture, fostered by the benign and tolerant Asaf Jah dynasty. The central antagonism of Deccani nationalism was not Hindu versus Muslim but rather Mulki (native Hyderabadi) versus non-Mulki.[135] Much of the impetus behind Deccani nationalism was a competition for employment in state services, which were disproportionately populated by Muslims from North India and which both Hindu and Muslim native Hyderabadis considered their rightful patrimony. Deccani nationalism was promoted by organizations such as the Osmania Graduates' Association, the Society of Union and Progress, and, from 1935, the Nizam's Subjects League. The Nizam's Subjects League raised the slogan "Long Live the Nizam, the Royal Embodiment of Deccani Nationalism."[136] Syed Abid Hasan's *Whither Hyderabad?* (1935), a manifesto of Deccani nationalism, committed the Nizam's Subjects League to "unflinching loyalty to the Asaf Jahi House," to communal harmony and equality in the state, to the protection of the "constitutional rights and privileges of Hyderabad as a sovereign State," and to the establishment of a constitutional monarchy under the aegis of the Nizam.[137] The Nizam's Subjects League advocated for joining the proposed Federation of India as a means of securing the Asaf Jah dynasty within a new constitutional order and of ensuring that Hyderabad played an important role in all-India affairs.

Political life in Hyderabad remained, however, highly constrained. Indeed, "political" activity was restricted in the state, and all gatherings had to be approved by authorities. The press was censored. Activists who were believed to have overstepped the bounds of propriety were arrested or fired from their jobs at schools, universities, or other state institutions. As a result, most organizations in the state were committed to cultural and educational development. For example, the Andhra Mahasabha, founded originally as the Andhra Jana Sangham in 1921, initially concerned itself with establishing libraries and promoting Telugu language, culture, and history. From 1930 it turned to social reform, and only in the late 1930s did it become an explicitly political organization. Rama Mantena has argued that, despite these limitations, a "thriving civil society" developed in Hyderabad over the 1920s and '30s.[138] Liberal reformers advocated representative institutions and civil liberties, with opinion generally cohering around a constitutional monarchy, a formal separation of powers, and civil liberties within the extant patrimonial system.[139] Although more explicitly loyalist and monarchist, these demands for constitutional government within Hyderabad and other princely states echoed those made by both imperialist princely sympathizers and the nationalists of British India.

Montagu's 1917 announcement helped ideas of "responsible government" become a key legitimizing discourse throughout the Raj. Supporters of the states, such as Lord Irwin (viceroy from 1926 until 1931), urged the princes to establish constitutional monarchies as a means of strengthening their position vis-à-vis British India and thus securing their dynasties.[140] Gandhi made the same appeal at the second Round Table Conference in 1931. He asked the states to introduce "elements—only elements—of representation on behalf of their subjects." Doing so would demonstrate to India and the world at large that they were "fired with a democratic spirit, that they do not want to remain undiluted autocrats, and that they want to become constitutional monarchs even as King George of Great Britain is."[141] If more of the princes, especially major states like Hyderabad, had undertaken substantial constitutional reform in the decades after 1917, the states would have perhaps been much better equipped to deal with nationalist onslaughts on their sovereignty from the late 1930s onwards. Yet the Nizam, and the princely order more generally, failed to act: not a single state implemented constitutional reforms that even came close to resembling "responsible government." Nor did they seek to negotiate with or come to an accommodation with the nationalists of British India in a way that would have made them less vulnerable in the postwar rush to decolonization. Rather than co-opt the language of civil liberties and the institutions of representative government, the Indian states largely prevaricated, fearing that any concessions would undermine the legitimacy of dynastic kingship. Instead, they gambled that loyalty to the British would continue to provide security for their dynasties. The remarkable success of the states in establishing their sovereignty and constitutional standing during the lead-up to the 1935 Act, in this respect, set them up for a confrontation with the nationalists of British India that they were unprepared to face. Coming only after, *and because of,* the Congress's electoral victory in 1937 and the subsequent mass actions in the states, constitutional reforms in the Indian states were reactive rather than preemptive, and ultimately inadequate and ineffective.

Mir Osman Ali Khan, under pressure from the British, first enacted constitutional reforms, or Qanuncha Mubrak, in 1919 to accompany the Montagu-Chelmsford reforms. The main result was the establishment of an executive council headed by a president, or sadr-i-azam. A legislative council composed of the chief justice of the High Court, inspectors-general of revenue and police, the director of public instruction, and the finance secretary was also established.[142] Yet the Nizam maintained sweeping executive powers, and all laws continued to be enacted by royal decree. The reforms were, in other words, largely administrative in nature. The Nizam ordered the first president of his executive council, Sir Ali Imam, to produce a report regarding political reforms, including "a substantial introduction of the elective element, direct voting, the representation of all important classes and interests, the effective protection of minorities, the condition of franchise," and a clear delineation of government powers and functions.[143] This initiative, however, never got off the ground. In his 1923 appeal to the viceroy regarding Berar, the Nizam promised, as a condition of restoration, to establish for Berar a "Constitution for a responsible Government with absolute popular control, under a constitutional Governor appointed by me as my Representative, of their internal affairs and complete autonomy in administration."[144] While he seemed to realize in the early 1920s that constitutional reforms offered a way to achieve his goals of securing territory and his dynastic sovereignty, the Nizam became increasingly mistrustful of any dilution of his powers.

While fairly extensive administrative, educational, and judicial reforms were implemented in the interim, it was not until 1937 that a committee under the chairmanship of S. Aravamudu Aiyangar was established on the orders of the Nizam to "devise a scheme of reform and expansion of the Legislature" with the aim of increasing the "association between my people and my Government."[145] The Reforms Committee, in their report submitted in August 1938, offered a new formulation of the Nizam's sovereignty: "The Head of the State represents the people directly in his own person, and his connection with them, therefore is more natural and abiding than that of any passing elected representatives. He is both the supreme head of the State and the embodiment of his 'people's sovereignty.'"[146] As the embodiment of the general will, the Nizam reserved vast executive powers as his sovereign prerogative: "Hence it is that in such a polity, the head of the State not merely retains the power to confirm or veto any piece of legislation, but also enjoys a special prerogative to make and un-make his executive or change the machinery of government through which he meets the growing needs of his people. Such a sovereignty forms the basis on which our Constitution rests, and has to be preserved."[147] The new constitution would "preserve" rather than constrain or more precisely define the Nizam's control over the functioning of his state. Hyderabad was hardly unique in this respect: in no Indian state was the ruler transformed into a constitutional head like the British monarch.[148] Nowhere was substantial power transferred to the people or their representatives.

The Nizam consented to the Aiyangar Committee proposals in 1939, although the Second World War delayed their implementation. They were partially implemented in 1946. The Aiyangar proposals were wide-ranging and thorough, amounting to a substantial standardization, codification, and bureaucratization of government throughout the Nizam's dominions. In terms of representative institutions, the plan called for a legislative assembly elected by functional representation. Constituencies, in other words, were to be economic rather than territorial. The aim was the "effective association of the different interests in the state with the government."[149] The legislature was to have eighty-five members, forty-three nominated and forty-two elected. As in other states, the franchise was circumscribed to a small percentage of the population. The legislature, moreover, had no authority over a number of important items like the Sarf-i-khas, the relations with the Paigahs, the Executive Council, the military, and, crucially, tax collection. The Nizam could veto any legislation and could enact laws not approved by the legislature.[150] The patrimonial and "feudal" character of the state was maintained, with the *jagirdars*, *watandars*, *deshmukhs*, samasthans, and Paigah nobles retaining jurisdictional rights.

The Aiyangar Committee settled on functional representation in order to circumvent the politics of numbers. They did so for two main reasons.

The first was the maintenance of rural hierarchies and, in a connected fashion, the balance of power between urban and rural Hyderabad. If the laboring peasantry, who made up the vast majority of Hyderabad's population, were to organize and gain substantial power it would have become a direct threat to the integrity of the state as it was constituted. State power and capital were heavily concentrated in the capital city. Urban political parties were also weak compared to their rural counterparts. Urban bourgeois dissenters and activists posed little threat compared to the Andhra Mahasabha, which attracted thousands of people to its gatherings and was organizing diligently throughout the Telangana countryside. Yet the Andhra Mahasabha was not given a role in the new "democratic" setup. Soon, under a young socialist leadership, the Andhra Mahasabha would instead lay the groundwork for the great revolution to come.

The second reason for functional rather than territorial representation was to achieve parity between Hindus and Muslims. Although the reforms called for joint electorates, the legislature and other representative bodies were to be divided equally between Hindus and Muslims, despite the latter numbering less than 15 percent of Hyderabad's population. In Hyderabad this minority problem was particularly acute because the Nizam was a Muslim and because Muslims benefited disproportionately from their predominance within state services and the patrimonial system. The Hyderabad government argued that parity was faithful to the vision, as the Nizam put it in his June 1947 declaration of independence, that Muslims and Hindus were the "two eyes of the State" and that the "importance of the Muslim community in the state, by virtue of its historical position and its status in the body politic, is so obvious that it cannot be reduced to the status of a minority in the Assembly."[151]

Hyderabad, went the argument, was free of the "communalism" of British India precisely because of the history of ethical kingship under the Asaf Jah dynasty that harmonized communal interests through forms of elite incorporation and beneficent government. Historians have argued that a "balance" between Hindus and Muslims did indeed exist in Hyderabad based on a "natural" distribution of economic and political power.[152] This balance was maintained through policies of "religious neutrality."[153] For some contemporary observers, such as the lawyer, political scientist, and polymath scholar H. K. Sherwani, the Aiyangar reforms formed "a bold, unique and definite departure from the principles which were supposed to have been the last word in the application of democracy to India."[154] Hyderabad "made history" by "dividing the Dominions into a series of *economic* rather than *geographical* constituencies."[155] A politics of interest, in other words, would avoid the pitfalls of the politics of numbers. Of course, as Ambedkar acerbically noted, Hyderabad's new constitution might "quite easily intensify class struggle by emphasizing class consciousness" and, crucially, would face new challenges "when every class will demand representation in proportion to its numbers."[156]

In light of the 1938–39 *satyagraha*, discussed in the next chapter, and the all-India context of the late 1930s discussed above, the new constitution came under attack as disingenuous and communal. The political scientist M. Venkatarangayya chastised Sherwani for his naïveté, arguing that "no change which does not involve a fresh arrangement or distribution of power deserves to be called a constitutional change."[157] For Ambedkar, although the scheme appeared "innocuous," its "real character" was essentially communal, unrepresentative, and antidemocratic.[158] For ostensibly secular and openly communal Indian nationalists alike, the new constitution merely affirmed that Hyderabad was both a feudal *and* a communal state in which the ruling dynasty enlarged the power of the minority at the expense of the majority. There was thus a convergence between the demands of secular and communal parties: democracy meant majority rule. In Hyderabad, majoritarianism was the shared legitimizing discourse for both secular and Hindu nationalist visions of democracy.

The Congress-led popular campaigns against the Indian states and the 1938–39 *satyagraha* against Hyderabad made the Deccan a flashpoint of all-India politics and, in so doing, nationalized politics within Hyderabad. The Mulki versus non-Mulki dynamic gave way to a majority-minority dynamic. With the ascendancy of a discourse of democracy as majority rule, the Majlis-e-Ittehadul Muslimeen set out to organize Hyderabad's Muslims as a single political entity that transcended social, economic, and sectional differences.[159] Originally started in 1927 to contain sectarian rivalry among

Hyderabad's Muslims, the Majlis under the leadership of Bahadur Yar Jung adopted an explicitly political program following the 1938–39 *satyagraha* and communal riots in Hyderabad City. Bahadur Yar Jung was a charismatic Hyderabadi nobleman known for his powerful oratory and *tabligh* work among the rural poor.[160] He came to be known as the Qaid-e-Millat, or "Leader of the Community." Under his leadership, the Majlis became a "representative cross-section" of the Muslim community by uniting Muslims of all sects and classes.[161] Bahadur Yar Jung opposed the appointment of the Aiyangar Committee, arguing instead for "administrative reforms."[162] A confidant of Jinnah, Bahadur Yar Jung invited the Qaid-e-Azam to Hyderabad in 1939 to convince the Nizam to preserve the numerical superiority of Muslims in the Legislative Council and to accept separate electorates.

The Majlis under Bahadur Yar Jang promoted the idea that Hyderabad was a Muslim state. As M. A. Moid and A. Suneetha argue, they took the Deccani nationalist conception of sovereignty and applied it to the Muslims alone. Popular sovereignty was defined "as specifically Deccani *and* Muslim."[163] The Majlis rejected the Aiyangar Committee's formulation that the Nizam was the "embodiment of his 'people's sovereignty.'" They suggested instead that he represented the "Muslim *awaam*" alone. Bahadur Yar Jung's theory of *ana'l-malik* held that sovereignty in Hyderabad was invested in the collectivity of Hyderabad's Muslims rather than in the personage of the Nizam.[164] He opened Majlis functions with the following invocation: "We are the Kings of the Deccan; the Throne and Crown of the Deccan are symbols of our own political and cultural sovereignty; His Exalted Highness is the soul of our Kingship and we form the body of his Kingship; if he ceases to exist, we cease to exist; and if we are no more, it will be no more."[165] In British India, the Muslim League turned to the idea of Pakistan as a way of escaping the minority problem. In Hyderabad, Bahadur Yar Jung and the Majlis committed to the preservation of the Asaf Jah dynasty. This called for a program of loyalty to the Nizam and support for his efforts to secure his sovereignty in the domains of imperial constitutionalism and, eventually, international law. The Majlis supported the Nizam's demand for the restoration of Berar and, ultimately, his bid for independence in 1947–48.[166]

Bahadur Yar Jung established the Razakars (volunteers) in 1938. Khaki-clad young men were trained at local gymnasiums. Until 1947 their activities were generally limited to parading, saluting the Nizam's Asaf Jahi flag, and maintaining order at public meetings.[167] Bahadur Yar Jung's project of reversing the physical degeneration of Hyderabadi Muslims and his belief that any successful political force required a paramilitary wing were hardly unique in late colonial India. After Bahadur Yar Jung's unexpected death in June 1944, the Majlis took a more radical route under Qasim Razvi, an Aligarh-educated lawyer from Latur, who became president of the Majlis in December 1946.[168] It was at this point that the purpose and function of the Razakars expanded dramatically, as they were mobilized to defend the integrity of the Nizam's state as he made his push for autonomy and independence. The Razakars arose out of and in response to a wider context of violent contestation in and around Hyderabad. From mid-1946, the peasantry of Telangana, under the leadership of the Andhra Mahasabha and the Communist Party of India, waged a revolutionary struggle, first against landlords and then against the Nizam's state itself. From August 1947, the Hyderabad State Congress, the Socialist Party, the Arya Samaj, and the Hindu Mahasabha set up camps on the western borders of the state and conducted armed campaigns of sabotage and guerrilla warfare. The provinces bordering Hyderabad raised tens of thousands of "home guards" and "village defense" parties. At the same time, the government of India instituted an economic blockade against Hyderabad, isolated it diplomatically, and prepared for military intervention. These events are examined in detail in the following chapter.

The Majlis, of course, did not simply conjure the idea of Hyderabad as a Muslim state out of thin air. For his part, the Nizam understood that both internationally and within the British Empire, Hyderabad's reputation as a Muslim state was a source of strength and legitimacy. In the face of an emergent popular politics and the specter of representative institutions, the Nizam increasingly relied upon the Majlis at home while playing off his reputation as a Muslim leader in all-India and international forums. What the Nizam recognized from the upheavals in his state and across princely India in 1938 was that his regime lacked a mass base. His turn to the Majlis from 1938 onwards was, in this sense, born of the Nizam's increasingly precarious position within India and the British Empire. Admittedly, the Nizam was widely revered, and only the Telangana uprising would pose any sort of existential threat to his state. In an era of mass mobilization and demands for "responsible government," the longevity of the Asaf Jah dynasty rested almost entirely on the Nizam's efforts in the domains of imperial constitutionalism and, eventually, international law.

IV. Hyderabad as a Muslim State

In his June 1947 *firman* declaring his intention to seek Hyderabad's independence, the Nizam, echoing Syed Ahmad Khan, argued that his "ancestors and I have always regarded the Muslims and Hindus as two eyes of the State and the state itself to be "the indivisible asset of all communities inhabiting it." He was "happy to say that there has not been in my state the same acute cleavage as had led to the recent events in British India."[169] The idea that Hyderabad was free of the "communalism" of British India was indeed a key legitimizing narrative of the Nizam's dynastic rule, as it was for other Indian states.[170] Yet the upheavals of 1937–40 sent Hyderabad's apparent communal harmony into a sustained crisis that would, ultimately, culminate in the violence of the 1948 Police Action.[171] The 1938–39 *satyagraha*, conducted jointly by the Hyderabad State Congress, the Arya Samaj, and the Hindu Mahasabha, demonstrated not only the extent to which the dynamics of all-India politics affected Hyderabad but also the extent to which pitting the rights of "the people" against princely sovereignty took on communal and majoritarian forms. While Muslims constituted less than 13 percent of Hyderabad's population, the idea of Hyderabad as a Muslim state worked, depending on the vantage point, to both legitimize and delegitimize the Nizam's Asaf Jah dynasty in the decades prior to 1947.

Hyderabad's "Muslimness," Beverley has argued, was central to discourses of ethical governance and legitimate sovereignty in the Deccan. Historical narratives linked the Nizam's rule to earlier Deccani polities and portrayed the Asaf Jah dynasty as a legatee of the Qutb Shahis or, at times, the Mughals.[172] By the late nineteenth century, Hyderabad had become "a nodal point in expanding Muslim intellectual networks" that extended beyond South Asia, with figures like the influential pan-Islamist Jamal al-Din Al-Afghani taking up residence in the state.[173] Server-ul-Mulk, an administrator for Osman Ali Khan's father, wrote in his autobiography that the Nizam possessed "the status of Amir-ul-Momineen and Khalifa with the Muslims in India."[174] The Islamist ideologue Maulana Maududi, born in Hyderabad and a beneficiary of state patronage, would later compare the fall of Hyderabad in 1948 to the Mongol capture of Baghdad in 1258, the expulsion of the Moors from Spain in 1492, and the end of the Mughal Empire in 1858.[175] The Nizams patronized Islamic scholarship and funded the Hajj for hundreds of thousands of Indian Muslims.[176] They funded Sir Syed's Muhammadan Anglo Oriental College at Aligarh, and many Aligarh-educated Muslims from North India found employment in Hyderabad.[177] Hyderabad became a center of Urdu and Islamic scholarship in its own right after the founding of Osmania University in 1918. India's first vernacular university, Osmania enhanced Hyderabad's reputation as an important center of culture and scholarship within India and elsewhere in the Muslim world.[178]

The British, who after 1857 proudly referred to their empire as the "world's greatest Mohammedan power," also worked to promote the loyal and subordinate Nizams as leaders of India's Muslims and, at times, of a global Muslim community that made up a significant proportion of their empire.[179] The English poet Wilfred Scawen Blunt, who promoted anticolonial and pan-Islamist ideals, asserted in 1909 that the Nizam "was the leader of the Mohammedans in India, and the people looked to him for their redemption."[180] Muslims formed the largest portion of the Indian Army, the linchpin of Britain's global power, and their loyalty became a subject of concern for imperialist thinkers and administrators.[181] During the First World War, the British called upon Osman Ali Khan, who became Nizam in 1911, to take up the mantle of leadership of India's Muslims, some of whom were wary of supporting a war against the Ottoman caliph. The Nizam complied, issuing a *firman* aimed at easing Muslim doubts over serving in the British war effort. He was rewarded with new titles—"Faithful Ally of the British Government" and "His Exalted

Highness"—and sought to affirm his preeminent status among the minor sovereigns of Britain's Indian empire by playing the role of the leader of India's Muslims.

Following the war, certain North Indian Khilafatists made efforts to establish the Nizam as a figure of both religious and political authority outside of the boundaries of his state.[182] Indeed, after the fall of the Ottoman Empire, the Nizam ruled over more people than any other Muslim monarch. Marmaduke Pickthall, an English convert to Islam who produced a widely read translation of the Quran, took up residence in Hyderabad and promoted the idea of the Nizam as an inheritor to the Caliphate. Pickthall envisioned Hyderabad City as "a sort of capital city for all Muslims," and as the seat of a "benevolent Islamic polity" that would further Britain's interests.[183] The Nizam himself seemed intrigued by this question of the Caliphate and from 1924 sent regular funding for the upkeep of the deposed caliph. In 1931, the Khilafat leader Shaukat Ali brokered the marriage of the Nizam's sons to the caliph's daughter and niece.[184] "Outlandish as it appears today," Faisal Devji notes, "the idea of situating Sunni Islam's central authority in a still colonized country where Muslims were a minority was not considered especially peculiar."[185]

The Nizam's curious position as the "premier prince" of the Raj, a particularly Deccani sovereign with deep roots in the region, and a potential leader of Muslims across and beyond South Asia was reflected in the "flurry of schemes" seeking to extricate Indian Muslims from their constitutional predicament after the 1935 Act and the 1937 provincial elections.[186] Indeed, Hyderabad seemed to occupy an anomalous yet integral position in Muslim visions of what Devji has called "non-national" futures.[187] Choudhry Rahmat Ali, for example, envisioned a Pakistan consisting of a fragmented yet subcontinental landscape of Muslim sovereignty. Aside from the Muslim-majority areas in northwestern and northeastern India that would later become West and East Pakistan, Rahmat Ali also proposed a Muinistan in Rajputana, a Haideristan in United Provinces, a Faruqistan in Bihar and Orissa, a Maplistan in Kerala, and, most significantly, an Osmanistan roughly adhering to the territorial boundaries of Hyderabad State. Yet while Rahmat Ali used the Nizam's name for his proposed Osmanistan, he rejected what he considered the "blunder" of "dynasticism" and dismissed the princely order as a legitimate basis for Muslim nationhood. He proposed instead that the extant Hyderabad state be utilized as a mechanism for creating a Muslim-majority nation-state in the Deccan: "The old demand of the Pakistan National Movement for the *de facto* recognition of the *de jure* sovereignty of Ala Hazrat the Nizam, which is essentially based on the solemn treaties with him as a sovereign ally, is no more than a prelude to the national construction of Osmanistan by a voluntary exchange of her Hindoo population with Muslim population of the neighbouring regions."[188] The Nizam's standing as a legitimate sovereign within the Raj's imperial constitution would, for Rahmat Ali, serve as the basis for a Muslim-majority sovereign formation in the Deccan.

In a 1939 book, *The Muslim Problem in India*, Dr. Syed Abdul Latif, a former professor of English at Osmania University, proposed the formation of four Muslim "cultural zones" in India, one each in the Northwest and Northeast, another in United Provinces and one in Hyderabad. These four zones were to be brought together in a loose federation with eleven Hindu cultural zones as the first step toward a full exchange of population that was to take place over a period of twenty-five years.[189] Latif argued that reorganizing India into cultural zones—including some defined by language—would accomplish the long-standing Congress demand for linguistic states. Indeed, the map of Latif's Indian federation looks much like the map of India after the States Reorganization Act of 1956, except that Latif proposed removing the Marathi-, Kannada-, and Telugu-speaking peoples of Hyderabad to their respective "homelands" and replacing them with Muslims from elsewhere in peninsular India. Despite its overwhelmingly Hindu population, Hyderabad was held up as a "Muslim Zone." As for Rahmat Ali, the dynastic sovereignty of the Asaf Jah was to serve as a transitional foundation for popular sovereignty based on an eventual Muslim majority. These two principles for territorial sovereignty—kingship and "the people"—coexisted in many of these plans just as they did in all official plans of federation.

In a 1938 pamphlet entitled *The Outlines of a Scheme of Indian Federation*, Sikandar Hayat Khan, the premier of the Punjab, proposed the reorganization of India into seven regional "zones" composed of both British Indian provinces and princely states.[190] The plan included princely representatives in both regional and federal governments but did not require any internal reform in the states and guaranteed internal autonomy and princely privileges, thus institutionalizing the princely system within an all-India federation.[191] *The Confederacy of India,* published in 1939 by the *nawab* of Mamdot (Sir Shah Nawaz Khan, president of Punjab Muslim League and member of the All India Muslim League Working Committee), suggested a division of India into five separate regional federations, or "countries," united in a loose confederation.[192] These federations included Muslim-majority "Indusstan" in the Northwest and a "Bengal Federation" in the Northeast. The British Indian provinces of United Provinces, Central Provinces, Bombay, Madras, and Assam were bundled into a "Hindu India Federation." The final two federations were composed of princely states: a "Rajistan Federation" combining the states of Rajputana, central India, and Orissa, and a Hyderabad-dominated "Deccan States Federation" linking the Nizam's dominions to Mysore, Bastar, and other smaller Deccani states. Here too was an uneasy combination of demographic and dynastic criteria for territorial sovereignty. Mamdot linked the fate of Hyderabad and Kashmir together: continued Hindu sovereignty in Kashmir was accepted as a "guarantee for the security of the Muslim minority and Hyderabad State" and "a Muslim Nizam in Hindu India."[193]

Sayyid Zafarul Hassan and Dr. Muhammad Afzal Husain Qadri, both professors at Aligarh Muslim University, published *The Problem of Indian Muslims and Its Solution* in 1939.[194] They proposed dividing India into four independent and sovereign states: Pakistan, Bengal, Hindustan, and Hyderabad.[195] In his review of the Aligarh Scheme, the Congress leader Rajendra Prasad noted that "Hyderabad commands a position which is exclusively its own.... Hyderabad with its restored territories should be recognized expressly as a sovereign State, at least as sovereign as Nepal. With Karnatak restored it will have a sea-coast and will naturally become the southern wing of Muslim India."[196] As discussed above, this demand for the restoration of Berar and other "Ceded Districts" was a consistent demand of the Nizam until 1947 and suggestive of the ways in which Hyderabad was imagined as an independent state, as a federated state, and vis-à-vis Pakistan. The pro-Muslim League branch of the Jamiat-ul-Ulema in the North West Frontier Provinces, for example, passed a resolution in 1940 calling for the "formation of an independent Muslim State consisting of Eastern Afghanistan, Tribal territory, the Frontier Province, Kashmir, the Punjab, Sind, Baluchistan," which was "to be placed under the Nizam of Hyderabad."[197]

While Jinnah refused to comment on any of these proposals, they were considered by other senior members of the Muslim League. In 1941, Sir Abdullah Haroon convened a "Muslim League Foreign Sub-Committee" composed of various authors of constitutional schemes, including Afzal Hussain Qadri, Syed Abdul Latif, and the *nawab* of Mamdot. The subcommittee's report offered a detailed territorial and demographic outline for their proposal that "one Muslim State can be formed in the North-West and another in the North-East."[198] In addition to these two federated states, they suggested that the League commit itself to "conserve and perpetuate the Muslim influence wherever it predominates in any form in non-British India." The Nizam's dominions should constitute a "Third Zone of Muslim Influence and Power": "Hence it is that all the native states, large or small, ruled by Muslim Princes, should be regarded for purposes of the Muslim constitutional plan as sovereign Muslim States. This must be made a basic demand. Of such Muslim States, Hyderabad with its vast territory is not a feudatory or creation of the British Government in the sense every other native state whether Muslim or Hindu is. Besides being the principal seat of the culture of Muslim India it is an independent state in its own inherent and historic rights."[199] The subcommittee emphasized Hyderabad's cultural importance and unique standing among the Indian states. An independent Hyderabad under the Nizam would, moreover, serve the interests of Muslims located in the nonmajority areas of India: "Who knows that in the fullness of time the Muslims of India might find it to their advantage to make Hyderabad their rallying point and the centre of their growing strength. This will thus be the third wide sphere of Muslim influence, the other two being those in the N.-W. and the North-East—the three forming a triangular stronghold of the Muslims in India."[200] Jinnah, for his part, considered the Indian states to be sovereign entities and argued that any settlement between the League, Congress, and the British would apply to British India alone.[201] The "independent states" referred to in the Lahore Resolution, then, very much included Indian states ruled by Muslim dynasties, Hyderabad most important among them. Jinnah was particularly keen to maintain the territorial integrity of the constituent units of the Raj, especially the provinces of Punjab and Bengal. Yet by refusing to include the princely states in a communal constitutional settlement, Jinnah gambled with the fate of Jammu and Kashmir. He encouraged the Nizam to stay out of an all-India federation after 1935 and to pursue independence in 1947. Yet the failure of federation, the Partition, and the founding of Pakistan ultimately left the Nizam on his own.

The desire to preclude a "triangular stronghold of the Muslims"—what Sardar Patel called a "Pan-Islamic bloc" on the eve of the Police Action—influenced the Congress's eventual concession of a territorial Pakistan limited to the northeast and northwest of British India.[202] Hyderabad became a key flashpoint in all-India contestations over sovereignty and democracy. This was not simply a story about the spread of "communalism" from British to princely India; rather, it was about a subcontinental contestation over sovereignty and the meaning of "the people" in late colonial India. To understand the Partition, then, we must account for the Indian states. The Indian states were key factors leading to the June 3 Partition Plan, and the terms of the settlement had enormous consequences for the fate of the states. The Partition and the Police Action were not merely contemporaneous events but outcomes of a shared history.

V. Partition and the Princes

The events of the late 1930s set the stage for the postwar sprint toward Partition. I have argued above that the Indian states were not merely a sideshow to the British Indian main event. They were integral to the development of all-India debates over sovereignty and democracy. The 1935 Government of India Act and the proposed Federation of India sought to codify and institutionalize the Raj's imperial regime of sovereignty by securing the sovereignty of the Indian states in an all-India polity. For the Congress this was straight constitutional skullduggery: federation would entrench British rule, perpetuate anachronistic autocracies, and undermine the territorial integrity of the Indian nation. They responded by demanding a sovereign constituent assembly for the entirety of India elected by universal adult franchise. In 1940, the Muslim League, seeking to "extricate Muslims from an untenable constitutional position," demanded Pakistan.[203] Thrust into the turbulent center of all-India politics, the Indian states ultimately rejected federation and clung to the perceived comfort of their indeterminate constitutional status as minor sovereigns within the British Empire. When the Second World War began, they once again pledged their men and resources to the king-emperor.

The June 3 Plan of 1947 and the Indian Independence Act would, ultimately, cut the Indian states out of the deal. This was a necessary condition for a settlement between the Congress and the League. The British unilaterally severed relations entirely with the Indian states, refused to recognize them as international entities, and, crucially, denied them entrance into the British Commonwealth. The states were both enticed and threatened to accede to either of the two new dominions of India and Pakistan. Mountbatten promised the Congress that he would work to deliver the states—a "full basket of apples"—to the Indian Union.[204] Indeed, the Congress accepted Partition, in no small measure, because it offered a solution to the problem of the princely states.[205]

For the Congress, the problem of the states was a problem of national unity. The Partition and the incorporation of the Indian states into the Indian Union were conceived of as part of the same historical process: the making of the territorial Indian nation-state. Partition, for academic scholars and Indian nationalists alike, is often articulated in terms of loss and severing, but it was also a process of consolidation and centralization. Building up a single national state out of the Raj's imperial regime of sovereignty was a complex and contested process. Hyderabad, in this respect, posed a great challenge to the territorial integrity of the Indian nation-state and to the project of a republican India. The Police Action was Partition's third front. Yet, unlike the Partition, it wasn't a border-making exercise. Just the opposite, the battle for the Deccan was a battle for the territorial heart of India.

The June 3 Plan represented a significant break from established frameworks of imperial constitutionalism, including the 1946 Cabinet Mission Plan. Much happened during the war that set the stage for the postwar isolation of the Indian states. The 1942 Cripps proposals offered the creation of a "new Indian Union" as an equal dominion within the British Commonwealth. Cripps promised that "steps shall be taken" to establish a constituent assembly after the war.[206] Yet that assembly would not be entirely sovereign; its decisions would need to be accepted by the British. Cripps committed the British government to accepting the constitution produced by the Constituent Assembly on two conditions. First, "any Province of British India" must be given the choice to refuse accession to the new union and, in that case, the province would "retain its present constitutional position." Moreover, such "non-acceding Provinces" could earn "the same full status as the Indian Union." That is, individual provinces could enter the Commonwealth as separate dominions. Second, the new Indian Union had to enter into a new treaty with the British covering "all necessary matters arising out of the complete transfer of responsibility" and providing for the "protection of racial and religious minorities." In keeping with the established practice of the princely veto, the Indian states were given the choice to join the union or, failing that, to "negotiate a revision of its treaty arrangements." If a state chose to accede, the ruler would be able to appoint representatives to the constituent assembly. Cripps further assured the princes that the British would "stand by our treaties with the States unless they asked us to revoke them."[207]

The proposed role of the Indian States influenced the Congress' rejection of the Cripps plan. They also objected to the "fettered and circumscribed" nature of the constituent assembly.[208] Allowing the rulers of the Indian states to choose delegates to the assembly amounted to "ignoring the ninety millions of the Indian States" and a "negation of both democracy and self-determination." The states, they argued, would "become barriers to the growth of Indian freedom, enclaves where foreign authority still prevails and where the possibility of maintaining foreign armed forces has been stated to be a likely contingency, and a perpetual menace to the freedom of the people of the States as well as the rest of

India."[209] The right of both provinces and states to stay out of the union would, Nehru reflected in *The Discovery of India*, create a situation of "separatism" in which "reactionary elements, differing from each other in many ways, would unite to frustrate the evolution of a strong, progressive, unified national state."[210] Nehru signaled his grudging acceptance of Pakistan if only as a means of preventing further territorial fragmentation along princely lines:

> Circumstances may force a partition of what logically and normally must not be divided. But the proposals put forward on behalf of the British Government did not deal with any definite and particular partition of India. They opened out a vista of indefinite number of partitions of provinces and states. They incited all the reactionary, feudal, and socially backward groups to claim partition.... If they were backed by British policy, as they well might be, it meant no freedom at all for a long time.... Thus this proposal was not a mere acceptance of Pakistan or a particular partition, bad as that would have been, *but something much worse*, opening the door to the possibility of *an indefinite number of partitions*. It was a continuing menace to the freedom of India.[211]

Walking away from the negotiating table, the Congress opted instead for mass mobilization, the last of Gandhi's great *satyagraha* campaigns. Launched in August 1942, the Quit India Movement saw the Congress leadership tossed behind bars for the duration of the war. The colonial government struggled to contain nonviolent and violent resistance, both of which brought administration to a grinding halt in multiple provinces. With over one hundred thousand arrested and mass fines implemented, the movement was a testament to the continued mobilizational ability of the Congress and to the tenuous grip of the colonial state over dissident populations. Both would be important factors in postwar constitutional negotiations. The Quit India movement in Hyderabad was by comparison far more modest, leading to the arrest of about four hundred Hyderabad State congressmen and another one hundred Arya Samajis.[212]

For the Indian states, the Cripps proposal pointed toward two possible futures. On the one hand was the possibility of acceding to an all-India federal polity along the lines of the Federation of India envisioned by the 1935 Act. On the other hand, Cripps raised the possibility of states, either individually or as groups, being granted dominion status. Thus, whether there was to be one successor to the Raj or multiple successors, the Indian states and their relationship to the British Crown would be preserved. The Indian states still had significant support among British politicians, and the Tories in particular. Viceroy Wavell noted in his journal in March 1945 that Churchill "seems to favour Partition into Pakistan, Hindustan, Princestan, etc."[213] The Nizam sought to distinguish Hyderabad from the other Indian states, informing Wavell that only those states "capable of standing on their own legs" should be allowed to survive.[214] Hyderabad's constitutional adviser, Ali Yavar Jung, argued in December 1945 for the advantages of the Indian states grouping together to form separate unions. He imagined Hyderabad (including Berar) forming a union with Mysore, Bastar, and the Northern Circars.[215] Yet, he presciently observed, it was important to keep in mind that the issues at stake "are political and not legal." "The period now opening," he warned, "will indeed be a period of tough political warfare."[216]

When constitutional negotiations resumed after the war, they initially proceeded in a familiar fashion. Wavell's 1945 Simla Conference proposals related to "British India only and do not make any alteration in the relations of the Princes with the Crown Representative."[217] Similarly, the 1946 Cabinet Mission Plan built upon the 1942 Cripps proposal. The Cabinet Mission proposed an all-India federation with a center exercising powers limited to defense, foreign affairs, and communications. Below the center was a middle tier of three subfederations composed of groups of provinces. At the bottom tier were the individual provinces themselves, which were provided with a mechanism for opting out of the subfederations but not out of the all-India federation. The Cabinet Mission proposed that acceding states would "retain all subjects and powers other than those ceded to the Union."[218] In many respects this was an updated version of the Federation of India proposed in 1935. This time, however, the Chamber of Princes formally endorsed the Cabinet Mission's proposals in June 1946. The Cabinet Mission, however, acknowledged that the end of paramountcy was imminent: "It is quite clear that with the attainment of independence by British India, whether inside or outside the British Commonwealth, the relationship which hitherto existed between the Rulers of the States and the British Crown will no longer be possible. Paramountcy can neither be retained by the British Crown nor transferred to the new Government."[219] In attempting to clarify this statement, the Cabinet Mission, however, muddied the waters:

> This means that the rights of the States which flow from their relationship to the Crown will no longer exist and that all the rights surrendered by the States to the Paramount Power will return to the States. Political arrangements between the States on the one side and the British Crown and British India on the other will thus be brought to an end. The void will have to be filled either by the States entering into a federal relationship with the Successor Government or Governments in British India, or failing this, entering into particular political arrangements with it or them.[220]

The Cabinet Mission conceptualized paramountcy as a contractual relationship between the Crown and the Indian states, in which certain powers were divided among the partners. The statement implied two potential outcomes. First, the Indian states, with all their rights "returned" to them, would, by virtue of the lapsing of paramountcy, immediately become independent sovereigns. Second, the Indian states would "have to" enter into "particular political arrangements" with the successor governments. This ambiguity surrounding the sovereignty of the princely states contributed to the Cabinet Mission Plan's undoing.

For the Congress, nonaccession of the Indian states was unacceptable, yet accession on parity with the provinces of British India was an equally objectionable institutionalization of princely autocracy. Moreover, recognizing the right of *all* the nearly six hundred princely states to federate would, in theory, have given constitutional parity to a wide range of entities among the states themselves, most of which were petty estates and *jagirs*. More troubling for the Congress would have been the inability of a center exercising powers limited to foreign affairs, defense, and communications to intervene in the administration of the states or to impose representative institutions on them.[221] As with the 1935 Constitution, the Cabinet Mission Plan, by maintaining the fragmented jurisdictional landscape of the Raj, would have foreclosed the possibility of a universal regime of citizenship rights. In the event of provincial grouping giving birth to two Muslim-majority groups in the Northwest and Northeast, a Hyderabad under the continued rule of the Nizam would have ultimately turned the map of India under the Cabinet Mission Plan into something akin to the proposals, discussed above, put forth by Sikandar Hyat Khan or the 1941 Haroon Sub-Committee.

The Nizam in 1946 had two main objectives: to maintain the territorial integrity of his dominions and his connection with the British Crown. This was a continuation of long-standing efforts to consolidate the sovereignty of his state and his dynasty. The Nizam settled on a wait-and-see approach. If there was to be a united India, it seemed likely that the Indian states would maintain a significant amount of integrity and autonomy as they had in previous federal plans—perhaps even more so, considering that paramountcy would lapse and with it the right of the government of India to intervene in their internal affairs. In this scenario, the Nizam's status as a subordinate sovereign would continue much the same as it had in the past, as would his relationship with the British Crown through the Commonwealth. The Nizam wrote to Sir Arthur Lothian, the British resident at Hyderabad, in May 1946 that "a united India would be much more advantageous to all concerned than the partition of India" and that "Mr. Jinnah is doing great disservice not only to British India and the British States but also he is ruining the interests of his own community by following a wrong path owing to his obstinate policy."[222] The Nizam opposed Pakistan because he thought it imperiled the interests of Hyderabad's Muslims and represented an abdication of the League's responsibility to Muslims in the areas of India where they were a minority. In their meeting with the Cabinet Mission, Hyderabad's delegates articulated a preference for a united confederal India with a central government with communal parity and limited to foreign affairs and defense.

In the case of Partition, the Nizam insisted that he would be unable to commit his state either to Pakistan, for obvious reasons of geography, or to India, for ideological reasons.[223] This ideological contradiction stemmed not only from the fact that India was Hindu but even more from Indian nationalists' commitment to a republican project of majority rule. Dynastic kingship was, of course, the key pillar of Hyderabad's patrimonial state. If there was to be Partition, the Nizam planned to seek dominion status for Hyderabad within the British Commonwealth and, eventually, recognition as an international entity. He would attempt, at the inception of the postwar international order, to become an "independent sovereign."

For advice, the Nizam engaged Sir Walter Monckton, a lawyer who had previously consulted on Hyderabad's constitutional affairs and had extensive contacts among Britain's ruling elite. In a February 1946 memorandum to the Nizam's executive council, Monckton made a number of recommendations. First, Hyderabad should neither commit itself to joining a proposed union nor refuse to consider the possibility. He warned that if Hyderabad decided against acceding to a federal union, "It might well find itself squeezed in later on on much worse terms."[224] He further argued that the Hyderabad government should take whatever action it could to strengthen its position vis-à-vis British India. Hyderabad's "main source of weakness" was that it was landlocked, so Monckton advised the Nizam to pursue a port facility in Goa. He recommended the immediate implementation of the constitutional reforms of 1939, improving administration, expanding health and education initiatives, and taking measures to develop industry. Monckton thought that in the event that Pakistan was granted, Hyderabad's case could be strengthened because there would be more than one successor government. Hyderabad could, by virtue of its size and history, legitimately claim to be one of multiple successors to the Raj. In terms of Berar and other territorial claims, Monckton warned that Hyderabad's legal case was strong but unlikely to pay dividends. Any decisions going forward "will be ultimately political" rather than legal, and he advised that the Nizam's treaty rights would best be used as bargaining chips in a political settlement.

The Nizam took a number of steps to press Hyderabad's interests in the all-India and imperial arenas, while inadequately addressing growing discontent within his state. Hyderabad once again demanded the return of Berar as well as the "Ceded Districts" of Bellary, Cuddapah, Kurnool, and Anantapur. The Nizam also asserted his treaty rights to the port of Masulipatnam and authorized secret negotiations with the Portuguese to obtain a port in Goa.[225] To the alarm of Nehru and other Congress leaders, Hyderabad was awarded a mining and railway concession in the neighboring state of Bastar in early 1947.[226] The Nizam agreed to implement, in part, the 1939 constitutional reforms in 1946. The elections to the Legislative Assembly were, however, boycotted by all the major parties excepting the Majlis, who won all of the Muslim seats in the Assembly. Indeed, the Andhra Mahasabha, the Hyderabad State Congress, the Socialist Party, Arya Samaj, and the Hindu Mahasabha were in no mood to cooperate and would eventually turn to armed insurrection against the Nizam's government. The revolutionary uprising in Telangana began in June 1946. The other parties, as they did in 1938–39, all set up camps in the Marathi-speaking areas along Hyderabad's northwestern border from mid-1947. This situation would come to haunt the Nizam, when, after August 1947, the Indian government would demand responsible government as a condition of a settlement with Hyderabad. There were no willing or able political parties to which the Nizam could have handed over responsibilities of administration. Indian officials reached the same conclusion immediately after the Police Action, and the state remained administered by unelected military officials, civil servants, and Congress party functionaries until after the 1952 elections.

The 1946 provincial elections and the establishment of the Constituent Assembly departed from conventional frameworks of imperial constitutionalism and, accordingly, were watershed moments in the refashioning of the Raj into the Republic. The Congress won the elections in Assam, Bihar, Bombay, Central Provinces, Madras, North West Frontier Province, and United Provinces. The League captured the Muslim-majority provinces of Bengal, Punjab, and Sindh. The Congress vote share in non-Muslim constituencies was over 90 percent, which gave them 923 of a total 1,585 provincial assembly seats across India. Under the terms of the Cabinet

Mission Plan, provincial legislatures elected members of the Constituent Assembly. Ultimately, the Congress won 208 seats and the League 73 seats in the Assembly out of a proposed total of 389 seats (93 of which were reserved for representatives from the Indian states). After joining the Interim Government in August 1946, the Congress exercised a commanding position within the cabinet of the government of India and had positioned themselves as the logical and rightful inheritors of the British. In sum, by mid-1946 the Congress had successfully translated its claim to represent "the people" into considerable institutional power and a predominant role in the crafting of India's future constitution. They were not in the mood to cede too much to either the League or the Indian states. In Britain, the landslide victory of the Labour Party in the 1945 elections gave the Congress a partner in the Attlee government, with whom they shared significant common ground. In December 1946, the Constituent Assembly resolved to "proclaim India as an Independent Sovereign Republic."[227]

Jinnah and the League, recognizing the commanding position of the Congress, withdrew their agreement to the Cabinet Mission Plan and refused to join either the Constituent Assembly or the Interim Government. On July 29, 1946, the League passed the Direct Action Resolution: "The Muslims of India would not rest contented with anything less than the immediate establishment of an Independent and fully sovereign State of Pakistan."[228] Direct Action Day on August 16 sparked communal bloodshed in Calcutta, an episode that set into motion a subcontinental event of violence that would reached its climax in the civil war, ethnic cleansing, and Partition of 1947. With the perceived obstructionism of Muslim League ministers in the Interim Government, unrest in the countryside, and communal violence raising the specter of civil war, the Congress began in the early months of 1947 to see Partition as a means of escaping the constitutional impasse. Equally worrying for the Congress was the persistent support for the Indian states by Muslim League ministers, who insisted that the central government had no right to interfere in princely matters.[229] Partition would, in a single move, sequester the League in a truncated Pakistan on the fringes of the subcontinent and allow the Congress to claim the rest of India, including the vast princely territories. At a March 8 meeting of the Congress Working Committee, Patel moved a resolution accepting the fundamentals of Pakistan. Supported by Nehru and Maulana Azad, the resolution was adopted unanimously by the Working Committee. Nehru clarified this position in April: "The Muslim League can have Pakistan, but on condition that they do not take away other parts of India which do not wish to join Pakistan."[230] Speaking as president of the All India States Peoples' Conference on April 18, Nehru declared that any princely state that did not join the Constituent Assembly would be considered "hostile" and made "to bear the consequences of being so regarded." His ultimate fear was the division of the country not "into one or two parts but into one hundred or more."[231]

This fear was the reason for Nehru's apoplectic reaction to the "Plan Balkan" approved by the British Cabinet and presented by Viceroy Mountbatten in Shimla on May 10, 1947. The plan would have transferred sovereignty to the provinces rather than the central government and would have allowed the princes to claim legal rights to independence and continued relations with the Crown. Nehru wrote to Mountbatten that instead of producing a "sense of certainty, security and stability" the plan encouraged "disruptive tendencies everywhere and chaos and weakness": "The proposals start with the rejection of an Indian Union as the successor to power and invite the claims of large numbers of successor States who are permitted to unite if they so wish in two or more States."[232] The implications of the plan, he concluded, would be "the Balkanisation of India" and, echoing the 1928 Nehru Report, the creation of multiple "Ulsters in India."[233]

It was in the wake of this encounter that Nehru and Mountbatten negotiated the Commonwealth solution that formed the basis for the settlement of June 3.[234] There would be a transfer of power to two new dominions of India and Pakistan, defined territorially by religious demography, within the British Commonwealth. The Indian states were essentially cut out of the deal. Britain would not recognize the states as international entities, and the only way the princes could maintain their relationship with the British Crown was via accession to either India or Pakistan.[235] It was this break from the established conventions of imperial constitutionalism that was Mountbatten's most significant innovation. In order to convince the Congress to abandon their long-standing commitments to complete independence and national unity, and to accept dominion status and Partition instead, Mountbatten committed himself to delivering the states to the Indian Union.[236] When the All India Congress Committee approved the June 3 Plan, Nehru sold Partition as a means of assuring Congress's unhindered control over a powerful central government.[237] The adoption of the resolution in favor of Partition was immediately followed by a resolution denying the right of any Indian state to declare itself independent.[238]

The Congress pushed for the transfer of paramountcy to the new dominion. As C. Rajagopalachari argued, "Paramountcy came into being as a fact and not by agreement, and on Britain's withdrawal the successor authorities must inherit the fact along with the rest of the context."[239] The Indian Independence Act, as we have seen, explicitly did not transfer paramountcy. Instead, the British unilaterally revoked all of their treaty and other relations with the Indian states. The Nizam understood this to mean that he would "resume" the status of an "independent sovereign." For the Congress, the British abandonment of the princes made the government of India the de facto paramount power. Nehru, in a June 1947 speech to the All India Congress Committee, argued that there was "a certain inherent paramountcy in the Government of India which cannot lapse."[240] The tensions between the legal and political domains of the imperial regime of sovereignty were not, by any means, immediately resolved in August 1947. Hyderabad would take its legal case all the way to the United Nations Security Council. Ultimately, the Police Action of September 1948 produced a new political fact, and subsequent legal developments grew out of that fact.

The key Congress decision makers, Nehru and Patel, approached the relationship between Partition and the Indian states in terms of the territorial integrity of the nation-state.[241] They were encouraged by Mountbatten and his constitutional adviser V. P. Menon, who argued that if Congress accepted both Partition and dominion status, India would accrue a net gain of territory by the accession of the princely states.[242] Patel was clear about the connection between Partition and the Indian states: "The country is saved from fragmentation by the accession of States. Otherwise, a

Raja-sthan would have been something worse than Pakistan. . . . I can tell you that if we had not accepted partition, India would have broken into bits. Now that we have been able to salvage a major part of India and have been able to build it up into an extensive single unit, let us make it powerful."[243] Patel's justification for Partition rested primarily on the counterfactual of a potential "Rajasthan": "I recall how only six months ago there was a general talk of a 'Raja-sthan' which, if it had materialised, would have meant that the whole body politic of India would have been covered with ulcers. Instead we have achieved integration and unity which have promised immense potentialities for glory and greatness."[244] Hyderabad, of course, was the greatest of these "ulcers." And unlike Nehru, who while favoring Partition nevertheless always spoke of it in terms of a lament, Patel openly sought to claim responsibility: "I would make no efforts to explain away the responsibility of the Congress for dividing the country. We took these extreme steps after great deliberation. . . . I felt convinced that in order to keep India united it must be divided now."[245] By dividing existing provinces on the basis of religious demography, the June 3 Plan departed from earlier federal schemes that maintained the territorial integrity of both the British Indian provinces and Indian states. The idea that provinces and states should remain intact had since the 1920s been a point of consensus among the British, the Muslim League, and the Indian states. It was on precisely this basis that the 1944 Gandhi-Jinnah talks failed, with the latter famously rejecting the partitioning of Punjab and Bengal as "a shadow and a husk, maimed, mutilated, moth-eaten Pakistan."

In earlier federal schemes, such as the 1935 Constitution, provinces and states were to come together as constituent units of a federation. In such schemes, the act of federating worked to affirm the sovereign status of the individual units and guaranteed their territorial integrity and internal autonomy. The Dominion of India, by contrast, inherited the Raj's unitary character. The Indian Union was not created as a federal state. Rather, its federal characteristics were developed later. The June 3 Plan, in other words, allowed for the accession of the Indian states to a unitary Indian Union on terms that did little to preserve their territorial integrity or internal autonomy. The Ministry of States, established in July 1947, moved swiftly under Patel's leadership to incorporate and dissolve princely territories. Initially, many of the states were grouped together into units like Madhya Bharat, PEPSU, Rajputana, and the Deccan States. By November 1949 only 6 of the 552 states that had acceded to India maintained their old territorial boundaries.[246] In this manner, then, the failure of federation followed by Partition made it possible for a very different sort of federalism to develop in the years after 1947, a system that some have credited with providing a foundation for Indian democracy in the decades since.[247] Hyderabad was broken up along linguistic lines in 1956 as part of India's first wave of federal reorganization.

In the short period between June 3 and August 15, 1947, almost all of the Indian states acceded to Pakistan or India, the vast majority to the latter. The mechanism was the same as prescribed by the 1935 Act: an Instrument of Accession. The Instruments were limited in nature. They asked the states to accede on three subjects alone: defense, external affairs, and communications. The Instruments explicitly affirmed the sovereignty of rulers "in and over" their states.[248] In this respect, they aimed to ease princely fears and lure them into the union. The terms of accession appeared very similar to their preexisting relationship with the government of India, with the states retaining a high degree of autonomy. In practice, however, the States Ministry was far more interventionist than the Political Department it replaced; rulers were ultimately reduced to mere figureheads with little real power, their sovereignty and territories replaced by that of the nation.

The Congress's success in convincing the vast majority of the princes to sign Instruments of Accession was due to an astute combination of coercion and incentive executed by Patel, Mountbatten, and V. P. Menon, who became secretary of the Ministry of States when it was created in July 1947.[249] In his overture to the states, Patel emphasized the patriotic duty of the princes to maintain national unity. The Congress, he reassured them, had no intention to "interfere in any manner whatever with the domestic affairs of the States."[250] Yet Patel also warned the states that failure to accede would lead to "anarchy and chaos which will overwhelm great and small in a common ruin."[251] Paramountcy and the Raj's imperial regime of sovereignty, Patel told the princes, were giving way to a new national regime of sovereignty based on popular sovereignty, or what he called "the ultimate Paramountcy of popular interests and welfare."[252]

Mountbatten, capitalizing on his status as a member of the royal family, took a similar route with the Chamber of Princes, a performance Menon described as the "apogee of persuasion."[253] The viceroy acknowledged the legal position, according to the Cabinet Mission Memorandum, the June 3 Plan, and the Indian Independence Act, that the states "have complete freedom—technically and legally they are independent."[254] Yet he argued that accession on the three subjects of defense, external affairs, and communications would give the princes "all the practical independence that you can possibly use and makes you free of all those subjects which you cannot possibly manage on your own."[255] If the states were to send representatives to the Constituent Assembly, they could, as Menon noted approvingly, "act as a brake on the headlong career of British India" and could "join hands with the Right Wing of the Congress" to combat the threat of socialism and communism.[256] Mountbatten and Menon also issued explicit warnings to the princes. If the states did not accede, the viceroy said, they "will be cut off from any source or supplies of up-to-date arms or weapons," rendering them helpless in the face of "external aggression."[257] He warned that the terms being offered to the states would no longer be available after August 15, so that this was the last chance for the states to secure their "internal autonomy or sovereignty."[258] "You cannot," he concluded, "run away from the Dominion Government which is your neighbor any more than you can run away from the subjects for whose welfare you are responsible."[259] In essence, the Indian states were presented with a fait accompli. Either they could accede or they would be left to face the Congress-controlled Indian Union government on their own.

VI. From Partition to Azad Hyderabad

In 1947, the British partitioned India and, in doing so, betrayed their most loyal partners in empire.[260] The abrupt departure from the conventions of imperial constitutionalism came as a shock to the Indian states. The *nawab* of Bhopal, the leader of the Chamber of Princes, desperately appealed to Mountbatten: "Are we to write out a blank cheque and leave it to the leaders of the Congress party to fill in the amount?" He pointed to the fundamental contradiction between republicanism and kingship: "How can we, the Rulers of independent States, throw in our lot with a political party whose resolution that India should become a Republic is still on the statute book. You cannot, my dear Dickie, mix oil with water."[261] When the details of the Indian Independence Act were made public in early July, the Nizam expressed his dismay at the "unilateral repudiation" of his treaties with the British, the "way in which my State is being abandoned by its old ally," and the preemptive foreclosure of Hyderabad's entrance into the Commonwealth.[262] The Nizam noted that the treaties guaranteeing Hyderabad protection against external aggression and internal disorder had been "constantly and solemnly reaffirmed," most recently by Cripps in 1942. As a result, Hyderabad was entirely unprepared to defend itself militarily and had not established industries to manufacture arms and other military equipment.[263]

In the weeks leading up to August 15, the Nizam and his representatives raised three main points with Mountbatten and the Congress. First, he was unwilling to accede to India. But he was willing to sign a treaty that covered the three subjects (defense, external affairs, communications) provided for in the Instruments of Accession. This difference between a treaty and an Instrument of Accession was a sticking point for both the Congress and the Nizam all the way up to September 1948. Under international law, treaties are made between two distinct sovereign and international entities. The Nizam argued that the Congress's insistence on an Instrument of Accession was a violation of the principles laid out in the Cabinet Mission Memorandum, and reiterated in the June 3 Plan, that referred only to "particular political arrangements" between states and the government of India.[264] The Congress refused to consider anything but accession, although they did give Mountbatten a two-month extension after August 15 to come to terms with the Nizam.

The second issue was that of Berar. On this, the legal position was quite clear. The Indian Independence Act clearly established, as Mountbatten put it, "the Nizam's sovereignty over Berar in law."[265] To the Congress, this was, in Gandhi's words, a "crime."[266] The Nizam made basically the same offer that he did in 1923: Berar would continue to be administered as a part of the Central Provinces, and Beraris would enjoy "all the freedom and responsible Government which they have now." Yet the Nizam would have the right to appoint Berar's governor. He argued that the continuation of the status quo in Berar would enable "the whole problem" with the Indian government to be "reasonably and amicably settled."[267] The Congress decided against negotiating with the Nizam regarding Berar and, instead, continued to administer the region as an integral part of the Indian Union. In the days before August 15, the Nizam raised the Berar issue as well as the potential restoration of the Northern Circars and Ceded Territories as conditions of any treaty deal with India.[268] He further insisted that a new treaty take into account provisions of the Commercial Treaty of 1802.[269] The Nizam was betting that, despite the revocation of treaties by the British, his legal case remained strong on the basis of centuries of international law and imperial constitutionalism, through which the sovereignty of his state and dynasty had been reaffirmed and reproduced. He would eventually take his case to the United Nations.

The third major issue raised by the Nizam was the state of relations between India and Pakistan. "The Partition of India," he observed, "has gravely complicated the problem for my State." He noted that Hyderabad was "necessarily closely concerned in various ways with what will now become the Dominion of India" but that "there are also many ties between my State and the future Pakistan Dominion."[270] As such, he wanted to maintain good relations with both dominions and was, as a result, bound to "wait and see how the relations between the two Dominions are regulated and developed."[271] As part of any treaty with India, he wanted assurances that Hyderabad and Hyderabadi forces would be able to remain neutral in the event of war with Pakistan.

Mountbatten warned the Nizam's representatives that "Hyderabad was militarily defenceless." The present chance, the viceroy continued, was the "last one and, if not seized at once, would be lost forever." The results would be "disastrous" if "his advice was not taken."[272] V. P. Menon warned of a blockade and serious "disorders" within Hyderabad and stated, in a thinly veiled threat, that "India would not stand by and see that state of affairs continue."[273] Popular agitation, in other words, would serve as a pretext for the annexation of Hyderabad by military means. Indeed, on the eve of the Nizam's June 1947 declaration of independence, Nehru warned Mountbatten that he would "encourage rebellion in all States that go against us."[274] This, as the next chapter demonstrates, was the exact strategy the Congress and the government of India would pursue between 1947 and 1948.

After June 3, the Nizam turned to Jinnah for advice, informing the Qaid that he would not take any decisions without his "concurrence and knowledge."[275] Jinnah's position had not changed much since the 1930s. "Constitutionally and legally," he argued, "the Indian States will be independent sovereign States" and could join India, Pakistan, or declare independence.[276] The Nizam hoped that Hyderabad's legal standing and its reputation as a "Muslim" state would allow him to find a place for Hyderabad within the communal settlement of Partition. Initially, Jinnah made efforts to assure both the Nizam and the government of India that the League, and Indian Muslims more broadly, would support Hyderabad. In July 1947, Jinnah warned Mountbatten that "if Congress attempted to exert any pressure on Hyderabad, every Muslim throughout the whole of India, yes, all the hundred million Muslims, would rise as one man to defend the oldest Muslim dynasty in India."[277] The Nizam explained to Jinnah that his commitment to a treaty rather than accession was driven partly by the fact that treaties could, as demonstrated by the British, be unilaterally revoked. A treaty would buy time to strengthen his state and, eventually, to seek independence and a bilateral treaty with Pakistan: "If and when Pakistan and Hyderabad are in a strong enough position to enable Hyderabad to resist political and economic pressure by the surrounding Hindustan, His Exalted Highness would review the position to make his ties closer with Pakistan and less close with the Dominion of India."[278] Before deciding "what attitude to adopt at this vital juncture," the Nizam wanted to know, "in black and white," what steps Jinnah would take in the event that India sought to pressure Hyderabad economically, militarily, or otherwise.[279]

Jinnah assured Hyderabadi officials that there should be "no doubt" that "Pakistan would come to the help of Hyderabad in every way possible."[280] Jinnah urged the Nizam to refuse to accede to India under any circumstances. According to Ali Yavar Jung, Hyderabad's constitutional adviser, Jinnah encouraged the Nizam to emulate the example of the Imam Hussain:

> He said that after all there was some such thing as standing for one's own right, despite every threat or provocation. If it came to the worst, one should die fighting rather than yield on a point of fundamental principle. Mr. Jinnah gave the illustration of what he called the greatest martyrdom in history, the example of Imam Hussain standing for what was right and giving his life for it. All the sanctions in the world then existing were applied against him and his followers but they withstood them and suffered wholesale butchery. It was a moral triumph and they gave their lives for it. That should be the attitude which the Nizam and his advisers and his people should adopt.[281]

Over the thirteen months between August 1947 and September 1948, Hyderabad was indeed put under tremendous pressure by the Indian Union, and Pakistan did little to come to the Nizam's aid. Ultimately, the Police Action resulted in significant anti-Muslim violence and an ignominious ending for the idea of Azad Hyderabad.

VII. The Incorporation and Dissolution of Hyderabad State

By the time August 15, 1947, arrived, massive transformations in the sovereign landscape of the subcontinent were already in full swing. The ruptures and upheavals of Partition would give further shape and substance to the new dominions of Pakistan and India. Yet contestations over sovereignty and territory were by no means resolved. Even though the vast majority of the Indian States signed on the dotted line, Kashmir and Hyderabad had not. The former would quite rapidly transform into an intractable international conflict central to the identities of the new territorial nation-states. Hyderabad, set adrift by its imperial benefactor and its Muslim allies, sought to find a place in the nascent postwar international order amid the sweeping changes brought about by decolonization, the "transfer of power," and Partition.

The thirteen months between August 1947 and September 1948 were uncertain and anxious, as the subcontinent reeled from the upheavals of Partition and as a multifaceted contestation over sovereignty in the Deccan escalated. Hyderabad became the site of three rival projects of sovereignty. The nascent Indian Union and its partisans faced off against the Nizam and the project of Muslim sovereignty in the Deccan. And in the Telangana region of Hyderabad, peasant revolutionaries challenged both the legitimacy of the Nizam's state and the Indian Union's claim to popular sovereignty. As Hyderabad's sprawling frontier with the Indian Union became a site of contestation and as Kashmir turned into an international battlefield, the Nizam signed a Standstill Agreement with the government of India on November 29, 1947. Doing so made Hyderabad's status as a sovereign but subordinate state much the same as it had been in the Raj. The agreement had five articles. The first article held that matters of common concern (including defense, external affairs, and communications) that had existed between the Crown and the Nizam would continue between the government of India and the Nizam. India, however, could not send military forces into Hyderabad except in a time of war and would not exercise any "paramountcy functions" in its relations with Hyderabad.[282] The agreement continued, in sum, the parceling of sovereign rights and prerogatives that was the cornerstone of the Raj's imperial constitution.

Further negotiations between Hyderabad and India continued along a long and tortuous path until their ultimate collapse in June 1948.[283] Although press accounts in India raised the specter of a Hyderabad-Pakistan alliance, Jinnah would ultimately do very little to help the Nizam realize the project of Azad Hyderabad.[284] Leading up to his death on the eve of the Police Action, Jinnah continued to publicly support Hyderabad's legal right to independence: "It is already well-known by both the Governments of Hyderabad and India that Hyderabad was an independent sovereign State and it was for its duly constituted authority to accede to India or remain an independent Dominion."[285] Yet he refused to meet Hyderabadi delegations or to commit the government of Pakistan to aid Hyderabad in the event of Indian aggression.[286]

Though major British and American newspapers published regular updates on Hyderabad affairs, the Nizam's international outreach largely fell on deaf ears. He made personal appeals to the king of England, Prime Minister Attlee, and President Truman to intervene on Hyderabad's behalf.[287] They all refused. American and British military strategists were keen to maintain stability in South Asia as the Second World War gave way to the Cold War. Indeed, Attlee publicly expressed sympathy for the Indian government's claim that Hyderabad was a domestic issue.[288] The Nizam was not entirely without international sympathizers. Churchill and Attlee had a contentious debate on Hyderabad and Kashmir in the House of Commons in July 1948. Churchill, of all people, compared Nehru to Hitler and argued that Britain should not "allow an independent State to be strangled, stifled, and overborne by violence."[289] He demanded that the British government defend the cause of Hyderabad at the United Nations and push for its admission as a member state. This encounter led the press in Pakistan to dub Churchill a "Mujahid" and Attlee a "Kaffir."[290]

The Nizam's appeal to the United Nations in August 1948 sought to bring his legal and historical claims to sovereignty from the domain of imperial constitutionalism into that of international law, where Hyderabad had last operated in the early nineteenth century. If Hyderabad's case at the UN had been given the opportunity to proceed, it is very possible that the Nizam could have succeeded in establishing himself as an "independent sovereign" and Hyderabad as an international entity. Expert opinion was divided. Some, like the American professor of international law Clyde Eagleton, argued that Hyderabad's legal rights were "embarrassingly clear." For Eagleton, the stakes of the Hyderabad case were of "fundamental importance" to the emergent postwar international order: the Police Action represented "the most clear-cut defiance which the Security Council has yet faced and, if left untouched, it will be the United Nations' most humiliating defeat, a precedent very dangerous for the future."[291] Eagleton's colleague at New York University, the former Ghadarite revolutionary and political scientist Taraknath Das, pointed to the long tradition of imperial constitutionalism, which held the Indian states to be sovereign entities within the British Empire but without international personalities.[292]

As it happened, the Nizam's appeal to the UN, by attempting to internationalize the conflict over Hyderabad, precipitated the Police Action. The political fact produced by the Police Action would ultimately trump any legitimate legal claims Hyderabad might have had. Hyderabad, like the other Indian states, was absorbed, subordinated, and dissolved in a highly ambivalent and in certain respects protracted manner. This process began in December 1947, when the states of the Eastern and Chhattisgarh political agencies were integrated into Orissa. The following month the states of the Kathiawar peninsula were united into Saurashtra. This was followed by the merging of the smaller states of the Deccan and Gujarat into Bombay Province and the merger of the Punjab hill states into the centrally administered Himachal Pradesh. Indore, Gwalior, and around twenty smaller states were combined in April 1948 into the Union of Madhya Bharat. The states of Rajputana were similarly merged into Rajasthan, the Punjab states into PEPSU, and Baroda into Bombay Province. By November 1949 only six princely states—Hyderabad, Mysore, Bhopal, Tripura, Manipur, and Cooch-Behar—maintained their old territorial boundaries.[293]

The republican Constitution of 1950 established India as a "Union of States" and distinguished between four different types of states (A through D). In certain respects, then, the categories of imperial constitutionalism were smuggled into the postcolonial constitution, only to be disposed of at a later date. These distinctions were done away with in 1956 by the Seventh Amendment to the Indian Constitution in order to implement the scheme of states' reorganization along linguistic lines. Linguistic reorganization marked the moment in which the modes of federalism examined in this chapter were abandoned at last.

Despite this subsequent outcome, the project of Azad Hyderabad was not merely a quixotic exercise in kingly vanity, nor was it the inevitable fate of a dying feudal order in a modernizing India. On the contrary, the Indian states were absolutely central to major political and constitutional developments in India in the decades prior to 1947. The complex and indeterminate nature of the Raj's imperial regime of sovereignty provided opportunities for a minor sovereign like the Nizam of Hyderabad to affirm

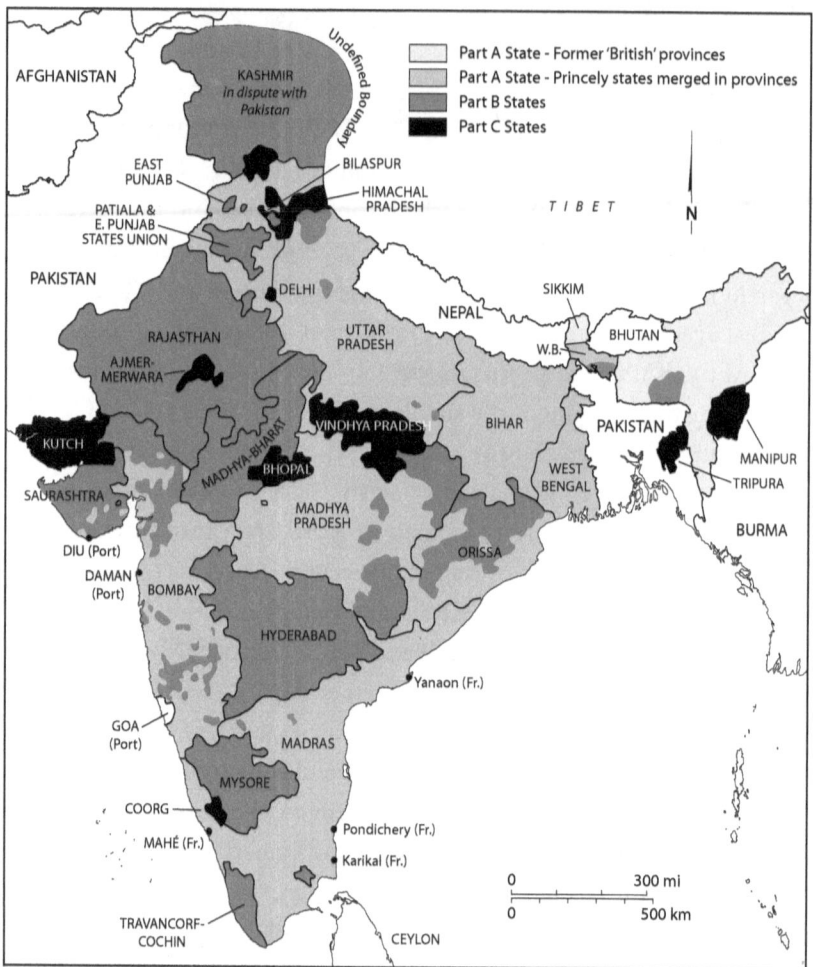

MAP 4. Republic of India, 1950.

and even expand his powers. The integral role played by the states was most obvious in the domain of imperial constitutionalism. I have argued above that in the two decades after the First World War, federation allowed the states to occupy an integral role in all-India politics. The Federation of India as envisaged by the 1935 Government of India Acts sought to codify the Raj's unwritten constitution. The Indian states played the determining role in the failure of federation. But their entrance into all-India politics brought them into direct confrontation with the dynamics of nationalist politics in British India. Out of this encounter arose two main consequences. The Congress adopted the demand for a constituent assembly based on a republican conception of popular sovereignty, and the Muslim League demanded Pakistan. The Congress waged *satyagraha* and conducted agitation in states across India, aided by newly established ministries in the British Indian provinces. The 1938–39 *satyagraha* against Hyderabad turned the Deccan into a major flashpoint of all-India contests over sovereignty and democracy.

It was in this context that Hyderabad came to occupy a central, if curious, place in the Indian political imagination. In addition to his prestige within the Raj's imperial constitution, the Nizam came to be widely regarded as a leader of Muslims. Hyderabad was seen as a Muslim state, a claim embraced, albeit inconsistently and nonsystematically, by the Nizam Mir Osman Ali Khan, as well as by his supporters and adversaries. In Hyderabad, the competition between popular sovereignty and dynastic kingship intersected with the democratic question of majorities and minorities. This dynamic had consequences both for the development of politics within Hyderabad and for Hyderabad's all-India significance. It led to a convergence of interests and rhetoric among secular and Hindu nationalists, resulting in a sort of majoritarian consensus around Hyderabad. The narrative of Hyderabad as a "communal" state, in which an autocratic Muslim minority dominated a nonconsenting Hindu majority, became the official line of the government of India after August 1947. The battle for Hyderabad, the third front of Partition, was an integral event in the violent making of the Republic of India.

CHAPTER TWO

THE BATTLE FOR HYDERABAD

THE INDIAN ARMY entered Hyderabad on the morning of September 13, 1948. The main force under Major-General J. N. Chaudhuri advanced east along the Sholapur-Hyderabad road. A smaller force entered heading west along the Vijayawada-Hyderabad road. Additional troops also moved into the state from the north and the south. Chaudhuri's forces consisted of two infantry brigades, one armored brigade, and a smaller strike force composed of Stuart and Sherman tanks. They were joined by 9,615 armed policemen from various provinces and states of the Indian Union. Air Force Tempests conducted aerial bombing raids in support of the advancing ground troops.[1]

The poorly equipped Hyderabad Army and the Razakars of the Majlis-e-Ittehadul Muslimeen were easily overpowered.[2] The Indian Army suffered the loss of only 10 men, compared with 807 and 1,373 for the Hyderabad Army and the Razakars, respectively.[3] Fully aware of the hopeless situation, Hyderabad's Major-General El Edroos issued secret orders for his forces to either fall back to the capital city or surrender to the Indian Army.[4] Although the orders were never carried out, Hyderabad's prime minister, Mir Laik Ali, ordered the demolition of all bridges on the roads leading to Hyderabad City, hoping to delay an Indian victory until the United Nations could intervene on Hyderabad's behalf.[5] On the fifth day,

September 17, the Indian Army was on the outskirts of Hyderabad City and the Nizam surrendered.

The Nizam, through a royal *firman*, established a new government under General Chaudhuri as military governor invested with full executive authority. This *firman* was the legal basis for the government of India's authority in Hyderabad until the adoption of the Constitution of 1950, when Hyderabad formally became part of India on January 26.[6] The Nizam thus stayed on the throne after the Police Action as a highly ambiguous and liminal figure: in his lawmaking capacity he maintained his sovereign status, yet he exercised no executive power or authority over his state. Indeed, the Nizam *never* signed an Instrument of Accession.[7] It was in this curious manner that Hyderabad was legally integrated into the Indian Union between the Police Action and January 1950. His "accession" consisted of a short November 1948 letter to India's governor-general (at that point still technically the representative of the British Crown) in which the Nizam stated that Hyderabad had no external relations "and never had any, whether before or after the 15th August 1947."[8] In November 1949, the Nizam issued a *firman* accepting the Constitution of India for Hyderabad.[9] And on January 25, 1950, the day before the Republic of India was established, the Nizam signed an agreement guaranteeing him a privy purse of Rs. 5,000,000 and the maintenance of his "personal" privileges, rights, dignities and titles.[10] The next day, the Nizam became Hyderabad's *rajpramukh*, the equivalent of governor, and remained so until the state was dismantled in the linguistic reorganization of 1956.

On September 20, 1948, three days after the Nizam's surrender, the Indian government informed the United Nations Security Council that the Nizam had sent orders on September 18 instructing the Hyderabad delegation to withdraw the case. India sought to reassure the council that "hardly any changes have been made" in Hyderabad and that the Nizam and his old administration were fully and willingly cooperating with the Indian Army.[11] Many members of the council, including the United States, criticized India's use of force in strong terms. The Americans warned that the "use of force does not alter legal rights" and that "not only members of the Security Council but all the Members of the United Nations will watch with interest the developments in Hyderabad."[12] On September 22, the Nizam sent another telegram, this time directly to the secretary-general, to withdraw the case. He said that the Hyderabad delegation "has now ceased to have any authority to represent me or my state."[13] This was another advantage, for the Congress, of keeping the Nizam on his throne. Although Hyderabad's case was kept on the agenda of the Security Council for years afterwards, it would, over time, lose its urgency and relevance.

India's leaders, Nehru in particular, were sensitive to the international implications of the Police Action and sought to keep events within Hyderabad tightly under wraps. As Indian forces entered Hyderabad, Patel remarked that "once we enter Hyderabad, it is no longer an international affair. It is a States Ministry's function."[14] As the Indian Army arrived in Hyderabad City, Nehru was clear that calling it a "Police Action" was consistent with their stance that Hyderabad was a domestic affair: "The first thing to remember is that our action was supposed to be a 'police action' against a recalcitrant State. We did not call it war and we must not therefore do anything now which might indicate that we consider it as a war against a foreign state. Indeed, we do not consider it as a foreign state, whatever its strict legal position might have been since August 15."[15] This removal of Hyderabad from the international sphere had major domestic implications as well. For Indian nationalists, the Police Action was a moment of fulfillment: the nation and the territorial nation-state were now commensurate. For the Hyderabadi Congress leader Swami Tirtha, the Police Action was "the last battle of Indian freedom," a freedom that was now "complete and whole."[16] V. P. Menon wrote of "universal jubilation at the swift and successful ending of the Hyderabad episode."[17] Nehru commended the Indian Army for its "brilliant success."[18]

For Nehru, the Police Action brought closure to a period of existential uncertainty opened up by the Partition and, in so doing, inaugurated a new phase of India's history. He compared the impact of the Police Action to the "magical effect" of Gandhi's entrance into Indian politics and argued that it confirmed his conception of a plural, secular Indian nation:

> By the example of Hyderabad, the fear in the people of India suddenly disappeared, be they Hindus, Muslims or Sikhs. Almost 90 per cent of

the fear has gone and mutual confidence has been restored. Each community feels reassured that its fear is unnecessary and that the other community is not interested in harming it. So the picture of India has changed completely and the people's hearts are lighter and calmer. This has immediately increased the strength of the country and the nation and every individual has gained by it. Such events have a magical effect on communities. As I told you, forty years ago, Mahatma Gandhi produced such a magical effect.[19]

This sense of relief must be understood in light of Hyderabad's perceived threat to the integrity of the territory of the Indian nation and, as a result, to the nation itself. In the thirteen months prior to the Police Action, a discourse regarding Hyderabad as an existential threat spread through official channels, the nationalist press, and more informal means, having a powerful influence on the perceptions of officials and the public alike. When he submitted the government of India's *White Paper on Hyderabad* to the Central Legislature on August 10, 1948, Vallabhbhai Patel declared that "an independent Hyderabad" would be "a standing threat to the progress and prosperity, indeed to the very existence, of the Indian Dominion."[20]

Such existential anxieties, what Arjun Appadurai has called the "anxiety of incompleteness," speak to the convergence on Hyderabad of fears over territory and national purity.[21] For nationalist leaders the stakes in Hyderabad were high, and they did not shy away from ratcheting up their public rhetoric about the dangers posed by Hyderabad. In particular, the conflict over Hyderabad threatened a full replay of Partition violence in the territorial heart of peninsular India. Dr. Pattabhi Sitaramayya of the Congress Working Committee issued a dire warning in this regard:

> The fact remains that the first reactions of an armed attack upon Hyderabad cannot but be the visitation of the "sins" of India upon the innocent Hindus of the State. Any hesitancy on the part of the Union forces in taking drastic action against the state forces for fear of injury to the innocents in the state would prolong the agony.... All the same there will be indescribable suffering. The near and distant repercussions of open warfare should be considered. The news of Hindus being butchered in

> Hyderabad is apt to endanger the lives of the 35 millions of our Muslim brethren all over India and the pogroms of September, 1947, may pale into insignificance before their enlarged and intensified edition of 1948. It is feared that this may in turn lead to a mass exodus of the one crore and twenty-five lakhs of Hindus from East Bengal to West Bengal ... which may become the scene of another man-made famine.[22]

The consequences of the Hyderabad conflict were thus seen to be far-reaching, potentially cataclysmic, and subcontinental in scope. Some even predicted renewed war between India and Pakistan. It was reported, for example, that Hindu residents, fearing a cross-border attack, fled en masse from Amritsar upon hearing of the Indian Army's entry into Hyderabad.[23]

In the weeks after the Police Action, it seemed as if the prophets of despair had been off the mark. Yet by mid-October, it was becoming increasingly clear that the Police Action's "magical effect" was largely an illusion. A stream of reports from Pakistani newspapers alleged large-scale anti-Muslim violence in Hyderabad.[24] By November, Nehru was receiving disturbing news from trusted sources. He had been informed of "the massacre of some thousands of Muslims by Hindus, as well as a great deal of looting etc."[25] After further inquiries, Nehru wrote that additional reports from Hyderabad presented an "alarming" picture:

> This picture is chiefly of the past, that is, of events in September-October, when it is said, large scale killings were indulged in by the civil population (Hindus). It is even more than the killings, it is reported, that looting was on a tremendous scale and as a consequence vast numbers of Muslims are completely destitute. The figure of killings mentioned are so big as to stagger the imagination. . . . The effect left by these accounts on my mind has been most distressing. . . . If there is even a fraction of truth in these reports, then the situation in Hyderabad was much worse than we had been led to believe. It is important that the exact facts should be placed before us. We want no optimistic account and no suppression of unsavoury episodes.[26]

A "profoundly saddened" Maulana Azad approached Nehru to do something.[27] As head of the Ministry of States, Patel refused to give permission for Azad to visit Hyderabad.²⁸ Nehru sent instead a "Goodwill Mission" to collect information and ease the fears of Hyderabad's Muslims.²⁹

This Goodwill Mission was led by Pandit Sunderlal and Qazi Abdul Ghaffar. Pandit Sunderlal was a long-standing Congressman, the vice president of the United Provinces Congress from 1931 to 1936, and a prominent advocate of Hindu-Muslim unity. Abdul Ghaffar was the former editor of the nationalist newspaper *Payam* in Hyderabad and a bitter critic of Qasim Razvi and the Majlis.³⁰ The Mission's report, known as the Sunderlal Report, was long considered lost, destroyed, or suppressed. However, I accessed the original version, along with fourteen pages of the Goodwill Mission's "Confidential Notes," at the Nehru Museum and Memorial Library in 2010.³¹

The delegations led by Pandit Sunderlal and Qazi Abdul Ghaffar toured nine of the sixteen districts of Hyderabad between November 29 and December 21, 1948. They visited seven district headquarters, twenty-one towns, and twenty-three "important" villages and interviewed over five hundred people who came from 109 villages that the Mission did not visit. They concluded that Osmanabad, Gulburga, Bidar, and Nanded were the districts worst affected by violence. In these districts, "the number of people killed during and after the police action was not less, if not more than 18,000." They estimated that in Aurangabad, Bir, Nalgonda, and Medak districts "those who lost their lives numbered at least 5 thousand." While these eight districts were the most affected, the report claimed that no district remained "wholly" free of "communal trouble." For Hyderabad as a whole, the report gave "a very conservative estimate that in the whole state at least 27 thousand to 40 thousand people lost their lives during and after the police action."³²

There is considerable evidence to suggest violence on a large scale, but it is impossible to either confirm or refute the figures presented in the Sunderlal Report. In light of this violence, however, we need to rewrite and recenter the history of the Police Action. The Congress, of course, commandeered the coercive institutions of the colonial state and deployed them in service of the national project. Yet in transitioning from an anticolonial mass movement into a ruling party, they did not simply give up popular mobilization.

Unlike in Punjab, where state sovereignty was built up through efforts to absorb and subdue violence by converting a highly mobilized situation into a settled order, in Hyderabad there was a dispersal and mobilization of violence. Neighboring provincial governments raised and armed tens of thousands of "home guards." Militant cadres from the National Congress, the Hyderabad State Congress, the Socialist Party, the Arya Samaj, and the Hindu Mahasabha waged a violent campaign of disruption and sabotage in and around Hyderabad. This subaltern violence was co-opted to reinforce rather than subvert the authority of the new nation-state. It created the pretext for the Police Action and served as a ground-clearing exercise for a state making claims to popular sovereignty.

Violence was integral to the resolution of the Hyderabad question and thus to the transformation of the Raj's imperial regime of sovereignty into a national one. The Battle of Hyderabad was, in this respect, a battle about sovereign kingship and majorities and minorities in a democratic India. For K. M. Panikkar, himself a former princely servant, the end of the Indian tradition of kingship resulted from the "revolutionary democratic urge of the people."[33] For Vallabhbhai Patel, the violence of the Police Action, and the political changes it wrought, constituted "nothing short of a revolution," a foundational coming together of the people and the state.[34] This new national regime of sovereignty was announced in explicitly majoritarian terms, and the Hyderabad conflict was central to the making of new national majorities and minorities from 1947.

I. Retaliation and Revolution

After the Police Action, both the Indian government and the nationalist press were conspicuously silent regarding violence in Hyderabad, refusing to respond to what they considered a hyperbolic Pakistani press campaign. Confidentially, however, there was an official consensus that the fact of widespread violence was irrefutable.[35] What was questioned was the scale suggested by the Sunderlal Report. "Your estimate and your appreciation of the position," a furious Patel wrote to Abdul Ghaffar, "lack balance and proportion."[36] After meeting with the Sunderlal delegation, Military Governor Chaudhuri described the report as "grossly untrue" and warned of "the danger of such a document getting into the hands of any interested Pakistani."[37] However, Chaudhuri's report to the Ministry of States in November 1948 painted a somewhat different picture: "Immediately after the military occupation started, a large majority of Hindus in all districts of Hyderabad, thought that Hindu Raj had come into being.... As a result of this retaliatory action by Hindus, some Muslims in certain districts suffered. The districts particularly affected were Bidar, Osmanabad, Gulbarga, Nalgonda & Warangal. Though accurate figures cannot be obtained yet of what the casualties were, it is estimated that about 2,000 Muslims may have been massacred. Almost all of this happened in the smaller villages off the main communications."[38] Nehru compared what had happened in Hyderabad to the "horrible deeds" and "inhuman atrocities" that had taken place in Punjab: "In Hyderabad, something of a like nature happened perhaps on a smaller scale."[39] According to an intelligence report from October 1948, "Muslims who did not have much to do with the Razakar organization have also been greatly victimised..... In Secunderabad several Muslim houses and shops were looted both day and night for about ten days from 18-9-48, with Indian troops not effectively intervening to stop the lawlessness. A further outbreak of looting was reported for about five days from 2-10-48..... Both in Hyderabad City and the mofussil it would appear that many sections of the irresponsible Hindu public looted and oppressed Muslims indiscriminately."[40] *Hyderabad Reborn*, a propaganda publication issued by Hyderabad's military government in March 1949, conceded that during the "disturbances" both before and after the Police Action thousands of families "lost their earning male members and were reduced to destitution," adding that "the worst sufferers of any holocaust are women."[41] The Hyderabad government gave out a fixed quota of 4,500 "widow pensions to the women whose husbands had been killed." Of these, "about 75 percent" were given to Muslims "who suffered immediately after the Police Action on account of the reaction."[42] According to government figures, then, at least 3,375 Muslims were killed during and after the Police Action.

The Sunderlal Report observed that the areas "worst affected" by the violence were previously "the main strongholds of Razakars" and that the people in these areas "had been the worst sufferers at the hands of the Razakars." On this account, the report concluded, "In this campaign of retaliation at least a hundred were made to suffer for the sins of each guilty individual."[43] This discourse of "retaliation" had long held currency in Indian politics, used by colonial administrators and Indian political leaders alike.[44] Hyderabad's home secretary observed that "following the taking-over of the administration, there was naturally some retaliation and it was understandable that there were quite a few cases of forcible occupation of places of worship or their desecration."[45] The chief civil administrator in Hyderabad dismissed the violence as "a retaliation against the brother villagers for their misdeeds committed by them as Razakars."[46] Chaudhuri explained that "as a result of this retaliatory action by Hindus, some Muslims in certain districts suffered."[47] Nehru proffered a similar interpretation: "About the time the Indian forces were entering Hyderabad, and the old governmental structure had broken down, there were upheavals of the Hindu population especially in the rural areas. These people, who had previously suffered from considerable repression from the Razakars, rose against them. They were joined by refugees who returned to Hyderabad. The result was that murder, arson and looting was committed."[48] The official line of Patel's Ministry of States held that Razakar "crimes were committed as part of a deliberate policy with the knowledge and presumably the connivance of the then administration of Hyderabad," whereas the crimes "committed by non-Muslims in the wake of the Police Action" were "the natural reaction against long years of oppression by a minority community and were committed in the heat of the moment."[49] The violence committed by Muslims was criminal, and the violence committed by Hindus was political.

Accordingly, a few weeks after the Police Action, Patel ordered that "all political detenus, under-trial prisoners and prisoners convicted for political offences whether they were involved in acts of violence or not, other than communists, should be released."[50] In June 1949, on Patel's instructions, the Hyderabad government granted amnesty to all "Hindus involved in retaliatory action just after the Police Action," although Chaudhuri ordered that "no publicity should be given to it."[51] One objective of the amnesty was to groom the State Congress to take over the reins of government in Hyderabad. The State Congress, Patel noted, had "extremely limited" influence within Hyderabad and included in its ranks "a considerable section of men who had taken to crime not entirely without mixed motives."[52] The amnesty's exclusion of communists was a recognition that the revolutionary *sangham* in Telangana was the only political movement in Hyderabad with a mass base. The amnesty thus aimed to use state power to turn the Hyderabad State Congress into a party that could claim to represent "the people." Indeed, the release of prisoners was done "in consultation with the local Congress organisation."[53] The military governor observed that the "release of persons at present undertrial for offences committed in the course of retaliatory activities will considerably rehabilitate the prestige of the Hyderabad State Congress."[54] Patel personally oversaw the efforts to build up the State Congress into a governing party with the aid of both the National Congress Party and the institutions of the state.

II. Geography of Violence

The Sunderlal Report tallied casualties in the Police Action by collating reports from the various districts of Hyderabad State. Considered alongside *Hyderabad Reborn*, a propaganda book published by Hyderabad's military government in March 1949 that aimed to demonstrate the legitimacy and effectiveness of the new administration, the Sunderlal Report illuminates a geography of violence in Hyderabad.[55] The Police Action plan developed by the Ministry of States called for teams of civil administrators to trail advancing Indian troops to take over government in "liberated" areas.[56] However, semifunctional governance was not established for weeks after the Nizam's surrender in large areas of the state. This gap, both sources suggest, roughly coincided with much of the violence. In Adilabad, the civil team did not reach district headquarters until the last day of September, a full two weeks after the Nizam's surrender. According to *Hyderabad Reborn*, it was during this period that "Muslims suffered through retaliatory action" in Kinwat and Nirmal *talukas*, located along or in close proximity to the Berar border.[57] When the Indian civil team arrived in Bidar, "the retaliatory instinct" of the Hindus "had to be

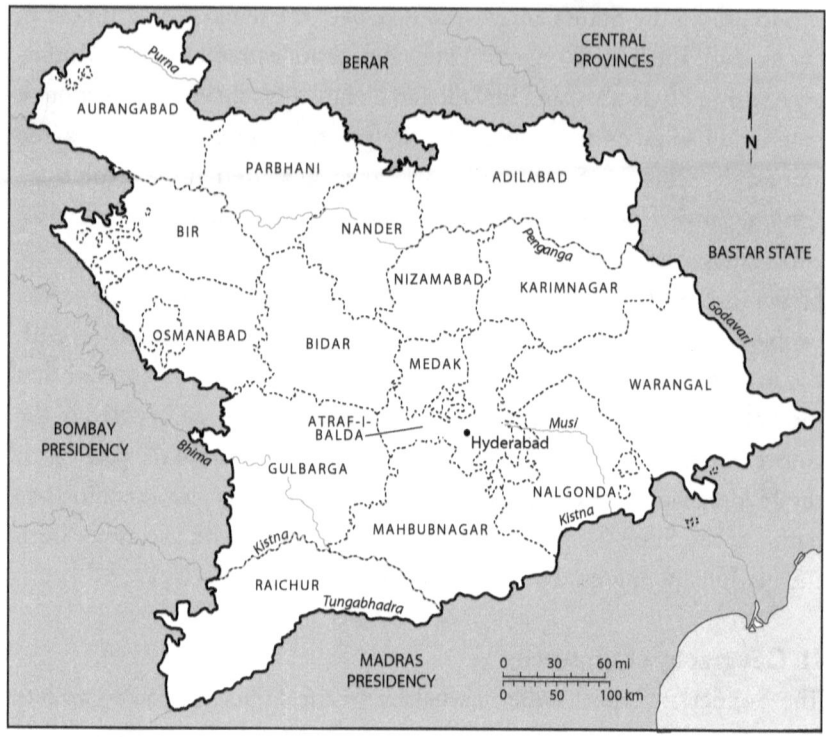

MAP 5. Hyderabad State.

held in leash." As a result, it took considerable time before law and order were reestablished.[58] The civil team in Gulbarga "was faced with the same problem as Bidar of controlling the majority community from wreaking vengeance on their erstwhile oppressors."[59] It took weeks to reestablish governance in the district, and the civil team had "settled down" only by early November. The Sunderlal Report claims that five to eight thousand Muslims were killed in Gulbarga during this time and that Bidar "fared at least as ill if not worse than Gulbarga."[60] In Nanded District, which shared a border with Berar, it was only "by the middle of October" that the "situation in the interior had come under control."[61] Military forces were withdrawn from the district only at the end of November. The Sunderlal Report estimated that between two and four thousand Muslims were killed in Nanded during this time.

Hyderabad Reborn had little to say regarding Osmanabad. Indeed, the Osmanabad civil team was later revealed to have participated in an auction of Muslim property conducted by the Hyderabad State Congress.[62] Later, a government-appointed committee led by Congressman Narsing Rao visited forty-seven villages in Osmanabad in 1951 and reported that there were "approximately" 2,500 widows and 6,000 orphans in these villages alone. The committee recommended that any government plan for rehabilitation should be based on the estimate of "approximately 10,000 widows and 25,000" orphans in Osmanabad District.[63] A 1950 report by Maulvi Hifzur Rahman, general secretary of the Jamiat-Ulama-i-Hind and a member of both the All India Congress Committee and the Constituent Assembly, claimed that there were about two thousand Muslim widows in Osmanabad District, with a further 1,222 in Aurangabad.[64] *Hyderabad Reborn* says little about Aurangabad District. The Sunderlal Report mentions that the civil team and military there were "exemplary" and "effective," yet concludes that between two and three thousand Muslims were killed in the district. According to *Hyderabad Reborn*, the "restoration of law and order and normal life" took two weeks in Medak District, during which time looting and occupation of Muslim property were common.[65] Anticipating trouble, many Muslims in Medak left their villages at the onset of the Police Action. In Nizamabad, the Indian civil team arrived on September 29. It "took a month and a half for the situation to return to normal." The primary challenge in this district was to assure "the Muslim population of all protection from retaliation."[66] However, Nizamabad was ignored by the Sunderlal Report and by later investigations. The same can be said for Raichur, although *Hyderabad Reborn* mentions its large "Razakar population," looting, and the kidnapping of women.[67]

The extent of violence remains unclear in the other districts of Telangana, where the communist-led peasant revolution had upended rural social structures and state authority since mid-1946. Initial reports, including the Sunderlal Report, indicated that Muslims were targeted in both Warangal and Nalgonda. Maulvi Rehman detailed attacks on Muslim property in Warangal.[68] The communist leader P. Sundarayya later claimed that "ordinary Muslim people" were "pounced upon and untold miseries were inflicted on them" during the Police Action. He fingered the Indian Army as the primary culprit. Sundarayya argued that areas in Telangana under revolutionary influence were relatively unscathed but that elsewhere "attacks on [Muslims] were widespread."[69] And yet, as part of a contentious intraparty debate on whether to continue the armed struggle after the Police Action, the Communist Party of India leader Ravi Narayan Reddy cited numerous incidents during which communist guerrilla squads killed unarmed Razakars, noting that "all the Razakars and soldiers killed this way were poor Muslims."[70]

In sum, it seems that while there was anti-Muslim violence in Telangana, the Marathwada and Karnatak areas of Hyderabad suffered the lion's share. Chaudhuri's successor and the first civilian chief minister of Hyderabad, Indian Civil Service officer M. K. Vellodi, described Marathwada as an area "where militant Hindu orthodoxy prevails, and where Hindu excesses have been gravest in the wake of Police Action."[71] Vellodi characterized these "excesses committed by the Hindus" as "exceptionally savage in nature."[72] L. C. Jain, chief secretary to the government of Hyderabad, similarly noted that "Marathwada has always been strongly communal in character. It is here that the greatest excesses against the Muslims were perpetrated in the wake of Police Action."[73]

Who, then, was involved in this event of violence? Among officials, the consensus culprits were the estimated five hundred thousand Hindu "refugees" who had fled Hyderabad during the previous year. This was part of a wider discourse that identified Partition refugees as the source of communal strife and as potentially subversive to state authority.[74] Many of the refugees from Hyderabad settled in the border areas of Bombay Province and Central Provinces (CP) and Berar, in cities like Sholapur or in the border camps set up by the Congress and the Arya Samaj. Young men joined the armed struggle against Hyderabad. In the second week of October 1948, the Ministry of States ordered the governments of the neighboring provinces to prevent any Hindus from returning to Hyderabad unless organized and supervised by the government. Chaudhuri was "greatly perturbed at the indiscriminate return of Hindu refugees," fearing this would lead to further "communal trouble."[75]

The Sunderlal Report generally agreed with the official explanation, but it also claimed that the "perpetrators of these atrocities were not limited to those who had suffered at the hands of Razakars": they also included

> individuals and bands of people, with and without arms, from across the border, who had infiltrated through in the wake of the Indian Army. We found definite indications that a number of armed and trained men belonging to a well known Hindu communal organization from Sholapur and other Indian towns as also some local and outside communists participated in these riots and in some cases actually led the rioters. Duty also compels us to add that we had absolutely unimpeachable evidence to the effect that there were instances in which men belonging to the Indian Army and also to the local police took part in looting and even other crimes.[76]

The report further observed that the "State Congress has failed to give an absolutely satisfactory account of itself during the period of trouble." The report presented a litany of charges against State Congress cadres, including "extracting money from panicky Musalmans," disrupting local administration, and auctioning property confiscated from Muslims for the benefit of the party. Chaudhuri came to a similar conclusion: "Certain members of the State Congress undoubtedly terrorized the Muslims."[77] The State Congress chief Swami Tirtha largely conceded most of these charges: "Soon after the Police Action, there was a great upheaval. People retaliated."[78] Yet, he argued, the State Congress was simply following the lead of the Indian Army:

> It was a natural reaction even though wrong and bad in character to the worse Razakar regime and sufferings of the people in those days. The communal minded section of the Military and Police also indulged in it and encouraged and even threatened the people to do it. That must give them [State Congress] a cover for their own acts.... Some of the Congress workers, who happened to be with these incoming troops, got implicated into it and strangely enough the whole phenomenon is taken by the Muslims and propagated by certain interested sections as the Congress sponsored game.[79]

This situation was used to promote factional interests within the State Congress. A liberal, moderate faction accused cadres from the border camps of "committing acts unworthy of congressmen."[80] Chaudhuri noted that rival factions had "given information against the members of the other group for having been concerned in the commission of atrocities after Police Action."[81] An intelligence report was more unequivocal: "It is known that in several areas, immediately after 'occupation' these 'volunteers' themselves took part in pillage, loot and rape.... Irresponsible 'volunteers' looted properties and molested Muslim women in Khammamet, Madira and Warangal, and were restrained by their leaders only with difficulty."[82] This situation was enabled by the way that officials treated the State Congress as an extension of the government. Immediately after the Police Action, Chaudhuri dispatched at least four hundred State Congress workers to the districts, armed with ID cards as proof of their official sanction.[83] Chaudhuri would later report, however, that "immediately after the Police Action members of the Hyderabad State Congress extorted money, sold property belonging to Muslims by auction and appropriated the proceeds to party funds, etc."[84]

For example, State Congress cadres were implicated in orchestrating looting and violence in the city of Latur in Osmanabad District. Osmanabad's district collector recalled "thugs" and "several thousand young men from the border camps" pouring into the city.[85] Noting that Latur was the hometown of Razakar supremo Qasim Razvi, the Sunderlal Report claimed that "the killing continued for over twenty days. Out of a population of about 10 thousand Muslims there we found barely three thousand still in the town. Over a thousand had been killed and the rest had run away with little else besides their lives and completely ruined financially."[86] Officials would later acknowledge that the State Congress had played a role in orchestrating the confiscation and auctioning of the property of Muslims in Latur.[87] Yet many of the leaders involved in the armed struggle and accused in the violence remained influential within the party.[88] Some were even made ministers in Hyderabad's first civilian government appointed by the States Ministry in 1950.

In his 1950 report, Maulvi Hifzur Rahman attributed a number of "atrocities" and "assaults" to the State Congress. He alleged that government

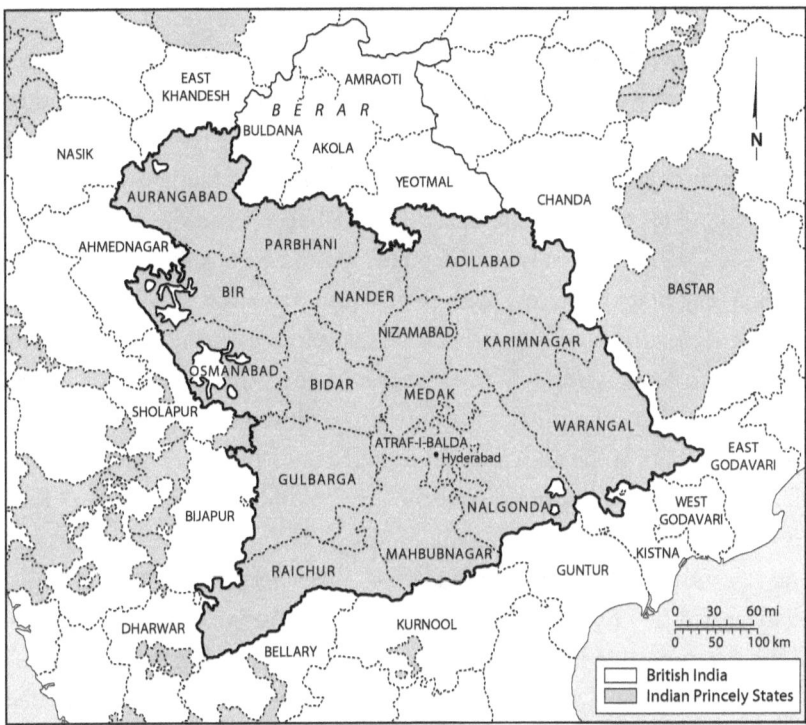

MAP 6. Political Subdivisions of Hyderabad and Surrounding Areas.

officers were colluding with the State Congress and other "unsocial elements" to seize Muslim property.[89] The Narsing Rao committee reached a similar conclusion the following year.[90] Gail Omvedt has argued that "a major source of conflict in Marathwada after the Congress takeover" was the land given to Dalits by the Nizam's government in the years preceding the Police Action as part of a program of cultivating Dalit support for the Nizam.[91] The Police Action, she argues, also involved "direct army atrocities against many of the poor and support for return of the worst landlord oppressors, as well as direct Hindu reprisals in many areas against Muslims and Dalits who were presumed to be 'pro-Razakar.'"[92]

The "well known Hindu communal organization from Sholapur" mentioned in the Sunderlal Report was, most likely, the Arya Samaj, which headquartered its activities in Hyderabad from Sholapur. According to the report, a "prominent Arya Samajist" converted the "local Arya Samaj mandir into a sub-jail." He arrested Muslims from the locality on "his own authority" and would release them only after extracting payments. If they refused or could not pay, they were handed over to the police as Razakars. As I explain below, the State Congress and the Arya Samaj were inextricably bound together in Hyderabad and had been since the *satyagraha* of 1938–39. Indeed, there was considerable overlap between the two organizations. Many State Congress leaders were also Samajists.

The accusations the Sunderlal Report leveled against the Indian Army are difficult to substantiate. The report conceded that "on the whole the Army has done splendidly well" but also claimed that at "a number of places members of the armed forces brought out Muslim adult males from villages and towns and massacred them in cold blood." Elsewhere, "They encouraged and even persuaded the Hindu mobs to loot Muslim shops and houses" and "even joined in the looting."[93] An October 1948 intelligence report noted that Sikh units in the Indian Army "actively assisted" sections of the "irresponsible Hindu public" in both Hyderabad City and the state's rural areas.[94] A confidential Communist Party of India document leveled similar charges.[95] The press in Pakistan produced a chorus of accusations against the Indian Army.[96] Chaudhuri rejected such accusations altogether but did concede that there was "indiscriminate arresting of Muslims in the districts by both troops and Union Police" during the Police Action.[97] This left Muslim families and property vulnerable to "certain unsocial Hindu elements."[98]

What is clear is that the violence in Hyderabad during and after the Police Action cannot be attributed to Hindu "retaliation" or to "refugees" alone. The Police Action was much more than a simple military operation against the Nizam's armed forces. It was a highly complex, multifaceted event that involved a number of actors and institutions. My concern here is not to assign responsibility or blame for the violence but to take the violence as a starting point for a fuller reconstruction of the Police Action as an event and to understand its political meaning in the context of the transformation of the Raj into the Republic. This was a foundational event of violence that brought together the actions of partisan militants and state forces and, in doing so, gave meaning and substance to the development of a new sovereign formation in the Deccan and in postcolonial India more broadly.

III. Mobilizing for Battle

In the thirteen months between August 1947 and September 1948, the Hyderabad State Congress, the Socialist Party, the Arya Samaj, and the Hindu Mahasabha all took up arms against Hyderabad State. Partisan cadres were active primarily along the Marathi-speaking areas of Hyderabad's border with Bombay and Berar, where they established a number of camps. The governments of all the provinces bordering Hyderabad also raised "home guard" units and authorized police actions along the border. This was a highly decentralized effort. Home guards were sanctioned by the state, but their actions were not necessarily controlled by officials. Added to this mix were state forces proper, including units of the Indian Army stationed along the Hyderabad frontier. The government of India also implemented a blockade on Hyderabad. All of these activities—the actions taken by political parties, home guards, and provincial governments—were undertaken with the consent and under the guidance of the national leadership of the Indian National Congress. The Police Action, from this perspective, witnessed the coming together of people, party, and state in an event of foundational violence. In its transformation from an anticolonial nationalist movement into a ruling party, the Congress utilized both state power *and* popular mobilization to achieve its political objectives. Indeed, such a combination was an integral part of the development of the Republic of India as a new sovereign formation after 1947.

The Nizam increasingly came to rely on the Majlis-e-Ittehadul Muslimeen in the years after the 1938–39 *satyagraha*. In 1947, the Nizam sought, with little success, to procure adequate arms for Hyderabad State forces. It was in this context that the Razakars were mobilized to defend Azad Hyderabad and, in doing so, took center stage in the dispute between India and Hyderabad.[99] The Razakars played a highly visible role in the nationalist imagination and in public discourses concerning the conflict over Hyderabad. The Razakars became a rallying point for the nationalist press and the government of India alike, as the conflict between the two states became framed as a conflict between two religious groups in increasingly loaded terms. As a paramilitary force, the Razakars were deployed to guard the border against incursions from British India and to suppress the peasant revolutionaries in the Telangana region of Hyderabad, who had since 1946 taken up arms against the Nizam's state and established what Communist Party of India leaders began referring to as India's Yan'an. Amid this multidimensional confrontation over Hyderabad State, the seeds of India's revolutionary future were being sown. In sum, the Deccan became between 1947 and 1948 a crucible of violent contestation over sovereignty and democracy in postcolonial India.

The State Congress–led struggle in and around Hyderabad has had a curious legacy. On the one hand, it was publicly disavowed by the Indian National Congress and the government of India. It finds only passing mention, if at all, in most history books. Press accounts highlighted the alleged outrages of the Razakars, while making only oblique references to the activities of the State Congress. On the other hand, the struggle became a point of pride within the Indian nationalist movement. It launched important political careers, most notably that of P. V. Narasimha Rao, who began his political career during the 1938 *satyagraha* conducted by the Hyderabad State Congress, the Arya Samaj, and the Hindu Mahasabha against the Nizam's government. Rao was expelled from his college in Warangal in late 1938 for singing the nationalist anthem "Vande Mataram," a protest begun by students at Osmania a few months earlier.[100] A decade later, he worked as a gunrunner out of a State Congress camp in Chanda, Maharashtra.[101] Rao's mentor was Swami Ramananda Tirtha, the president of the Hyderabad State Congress and the leader of the party's "radical" faction that engaged in armed struggle against Hyderabad. Tirtha was also the main instigator behind the move to *satyagraha* in 1938. Indeed, the infrastructure established over the course of the 1938–39 *satyagraha*, the border camps in particular, would be reactivated and redeployed to great effect in 1947–48. Hyderabad was central to the major political developments in India in the late 1930s and would, a decade later, find itself once again in the midst of an all-India political storm.

In 1938, *satyagraha* against Hyderabad was initiated on two fronts.[102] On the one hand, the Hyderabad State Congress, founded that very same year, demanded constitutional reforms and responsible government. The *mulki* politics of groups like the Nizam's Subjects League gave way to a nationalized political discourse of responsible government and popular sovereignty, with the latter increasingly coming to be articulated in terms of majority rule. The *satyagraha* was part of an India-wide political storm demanding reforms in the Indian states. This storm was, in no small measure, a direct result of the Indian National Congress's 1938 Haripura Resolution, which held the states to be "an integral part of India" and advocated for the "same political, social, and economic freedom in the States as in the rest of India." As part of their efforts to "break" the federation proposed by the 1935 Constitution, the Congress issued a demand for a constituent assembly in which sovereignty would be vested in "the people" rather than the rulers of the Indian states or, indeed, the British Parliament. The All India States Peoples' Conference (AISPC) considered Hyderabad, as the "premier" state, to be the keystone of the entire princely order: "If we could succeed there, we should have success all through."[103] The Congress's triumph in the 1937 provincial elections not only gave impetus to "people's" movements in the states but allowed new Congress provincial governments to facilitate them. "The State Congress people," Gandhi noted in 1938, "have been acting under my advice."[104] The congressman and Akhand Hindustan proponent K. M. Munshi assisted the 1938–39 *satyagraha* against Hyderabad as the home minister of Bombay province and reprised this role when he returned to Hyderabad as India's agent-general after the signing of the Standstill Agreement in November 1947.

Established in July 1938, the Hyderabad State Congress was still a relatively small organization by the time the *satyagraha* was launched three months later. Its leadership was composed mostly of liberals of a moderate bent, although there was a younger and more radical faction, based primarily in Marathwada, who tended toward socialism and the more militant position of the Arya Samaj. The State Congress rejected the proposals for constitutional reform put forth by the Aiyangar Committee in August 1938. They argued that the proposals, including those for functional representation, denied the principle of majority rule and sought to shore up the extant distribution of power in Hyderabad. The State Congress, almost exclusively composed of Hindus and clearly coordinating with the Indian National Congress, was immediately banned after its formation. This was the context in which a Committee of Action was established and *satyagraha* initiated in late October 1938. On December 24, exactly two months after it began, the *satyagraha* was called off by the Hyderabad State Congress on the advice of the national leadership. At that time there were three hundred State Congressmen in prison in Hyderabad. By June 1939, nearly eight thousand *satyagrahis* crowded the Nizam's jails, most of whom were associated, not with the State Congress, but with the Arya Samaj and the Hindu Mahasabha.

The second front of the 1938–39 *satyagraha* was waged by the Arya Samaj and the Hindu Mahasabha as a campaign for civil liberties and religious freedom.[105] They too deployed a language of majority rule. This discourse was common ground between the secular Congress and the Hindu nationalist groups. While the State Congress's conceptions of "the people" and the "majority" were stated in universalist terms, there was, in practice, considerable slippage between, and convergence with, Hindu nationalist idioms. The Congress's liberal critique of autocratic kingship was entirely compatible with, indeed complementary to, illiberal Hindu nationalist arguments about Muslim tyranny and minority rule. Indeed, by 1947 it was often difficult to distinguish the Samaj from the State Congress. There was considerable overlap between the organizations, with many Samajists holding leadership positions in the State Congress. This was particularly true in Marathwada, where "the Arya Samaj provided the required wherewithal to the struggle."[106]

Unlike the brand-new Hyderabad State Congress, by 1938 the Arya Samaj and Hindu Mahasabha had been organizing in Hyderabad for decades. This was a period in which political life in Hyderabad was highly constrained. In 1921 and then again in 1929 the government passed orders (*Gashti* 52 and 53, respectively) first banning any meeting "creating political issues" and then requiring prior approval for meetings that could potentially be deemed political in nature.[107] As a result, most organizations in Hyderabad were formally committed to projects of cultural and educational development. The Indian National Congress's policy of noninterference in the Indian states left a void in Hyderabad filled by the Samaj, the Hindu Mahasabha, and the Andhra Mahasabha. Samaj activities geared up in the state in the late 1920s and early 1930s, as their program of *shuddhi* competed with the *tabligh* efforts of Bahadur Yar Jung and the Majlis. Historians have largely attributed to the Samaj a key role in the development of "communalism" in Hyderabad over the course of the 1920s and 1930s.[108] By 1938, there were 250 Samaj branches in Hyderabad, and they commanded a considerable following, particularly in Marathwada.[109]

The 1938–39 Samaj-Mahasabha *satyagraha* was a collaborative effort between two national organizations that sought to nationalize Hyderabad as an archetype of Muslim tyranny and threat to the integrity of the Hindu *rashtra*. For Hindu nationalists today, Pakistan stands for the instantiation of the Muslim other in a state form. For the founders of the modern Hindu nationalist movement, many of whom were from Maharashtra, that role was played, historically, by Hyderabad.[110] As Manu Bhagavan has observed, Hyderabad was seen by Hindu nationalists to be the primary obstacle to the attainment of Akhand Hindustan.[111] The 1938–39 *satyagraha* was coordinated by the president of the International Aryan League, G. S. Gupta (also speaker of the Central Provinces Assembly and member of the Congress), and V. D. Savarkar, president of the Hindu Mahasabha. Their initial plan called for agitation to begin in early 1939, but the Samaj and the Mahasabha followed suit when the State Congress launched their *satyagraha* in October 1938. While the State Congress campaign was abandoned in December 1938, the Samaj-Mahasabha campaign continued until the end of July 1939. Most of the *satyagrahis* that filled the Nizam's prisons were not from Hyderabad. The Mahasabha sent approximately five thousand cadres from across India to Hyderabad. They declared in the *Hindu Outlook* that "on the success or failure of Dharmayuddha [in Hyderabad] depends the political existence of the Hindus of Hindusthan."[112] Nathuram Godse was a "dictator" of the first Mahasabha *jatha* arrested in November 1938.[113]

Later, during his trial, Godse attributed the decision to kill Gandhi, in no small measure, to the Mahatma's indifference to "attacks on the Hindus in Hyderabad State" and the alleged appeasement of the Nizam by the Congress government.[114]

The Samaj and the Mahasabha based their 1938–39 campaigns out of Sholapur and Nagpur, respectively. This infrastructure was reactivated in 1947–48, when the Samaj organized camps at places like Sholapur, Pandharpur, Barsi, Bijapur, Umarkhed, Buldhana, Ahmednagar, Pusad, and Chanda.[115] Samajists from these "*satyagraha* camps" agitated against Hyderabad under the command of "Field Marshal" Swami Swathantra and Mahatma Narayan Swamiji.[116] In certain respects, the area including the Marathwada region of the Nizam's dominions and the Marathi-speaking districts of Bombay and CP and Berar was the epicenter of Hindu nationalism in India. The Rashtriya Swayamsevak Sangh (RSS) and the Mahasabha had been organizing youth in the area since the mid-1920s.[117] Throughout the 1940s they set up a network of training camps in western and central India providing arms and ideological training. There was, additionally, B. S. Moonje's Central Hindu Military Education Society and the Bhonsle military school at Nasik, which received support from both British and Congress governments.[118] Moonje and other major Hindu nationalist leaders like Bhai Parmanand sought action to alleviate the "grievances of Hindus" in Hyderabad State.[119] The Mahasabha vociferously opposed the Nizam's independence bid and called for armed intervention by the Indian state.[120]

The Intelligence Bureau reported from Nagpur in September 1947 that "the news of the colossal oppression of Hindus in Hyderabad has inflamed public opinion."[121] Samaj and Mahasabha propaganda regarding Hyderabad alleged the defilement of temples, suppression of religious rituals, and discrimination against Hindus, including killings perpetrated with impunity.[122] An Arya Samaji attempted to assassinate the Nizam in 1949, and a member of the Hindu Mahasabha threw a grenade at the Nizam's car after his swearing-in ceremony as rajpramukh in January 1950. In sum, Hyderabad and the Nizam occupied a position in nationalist discourse as a Muslim state and an autocratic monarch, respectively, which were inherently threatening to the Hindu majority within the state and to the Hindu character of the Indian nation more broadly.

IV. Making a Majority

Hindu nationalists weren't alone in ratcheting up the rhetoric about the dangers posed by Hyderabad to both national unity and the lives of Hindus living in the state. As far back as 1924, Gandhi accused the Nizam of sponsoring a secret program that coerced Hindus to convert to Islam.[123] The government of India's *White Paper on Hyderabad*, authored by the States Ministry and submitted by Sardar Patel to Parliament in August 1948, echoed Hindu nationalist tropes about Hyderabad. It began by referring to Hyderabad as "founded by the agents of foreign invaders" and ruled by a "fascist minority."[124] Hyderabad was a "communal" state in which "the minority monopolises all rights and privileges and the majority has no civil liberties and lives in a State of utter serfdom."[125] The government of India alleged, moreover, that Hyderabad had a "network of agents throughout India" who smuggled arms, formed centers "responsible for creating communal tension," and induced "Muslims from India to emigrate to Hyderabad and to terrorise and force the majority population to migrate to India."[126] These activities were "carried on under the inspiration and support of the Nizam and his Government" and constituted "a grave menace to the public tranquility of India."[127] The *White Paper* emphasized the role of the Razakars and the Majlis, a strategy that sought to capitalize on reports of "atrocities," "border raids," and other alleged misdeeds of Hyderabad's Muslims that circulated widely in newspapers across India from the summer of 1947.

The *White Paper* exemplified two primary lines of argument. The first was that Hyderabad was an essentially illegitimate Muslim state, foreign in origin and propped up by colonial rule, in which a Muslim minority dominated over an oppressed Hindu majority. Hyderabad was, as examined in the previous chapter, widely considered by supporters and detractors alike to be a "Muslim" state. Like their opponents, Bahadur Yar Jung and the Majlis sought to link the fate of the Nizam's state to that of Hyderabad's Muslims: "He cannot exist without us and we cannot survive without him."¹²⁸ The second argument was about security: Hyderabad was a threat to India, and Muslims, both in Hyderabad and elsewhere in India, were as a result potential fifth columnists. The Police Action was justified by the government of India, not on the basis of law or the constitutional standing of Hyderabad, but on the basis of security. As in the partitioned Punjab, a violent crisis was transformed into a legitimizing narrative that equated the sovereignty of the Indian nation-state with peace.

Shortly after August 1947, rumors began circulating that the Nizam and the Razakars were preparing an attack on Hyderabad's Hindus with the object of transforming Hyderabad into a Muslim-majority state.¹²⁹ A number of constitutional proposals put forth by Muslims in the late 1930s had indeed proposed an exchange of population in the Deccan. The author of one such plan, Dr. Syed Abdul Latif, a former professor at Osmania, publicly urged Hindus to leave Hyderabad in October 1947.¹³⁰ The Nizam's reputation as a leader of Muslims and Hyderabad's reputation as a Muslim state led, by one estimate, around seven hundred thousand Muslims to move from the Indian Union to Hyderabad between August 1947 and September 1948.¹³¹ Coming from UP, CP, and elsewhere, they looked to the Nizam for protection and patronage, which his administration made considerable efforts to provide.¹³² The government of India took various actions to stem this movement, which suspicious officials saw as the work of the Nizam's agents working covertly in India. As early as October and November 1947, orders were issued to provincial governments not to permit sales of railway tickets to destinations in Hyderabad without the approval of a district magistrate.¹³³ In this way, the conflict over Hyderabad raised the specter of a replay of Partition in the territorial heart of peninsular India.

B. G. Kher, the chief minister of Bombay, reported to Patel in October 1947 that there were "strong rumours and also information from Criminal Investigation Department that on and from fourteenth instant Hyderabad Nizam Muslims intend starting trouble against Hindus on a mass scale." He assured the Sardar that "we are watchful" and asked the central government to "make military and other arrangements."¹³⁴ That same month the *Indian Express* reported that a "well-laid Scheme to massacre, on a vast scale, the Hindus of Hyderabad is almost complete."[135] Patel also received alarming reports from, among others, Kashinath Rao Vaidya, a Congress leader of Hyderabad, who warned that "any action of the Government of India delayed will cost several thousand Hindu lives."[136] Syama Prasad Mookerjee, prominent Hindu Mahasabhaite and minister of industry and supply in the Union Cabinet, forwarded a December 1947 report to Patel claiming that "within a short time over a lakh of poorer class Hindus would have been butchered."[137] The nationalist press and major political leaders reinforced the perception of a secret alliance between Pakistan and Hyderabad and questioned the loyalty of Indian Muslims. The *Hindustan Times* reported that "the Nizam's police and military were ravaging village after village in the front rank of the people's struggle and the Ittehad-ul-Muslimeen was rushing on with Fascist plans of creating another Pakistan in the heart of India."[138] The socialist leader Dr. Rammanohar Lohia warned in May 1948 that "the bluster and tyranny of Hyderabad's rulers is directly due to Pakistan's encouragement. The Government of India are not standing up manfully to this and are allowing this great fifth column base in the south to grow in strength."[139] Jinnah made similar intimations when he warned Mountbatten that "every Muslim throughout the whole of India, yes, all the hundred million Muslims, would rise as one man to defend the oldest Muslim dynasty in India."[140]

No one, however, was more forceful in his demand for Muslim loyalty than Sardar Patel, who was India's deputy prime minister, home minister, and head of the Ministry of States (the department in charge of the princely states).[141] And unlike Nehru, who preferred to stay above the fray of party politics, Patel not only commanded a loyal following within the Indian National Congress but was also deeply engaged in party affairs at the moment when the Congress took over the colonial state. Patel insisted that for India's Muslims "mere declarations of loyalty to the Indian Union" would not suffice. They "cannot ride two horses," he claimed, and what was needed instead was "practical proof of their declarations."[142] For Patel, unlike Nehru, Muslims held little if any import for the nature of Indian citizenship and were certainly not essential to the legitimacy of the Indian state. "Both of us cherish one goal," the Sardar told the RSS chief M. S.

Golwalkar in 1949, "but difference in emphasis—four crore Musalmans here—place for loyal ones—not for others."¹⁴³ For Patel, as for many other Indian nationalists, the conflict over Hyderabad became a crucial litmus test for Indian Muslims. The socialist leader Acharya Kripalani, for example, argued that it was "the duty of the Indian Muslims to tell the communal leaders of Hyderabad that their present activities might spell disaster."¹⁴⁴

The suspicion surrounding Muslims was, of course, given existential stakes by the Partition and its epochal violence. The conflict over Hyderabad fed on the anxieties and pathologies stemming from Partition. Patel spoke of Hyderabad as an "ulcer" in the "whole body politic of India," "a cancer in the belly of India," and a "veritable poison."¹⁴⁵ For Patel, the Police Action was a "surgical operation," necessary for the very survival of the body politic.¹⁴⁶ In this way Hyderabad was "nationalized" over the course of 1947–48. Muslims, and especially Muslims in Hyderabad, were constructed as threatening to the very life of the nation. Patel ordered the confiscation of arms from all Muslim licensees in CP and Berar, even while, as discussed below, arms were being liberally distributed to Hindus.¹⁴⁷ Several hundred Muslims, including members of the Legislative Assembly, were arrested in the border areas of Bombay, Madras, and CP in the weeks preceding the Police Action.¹⁴⁸

Rumors of impending danger led around four hundred thousand to five hundred thousand Hyderabadi Hindus to leave Hyderabad State for places like Sholapur, Pandharpur, Poona, Barsi, Bijapur, Bezwada, Ahmednagar, Nagpur, Wardha, and Chanda, and even as far away as United Provinces (UP).¹⁴⁹ Yet officials also acknowledged that the "press accounts of atrocities and panic seem to be a result of the part of the [Congress] programme."¹⁵⁰ Indeed, much of the reporting on Hyderabad in many of the major national and international newspapers and on Indian government radio was derived from press releases put out by the "publicity offices" established by the Hyderabad State Congress Committee of Action in Bezwada, Sholapur, and elsewhere.¹⁵¹ After the Police Action, Military Governor Chaudhuri conceded that "the figures of Razakar atrocities investigated so far do not tally with the figures released . . . by the Hyderabad State Congress to the world outside by way of propaganda before Police Action," which were "deliberately inflated for propaganda purposes or were unreliable."[152] A delegation of Congressmen, led by a member of the Legislative Assembly from Sholapur, reported in January 1948 that the many newspaper reports of "*goondas* from Nizam's State playing havoc on the borders of Barsi taluka of Sholapur District" were "far from correct." Indeed, they reported that security arrangements along the border were sufficient and that, if anything, it was "*goondas* from the Indian Union" that had been extorting "money in the name of the Hyderabad State Congress" from villagers within the Nizam's domains.[153]

Even more duplicitously, Razakar attacks on the communist-led peasant revolutionaries of Telangana were reported as attacks on Hindus *as* Hindus. Government propaganda and the press campaign regarding Hyderabad thus effectively tapped into a discursive reservoir regarding Muslim tyranny in Hyderabad that had been propagated by Hindu nationalists since at least the 1930s. The Indian government brought the Razakars to the center of public discourse about Hyderabad and of the private negotiations with the Nizam's government. The *White Paper* framed the issue in these terms: "The Ittehad and the Razakars have embarked upon a virulent anti-Indian campaign, and are indulging in most provocative anti-Indian activities. In many parts of the State, their savage atrocities culminating in a large number of incidents have brought about a virtual collapse of law and order. The contiguous districts of the three Indian Provinces, Bombay, Madras, Central Provinces and Berar, have been raided again and again."[154] Press reports of Razakar raids galvanized popular opinion in favor of a military solution to the impasse. By early 1948, the Indian government made banning the Majlis and the disbanding of the Razakars a condition of any agreement with the Hyderabad government.[155] The *White Paper* devoted an entire chapter to "border incidents," in which Razakars and Hyderabad police were portrayed as the sole aggressors, their victims as helpless civilians, and the government of India as needing to intervene to restore security.[156]

In early September 1948, Patel and Nehru made the case for military intervention to Parliament. Patel stated that the "campaign of murder, arson and loot going on in Hyderabad rouses communal passion in India and jeopardizes the peace of the Dominion."[157] Nehru read from the same playbook. The Indian government had, "for the last time," asked the Nizam to disband the Razakars: "No civilised government can permit such atrocities to continue to be perpetrated with impunity within the geographical heart of India; for this affects not only the security, honour, life and property of law-abiding inhabitants of Hyderabad, but also the internal peace and order of India. We cannot have a campaign of murder, arson, rape and loot going on in Hyderabad without rousing communal passions in India and jeopardizing the peace of the Dominion."[158] At a press conference three days later he echoed these remarks, insisting that the "real reason" for "taking action" was not "political"; rather, "inside Hyderabad and on the borders conditions were worsening and this was affecting the whole of south India and, to some extent, the rest of India."[159] On both occasions he spoke at length of the Razakars, to whom he attributed the alleged "anarchy" in the state. Hyderabad was thus constructed as a security problem that posed an existential threat to the nation at the very moment of independence.

V. Sovereignty from Below

India's military intervention, as a "Police Action," was premised on eliminating internal threats and restoring order. The Razakars were, undoubtedly, a threat *within* Hyderabad but, as demonstrated by the Police Action, hardly constituted an existential threat to the nation. In response to the government of India's demands for the disbanding of the Razakars, Hyderabad's prime minister, Mir Laik Ali, insisted that the entire raison d'être of the Razakars was to defend Hyderabad from "raiders armed with modern weapons" coming across the border, "derailing trains and destroying life and property."[160] India's blockade of Hyderabad had left state forces and police inadequately "armed and equipped to enable them to cope with the raiders."[161] Laik Ali argued that it was impossible, in this context, for Hyderabad to meet India's basic demand, thus making a peaceful settlement impossible.

Laik Ali was right. The Congress, and Sardar Patel in particular, were not interested in a negotiated settlement, although they did use the campaign of sabotage against Hyderabad as leverage in negotiations.[162] The Congress did not pay the price of Partition simply to let the Nizam have his way. Under the guidance of Patel and with the support of Congress provincial governments in Madras, Bombay, and CP and Berar, the Hyderabad State Congress, the Socialist Party, the Arya Samaj, and the Hindu Mahasabha conducted a violent campaign in and around Hyderabad between August 1947 and September 1948. Their aim was to manufacture a "law and order" crisis, which would, in turn, give the Indian government a pretext for military intervention.[163] Hyderabad's fate would not, ultimately, be decided via a legal or constitutional settlement. It was to be a political affair.

According to the State Congress leader M. Narsing Rao, the armed campaign was part of a three-stage plan adopted by the Hyderabad State Congress in May 1947:

> The working committee was authorised by a resolution of the general session, to take all necessary steps for securing Hyderabad's accession to Indian Union and immediate establishment of Responsible Government. The Working Committee appointed a committee of action which started and carried on the struggle. The committee of action prepared a plan of struggle consisting of 3 stages to be extended over a period of 3 or 4 months at the most. The first stage consisted of civil dis-obedience, and satyagraha, and the 2nd stage of non-payment of levy and taxes, and cutting of toddy trees and breaking of forest laws and causing economic damage to the Nizam State Government. The 3rd stage was to be reached by creating what were called "Border incidents" indulging in acts of sabotage, destruction of means of communications, demolition of customs and police choukies etc. It was also planned that students, lawyers, village officers, etc. should non-co-operate by boycotting their institutions. It was intended to paralyse the Government in all these ways. This plan was further modified as the period of the struggle became greater, in order to fight by violent resistance against the atrocities of Nizam's Government and Razakars. In this way our struggle has been a curious mixture of violent and non-violent methods.[164]

Patel approved this plan and directed Congress provincial ministries to aid the agitation.[165] In June 1947 the government of CP and Berar wrote to Patel that they had

> posted on our border trusted Hindu DCs and DSPs with instructions to help those who are working in Hyderabad. Such workers can agitate in Hyderabad and when pursued can cross back into CP and Berar districts. I have requested Morarji Desai to make similar arrangements in their border districts. Shri Ramanadji has gone to Bombay to see Shri Desai. When I visited Mysore in March I had spoken to Reddiar and Bhashyam, the two veteran Mysore Congress leaders, to help the Hyderabad workers on the Mysore border. If a similar situation could be created by Dr. Subbarayan on the Andhra border, I think we would have succeeded in *throwing a ring round this treacherous State*. Of course *all this is subject to your approval* and you will kindly instruct Guptaji accordingly.[166]

After the Nizam announced his intention to pursue Hyderabad's independence, the State Congress first organized nonviolent protests. Mass meetings, strikes, and various forms of civil disobedience were held across Hyderabad, culminating in a "Join the Indian Union Day" on August 7 and further protests on August 15. More than 7,103 State Congress supporters ended up in Hyderabad's prisons over the next six months. Pandit Narendra, the Samajist leader in Hyderabad, backed the Join India Movement and committed his organization and its resources to the State Congress "*satyagraha*" program.[167]

Shortly after August 15, Tirtha, president of the State Congress, met with Patel in Bombay to finalize the Hyderabad strategy. "Volunteer squads," he later wrote, were then "organised and most of these functioned on the border."[168] Tirtha was convinced that the "final phase of the freedom struggle in Hyderabad would have to be a clash of arms with the Indian Union" and that "nothing short of an armed action on part of the Government of India would force the issue." The armed campaign, he concluded, "hastened the process of impending Police Action."[169] State Congress leader D. G. Bindu later confirmed that the Home Ministry permitted the functioning of the border camps and approved of their violent tactics.[170] The State Congress, of which the Hyderabad branch of the Socialist Party was an integral part, organized over 1,600 men in seventy-nine camps along Hyderabad's borders.[171] The majority of these were located in the Marathi-speaking areas along the Bombay-Hyderabad border and the Berar-Hyderabad border. The first training camp was established at Manmad at the beginning of August 1947, and saboteurs were sent into Hyderabad at the beginning of September.[172] Militant cadres from the border camps burned customs posts, attacked police stations, cut telephone and telegraph lines, and sabotaged the railways.[173] The "main object," reported the deputy inspector-general of police of Bombay Province, was to "break the Government machinery of the State."[174]

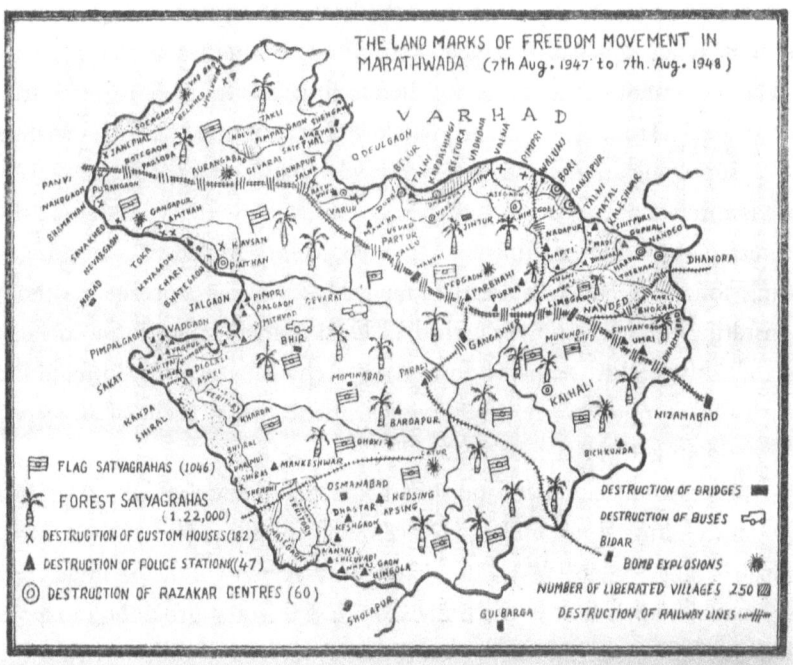

FIGURE 1. The Landmarks of the Freedom Movement in Marathwada. Source: Hyderabad State Congress, *Thus Fought Marathwada*, Maharashtra Provincial Office, Bombay, 1948.

With financial support from socialist leader and hero of the Quit India movement J. P. Narayan, the State Congress's "Committee of Action" established an office in Bombay that was attached to the Congress Party office. The State Congress and the socialists released statements to the press describing their border activities and the heroic deeds of the "Kisan Dals."[175] The State Congress office in Bombay published a pamphlet entitled *Thus Fought Marathwada* that detailed their sabotage activities in the Marathwada region of Hyderabad State and claimed they had killed 844 people, mostly Razakars and police, while losing only seventeen "martyrs."[176] Militant cadre encouraged villagers in the border areas to declare "independence" from Hyderabad and to form "Gram Raj."[177] The Socialist Party was particularly active within Hyderabad State and along the CP and Berar border, with Chanda being a major center of socialist activity.[178] Narayan toured Chanda, Bezwada, Kurnool, and the Bombay-Hyderabad border in mid-1948.[179] He criticized the Indian government for not taking military action against Hyderabad and, citing Junagadh, argued that a parallel government should be established to force the Indian government to intervene.[180] Aruna Asaf Ali and Ashok Mehta confirmed that the socialists were "supplying arms to the people of Hyderabad" and responded to critics by claiming that they were acting in consultation with V. P. Menon, the secretary of the States Ministry.[181] Indeed, Mehta argued that "nothing is being done by the Socialist Party, so far as Hyderabad is concerned, without consulting the Government of India." During the Maharashtra Socialist Party's "Hyderabad Week" in June 1948, Achyut Patwardhan offered the party's full support to the Indian government in the "event of an armed show-down with Hyderabad State."[182]

More than fifteen thousand students responded to the All Hyderabad Student Union's "Quit College Movement" and some joined the "armed squads" at the borders.[183] M. P. Venkatswamy, secretary of the Secunderabad Students Union, wrote in the State Congress prison journal the *Democrat* that the "offices on the borders and the underground offices within the State are mainly manned by these students. The work on the borders is mainly that of the students.... The training camps are run by the students. The student volunteers, who form the great part of the State Congress volunteers, are always at the beck and call of the people of the State."[184] For many progressive students, socialists, and, indeed, the communist-led peasant revolutionaries of Telangana, the battle against Hyderabad was against the reactionary forces of feudalism and imperialism. "It was impossible," Nehru stated in June 1948, "for a feudal state like Hyderabad to continue for long as such in modern India."[185]

Of course, it was not all heroism and derring-do. Officials in the border districts of the Indian Union reported an alarming increase in criminal activity.[186] The most infamous State Congress raid was known as the Umri Bank Affair, during which about seventy State Congressmen attacked the police station, bank, and railway station in Umri, killing three policemen and two bank employees and making off with Rs. 200,000.[187] There was also foreshadowing of the anti-Muslim violence of the Police Action. In October 1947, State Congressmen attacked a village in Hyderabad's Raichur district and destroyed the local mosque.[188] The next month the Bombay government reported that houses of Muslims in three different villages in Hyderabad State were burned by "a mob" and that "an armed mob of 60/70 persons attacked Officers and Muslims of Bhanasgaon village in State limits, routed the whole of the Muslim population and set their houses on fire."[189]

Laik Ali accused India's agent-general to Hyderabad, K. M. Munshi, of organizing the border activities of the State Congress.[190] Patel's decision to send Munshi, a conservative Gujarati Brahmin and founder of the Akhand Hindustan movement, as India's representative to Hyderabad suggests that the Sardar was not interested in developing cordial relations with the Nizam's administration.[191] Immediately upon his arrival, Munshi began a turbulent and antagonistic relationship with Hyderabadi officials.[192] As home minister of Bombay Province, Munshi had actively supported the 1938–39 *satyagraha* conducted against the Nizam by the State Congress, the Arya Samaj, and the Hindu Mahasabha.[193] He was also instrumental in organizing the popular mobilization against Junagadh after that state refused to accede to the Indian Union. Munshi's Akhand Hindustan movement and his leadership of the *akhada* (gymnasium) movement in Bombay were supported by the Hindu Mahasabha and the RSS. Munshi "knew very well" many RSS organizers in Poona and Nagpur, with whom he had long associations dating back to the 1930s.[194] These activities had led Gandhi to temporarily expel Munshi from the Congress at that time.[195] Manu Bhagavan has suggested that Munshi was involved in a conspiracy between Hindu Mahasabha militants, personnel in Hyderabad's military, and the Indian Army.[196] The British journalist Maurice Cheesewright reported in September 1948 that "almost alone, he is responsible for the spread of exaggerated reports of chaos in Hyderabad. The stories of attacks on Hindus, eagerly and naively reported by the Indian Press, nearly all came from him."[197] In May 1948, Munshi wrote to Patel that the "suppression of border incidents is not an end in itself," because the "border incidents only provide justification for the exercise of defence power under the Standstill Agreement and otherwise. If the Nizam's Government restrains the Razakars from indulging in border incidents, our end will not be gained. . . . This, to my mind, is the only point of view which would justify our action in the eyes of the world."[198] The strategy of the Indian government was to manufacture border incidents and other disorders in order to justify military intervention in Hyderabad. Nehru too was in on this game, although from a distance: "It is rather difficult to find out who the raiders and aggressors are. Sometimes the State Congress people are responsible for these raids etc."[199] He wrote to the chief ministers in July 1948 that India was pressuring Hyderabad by imposing an economic blockade, severing financial ties, cutting communications, and, cryptically, "other ways too which I need not mention here."[200] Publicly, however, both Nehru and Patel stayed on message by attributing the "law and order" crisis in Hyderabad to the Razakars alone. Munshi even published a book, *Report on the Razakars of Hyderabad*, consisting of more than a hundred pages of alleged misdeeds committed by the Razakars and the Majlis.[201]

The collaboration between the nascent Indian nation-state and partisan groups continued during the Police Action itself. The *Hindu* reported that "3,000 cadets of the State Congress served as guides to the Indian Army when it entered."[202] In this, they were not alone. Home guards from neighboring British Indian provinces also accompanied the army into Hyderabad.[203] The frantic raising of home guard units after August 1947 was part of a more comprehensive plan by the Congress and the government of India to put, as Nehru put it, increased "pressure" on Hyderabad.[204]

VI. Home Guards and the Nation-State

What the connections between State Congress (and other) partisans, the National Congress Party, and the nascent Indian nation-state illuminate is a highly complex process of building a new sovereign formation out of the wreckage of the Raj. The Congress did not insist on a state monopoly of violence. On the contrary, they saw a dispersal of violence into the body politic as working to affirm rather than subvert the sovereignty of the nation and the nation-state as the embodiment of "the people." Between 1947 and 1948, the Congress and the Indian government promoted the raising of "home guard" forces throughout India, but especially in the areas surrounding Hyderabad.[205] Home guards occupied a liminal space, endowed with the capacity to exercise violence on behalf of the state but not being properly of the state. The democratization of the state was, in this sense, accompanied by a democratization of violence. The home guard, disciplined and apparently willing to sacrifice himself for the state, now emerged as an idealized national subject working to build the state at the lowest level: "The ignorant, illiterate and rough villager from the remotest corner of the province, had within three months of training, proved an efficient and well disciplined Home Guard who while affording protection in times of emergency also helped to reconstruct the villages according to Mahatma Gandhi's ideals."[206]

In November and again in December 1947 Nehru wrote to the chief ministers expressing the urgent imperative for home guards in all provinces, but particularly those surrounding Hyderabad.[207] A similar effort was undertaken in Kashmir, where the Indian government began arming people's militias after the fall of Baramulla.[208] A week after the assassination of Gandhi, Nehru ruminated over the appeal of the RSS, which was estimated to have upwards of six hundred thousand *swayamsevaks*. He diagnosed a societal requirement for both violence and discipline, and he sought to channel these urges into constructive purposes. The home guard, he thought, could substitute for the *swayamsevak*. Nehru was "rather impressed" by the Raksha Dal in UP and wrote to the chief ministers suggesting that similar organizations

> should be formed on a fairly extensive scale in other provinces. The question of arms does not come in. Where possible the Raksha Dal volunteers may be taught how to use a rifle. But they need not be given rifles. Indeed rifles are not available. But the arms part is the least significant. What is necessary is to discipline them and give them some training. . . . This will have a salutary effect on the public mind and more specially on the mind of those engaged in this training. There is a strong demand for such training and the success of some organisations like the R.S.S. has been largely due to their supplying this need.[209]

The old Congress strategy of "discipline and mobilize" was to be converted from a technique of displaying the illegitimacy of the colonial state into a means of establishing the sovereignty of the postcolonial nation-state from the bottom up.[210] Provincial governments requested almost two hundred thousand rifles for the home guards, and at least sixty thousand rifles were distributed to the provinces.[211] Nehru considered the matter as "one of great urgency" and urged that "people on the borders [of Hyderabad] should also be taught to organise themselves in self-defence."[212] The provinces that bordered Hyderabad—Bombay to the west, Madras to the south and east, and CP and Berar to the north—raised tens of thousands of home guards. In CP and Berar they were trained by military personnel and ex-Indian National Army officers. The defense minister requested that "in view of the gravity of the situation on the Hyderabad-C.P. border," home guards "be placed at the disposal of the Government of India."[213] The Bombay government's "ultimate object," in light of "the incidents in the districts bordering Hyderabad State," was to have a "Village Defence Party in each village."[214]

By the end of May 1948, the government of Bombay had raised fifteen thousand home guards out of a target forty thousand.[215] Bombay's chief minister, B. G. Kher, exhorted villagers to collect weapons and organize village defenses.[216] In a note to the States Ministry, his government approvingly noted that "Hindus on the borders of the Nizam's State are collecting arms and ammunition."²¹⁷ A "Special Officer for Border Areas" was deputed to Ahmednagar District to organize village defense parties to be led by local congressmen along the Hyderabad border.²¹⁸ The district magistrate of Sholapur reported that he was "issuing weapons very freely in bordering villages."²¹⁹ In Sholapur, which had six *talukas* bordering Hyderabad, the local authorities deployed armed police and aided the formation of village "defense squads" in at least 254 villages, in many cases recruiting Hindus displaced from Hyderabad.²²⁰ Police constables from the district accompanied a group of three hundred state congressmen to attack a Hyderabadi police outpost in February 1948.²²¹

After coming to office in 1946, and with growing urgency during 1947–48, the Congress Ministry in CP and Berar under Ravi Shankar Shukla implemented a program to give military-style training to the "young, well-built and able bodied" for the purpose of "self-defence."²²² The CP government positioned home guards, extra police, and small detachments of the Indian Army to "protect the frontier" with Hyderabad.²²³ Shukla argued that the home guards were necessary for defense from "the inhuman atrocities perpetrated by the Razakars." He boasted that the home guards had won praise from Mountbatten, Nehru, and Patel.²²⁴ By mid-May 1948, there were more than five thousand home guards in the rural areas of Berar (a territory claimed by the Nizam), all trained and armed by the provincial government.²²⁵

The first Congress premier of CP and Berar, N. B. Khare, later became the president of the Hindu Mahasabha. His successor, Ravi Shankar Shukla, the chief minister from 1946 until 1950, and of Madhya Pradesh until 1956, referred to the Muslims of his state as "fifth columnists" in a July 1948 letter to the Ministry of States.²²⁶ The governor of CP and Berar reported in July 1947 that Shukla's ministry considered "every Muslim as a Pakistani" and that Muslim policemen were being coerced to leave the province. A few days after the adoption of the June 3 Plan, Shukla reviewed cadets of the Hindustani Seva Dal, noting that "even though religious and cultural freedom may be conceded to the Muslims living in Hindustan they will have no representation in the legislatures or in the services."²²⁷ Around the same time he suggested that Muslims in India be designated as foreign nationals.[228] Three days after Gandhi's assassination in January 1948, concerns over the influence of the RSS in the home guard units in CP were raised in a meeting of the Union Cabinet and provincial governors.[229] Shukla worked to inflame Hindu opinion against Hyderabad, charging the Nizam's administration with systematically depriving Hindu cultivators of their land, forcibly converting Hindus to Islam, and colluding in the kidnapping of thousands of Hindu children.[230] He wrote to Nehru in July 1948 that the "tales of atrocity and woe" brought by Hindu refugees from Hyderabad "naturally inflame the feelings of Hindus in our districts, many of whom have friends or relations amongst the refugees. Unfortunately the actions of the local Muslims, amongst whom there are signs of increasing fifth column activity, are not exactly calculated to assuage the outraged feelings of the local population. The result is that the problem of maintaining peace and order and preventing an outburst against the local Muslims is becoming increasingly difficult."[231] Shukla's prediction of an "outburst" would be prescient.

In addition to agitating partisans, home guards, and provincial police forces, units of the Indian Army were posted along the Hyderabad border from January 1948.[232] Nehru ordered the military and police to pursue any "raiders" into Hyderabadi territory so that they might be captured or otherwise punished.[233] The Hyderabad government, in response, accused the Indian Army of aiding the State Congress militants.[234] Although they vigorously denied it, especially after reporting by international newspapers like the *Manchester Guardian*, the Indian government also imposed a near-complete economic blockade on Hyderabad.[235] Nehru ordered that "with the exception of articles of food, salt, medical stores and chlorine for purifying the water supply, all other articles should be denied entry into Hyderabad State and strict blockade should be maintained in regard to these other articles."[236] There is evidence that the blockade went even further than this. Shukla reported that the CP government had "sealed off all movements of goods into the state."[237] The *Times of India* reported that the blockade "went beyond the stopping only of articles and commodities required for military preparations and, therefore, soon paralysed the economy of the state."[238] Munshi informed Patel that "our unofficial blockade ... imposed a severe strain on Hyderabad's economy."²³⁹ Nehru wrote to the chief ministers in July that "Hyderabad has suffered a lot from the economic blockade" and that "the conditions in Hyderabad are bad for the people."²⁴⁰ Hyderabad officials complained that they were running low on essential medical supplies and chlorine and approached the government of India for a loan of wheat in June 1948. Indian officials denied this request, despite acknowledging that Hyderabad had a fifty-thousand-ton food grain deficit.²⁴¹

In sum, the Indian nation-state achieved a sovereign presence in the Deccan through ambivalent efforts to incite, control, and subdue violence. Rather than seek to monopolize violence, the Congress sought to disperse and democratize it. It was in this multifaceted way that violence worked to forge a new relationship between the state and "the people." Hyderabad became a convergence point for antimonarchical republicanism and Hindu majoritarianism, in which the unity of the people was created through opposition to a Muslim monarch. The battle for Hyderabad was foundational of the transformation of the Raj into the Republic.

VII. Making a Minority

In a classic essay, Gyanendra Pandey asked a provocative question: "Can a Muslim be an Indian?"²⁴² Yet within mainstream Indian nationalism as exemplified by the Congress, the potential of Muslims to be Indian was rarely in doubt. What was questioned was their proper place *within* the Indian nation. Partition and the founding of Pakistan were, of course, transformative events in this regard. The quest for Azad Hyderabad, the multifaceted mobilization of violence it provoked, and the aftermath of the Police Action were also integral aspects of the historical context in which Muslim belonging after August 1947 was contested and experienced.

The battle for Hyderabad and the Police Action were key events in the development of a national regime of sovereignty premised on the establishment of national majorities and minorities. Minorities, Pandey reminds us, were the very means of making national majorities. If the campaign against Hyderabad leading up to the Police Action was marked by a discourse constructing Hyderabadi Muslims as a menacing and illegitimate other, the violence against them was an act of incorporation, of internalizing Muslims as a minority within a new national sovereign formation. After 1947, Indian Muslims, as a minority, were emptied of their political character inasmuch as they ceased to have a claim on the exercise of state power or to certain rights as Muslims. They were certainly no longer a minority in the political sense of electoral or representative politics. As a minority religious community, however, the place of Indian Muslims in the nation became the primary measure of the secular character of the nation-state. This transformation was on stark display in Hyderabad, where violence evacuated sovereignty from the Asaf Jah state and the political content of the Muslim community. Indian Muslims, as a religious minority divested of political power and, indeed, their political character more broadly, were expected to behave in a certain manner and to play certain roles assigned to them by the majority. What emerged in Hyderabad, and in India more generally, was an ambivalent combination of majoritarianism and trusteeship, the former most closely associated with Patel and the latter with Nehru.

Violence in Hyderabad before, during, and after the Police Action often took on explicitly symbolic and ritualized forms. The Sunderlal Report claimed that "forcible conversions" were

> a universal factor almost everywhere we went. After the adult males of a locality had been killed the women and children were generally "persuaded" to adopt the Hindu faith. We came across hundreds of Muslim women who had been forcibly tattooed on the forehead in the orthodox Hindu style as a mark of their conversion. Some had even their new Hindu names tattooed on their fore-arms. We saw children whose ears had been freshly bored in the Hindu style. Beards had been shaved off and choties[243] kept. We saw the sacred thread hanging around the neck of Muslims.[244]

Similarly, an intelligence report noted that "instances of demolition of mosques, desecration of the holy quran, forcing Muslim women to tattoo their foreheads and compelling Muslims to shave off their beard have been reported from Bidar, Nander and Gulbarga districts."[245] By the emptying out of a symbolic world of meaning, such violence sought to evacuate the sovereign content from the Muslim body.[246] We can, I think, also understand it as a response to the overwhelming ambivalence and anxiety that arose out of the Nizam's quest for Azad Hyderabad. Ritualized tattooing, as acts of naming and incorporation, can be seen as acts of ordering that produced certainty out of such ambivalence.[247] Tattooing, in particular, could be understood as a marking of Muslims, not as the irreconcilable other, but as one's own. The symbolism of incorporation was similarly visible in the installation of Hindu idols in hundreds of rural mosques throughout Hyderabad. Much the same could be said about the forms of sacrificial violence that were reported during and after the Police Action.[248] Yet unlike in Punjab, in Hyderabad violence against Muslims was not necessarily about pushing them out but rather about pushing them down. Violence forged, at once, a relationship of association and submission. For example, in December 1948 Abdul Karim Ghudabhai Lunje, a member of the All India Congress Committee and Executive Committee of the Maharashtra Provincial Congress, wrote to Chaudhuri and Nehru that Hindu "*gunda*s" in Hyderabad were threatening Muslim widows and their daughters to marry Hindu men. If they refused, they were being forced to go to Pakistan.[249] There was a choice between submission and incorporation, or expulsion from the nation altogether.

This incorporation was, ultimately, conditional. Discourses of loyalty, as Pandey highlights, were central to the forging of a postcolonial regime of citizenship in India. What was demanded of Muslims were performances of speech and, at times, silence. In the period between August 1947 and September 1948, Muslim leaders across India were asked to publicly voice their loyalty to the Indian Union and to denounce Hyderabad or the Razakars. Similar demands were issued after the Police Action, with many prominent Muslims and Muslim associations issuing statements in support of the Indian Union.[250] After the Police Action, however, Muslim security and belonging were conditional on silence. In his study of a village near Hyderabad City conducted in 1951–52, the anthropologist S. C. Dube noted that "after the Police Action, when Hyderabad was no longer a feudal Muslim State, the Hindus had their revenge by pouring scorn openly on Muslim religion and society. It was now the turn of the Muslims to observe silence, and tolerate humiliation and insults."[251] In March 1949, M. A. Shakir, a Bombay-based journalist for the Urdu-language *Nakhuda Weekly*, sent a letter to Chaudhuri and Nehru. Shakir began by declaring, "I am a Congressman of 20 years' standing having complete faith in the declared policy, creed, and principles of that great organization." He then offered details of his investigation of Bidar, Gulbarga, and Osmanabad districts after the Police Action. Shakir wrote that local officers admitted "large scale murders, loot, arson" and that "forcible conversions, abductions, rape, house-breaking, thefts, arson etc. are still being resorted to." Shakir concluded his letter by pointing out that although "all or most of the male members of the Muslim community have been killed at many places and only women and tiny children are surviving," he refused to go to the press with such information.[252] Shakir offered his silence as proof not only of his loyalty and honesty but also as part of his perceived duty within a reciprocal ethics that was seen to be essential to an effective regime of secular democracy. National Muslim leaders like Maulana Azad, fully aware of events in Hyderabad and urging action behind the scenes, maintained a steady public silence.

In late colonial India, the terms *majority* and *minority* largely retained their original meanings as a vocabulary of electoral or representative politics, even as they became attached to distinct religious communities. As such, they were inseparable from the question of participating in political power. After August 1947, however, Indian Muslims became a substantially different type of minority. In his address to Delhi's Muslims in October of that year, Maulana Azad, as he had for years, urged Muslims to cast off their fear of being a minority. He argued that India's Muslims had "adopted an attitude towards freedom which was characteristic of a community heading towards extinction." He advised Muslims to abandon the fear that had led them to support Pakistan and consequently put them in their vulnerable position in postcolonial India.[253] Azad saw the foundation of Pakistan as giving "permanent constitutional form" to the "enmity between Hindus and Muslims," thus requiring Indian Muslims to adapt to their status as a "weakened" and newly disenfranchised minority.[254] He suggested that the way forward was for Muslims to become a nonpolitical category: "We shall not establish any Muslim organisation in the political field." For Azad, Muslims, *as Muslims*, should withdraw from the political sphere altogether. Azad framed secular citizenship as a set of reciprocal duties between the majority and minority: "So you [Muslims] will have to eliminate communalism and shut the door of Muslim League, which the Muslims had opened. If it is not shut, *you shall be held responsible*, and all of our efforts to improve the climate of the country shall be impeded."[255] Like Azad, Nehru saw secular citizenship emerging from an ethics of coexistence in which the majority and the minority had reciprocal duties. Muslims were expected to exhibit proper behavior—loyalty to the state and docility being the chief criteria—in exchange for state protection from the wider social, economic, and political forces ranged against them. The duty of the majority, Nehru insisted, was to recognize its position of strength and accommodate the fears of the minority: "By virtue of numbers and in other ways, [the majority community] is the dominant community and it is its responsibility not to use its position in any way which might prejudice our secular ideals."[256] Nehru's hope, of course, was that after Partition majorities and minorities would no longer be thought of solely in terms of religion but would instead be dynamic and contingent arrangements determined by ideology and interest. Nehru was majoritarian in the sense that he did not believe in the necessity or the absolute right of the minority to participate in state power. Rather, he thought that the majority should wield power in a responsible manner that acknowledged the vulnerability of the minority, essentially adapting Gandhian notions of trusteeship to a statist order. Under Nehruvian secularism the minorities would be given assurances, not of jobs and seats in assemblies, but of the security of their culture and lives.[257]

In this respect, there was something of a majoritarian consensus among Nehru, Patel, and Hindu nationalists both within and outside of the Congress. The major difference between Nehru and Patel was that the latter thought it was primarily the responsibility of minorities to behave appropriately. For Nehru, however, the legitimacy of Indian democracy would be measured in terms of the effectiveness of state protection of Muslim life and property. In 1949, he lamented the corrupt and unjust approach of the custodian of evacuee property and other officials toward Muslims in UP: "Gandhiji's face comes up before me, gentle but reproachful. His words ring in my ears. Sometimes I read his writings and how he asked us to stick to this or that to the death, whatever others said or did. And yet those very things we were asked to stick to slip away from our grasp. Is that to be the end of our lives' labour? I have been upset about many things, but these recent developments in regard to Muslims, evacuees or others, have come as a great shock to me."[258] Nehru thought Muslims were essential to the very idea of the Indian nation. There could be no India without Islam. This was, of course, a factor in his commitment to Kashmir as an integral part of India. The Police Action coincided with calls for an exchange of population in Bengal as had taken place in Punjab. Nehru worried that "every Moslem in India would feel an alien and in effect we would have established a Hindu State."[259] He feared that the Indian state's mistreatment of Muslims after 1947 would bring the entire ideological project of the Congress, and thus the legitimacy of the state, into crisis: "All of us seem to be getting infected with the refugee mentality or worse still, the R.S.S. mentality. That is a curious finale to our careers."[260] The ethical burden of secularism should, Nehru insisted, be borne primarily by the majority.

Yet for Nehru a healthy democratic life could come only through reciprocal ethical commitments between majorities and minorities. Here too he drew on Gandhi, arguing that rights, even though in theory unconditionally guaranteed by the future constitution, were in practice conditional upon the performance of duties. In a January 1948 address at Aligarh Muslim University, he issued a challenge to the Muslim students: "Do not think that you are outsiders here, for you are as much flesh and blood of India as anyone else, and you have every right to share in what India has to offer. But those who seek rights must share in the obligations also. Indeed, if the duties and obligations are accepted, then rights flow of themselves."[261] A few months earlier, Nehru had responded to comments made by Ravi Shankar Shukla, the Congress chief minister of CP and Berar, that Muslims in India should be designated as foreign nationals by arguing instead that "citizenship in India will certainly not be a matter of religion but of fulfilling certain qualifications and of allegiance to the state."²⁶² This lack of "allegiance to the state" was, of course, seen to be the great sin of Hyderabad's Muslims. Nehru accordingly went along with Patel's fiery rhetoric regarding Hyderabad, as we have seen in the *White Paper*.

After the Police Action, Nehru publicly denied any violence in Hyderabad and defended India internationally. At the same time, he expressed grave concern through private and official channels and demanded action. Muslims from Hyderabad made appeals directly to the prime minister, pointing to his curious role after 1947 as a leader of Indian Muslims, tasked with protecting them from the very state and political system that he ostensibly controlled.²⁶³ In November 1948, he ordered a "policy of minimum interference in the administration" of Hyderabad. He was upset over changes that had "been made rapidly and on an extensive scale" and that he believed had "given rise to widespread fear among the Muslim population" that an attempt was being made to "Hinduise the entire administration."²⁶⁴

Nehru's concerns were justified. That same month, V. P. Menon, secretary of the Ministry of States, and Military Governor Chaudhuri agreed to reconcile the "communal" proportion of the civil and military services in Hyderabad along demographic lines according to census data.²⁶⁵ Muslims had held a disproportionate number of posts under the Nizam, especially at the higher levels, so such an order was in effect a Hinduization of the administration. From January 1949 until September 1950 the Hyderabad government issued a Secret Circular Letter requiring government departments to restrict Muslims from numbering more than 12.5 percent of the government workforce.²⁶⁶ This policy was defended by Chaudhuri's appointed civilian successor, the Indian Civil Service officer M. K. Vellodi: "The policy of preferential treatment based on communal considerations was the only policy that any sane Government in Hyderabad, could have adopted after the Police Action. Any other policy would, in my view, have been criminal madness at the time."²⁶⁷ Vellodi maintained it was inevitable that the demobilization of the Hyderabad Army and administrative reforms would cause mass unemployment among Muslims.²⁶⁸ The Indian government also deported or repatriated thousands of Afghans, Arabs, and others from Hyderabad.²⁶⁹

After the Police Action, approximately 17,550 suspected Razakars were "rounded up" by the new military government. Around the same time when Hindus were granted amnesty in mid-1949, 1,535 suspected Razakars remained in prison as under-trial prisoners, while an additional 563 individuals were "held in detention as detrimental to the security of the State."[270] Pointing to the hypocrisy of the selective amnesty, Maulvi Hifzur Rahman wrote to Nehru that this "discrimination undermines the very secular status of the State."[271] Nehru agreed. In late 1950, with hundreds of Muslims still in detention, he asked Patel to implement a universal amnesty:

> Much has happened during these years which has changed the face of Hyderabad almost completely. Still it is possible to follow these changes and more particularly what passes in people's minds there. I have not been happy about this at all, as I have sensed repeatedly that things were not well and sometimes were even deteriorating.... What I have noticed in the course of the last two years or more is a big hiatus between the administration and the people. The administration did its best, at the top at least, but it remained completely apart from the people not only in the official way but more so in the human way. It did not therefore understand or appreciate the feelings of the people. This applied even more so to the Muslims of Hyderabad, who had been completely broken up by events. Many of these Muslims were examples of a particular and rather attractive culture, which had grown up in Hyderabad both among Muslims and Hindus.... All these persons were suddenly frustrated and there was little in the way of a gesture of friendship and welcome. The past pursued them and us and this past was represented, more especially, by innumerable trials and detentions and the rest of it.[272]

Nehru emphasized government action to restore the faith of a disenfranchised minority. He argued that it was the ethical duty of the majority, or those claiming to act on behalf of the majority, to act with mercy and forgiveness. Nehru thought forgiveness rather than forgetfulness was the key to forging a harmonious political future.[273] He compared government actions in Hyderabad with the response to Partition violence:

There is no doubt that horrible deeds were performed in Hyderabad by the Razakars first of all and later, immediately after the police action, by the Hindus against the Muslims. Something equally horrible, or perhaps more so, occurred in Delhi in September and October 1947, and in East Punjab and of course West Pakistan, on an enormous scale. It was astonishing how decent people committed inhuman atrocities. We survived that and we did not go about searching for the culprits. They live amongst us today, many of them, as respected citizens. A madness seized the people, fear and a lust for vengeance. We paid ultimately the heaviest penalty of all for it in the death of Bapu.[274]

Nehru thought the punitive approach taken in Hyderabad was both counterproductive and unethical: "In Hyderabad, something of a like nature happened perhaps on a smaller scale. It is difficult and not desirable to punish vast numbers of people. The change in Hyderabad and the frustration and fear that this brought about, was a very big one. The future became dark with no hope in it. The main problem was not to punish a few more, but to remove this overhanging sense of fear."[275] Nehru was keenly attuned to the affective and psychological dimension of political life and the ethical demands it made on those who exercised state power. He was sensitive, as Sunil Khilnani has argued, to the "destructive potentialities of politics," and thus the need to wield power with circumspection.[276] He concluded his appeal to Patel by pointing to Hyderabad's uniqueness: "Historically and culturally, Hyderabad represents certain traditions. It is always a rather dangerous thing to uproot deep historical and cultural forces. Or rather, it may not be difficult, but it is very difficult to replace them by something constructive and substantial."[277] Patel's response distilled the tensions within the Congress and the republican project in India more broadly. His message was essentially majoritarian: the duty of the government was to express the popular will. The pursuit of justice should, as a result, reflect the interests of the majority. Addressing the idea of a general amnesty, he admitted that it "might create some impression among the Muslims." But, he averred, both "those who have suffered at the hands of Razakars and Government servants" and those "not directly affected" were "very bitter about these things." Their reactions to an amnesty for

Muslims "would be most adverse." Patel "naturally counseled a generous and lenient attitude" but warned Nehru that "clemency" would not be "upheld by public opinion."[278] In other words, popular will demanded punishment, not mercy, and Patel thought that government action should reflect that. In this way the violence committed by the Muslim minority, unlike that of the Hindu majority, was essentially criminal and needed to be handled by the state as such.

Patel argued that the violence of the majority, in contrast, was a "popular reaction and revulsion against the old order" that was "inevitable."[279] This was, of course, the same argument he used to justify amnesty for Hindus. Patel asserted that the violence of the majority was essentially political and, as such, integral to the establishment of a new sovereign order in the subcontinent:

> All changes of the established order must bring about a certain amount of suffering, and all that we, who to some extent control events, can do is to endeavour to minimize suffering. If you remember the nature of the treatment which the Hindu population had been receiving at the hands of the Razakars, the wonder is that the retaliatory violence after the sharp change in the situation after the Police action was so little. In fact, it was probably the assurance that suitable penal action would be taken against the Razakars by the Government that somewhat assuaged mob fury.[280]

Punishment of suspected Razakars and former officials of the Nizam's government was, by this logic, necessary to protect the Muslim minority, allowing them to take their proper place in the new national order. Patel argued that, if anything, "There was a general criticism of those days that we were far too mild and conciliatory." Patel further dismissed Nehru's concerns about the value of Hyderabad's history and culture, which, "in spite of its attractive features," could never be "regarded as indigenous." It was, rather, purely a creation of British colonialism; it owed "its existence and prosperity to the stimulus from the ruling powers." It was, then, "inevitable that the political changes which displace the Muslim rulers from their favoured position should affect this culture to the same extent."[281] In this respect

Patel viewed the Police Action and its violence as essentially revolutionary in nature: that is, as an integral part of the collapse of an older sovereign order and the foundation of a new one based on popular sovereignty. "I think we should be under no illusion," he argued, "about the magnitude of the change which has taken place in Hyderabad." "Everything considered," he concluded, "it was nothing short of a revolution."[282]

In February 1949, during his first visit to Hyderabad after the Police Action, Patel spoke to a crowd of four hundred thousand at Fateh Maidan. "The terrible nightmare happily ended in Hyderabad," he told them, "and now the old organisation" had to be "substituted by a new one." The "dirt of the past" must be "completely washed away."[283] He issued two warnings. The first was to Hyderabad's Muslims, telling them that if they still believed in the two-nation theory they should leave for Pakistan. After the Police Action, Muslims in Hyderabad, as elsewhere in India, did indeed withdraw significantly from the political sphere, as advocated by Azad, Nehru, and Patel, among others.[284] The years after 1948 have been characterized as the "political wilderness of the Muslim masses" in Hyderabad.[285] Many of Hyderabad's Muslim elite and much, if not most, of the educated classes left for Pakistan or elsewhere after the Police Action, with more to follow after the dissolution of Hyderabad State in 1956.[286] The Majlis-e-Ittehad-ul-Muslimeen was initially banned and then remained dormant until Qasim Razvi's release from prison and migration to Pakistan in 1957. The refounded Majlis have since practiced a form of identity politics that seeks to articulate Muslim interests as a minority in a secular India.

VIII. The State and the Sangham

The second warning that Patel issued during his speech at Fateh Maidan was directed at the communist-led revolutionaries in Telangana. The Sardar assured the audience that he would not "let our hard-earned freedom go to blazes" and that he would "not allow one Communist to remain alive because it will poison not only the State but the whole of India."[287] A month before the Police Action, Munshi wrote to Patel that Hyderabad involved a "double problem" of "liquidating the Razakars as well as the Communists." In contrast to the Indian government's public stance that the Razakars represented an existential threat, Munshi predicted that solving the Razakar problem would be "easy." The communist problem, on the other hand, was allied to "the problem of the whole of South India and connected with the Communist policy in South East Asia." A communist "infiltration in South India," Munshi warned, "would prove a danger to the National Government if not firmly and thoroughly handled."[288] Patel agreed. In an Independence Day broadcast on August 15, 1948, he assured the nation that the government was determined to use "a firm hand" against "undesirable elements" in order to prevent the spread into India of the "chaos" found in China, Burma, Malaya, Indonesia, and Indo-China.[289]

Within three days of the surrender of the Nizam's forces to General Chaudhuri, the new military governor ordered "vigorous military and Police Action" against the communists in Telangana.[290] Two brigades of the Indian Army and nearly ten thousand armed policemen were dispatched to Telangana.[291] In a message sent to chief ministers shortly thereafter, Patel warned that the "Communist menace demands constant vigilance" and, once again referring to China and Southeast Asia, demanded that it should "never be allowed to deteriorate beyond a police problem and even there the less of a problem the better."[292] V. P. Menon, Patel's deputy and former constitutional advisor to the viceroy, wrote to Mountbatten in late October 1948 that "the resistance of the Communists in Warangal and Nalgonda" was "more determined" than anticipated. He vowed to "take all powers to liquidate them as effectively and rapidly as possible."[293] It was no surprise that the Communist Party of India believed the real reason behind the Police Action wasn't the Nizam or the Razakars but the "democratic revolution" in Telangana.[294] For the government of India, after the Nizam was vanquished, the threat of revolution remained. And unlike the aspirational and ultimately impotent monarch, Telangana represented a more fundamental challenge to the claim of the Indian National Congress and the government of India to represent "the people."

CHAPTER THREE

FOUNDATIONAL VIOLENCE
State and Society in Partitioned Punjab

TODAY, TOURISTS GATHER at the border crossing in the town of Wagah to watch Indian and Pakistani soldiers perform an elaborate border-closing ceremony. Wagah now symbolizes the banal reality of these two territorial nation-states as exclusive yet intimate entities. Yet prior to 1947, Wagah was nowhere near a border. It was a small village located on the Grand Trunk Road between Lahore and Amritsar in the heart of the vast and populous region of Punjab. "Between the two cities," observed the imperial historian and jurist Reginald Coupland in 1943, "there is no natural dividing line of any kind." Any border between them, he noted, "would be wholly artificial, geographically, ethnographically and economically."[1] The border that now divides Indian Punjab from Pakistani Punjab is thus an artifact of a particular historical contingency, one in which violence was the critical factor in transforming an imperial space into two exclusive national territories. Violence precipitated the collapse of colonial power, a social crisis, and a process of ethnic cleansing. It also provided the context for claims to sovereignty and citizenship in the months and years from August 1947. In telling this story of the violent linking of nation, state, and territory, this chapter examines the Indian state's contested and contingent efforts between 1947 and 1948 to fix national subjects to a clearly demarcated national territory. The unmixing of Punjab's socially heterogeneous population was a means by which the event of Partition was sutured. Violence and displacement were converted into a normative, settled order. Out of this violent process, a new regime of sovereignty and citizenship emerged.

In the months after August 1947 Punjab was the site of overlapping sovereignties. Both India and Pakistan made claims to individuals and populations outside of their territories as demarcated by the "award" issued by the Boundary Commission. The normative ideal of national sovereignty as absolute, singular, and exclusive was not simply conjured into existence by fiat on August 15, 1947; it had to be made. In October, Jinnah cited the exchange of population as an affirmation that the two-nation theory was "not a theory but a fact."[2] The exchange of populations and the establishment of two sovereign nation-states did indeed internationalize the question of Muslim nationality. Muslims remaining in the Indian Union navigated a highly precarious situation as they transitioned from a separate nation to a religious minority within an emergent postcolonial regime of sovereignty and citizenship, as in the case of Hyderabad.

Yet the June 3 Partition Plan, as Yasmin Khan has pointedly observed, left crucial questions unanswered: Where was India and where was Pakistan? Who was an Indian or a Pakistani?[3] In one sense, the answers to these questions were matters of cartographic and demographic knowledge. The Boundary Commission, led by the English lawyer Cyril Radcliffe, issued its award primarily on the basis of the religious demography of the various districts of the province. Colonial statistical knowledge and the administrative categories of the ethnographic state formed the basis for determining membership in the two new national communities and for demarcating their territorial contours. Radcliffe's boundary award, however, wasn't announced until August 17. Both the Congress and the League remained in the weeks after June 3 opposed to a transfer of populations, which they saw as contrary to the interests, ideals, and identities of their respective national projects. Violence provided more or less definitive answers to the questions left unanswered by the June 3 Plan. It forced the issue of a population exchange and authorized enormous state operations aimed at securing national territories and protecting and controlling displaced populations. Violence did not, as Khan suggests, "threaten the existence of the two new states"; rather, it was constitutive of them.[4] Partition as "a history of broken bones and broken lives" can, in this light, also be understood as a history of sovereignty and citizenship.[5]

The great unmixing that took place from mid-1947 made Punjab a key site of a global twentieth-century transformation: the making of exclusive national territories and a new international order out of socially heterogeneous imperial spaces.[6] In India, as in Europe and elsewhere, certain communities were displaced and victimized as they were forced from their ancestral homelands and initiated into new national ones or cast into the liminal zone of the refugee. The sovereignty of the nascent Indian and Pakistani nation-states was staked on the maintenance of this northwestern border, giving birth to their mutually constitutive dialectic. The role of violence was integral to this historical process of border making. India's border with Bangladesh (the former East Pakistan) and its contested frontier with China, in contrast, remain indeterminate and disputed to this day.[7]

British Punjab was divided into Pakistani West Punjab and Indian East Punjab, the former with a Muslim majority and the latter with a "non-Muslim" majority. Yet these majorities, especially in the central districts of the province, were statistical abstractions that obscured a much more complex social reality. Religion was not the only marker of identity in pre-Partition Punjab, and the official emphasis on religion did not account for the caste, class, and gender dynamics of a predominantly rural Punjabi society. The process of unmixing and sorting heterogeneous populations was, as a result, characterized by a "gap between a chaotic reality and the clean distinctions of legal theory."[8] Leaders in both countries wanted to see the logic of Partition fully carried through with a decisive stamping of people as belonging to one nation or the other. This was in many respects a protracted and incomplete process, a "long Partition," as Vazira Zamindar has shown.[9] Yet the vast majority of movement between West Pakistan and India took place in the three or four months after June 1947. A permit system was first introduced in July 1948, giving a border forged in violence a formal legal architecture and converting a space of multiple sovereignties into two distinct and exclusive sovereign spaces.[10] Between June 1947 and July 1948, there was considerable confusion and contestation over the national status of certain communities and individuals. This included the status of certain subaltern groups, including Scheduled Castes and Tribes, Christian converts, and abducted women.

People caught up in the chaos of the Partition moved through a series of camps en route to their new national homelands, where "their" state would, in theory and often in practice, endeavor to provide them with welfare. In most districts of West Punjab, the Indian government established "evacuee" camps, where potential Indian nationals were collected before being moved to "transit" camps at the border, and then "refugee" camps in East Punjab and elsewhere in northern India. From there they would be resettled on agricultural land; moved to urban settlements, sites of state-led industrial production, and "model" cooperative settlements; and sent to labor on iconic nation-building projects that came to define the Nehruvian developmental state. The camps of Punjab were thresholds to the nation and a new regime of citizenship and sovereignty.

I. Civil War and State Sovereignty

Shruti Kapila has recently argued for conceiving of the event of Partition as a civil war, in which the concern with fraternity was "transfigured into the domination of the language and pursuit of sovereignty."[11] It was out of civil war, Kapila observes, that "the people" were at once revealed as the source of sovereignty and as a means of constituting new national territories "demarcated in blood." What distinguished the Partition as an event of mass violence from its contemporary counterparts was that violence largely emanated from society rather than from the modern state. In this respect, the civil war of 1947 was a Hobbesian *bellum omnium contra omnes*, "the war of all against all," out of which a new regime of sovereignty emerged. Normative time was suspended, the extant colonial regime of state sovereignty dissolved as an already tenuous colonial administration went into free fall, and communities were fractured and dislocated. Of course, the princely states, local administrators, and certain military units were involved in organizing and effecting violence.¹² Violence, nevertheless, was decentralized and diffused across the body politic.

Violence cleared space, quite literally, for the growth of a new regime of state sovereignty premised on a new social contract that authorized its power. This process of state formation worked not through a complete monopoly over violence but through the absorption and channeling of violence into bureaucratic processes of protecting and managing vulnerable and displaced populations. Through institutional practices of care and control—"refugee relief and rehabilitation"—the violent, victimized, and displaced people of Punjab were converted into docile, settled, and ostensibly rights-bearing ones. State sovereignty, in other words, was conceived as a project of social peace—that is, of security—and of new beginnings. "The fear of death and the concern with corporeal safety," Uday Mehta has noted in his commentary on Hobbes, "was thus the enduring and underlying basis of politics."¹³ A new regime of citizenship and sovereignty was constituted out of the suturing of this event of civil war.

To say that violence emanated from society is not to say that it was entirely uncoordinated or completely random. A plethora of organizations mobilized during this period in Punjab and North India: the Muslim League National Guards, the Khaksars, the Ahrars, the Rashtriya Swayamsevak Sangh (RSS), the Hindu Mahasabha's Ram Sena, the Akali Fauj, and factions of the Congress Party. Paul Brass, for example, highlights the role played by the Sikh princely states and the Akali Dal, even as he points to the highly decentralized nature of the violence.¹⁴ Virtually every Indian political organization in the interwar period had paramilitary or militant youth wings in which young men engaged in physical drilling and ideological indoctrination. Militia-style groups were part and parcel of India's "militant publics."¹⁵ They were also part of a wider global interwar landscape, with similar mobilizations occurring both elsewhere in the colonial world and throughout Europe.¹⁶ In India, such groups were essential to both nonviolent campaigns of civil disobedience and community "self-defense" during rioting and violent opposition to the colonial state.¹⁷ They offered divergent visions of the "nation" and its ideal subjects. As sovereignty increasingly came to be seen to reside in the people, fierce contestations were unleashed within Indian society. Following World War II, and particularly from early 1946, informal militant outfits proliferated across North India, adding to the tension produced by the high-stakes constitutional negotiations regarding the future of India. Demobilized soldiers, students, party activists, criminals, and young men of all sorts steeled themselves for an uncertain future and potential confrontation.[18] As Indian society became increasingly mobilized rather than demobilized after 1945, the colonial state's monopoly on violence deteriorated.

The wave of communal violence that swept westward across North India after the Great Calcutta Killings of August 1946 was the immediate catalyst of the June 3, 1947, Partition Plan. Riots in the Punjab in early 1947 pushed the Congress toward Partition and the British toward an abdication of their Indian empire. Frustrated by the experience of governing in coalition with the Muslim League and by deadlocked constitutional negotiations, the Congress leadership saw Partition as a way out of the impasse, as a means of bringing an end to violence, as a way to consolidate their power while pushing the League to the margins of the subcontinent, and as an opportunity to undermine the status of the princely states. In terms of violence, the June 3 announcement had, of course, the opposite effect. Observers and officials in Punjab had been warning of a brewing civil war for months, and by mid-July the provincial government was both unable and unwilling to control the situation.[19] British officials withdrew, and the government essentially ceased functioning. Radcliffe's "award," moreover, was not announced until August 17, creating an intense sense of uncertainty. With the location of the border still uncertain, ethnic cleansing aimed to alter demographic realities on the ground, setting into motion what Brass has called a "retributive genocide."[20]

Both the Congress and the Muslim League remained opposed to a formal exchange of population until the end of August, when the sheer scale and intensity of violence forced their hand. When violence began to escalate in July, the first, and ineffectual, step in what would eventually become a massive state operation was the establishment of the Punjab Boundary Force.[21] Yet violence could not be tamed by violence: not only was the size of the force inadequate considering the scale of the problem, but certain units of the PBF itself became implicated in the violence.²² On August 27, it was announced that all Muslims in East Punjab would be evacuated to Pakistan and all "non-Muslims" in West Punjab would be moved to India. Both governments established Military Evacuation Organisations (MEOs) in the first week of September, and Ministries of Refugee Relief and Rehabilitation shortly thereafter. On September 3 the government of East Punjab opened the East Punjab Liaison Agency (EPLA) in Lahore, and the government of West Punjab set up its Liaison Agency in Jalandhar.

Initially, the MEOs did the bulk of the heavy lifting. The British Indian Army was undergoing its own division into two distinct forces. This transition was extraordinarily complex and fraught with troubles of its own. Nevertheless, in the twelve weeks from the beginning of September to the end of November, the Indian MEO evacuated 2,300,000 "non-Muslims" from the districts of West Punjab by *kafilas* (foot convoys), military transport lorries, and rail.²³ During the same period, more than an estimated 3,500,000 Muslims left Indian East Punjab for Pakistan. The Indian and Pakistani MEOs together moved an estimated 5,757,909 people during these three months.²⁴ Later estimates of the number of people who migrated between India and Pakistan by the end of 1950 run as high as 14,000,000, with an estimated 5,000,000 moving from West Pakistan into India.²⁵ One of the largest mass migrations in history took place over a few intense, violent months.

Violence and mobility were at their peak between July and the end of November. Most of the iconic images of Partition date from this period: long *kafilas* trudging along in desperate conditions, people packed onto overburdened trains, and sprawling and squalid camps. While millions moved, many others remained in uncertain and precarious situations for months and even years afterwards. Tens of thousands of women were raped, abducted, converted, and forcibly married.²⁶ India and Pakistan engaged in a contentious public tussle over the status of these "abducted women." The social panic in Punjab became, immediately from August 1947, a political matter at the heart of an emergent regime of sovereignty and citizenship. Abducted women were, however, one group among many whose national status was uncertain and contested. Scheduled Castes, converts to Islam, Christians, tribal people, and criminal convicts all complicated and confounded the Hindu-Muslim-Sikh paradigm of the Partition plan. The task of unmixing, of disentangling individuals and communities, fell largely to the Liaison Agencies.

The EPLA was headquartered at the office of the chief liaison officer (CLO) in Lahore.[27] The CLO and the district liaison officers (DLOs) were assigned to the staff of the deputy high commissioner of India. DLOs were initially sent to all the districts of West Punjab. The transfer-of-population agreement divided responsibilities between military and civil authorities uniformly in both countries. The MEOs were tasked with arranging the movement of "refugees," protecting them en route, guarding evacuee camps, and aiding "the civil power in maintaining law and order."[28] The EPLA's primary responsibility in September and October 1947 was to establish at least one "evacuation" or "transit" camp in each district of West Punjab in which "non-Muslims" were collected, protected, and, eventually, transported to India under military guard. District liaison officers compiled information regarding the locations of non-Muslim populations and abducted women. They would then work to facilitate their evacuation with the aid of the Indian or Pakistani military or, as was often the case, the local police or civil administrators. The EPLA was supposed to be aided by the two refugee commissioners appointed by the West Punjab government as well as district commissioners. The EPLA supplied the MEO with "all information regarding evacuees, their numbers, state, and location to enable the Military to evacuate them in the quickest and most efficient manner."[29] The CLO, according to the initial plan, was the paramount official for the movement of Indian nationals from West Punjab to India.[30]

The EPLA and other civilian authorities were, however, unable to function effectively throughout the crucial period between September and November, when the bulk of people were on the move. During this time, the MEO was the principal institution for managing the transfer of population. This was due to the near collapse of administrative power in Punjab. As Nehru noted at an August 28 press conference, "The East Punjab Government had to start from scratch ... with hardly an apparatus of Government."³¹ Officials lacked sufficient information and transportation, faced severe fuel shortages, and experienced significant communication difficulties. India's CLO and DLOs refused all-Muslim military guards and had difficulty obtaining the necessary forces for conducting their operations.³² In October and November, the chief liaison officer reported "quite nominal" progress in the "recovery of abducted women and the clearing of small pockets which invariably are full of converts." On November 27, the MEO changed its primary task from the mass evacuation of large population concentrations to what was referred to as the "clearance" of non-Muslim "pockets" and the "recovery" of "abducted women."³³ A few days later, the head of the MEO confidently predicted that "mass evacuation having finished, main mopping up is expected to be completed within the next two weeks."³⁴ The MEO estimated the number of non-Muslims in such "pockets" in West Punjab and the North West Frontier Provinces to be about 419,600.³⁵ In early December, an "Inter-Dominion Agreement" was reached between India and Pakistan regarding the procedures and administrative infrastructure required for the tasks of "recovery" and "pocket clearance." From January 1948, the EPLA took the lead in "pocket clearance" and "recovery," with the MEO moving into a support role. India's MEO was eventually withdrawn from Pakistan in July 1948, at which time an estimated 28,800 "non-Muslims" remained in West Punjab.³⁶

As people moved to "evacuee" camps in West Punjab and then to "transit" camps at the border and onwards to "refugee" camps in India, they were inducted into a new regime of sovereignty and citizenship. State efforts at refugee relief and rehabilitation were foundational to the "social security commitments" of the postcolonial Indian state.³⁷ In this way, violence was integral to the transformation of the colonial state into the developmental national state. Confronted with the task of preserving and improving the life of its subjects on an unprecedented scale, the Indian state worked to transform displaced and victimized refugees into manageable and productive populations. Projects of resettlement and rehabilitation completely altered the social, economic, and political landscapes of many areas of northern India, especially Punjab, present-day Haryana, and Delhi.

Some of the refugees in camps like the one at Kurukshetra were later moved into planned "model" townships. Such townships were equipped with housing, water and power connections, hospitals, schools, and other basic infrastructure. Some of them, like Faridabad, seventeen miles southeast of Delhi, were planned in conjunction with new industrial projects.[38] The Indian Civil Service officer M. S. Randhawa, who directed rehabilitation efforts in East Punjab, wrote that the "partition has provided great opportunities for planning and rebuilding life on a new pattern."[39] This relationship that arose between a displaced population and a nascent state-building project created a zone of interaction where claims of citizenship and sovereignty were negotiated and gave impetus to the growth of the postcolonial developmental state. "Rehabilitation" was thus linked to "development" at a foundational moment. Officials were anxious to move the huge numbers of people out of the camps and into productive roles. Refugees became valuable sources of labor for state-led development measures. The underlying premise was that a return to normative economic behavior was not only beneficial to the national economy and national state but also a means of remaking normative social life after the traumatic violence of Partition. Rehabilitation, Ritu Menon notes, was "as much about *restoring a way of life* as it was about claims and compensations."[40]

Converting refugees into "useful citizens" also generated new power hierarchies and disciplinary regimes. In July 1948 the East Punjab government announced that free rations in the refugee camps would be stopped if "employable persons" refused to work. At least eighty-seven thousand people had their rations stopped immediately as a consequence. For the director-general of relief and rehabilitation in East Punjab this was a necessary step, not only because the free rations were unsustainable, but also because the "Government required 52,000 persons for the Bhakhra dam project."[41] One of the Nehruvian state's most prominent symbols of modernity and progress was built by refugee labor. Mridula Sarabhai, head of the women social workers aiding in the "recovery" of abducted women, suggested that refugees "should be sent to Bhakra Dam or anywhere where there is a labour shortage" because they should not "get out of the habit of doing hard labour."[42]

For many officials, and for Nehru in particular, refugees were a political problem as well as an economic one. As such, they were a source of anxiety, not least because they were seen as both victims and potential threats. The prime minister saw refugees as potentially disruptive of efforts to restore communal peace after August 1947 and as giving impetus to a renewed push to convert India and the Congress into a Hindu state and party, respectively. Nehru went as far as to propose a "voluntary conscription of all refugees who want relief" into a "semi-military regime of discipline and work."[43] He aimed either to shed state responsibility for refugees or to allow the state to "deal with the refugees more thoroughly and we can send them where we like."[44] This obligation to "do some kind of work involving manual labour," Nehru argued, was "useful not only for keeping the people in good mental and physical condition, but also in the larger interests of the State."[45] He conceded that it was "the duty of the State to rehabilitate millions of displaced persons from Pakistan" but argued that "no state can accomplish such a tremendous task unless it is given active cooperation of the people." For Nehru, this forging of a new relationship between the people and the state on the basis of reciprocal duties was essential to overcome the colonial legacy in which the state "functioned as something apart from the public."[46]

Nehru also saw in the crisis in Punjab an opportunity to expedite the transformation of the state into a centralized planning and developmental apparatus. He called for a Development and Rehabilitation Board with "large executive powers" over the "whole of India" so that it might be able to "achieve results with speed and without the delays normally accompanying governmental procedure."[47] The urgency of both rehabilitation and development, in other words, called for the centralization of broad powers akin to wartime measures. By early 1950, however, Nehru became convinced that an overly technical and bureaucratic approach to rehabilitation was counterproductive in terms of building up a democratic state and society. Rehabilitation had, in his view, been reduced to a "mechanical process, as if we were dealing with chattels and not with human beings possessing minds and spirit, which have passed through a period of terrible abnormality and have to be made normal again."[48] He was concerned that rehabilitation would inhibit rather than facilitate the cultivation of a free and democratic society. This demanded not simply returning to the status quo ante but, rather, imbuing the relationship between state and society with new meaning and purpose. He was inspired by the model townships such as Faridabad and Nilokheri ("the brightest example of rehabilitation that I have seen anywhere"),[49] which were based on a cooperative model with a "human touch."[50] He envisioned these small-scale rehabilitation efforts as models for local development throughout India, particularly the way in which local inhabitants needed to be actively involved and vested with a sense of partnership and purpose in the developmental project. Cooperative settlements that initially pioneered as refugee rehabilitation projects served as the model and inspiration for fifty-five community projects that were launched in 1952 and covered about seventeen thousand villages. These community projects, along with the national extension service started the following year, were expanded nationwide by 1955.[51] For Nehru, the national extension service and the community center schemes, based on the "experience in the Punjab," were "the seeds of a great revolutionary change in India."[52]

II. Caste and Nation

Partition forced a confrontation with long-standing debates over the status and identity of Punjab's lower castes. The religious identities of the lower castes, and of the populous Chuhra and Chamar communities in particular, had been a source of contention in the Punjab since at least the late nineteenth century.[53] The new nation-states sought to use the categories of "Muslim" and "non-Muslim" to determine nationality, yet this ostensibly clear-cut formula ran aground of a much more complex social reality. At a foundational moment, the civil war in Punjab forced the nascent Indian nation-state to directly address the caste question.[54] The Dalit experience of Partition was, moreover, conditioned by a number of variables, including popular religious practices, political activism, religious conversion, rural labor relations, and official concerns relating to urban governance.

The relationship between Dalits, Hinduism, and Indian nationalism had been a matter of long-standing contention. B. R. Ambedkar rejected

Hinduism and argued that Dalits should be accorded separate political representation similar to that granted to Muslims. The 1932 "Communal Award" expanded the system of separate electorates to include most religious groups and what were at the time called the "depressed classes." The award was the result of the second Round Table Conference held in 1931, where Muslim, Dalit, Christian, and Anglo-Indian representatives formed a "minorities pact." The pact sought to disprove the idea that India possessed a Hindu majority and to suggest that the Congress represented caste Hindus rather than the nation as a whole. The Congress saw these developments as an intensification of colonial divide-and-rule policies, a threat to national unity, and an attempt to fracture the Hindu community along caste lines. Gandhi's fast unto death forced Ambedkar to sign the Poona Pact giving up separate electorates in exchange for reserved seats for Dalits. The 1935 Government of India Act codified this arrangement and, further, grouped all the Untouchable castes in India into a single distinct constitutional category: the Scheduled Castes. A heterogeneous collection of communities with no common language, profession, or geographical location was consolidated into a single nationwide juridical and political category.[55]

Ambedkar, the figure most responsible for the nationalization of the caste question, entertained, for a time, the possibility of an alliance between Muslims and Untouchables.[56] He took the idea of Pakistan seriously, immediately recognizing its power and potential.[57] Ultimately, Ambedkar became disenchanted with the Muslim League and Jinnah's bad faith. However, the Scheduled Castes Federation (SCF; founded by Ambedkar in 1942 as an all-India party) and other regional leaders continued to see potential in a Dalit-Muslim alliance up until and, in certain cases, even after 1947. There was a formal alliance between the SCF and Muslim League in Bengal, United Provinces, and Punjab. Certain members of the SCF actively extended support for the League's Pakistan demand. This was also the case in Hyderabad, where the two major Dalit leaders threw their weight behind the Nizam's bid for independence.[58] The leaders of the SCF, Ad Dharmis, Ravidasis, and other lower-caste organizations supported the Muslim League's Pakistan demand.[59] Jogendranath Mandal, the Dalit leader of Bengal, carried the Dalit-Muslim alliance across the 1947 divide, taking up a ministerial post in the Muslim League government in Bengal in 1943 and again in independent Pakistan's first cabinet. Mandal's alliance with the Muslim League arose from the fact that, in Bengal, the vast majority of Dalits and Muslims lived as agricultural laborers, while caste Hindus controlled land and capital in a long-standing pact with the colonial state.[60] In Bengal, Hindu congressmen and the Hindu Mahasabha pushed for partition, while Mandal's chapter of the Scheduled Castes Federation and the Muslim League argued for a united Bengal. A large proportion of Dalits were living in East Bengal, and a significant portion of these stayed on in East Pakistan after 1947. The Partition in Bengal "was as much about a nationalist resolution of the caste question" as it was about the Hindu-Muslim conflict over the distribution of political power.[61]

As in Bengal, the dynamics of caste politics in Punjab were marked by particularities unique to the province. These included Punjab's religious demography and the competition over numbers it engendered, the popularity of conversion to Christianity, Sikhism, and Islam among Dalits, and efforts by religious "reform" groups to cultivate separate identities and to make claims to represent Dalit communities. Beginning in the 1870s, large numbers of Dalits drawn largely from the Chuhra community converted to Christianity, opting out of Hinduism altogether as a means of asserting their dignity and social equality.[62] The Chuhra community was largely concentrated in the western areas of Punjab. Indeed, the vast majority of Punjabi Christians lived in the Muslim-majority areas that became Pakistan: of an estimated 486,038 Christians in the undivided Punjab in 1947, only 60,955 lived in East Punjab.[63] Partition led to another wave of conversions, and a significant proportion of the Dalits who remained in West Punjab after 1947 belonged to the Christian community. The movement of some Dalits toward Christianity from the last decades of the nineteenth century fueled the rapid growth of the Arya Samaj in Punjab, as well as its competition with the Sikh Singh Sabha, Sunni Anjumans, and the Ahmadiyya.[64] Beginning in the 1880s, most Dalits were, by default, classified as Hindus in the colonial census. Conversion was thus a direct threat to the size of the Hindu population as numbers became increasingly connected to claims to political power. Political anxieties over numbers stemmed from the introduction of the census in the late nineteenth century and of "communal" representation from 1909. The Samaj sought to consolidate the Hindu nation into a single body. They developed a fairly effective and extensive repertoire of establishing schools and service organizations aimed at social betterment as well as spreading their ideals of a modern caste-less Hinduism. In Punjab, the Arya Samaj grew rapidly in popularity among urban Hindus of the mercantile castes, who provided the funds for the Samaj's outreach efforts. With the percentage of the Hindu population in Punjab steadily declining from the late nineteenth century onwards, the Samaj launched a concerted campaign of *shuddhi*, or purification, which sought to bring Muslim or Christian Dalits "back" into the Hindu community. These efforts heightened social tensions in the province.

In the 1920s, Dalit activists led by Mangoo Ram broke away from the Samaj to found the Ad Dharm, the "original faith."[65] The Ad Dharm movement sought to provide both a new religion and a political organization for Punjab's Dalits. It was the Punjabi iteration of "Adi" movements elsewhere in India, such as the Adi Dravida movement in the South led by M. C. Rajah and the Adi Hindu movement in UP.[66] The shared premise of these movements was that Dalits were the original inhabitants of India who were subsequently subordinated by the Aryans and made into outcastes of Brahminical Hindu society. As such, they were a distinct *qaum* from Hindus (and from Muslims and Sikhs, for that matter) and deserving of special political representation.[67] The Ad Dharm's big coup in this regard was the 1931 census, when nearly half a million Dalits in Punjab identified their religion as Ad Dharm, accounting for approximately a tenth of the Dalit population in the province. This made them roughly the same size as the Christian community. Sixteen percent of the nearly two million Chamars in the province registered as Ad Dharmi, while out of the 1.5 million Chuhras, Christians numbered 30 percent and Ad Dharmis another 6 percent. The change was striking. As Navyug Gill has noted, within the decade leading up to the 1931 census, nearly one-third of Hindu Chamars and one-half of Hindu Chuhras had changed religions.[68] While the Ad Dharm movement was largely centered on Jalandhar, more than 50 percent of the Scheduled Castes in the West Punjab provinces of Lyallpur and Gujranwala reported as Ad Dharmis, with significant numbers in at least four other districts of what would later become Pakistan.

The religion developed by the Ad Dharm centered on the veneration of the *sants* Kabir and Ravidas, a practice with deep roots among Punjab's Dalits. These gurus were popular among the lower castes because they conveyed a message of social equality and because Dalits were denied access to the texts, temples, and priesthood of Brahmanical Hinduism. Ravidas himself was from the Chamar community, who made up much of the membership of the Ad Dharm. Additionally, a movement that took the author of the Ramayana, Valmiki, as its guru spread among the Chuhra community in the early decades of the twentieth century, particularly in urban areas. The Balmikis constituted something of a parallel movement to the Ad Dharm, with whom they made common cause during the interwar period. The veneration of Valmiki, however, didn't seek to make a complete break with Hinduism as the Ad Dharm claimed to do. Rather, it connected the Chuhra to the Brahminical tradition while at the same time rejecting Hindu society's hierarchies and instilling a sense of pride and dignity in their community.[69] Moreover, it was common for lower castes in Punjab, as elsewhere, to associate themselves with the religious identity of the dominant community where they lived. In areas with Muslim landlords, Chamars had become Mochis. Where Sikh cultivators dominated, Chamars became Ravidasia and Chuhra became Mazhabi Sikhs. In the decades preceding Partition, the Mazhabis too had sought to carve out a separate political identity from that of the Jat-dominated Akalis. At one point they demanded an autonomous "Mazhbistan"—distinct from the Akali demand for a Khalistan or Sikhistan—in the event that Punjab was partitioned.[70]

In sum, when it came to the actual work of partitioning, the binary of Muslim and non-Muslim ran aground Punjab's complex sociopolitical matrix, and there was considerable confusion among both officials and many of the lower castes themselves when the mass migrations began. Pakistani officials at nearly every level of government objected to what they considered inappropriate encouragement of Scheduled Castes to leave for India. Pakistan's refugees and evacuees commissioner wrote to India's deputy high commissioner in November 1947 that the "depressed classes are quite contented where they are" and complained that Indian district liaison officers were "causing great uneasiness amongst them" by "inducing" them to leave Pakistan.[71] Pakistan's Ministry of Relief and Rehabilitation subsequently informed the chief liaison officer that "the original agreement between the two Governments on the subject of evacuation did not cover the Scheduled Castes."[72] According to the Inter-Dominion Agreement, district liaison officers were to be aided in their efforts by local administrators and police officials. Indian DLOs reported, however, that their attempts to contact and evacuate Scheduled Castes were being obstructed, with the notable exception of Lyallpur District.[73] Local officials in West Punjab drew on long-standing debates by arguing that Mazhabi Sikhs and Balmikis, among others, were neither Sikhs nor Hindus and thus were ineligible for evacuation.[74]

Dalit labor was crucial to Punjab's pre-Partition economy in both urban and rural areas. District and municipal governments throughout West Punjab passed "Essential Services" ordinances that prohibited sweepers—largely drawn from the Chuhra community—from ceasing work or leaving for India. Pakistani officials pleaded that such essential services should not be compromised at a time when governments on both sides of the border were in a state of crisis. Indian officials agreed that sweepers should continue to work while they prioritized the evacuation of other non-Muslims. As elsewhere in India, however, the vast majority of the Scheduled Castes in Punjab worked in agriculture.[75] Many were *kamins*, landless laborers bonded to certain landholders.[76] Others performed agricultural labor as *siris* who worked for, and often alongside, landholding castes. *Siris* were contracted to work for an entire growing season in exchange for a small proportion of the harvest, as well as cash advances and other forms of patronage.[77] In 1947–48, village *lambardars*, with the support of officials at Pakistan's Refugee and Evacuee Department, often insisted that Scheduled Castes who wanted to leave for India must first pay both land revenue and *tawan*, or compensation.[78] Debt was an important dimension of caste-based labor, land tenure, and social hierarchy in rural Punjab. The DLO in Sialkot reported that potential evacuees were being detained on the premise that they must pay off their debtors in Pakistan before going to India.[79] Well into 1948, Dalits reported to Indian officials that they planned to wait until the next harvest was completed before moving to India.[80]

EPLA records refer often to forced conversions of Scheduled Castes to Islam as a means for landlords to retain control over their labor. The Inter-Dominion Agreements considered all conversions that took place after March 1, 1947, as invalid. Yet Pakistani officials argued that efforts to evacuate recent converts risked creating further disorder and violence. The major-general of Pakistan's MEO wrote to his Indian counterpart in November 1947 that he needed civilian help to "avoid any possibility of removing converts to Islam and thereby upsetting the local population."[81] A month earlier the Indian DLO at Sialkot reported that "lumbardars and members of the village committees do not permit us to evacuate those who have been forcibly converted to Islam and the untouchables and the abducted girls who are said to have accepted Islam."[82] For some Dalits, conversion was a strategy for negotiating a violent event and, potentially, an opportunity to better their socioeconomic standing. Conversion, in certain cases, provided an opportunity for tenants and agricultural laborers to lay claim to property after the departure of Sikh and Hindu landlords. In Montgomery District, for example, many of the Balmikis, Mazhabi Sikhs, Chamars, and Ad Dharmis who were laborers and *kamins* of Sikh and Hindu landlords stayed on the land as Muslim converts after Partition.[83]

Partition also led many of Punjab's Dalits to convert to Christianity, which created another point of contention between India and Pakistan. Such conversions were continuous with a longer history of conversion to Christianity in Punjab and offered the potential for Dalits to extricate themselves from the communal dynamics of the civil war. The Inter-Dominion Agreement held that converts could "only be sent to the Indian Union if they are willing to go."[84] Converts were, in theory, given a choice whether to stay in Pakistan or go to India. Officials, however, disagreed over how such a choice was to be exercised. Raja Ghazanfar Ali Khan, Pakistan's minister for refugees and rehabilitation, argued that converts to Christianity were different from forced converts to Islam and that, as a result, Indian officials should not actively encourage their migration to India.[85] This became Pakistan's official policy in January 1948, and in June the government of West Punjab issued a directive that because Indian officials were "persuading Christians to migrate to the Indian Union even if they did not wish to do so," "no District Liaison Officer or other staff of Military Evacuee Organization should be allowed or helped by subordinates to proceed to any village except where there are Hindu Sikh pockets."[86] Indian officials, for their part, saw such efforts as thinly veiled attempts to prevent evacuation of Dalit converts to Christianity, Mazhabi Sikhs, and other lower castes who "provide labour for agricultural operations."[87]

For those Dalits who did move to India, the experience of Partition was, as Ravinder Kaur has noted, "distinctive."[88] They faced discrimination throughout the process of evacuation and rehabilitation, pointing to the ways in which the category of refugee was not caste neutral. It elided social hierarchies that, in turn, became entrenched in postcolonial citizenship regimes. In every district of West Punjab, caste Hindus and Sikhs were evacuated before Dalits. By mid-November 1947, the vast majority of "non-Muslims" remaining in evacuee camps and villages in West Punjab belonged to the Scheduled Castes.[89] At that time, officials reported from the EPLA camp in Lyallpur that "not a single Scheduled Caste family has been evacuated."[90] By December 1948, 80 percent of the estimated 20,290 Indian nationals yet to be evacuated from West Punjab belonged to the Scheduled Castes.[91] Indeed, officials recruited members of the Scheduled Castes to perform menial duties within the evacuee and refugee camps until the upper castes were evacuated or resettled.[92]

Dalits, as mere tillers of the soil rather than property owners, faced similar discrimination by resettlement programs that awarded land and other state resources to those refugees who owned land and businesses in West Punjab. According to the Punjab Alienation of Land Acts (1901 and 1907), the ownership of agricultural land was limited to certain "agriculturalist" castes (the legislation referred to them as "tribes").[93] Dalits and other lower castes were denied the right to own land. In this way, their status as *kamins* was reinforced by the legal and institutional apparatus of the colonial state. As a result, Dalits were denied a claim to land in the massive effort of resettlement and redistribution that was undertaken from 1947. State intervention was central to the way in which caste and class hierarchies shaped both the experience of Partition and the remaking of normative social and economic life in the following years. The regime of citizenship that arose out of Partition violence and the processes of refugee relief and rehabilitation was differentiated, in that certain groups were seen to be deserving of particular rights on the basis of their caste. While Jats and other "agriculturalist" castes were given land as part of the relief and rehabilitation program, Dalits were resettled in distinct "colonies" and given employment as sweepers or encouraged to take up other "traditional" caste-based occupations.[94]

Gyanendra Pandey has argued that the Dalits of Punjab were "nobody's people" in 1947–48 because neither India nor Pakistan "spoke for them in the way in which they spoke for Hindus, Muslims, and Sikhs."[95] Ambedkar, then the minister for law and chairman of the Drafting Committee in the Constituent Assembly, wrote to the prime minister in mid-December 1947 with a litany of discrimination and oppression suffered by the Scheduled Castes of Punjab.[96] Writing with a sense of great urgency, Ambedkar insisted that Nehru take immediate action: at stake were fundamental questions about the meaning of citizenship in a free India. In his letter, Ambedkar charged the Pakistan government with obstructing the evacuation of Scheduled Castes from Pakistan. He demanded that the MEO be empowered to take effective action and that the Ministry of Relief and Rehabilitation dispatch special officers from the Scheduled Castes to every district in West Punjab.

For Ambedkar, evacuation was just the first step in a comprehensive plan for transforming Punjab's Dalits into rights-bearing citizens and equal members of the Indian nation. He insisted that Scheduled Caste evacuees, many of whom were excluded from government-run refugee camps, should be given rations, clothing, and other welfare being provided to caste Hindus. He argued for the inclusion of Dalits in any distribution of land by the government, the removal of their legal status as *kamins*, and the repeal of caste-based restrictions to land ownership in East Punjab. As a means of ensuring that these policies were implemented, he demanded that both the Punjab and Indian governments recruit Scheduled Caste officers into their civil and police forces.[97] Ambedkar, in sum, wanted Dalits invested with a stake in the new nation-state and enfranchised as rights-bearing citizens. The rupture of Partition was, in this sense, an opportunity to radically alter caste dynamics in Punjab. The return to normative social life after the event should not, Ambedkar argued, simply be a return to the status quo ante. Indeed, for some Dalit communities in Punjab, their encounter with evacuation officials during the partition and their subsequent "rehabilitation" in India, despite being fraught at every step with discrimination and inequality, was the first time they had received support from government as a matter of right. And while Dalits were considered lesser members of the national community and were treated as such, the Indian state nevertheless made sovereign claims over them. At stake in this decisive stamping of individuals as belonging to one nation or the other was nothing less than the sovereignty of these newly founded nation-states.

III. From "Burden on the Nation" to "Useful Citizens"

In November 1947, the Indian minister for refugee relief and rehabilitation, K. C. Neogy, ordered the EPLA to "take special steps for the quick and complete evacuation of the scheduled castes people."[98] He dispatched R. L. Jadhav as an officer on special duty to evaluate and monitor the evacuation of the Scheduled Castes. In the following months, Jadhav toured almost every district of West Punjab and reported that nearly everywhere the Scheduled Castes were victims of aggression and violence. They constituted the vast majority of non-Muslims remaining in the province and were systematically discriminated against by Indian evacuation officials.[99] Jadhav encouraged DLOs to make specific arrangements for the protection and care of the Scheduled Castes. His reports to the government of India emphasized the vulnerability of these groups as the basis for state action, pointing to the way in which mass victimization fed into an emergent regime of citizenship and state sovereignty. The concerted efforts to evacuate caste Hindus and Sikhs indicate that they were, by default, considered full citizens and members of the nation deserving of state protection. Indeed, the resilient Punjabi refugees—virile, disciplined, industrious—would in the years after 1947 come to stand in as the ideal national subjects, having overcome tragedy and committed themselves to the patient work of building the new nation.[100] Indeed, this narrative of Partition as an episode of a longer nationalist story of sacrifice, discipline, and collective effort became, as the next chapter explores, a founding narrative of the postcolonial nation-state.

The discriminatory behavior of Indian officials in West Punjab indicates that the place of Dalits in the nation, and thus the responsibilities of the nation-state toward them, was fraught, deeply ambivalent, and conditional. Jadhav realized that officials would not prioritize protecting and evacuating Dalits as a matter of course. His reports often included descriptions of why these communities were potentially valuable "assets" to the nation. "The Scheduled Castes who reside in these parts," he wrote of Narowal and Sialkot districts, "are a great asset to our country, as they are weavers and farmers. Besides they are very good fighters."[101] Jadhav described the Megh community as "the best stock of Scheduled Caste members in West Punjab," being professional weavers, "good cultivators," and "well skilled in sports work, manufacture of surgical appliances, etc." He noted that it "would be a pity if they are left behind."[102] He put forth similar arguments for the other Dalit communities in Punjab. For Jadhav, the process of evacuation and rehabilitation was about the transition of Dalits from social outcastes into rights-bearing citizens and integral members of the national community. He sent copies of all of his reports to Ambedkar, who sought to effect a similar transformation in constitutional terms on a national scale. Yet Jadhav's arguments about the value and utility of the Scheduled Castes alone cannot explain the Indian state's claims over populations and individual bodies located in Pakistan. These were sovereign claims of the Indian state's exclusive right over the bodies of its subjects. State efforts directed toward groups who were considered undesirable or burdensome are illustrative in this regard.

Take, for example, the case of the Bazigar, at the time classified as a Criminal Tribe and now as a Scheduled Caste. The Bazigar were an itinerant people involved in a range of occupations from trade to livestock, but their "traditional" occupation was as performers or acrobats (*bazi*). They spoke a language of their own, and their religious practices were eclectic, not clearly belonging to Hinduism or Islam. In January 1948, when a convoy of about fourteen thousand Bazigar with three thousand camels and five hundred goats attempted to leave Montgomery District for India, the deputy commissioner stopped the convoy on the suspicion that the Bazigar were Muslims and ordered an inquiry. In his statement to the authorities, a Bazigar lambardar claimed that his people had converted to Islam in the previous months to protect their camels and other property and had intended to stay in Pakistan. When the looting continued, however, they had decided to move to India. The DC concluded that the Bazigar were "non-Muslims" and ordered that the convoy be permitted to proceed. However, Pakistan's minister for relief and rehabilitation, Raja Ghazanfar Ali Khan, ordered the convoy stopped again. He too conducted a personal inquiry, and only after this was the convoy allowed to proceed to India. Throughout this episode, India's CLO endeavored to convince Pakistani officials that the Bazigar were Indian nationals.[103] Yet after the Bazigar had crossed into Indian territory, the CLO wrote to the East Punjab government:

> It has to be remembered that they are mostly beggars and although some of them may have been dealing in camels, quite a large number of them have been a burden on the nation rather than an asset. They do not appear to be imbued with any national or religious motives.... I take it that it is the policy of Government that all these bazigars who are willing to come over to the East Punjab must be evacuated, but I hope that the question of converting them into useful citizens is also engaging the attention of Government.[104]

State action to protect and preserve the life of vulnerable populations also inducted them into a new disciplinary regime. The apparatus of the colonial "ethnographic state" was after 1947 repurposed to construct India's heterogeneous population into a national sovereign formation in which governmental means of care and control were deeply intertwined. Indian officials, for example, endeavored to have non-Muslim convicts and undertrial prisoners sent from Pakistani prisons to Indian ones, efforts marked by the tragic absurdity of Manto's Toba Tek Singh. India's CLO took on the responsibility of sending food and other supplies to non-Muslim prisoners in Pakistan.[105]

The Criminal Tribes, much like prisoners, were incorporated into the state's juridical and disciplinary apparatus as undesirable and subversive subjects. The EPLA worked in conjunction with the East Punjab government's deputy commissioner for Criminal Tribes to evacuate "non-Muslims" from Criminal Tribe settlements in West Punjab.[106] Certain members of the Criminal Tribes were, however, converts to Islam or Christianity. For example, one Khanu was being held at the "Reformatory Settlement" in Amritsar. Even though he had converted to Islam three years earlier, he expressed his desire to stay in East Punjab to be with family members that had moved to the Indian side of the border. The government of West Punjab demanded his evacuation to Pakistan, yet the government of East Punjab refused on the basis that the Inter-Dominion Agreement did not allow for converts to be evacuated against their consent and said nothing in particular about tribal people.

Nationalist leaders in both countries wanted a decisive stamping of communities and individuals as belonging to either one nation or the other, regardless of how inconsistent or arbitrary such a process was in practice. Individual bodies became, as a result, sites of contestation over national sovereignty. For example, one Lachhman Singh was arrested upon his arrival in Lahore from Amritsar in June 1948. He was born a Sikh but claimed to have converted to Islam and presented his recent circumcision as proof. Unconvinced, Pakistani authorities handed him over to Indian police at the border, where he was detained while officials debated which side of the border he properly belonged to.[107] Here was someone with a Sikh name but a Muslim body, caught between two nation-states. There was also the case of one Surrinder Kumar, who converted to Islam after his family was killed during an attack on a train at Kamoke, Gujranwala, in September 1947. He subsequently worked with the police to help locate the hundreds of women and girls who had been abducted during the attack. When he later petitioned the Indian government for evacuation to India, he requested an official certificate explaining his circumcision.[108] Ultimately, however, it was the disputed status of women's bodies that gave rise to a charged public debate and to new forms of state action.

IV. Abducted Women, Sovereignty, and the New Social Contract

The months of mass violence beginning in mid-1947 were marked throughout by widespread violence against women. It is now understood that tens of thousands and perhaps even hundreds of thousands of women were raped and abducted by members of the "other" community. Over the last three decades, the most important and theoretically insightful work on Partition has emphasized the gendered nature of Partition violence.[109] For these authors, what was important was not only the fact of physical violence against women but what came after the initial event. Some have offered searing critiques of the efforts by the Indian and Pakistani nation-states to "recover" abducted women, which became a matter of national honor. The loss of control over women, their bodies, and their sexual and reproductive functions created a social panic that, in turn, precipitated state action. The state's "quest for justice on behalf of abducted women and children," Veena Das writes, "led ironically to new kinds of suffering imposed upon them."[110] By linking together borders and bodies, abduction and recovery were generative of a new regime of citizenship and sovereignty.[111] For Das, the story of abduction and recovery had "implications for the staging of sovereignty" and became "the foundational story of how the state is instituted and its relation to patriarchy."[112] The event of Partition as a Hobbesian *bellum omnium contra omnes* was "defined as one in which Hindus and Muslims are engaged in mutual warfare over the control of sexually and reproductively active women."[113] Reinstating "proper kinship" by returning control over women to the "right" men was, then, integral to the transition from an exceptional event of violence to a normative regime of national sovereignty. The social contract inaugurating the nation-state as a rational guarantor of order out of an event of social chaos was, ultimately, grounded in a sexual contract. In this respect, an attempt was made to instate the sovereign nation as a "pure" and masculine space.[114]

The impetus behind the recovery program came from the public and in particular from refugee families and communities. Thousands of sisters, mothers, husbands, brothers, fathers, sons, and other relations returned under dangerous circumstances to West Punjab to act as "guides" to help Liaison

Agency officials locate and evacuate their wives, daughters, sisters, and mothers.[115] The names of "recovered" women were published in newspapers in East Punjab, New Delhi, and elsewhere in North India. Officials were inundated with letters expressing eagerness to receive their female kin back into their families.[116] Some abducted women clandestinely wrote letters to Indian authorities requesting their own "recovery."[117] One Sarjit Kaur, for example, was being held against her will in Gujrat District when she sent a secret message to the DLO, who then came with an armed guard.[118] The recovery program reflected a new social investment in the state and authorized state intervention in society in new and profound ways. This transformation of the Indian state vis-à-vis Indian society—from an instrument of foreign domination to an agent of popular will—was a distinctly gendered process that generated new hierarchies and power relationships.

In late November 1947, the Indian government established the Women's Section of the Ministry of Relief and Rehabilitation. At the same time, the CLO wrote to district officials in West Punjab:

> In a recent conference between the representatives of the two Governments it was decided that women abducted during the disturbances, irrespective of their consent, should be restored to the community to which they originally belonged. The mere fact that they show unwillingness to go out should not prevent the authorities from sending them out or delivering them to their relations or to the representatives of their Government. Both the Governments are exceedingly anxious to recover and restore them and they have now set up a special Agency for the recovery of such women. I shall therefore feel grateful if you will kindly ask the police to act on this principle and deliver the girls recovered to our representative without taking the trouble of enquiring whether such women are willing to go or not.[119]

This became official policy with the December 6, 1947, Inter-Dominion Agreement and later with the 1949 Abducted Persons Restoration and Recovery Act. The agreement assigned primary responsibility for "recovery" to the local police. The MEO was ordered to guard transit camps and escort "recovered persons" to their respective dominions.[120] Women social workers were tasked with looking after the camp arrangements, receiving the abducted persons, and collecting information to be supplied to the DLOs and local police. DLOs were made responsible for facilitating coordination between the local civil administrators, police, social workers, and the MEO.[121] The EPLA functioned as the principal organ of India's "recovery" efforts and the clearance of "non-Muslim pockets" until it was closed in November 1948.

These arrangements were put in place in December 1947 and January 1948 in all the districts of West Punjab except for Rawalpindi, Campbellpur, Jhelum, Gujrat, and Sialkot. Owing to the conflict in Jammu and Kashmir, the Indian MEO and DLOs were not permitted to operate in these "closed" districts.[122] All responsibilities for "recovery" and "pocket clearance" in these districts were entrusted instead to superintendents of police.[123] Although efforts would continue until 1956, the majority of "recoveries" were made in the months immediately following the agreement. The number of recoveries dropped precipitously following the removal of the MEO in July 1948, by which time 9,362 women were sent from India to Pakistan and 5,510 from Pakistan to India. One aspect of the recovery program that scholars have critiqued was the denial of "free choice, freely exercised."[124] That the "wishes of the persons concerned are irrelevant" was an obvious violation of women's rights.[125] This lack of choice contrasted with policies toward Christians and Dalits. Yet state officials were not the only obstacles to the free exercise of free choice. The recovery program, by allowing abducted women to return to their families, also offered opportunities to women that would not have existed otherwise.

The EPLA's district liaison officers were tasked with coordinating recovery efforts with local police officials in West Punjab. Indian officials, however, regularly accused local police of obstruction and, even worse, of actively participating in the abduction and trafficking of women and children. The CLO noted in February 1948 that "women and girls were in the possession of influential persons, big zamindars, their tenants, notorious Badmashes and even with the subordinate police officials themselves."[126] Testimonial statements given by "recovered" women and other evacuees similarly point to the role of the police and other power brokers.[127] Some reported that police officials offered to facilitate their evacuation to India as a pretense for abducting women.[128] Kamla Patel, the Gandhian social worker in charge of the women's camp in Lahore, noted that "propaganda" made abducted women fearful of returning to India: "They were told that their relations were all dead. Even if they happened to be alive, they would not be accepted by their families; that there was not enough food in India and a bucket of water costs five rupees. They were being sent to India only to be handed over to the Sikhs in the army. It was but natural that after hearing such propaganda, women were scared and not ready to return to India."[129] The DLO in Sialkot likewise reported that "abducted girls are frightened by the prospect of having to return to an impoverished land where food is scarce and where they will be made over to Sikh goondas for prostitution, which facts are propagandised by the Pakistanis."[130] There was a widespread belief, moreover, that abducted women would be rejected by their original husbands or natal families on account of patriarchal norms of honor and purity. The CLO reported that "a few girls . . . were brought out with some difficulty and that they were unwilling to go out to India. They were talked to and the main reason for their reluctance appeared to be a sense of uncertainty about their future."[131] It remains unclear, however, how common such rejections by families actually were. Indian officials and the nationalist leadership argued that, in light of such coercion and confusion, abducted women were unable to make a free choice regarding their desire to go to India or stay in Pakistan. They arrogated this decision as a sovereign prerogative of the nation-state. The pathway from "abducted woman" to rights-bearing citizen must, they insisted, go through the state.

In practice, official policies were implemented in a contingent and arbitrary manner. They were also resisted and subverted. The policy regarding consent was altered in April 1948, when both governments agreed that pregnant women and "doubtful and resisting cases . . . should be dealt with from a human angle."[132] Such cases were reviewed by a tribunal consisting of officials and women social workers from both countries. Some women, after considerable delay, were allowed to remain in Pakistan.[133] Others secretly absconded from the camps where they were held, occasionally with the aid of social workers.[134] A "neutral camp for the difficult and resisting cases of recovered Muslim women" was established in Jalandhar in April 1948. The fates of these women were to be determined by a tribunal consisting of three women social workers, one Hindu, one Christian, and one Pakistani Muslim. Yet the tribunal was essentially nonoperational, leaving a pair of superintendents of police, one each from West and East Punjab, with the authority to "forcibly" send women to Pakistan, to their remaining relatives in India, or back to their abductors.[135]

Some women who refused to cooperate with officials viewed "recovery" efforts as yet another unwanted imposition and intrusion, likely leading to further betrayal. The Gujranwala DLO reported that "some of the girls genuinely felt that their men had run away having left them at the mercy of the Muslims and therefore they had no faith in their Hindu men folk." They believed that their husbands and parents "did not care for them and had altogether written them off their records." Some questioned the practicality of the scheme: "I have lost my husband and have now gone in for another. You want me to go to India where I have got nobody and, of course, you do not expect me to change husband every day." Even the gendered nationalist logic that emphasized restoring control over female sexuality to the men of the "right" religion was scrutinized: "But why are you so particular to take me to India? What is left in me now—religion or chastity?"[136] Some even pointed to the betrayal at the heart of Partition: "How can I believe that your military strength of two sepoys could safely take me across to India when a hundred sepoys had failed to protect us and our people who were massacred?"

As the nascent nation-state arrogated the role of *parens patriae*, the adjudication of domestic matters became an integral aspect of state policy. In this role, as Das has shown, the state transformed patriarchal kinship norms into law. In practice, this was a contingent and arbitrary process: sovereign decisions were wielded inconsistently and arbitrarily. Archival fragments point to divergent outcomes and the ways in which women exercised agency. For example, the husband of seventeen-year-old Ray Rani of Jhelum District sought to have her brought to India. Ray Rani, who was without any remaining natal family, had left her husband a year and a half earlier with one Niwagas Ali. She had converted to Islam and told Indian officials that she wanted to stay in Pakistan. Indian officials were legally obliged to return Ray Rani to her husband in India, yet they allowed her to remain in Pakistan on the basis that she had initially left her husband because her "mother-in-law was not treating her nicely."[137] One Charanjit Kaur refused to return to her husband in Jalandhar unless one of his houses was allotted in her name and only if officials guaranteed that his other wife "would not trouble her."[138]

Institutions such as the Gandhi Vanita Ashram in Jalandhar and the Destitute Women's Home in Hoshiarpur were established as recovered women became wards of the state. A marriage board was constituted to arrange marriages of "recovered girls whose relatives are not traceable and who are willing to marry."[139] The Indian state sought to suture the exceptional event of Partition by mediating a return to normative social life, even if this required denying women a right to choose, refashioning extant norms, or creating new spaces in which women could remake their lives. The "abducted woman" was a "legally constituted category, which framed the differential terms of inclusion of women into the new nation-state."[140] The contingent and inconsistent nature of the process of stamping individuals as belonging to one national community or the other illustrates how violence was integral to the historical processes through which national communities and its boundaries were constructed. The ability to decide who was included and who was excluded from the political community was articulated as a sovereign prerogative.

As the Punjab was transformed into an international border, the abstractions of nationalist imaginaries and colonial demography, were, in the months from June 1947, violently forged into material, territorial realities. Mass displacement and state-led efforts to "recover" abducted women and "evacuate" others not only generated new forms of territoriality but necessitated the unprecedented state management of large and vulnerable populations. Indeed, the very vulnerability and victimization produced by Partition violence became the basis for state action and a newfound social investment in a state previously seen as an external, foreign entity. For the Congress leadership, the crisis provided an opportunity to transform the repressive, minimalist colonial state into an apparatus of national development and social welfare. For "refugees," displacement and victimization provided the basis for making claims of restitution and welfare upon the state as a matter of right. This exchange of protection for submission was a central component of a new social contract between subjects and sovereign.

These "refugees" were not, of course, stateless people. On the contrary, their precarious and liminal status was a direct result of their putative membership in a national political community. The indeterminate status of many individuals and communities resulted instead from the abstraction of the two new nations running up against the realities of Punjab's complex, heterogeneous socioeconomic landscape. A highly contested process of unmixing, of fixing national subjects to national territories, was integral to Punjab's transformation into a border between two sovereign nation-states. This process of "making Indians" occurred through an "incorporation regime" that allocated membership in the nation in differential and hierarchical ways.[141] While the new Indian nation-state made sovereign claims over these people, it did not always take responsibility for them. Claims over bodies were premised on securing life but were not always followed up by substantive action to transform vulnerable subjects into rights-bearing citizens. Indeed, in many cases the Indian state insisted upon its rights over bodies located in Pakistani territory while simultaneously evading responsibility for providing welfare for the same people. Ultimately, this inextricable duality—the right to both preserve and dispose of life—was fundamental to articulations of sovereignty at this foundational moment.

While Partition as an event was, as Das has observed, "not simply constituted by forms of the social," it was "not wholly its other either."[142] As we have seen, while violence was universal to the experience of the event, it was not homogenous or homogenizing. It affected different individuals and communities differently. Violence threatened social hierarchies: upper castes were exposed to violence that was, arguably, part of normative social life for Dalits. The reinscription of caste and gender hierarchies, even in the refugee camps themselves, was integral to the suturing of the event. The state was deeply implicated in this process. Partition violence, in this sense, was not equalizing, a force that affected people uniformly. Rather, social hierarchies were internalized within the nation as "the people" became the basis of a new regime of sovereignty and citizenship in India.

CHAPTER FOUR

NATION AND NARRATION
Testimony, Citizenship, and Sovereignty

IN EARLY 1948, the government of India established a Fact Finding Organization (FFO) to establish a "true and authoritative account of the happenings in West Punjab, the North-West Frontier Province and Sindh."[1] Under the leadership of G. D. Khosla, a judge of the East Punjab High Court, the FFO recorded interviews with thousands of refugees displaced from Pakistan. These interviews formed the basis of a book, published in 1949, that summarized the FFO's findings. Khosla's handling of these interviews was lawyerly: he rejected evidence that "lacked corroboration" and emphasized that "every effort has been made to verify and check the correctness of the narrative."[2] In order to establish the documentary rather than representational nature of these interviews, Khosla opted for "drab understatement" over "picturesque probability." The story of Partition was told as a "stern reckoning." Evacuating emotions from refugee narratives would, Khosla argued, make his account "as near the truth as is possible in any historical narrative."[3]

The Fact Finding Organization and Khosla's subsequent book held the truth of Partition to be grounded in first-person testimonies of the refugee experience. The original speech acts in the refugee camps underwent a process of bureaucratic mediation to become absorbed into a national, state-authorized Partition narrative. Khosla situates the interviews within a wider historical narrative that seeks to explain Partition's causes and consequences rather than explore individual experiences of Partition violence. It was precisely the claim that these individual testimonial statements represented historical truth that allowed them to be redeployed in service of the nation-state. The telling of individual Partition experiences was, in this way, captured by the Indian state at a foundational moment.

Since the publication of Urvashi Butalia's landmark *The Other Side of Silence* (1998), historians and other scholars have critically explored the ways in which Partition and its experience has, or has not, been articulated. Demarcating what can or cannot be said about Partition was, they have discovered, a matter of power.[4] Speaking openly about Partition was politically subversive and socially transgressive. Veena Das locates the silence around Partition within kinship networks and their attendant norms of honor and acceptability. Suffering borne in silence was a strategy for remaking social life in the wake of "world-annihilating" violence.[5] In recent years, efforts by scholars, journalists, artists, activists, and online archives have sought to overcome this silence through a public recounting of individual experiences of Partition.[6] In addition to oral and family histories, there has been a sustained engagement with literature, poetry, and film in order to shed light on the "human dimension" of Partition.[7] These efforts have radically expanded our understanding of the archive of Partition. An underlying assumption in much of this work is that speech, as a means of bearing witness, is potentially cathartic. If Partition and its violence are understood as an unresolved and open traumatic wound that continues to haunt the subcontinent, then speaking truth to power becomes a precondition for recognizing, confronting, and ultimately overcoming historical trauma. In this light, the concealment of the fifteen thousand refugee interviews recorded by Khosla's FFO "constitutes an absence in the public archive that continues to haunt the collective imagination."[8] If the Partition was constitutive of a sovereign territorial Indian nation-state, it was also a betrayal, not only of Indian Muslims, but of non-Muslims in Pakistan. Non-Muslims in Pakistan were betrayed, but they were not abandoned: the Indian state made sovereign claims over them, and they in turn made claims upon the state as a matter of right. At this moment, speech rather than silence was constitutive of a new regime of sovereignty and citizenship.

While the archive of Khosla's FFO remains, to the best of my knowledge, unavailable to the public, dozens of first-person testimonial "statements" can be found scattered throughout the archive of the East Punjab Liaison Agency (EPLA), held at the Punjab State Archives in Chandigarh. The EPLA was responsible for the evacuation of non-Muslims from West Punjab and for the so-called recovery of abducted women from late 1947 until November 1948. Some evacuees and recovered women gave statements to government officials upon their arrival in evacuee camps in West Punjab or refugee camps in East Punjab. These statements were products of particular historical encounters between vulnerable subjects and functionaries of a state claiming sovereignty over them. The power dynamics of these encounters gave both form and function to the narratives. By attending to the "processes of production, relations of power in which the archives are produced, sequestered, and rearranged," this chapter argues for understanding these testimonial statements as part of a history of sovereignty and citizenship.[9] I locate sovereignty in a discursive domain of claim making and interpret narratives of victimization as invitations for the state to undo harm. These narratives frame their subjects as virtuous victims and, as such, deserving of state action on their behalf. Vulnerability and suffering came to authorize the Indian nation-state's sovereign claims. Such a perspective is common to virtually all Partition narratives, which are rarely told from the perspective of the perpetrator. Killing is either elided entirely, framed as sacrifice, or sublimated into stories about the perseverance and protection of life.

Suffering, and the Partition experience more broadly, were incorporated into elite and state-sponsored nationalist discourses. Nationalist leaders held up refugee "relief and rehabilitation" as a marker of state legitimacy and, in so doing, connected the stories of individual experience in the Punjab to the rest of India and, more specifically, to the project of national sovereignty. Narratives of victimization became stories of sacrifice that cast the nationalist project of state sovereignty as one of peace. The exchange of submission for protection was part of a wider process of forging a new social contract amidst the upheavals of 1947. The statements also made explicit claims upon state resources and tasked the state with rectifying wrongs. Such claims were of "critical significance for the invocation of citizenship" as much as the "migrant" was "crucial to the affirmation of the sovereign identity of the nation."[10] In this way, these first-person testimonial statements can be read alongside letters sent by families to state officials, and petitions sent by refugees who formed collective organizations to secure what they perceived to be their rights as citizens of a free India. Testimonial statements were also instrumentalized as primary sources for the state's information order. The reconstruction of bureaucratic power in the divided Punjab necessitated building up a new epistemological order. First-person testimonial narratives were collated into official reports, formed the basis for state action, and were used by state officials as evidence to further a variety of objectives. They served much the same truth-making function as they did for Khosla. Yet the form and function of the statements, in many respects, obscured the subjects they claimed to represent. They nevertheless offer glimpses into subaltern subjectivity and authorship.

I. Violence and the Social Contract

Violence forged new relationships between Indians and the nascent nation-state. This was especially true for those directly affected and displaced by Partition in Punjab. The contrast with Bengal is startling, where more protracted migrations were met with disavowal and apathy.[11] As part of their sovereign claim to have made peace out of civil war, the leaders of the new nation-state claimed that violence authorized a new role for the state vis-à-vis Indian society. As such, it constituted not merely a test of state legitimacy but a new social contract altogether. India's chief liaison officer reported from Jhang in October 1947 that when he "walked into the Camp all men, women and children—old and young, tears in their eyes, fell on our feet and asked for food."[12] A few weeks later, he noted that he was "greatly impressed with the pitiable condition" of the "women and children, who prostrated on the ground praying for help and evacuation."[13] "We owe," he wrote with grim understatement, "great responsibility to the unfortunate victims of the riots."[14] Such sentiments were echoed by national leaders. In a national broadcast on August 19, 1947, Nehru declared, "We cannot restore the dead, but those who are alive must certainly receive aid from the State now, which should later rehabilitate them."[15]

Through petitions and testimonial statements, refugees explicitly assigned the state new responsibilities and articulated claims for restitution as a matter of right. Some formed civil society organizations dedicated to securing communal and individual rights. For example, the secretary of the "Punjab and Frontier Hindu and Sikh Refugees Committee" wrote to the East Punjab government from Srinagar in October 1947, demanding that Punjabi refugees in Kashmir be sent to East Punjab and that the Indian government also immediately evacuate the "ten thousand Hindus and Sikhs" remaining in Rawalpindi:

> The reports daily reaching us here relate the tragic happenings in Rawalpindi where the assassin's knife is taking the toll of 15 to 20 lives daily. Unless these persons are evacuated at once they are bound to perish and leave behind a sad and heartrending page in the history of India's dawn of liberty, and the responsibility for this unfortunately will be entirely yours.... We are after all your subjects, who have managed to escape from the "enemy" country (Pakistan).... Now it is your Government's business to evacuate us from here by all the forces at your command. We have no claim on others, but we have every right upon you to demand protection to our lives and property.[16]

Such forms of claim making engaged in a discourse of sovereign duty, explicitly framing their demands as a test of the legitimacy of the new nation-state. This discourse centered on the security of life and property within a new regime of citizenship and sovereignty. In early September 1947, the Minority Protection Board in Dera Ghazi Khan District appealed directly to a number of top government officials, including Nehru, Patel, and India's deputy high commissioner in Lahore, to "come to their immediate rescue." Their petitions demanding evacuation were grim: the "terrible spectacle of a caravan of forlorn and miserable reduced to abject poverty," "mangled bodies, dismembered limbs, smashed skulls," and "a ruthless campaign of loot, arson, conversion, abduction and general massacre."[17] Following attacks on non-Muslims on September 7 and 8, 1947, the Fort Refugees Relief Committee in Peshawar sent a petition to India's Deputy High Commission that listed five major grievances and thirteen different demands, including immediate evacuation to India, the recovery of abducted girls, and monetary restitution "to make a fresh start in life."[18]

Such petitions foregrounded the preservation and protection of life and property—security—as the basic responsibility of the sovereign vis-à-vis its subjects. India was positioned as a refuge and sanctuary, in direct opposition to Pakistan and as distinct from the colonial state. For example, Ram Lal Juneja, a paper merchant from Gujranwala, wrote to the governor of East Punjab regarding the evacuation of his family from Nankana Sahib:

> I have made so many applications to the different authorities . . . but my applications seem to have been treated like waste paper. . . . Sir, we are subjects of the Indian Union Government and Government should have every possible step to safe-guard the life and property of her subjects and pay full attention to their grievances. I fervently hoped and still hope that when India has attained Independence, the people of India will have, unlike the previous system, full access to the authorities for the redress of their grievances and with the same hope I have ventured to approach you with the request that immediate help be rendered to me.[19]

While the affluent, educated, and upper castes had greater success in mobilizing the state to address their concerns, such a discourse was also deployed by the poor and marginalized.[20] Sohag Wanti, a refugee from Gujrat, had a petition transcribed upon reaching Jalandhar. She was primarily concerned with having her husband and three children evacuated from their home village, where they were being forcefully detained.

> I am now a destitute without a home and also without means of support and livelihood. . . . I have been left without my husband and children, who have been unfortunately with a sheer force of aggression and as well as in the absence of means of transport on account of the fact that our family is hardly hit by extreme poverty and to state the truth there is no voice of the poor in these days although Congress Raj,

which we people thought to be a blessing for the poor, but which, I regret to say has miserably failed to afford help to the poor, has been rotting in Pakistan at Kotla Sohian P.O. Jalalpore Jathan Distt. Gujrat.[21]

Signing with her thumbprint, Sohag Wanti tasked the state with upholding the promises of the nationalist movement. Indeed, failing to receive a response, three weeks later she, like thousands of others, wrote directly to Gandhi, Nehru, and Patel.[22]

In a similar fashion, the testimonial statements given by refugees in the camps often included explicit claims for restitution. Indeed, it is clear that many refugees considered giving their statements to authorities as part of a process of establishing a documentary basis for making claims upon the state. For example, after describing an attack on his train following the withdrawal of the Indian military guard, the statement of Ram Nath Kapur of Dipalpur, Montgomery District, concludes with a contractual claim: "We wish compensation for all the losses through our Indian Government."[23] To this end, the statements often noted the exact value of property lost by refugees. Take for example, the short statement attributed to ten-year-old Priya Kaur[24] of Montgomery District:

> During the August 47 disturbances all my kith and kin comprising eight members were murdered and I was the only survivor of that family. Our house was just near to that of Naib Tehsildar Awal Khan. He took me to his house and employed me for kitchen work, grinding of corn and pulling for hours of the old type of cloth ceiling fan. I was kept as a servant and was not allowed to play with his children of my age. I was beaten by wife of Barkat Ali daily for no fault of mine other than being a Hindu. I underwent these circumstances for a period of about ten months after which fortunately police raided his (Awal Khan's) house and I was taken into custody. All this happened in such a surprising manner that there was no other way left for Tehsildar than to hand me over to the police. All our household belongings were also taken away by the same Naib Tehsildar who was present on the scene. He was still in his possession our 2? seers of silver and gold ornaments of several tolas which may please be taken from him and given to me.[25]

The statement claims to be a faithful narrative of Priya Kaur's experiences, but the language, content, and structure are clearly a product of state functionaries. Her speech act, given in the context of the refugee camp, was mediated through, and appropriated by, the state.

II. Speaking Like a State

The first-person testimonial narratives of the EPLA archive were products of specific historical encounters between vulnerable, displaced individuals and officials of a state claiming sovereignty over them. These encounters largely determined both the form and content of the statements. Subalterns, to borrow Shahid Amin's twist on Marx, "make their own memories, but they do not make them just as they please."[26] These statements were testimonial speech acts mediated through the bureaucratic machinery of refugee relief and rehabilitation. It was in this way that the speech of refugees was appropriated by the state and incorporated into a state-authorized master narrative. The most obvious sign of this appropriation was language itself: the vast majority of statements were translated from Hindi, Urdu, or Panjabi into a stale bureaucratic English prose. As first-person narratives, the statements claim to represent individual experience, but the imprint of the state is inescapable.

As part of a state-sponsored effort in truth making, the statements generally adhere to strict documentary criteria. In this sense, they resemble more familiar staples of colonial bureaucracy, such as First Information Reports (FIRs), that became integral features of postcolonial writing practices. Documentary characteristics include the explicit marking of chronological time and the identification of places, people, and possessions. Consider, for example, the statement attributed to twenty-year-old Kaushlya Bai that describes a January 1948 attack in Gujrat district on a train carrying refugees from Bannu in the North-West Frontier Province:

> At 8 A.M. on 12.1.48, the tribesmen with Gujratis, National Guards and Pakistan Military & Police fell on the train. Breaking open the windows and doors they snatched away from us all cash and jewellery. A cash a/t of Rs. 2000/- and a ring of 9 mashas were snatched away from my husband. My ear ornaments were so severely robbed from me

that I got my left ear cut down. The neck ornament (Shingar patti) was also robbed of me. They abducted me and took me to a garden nearby and covered me with a quilt there. The Gujrati Muslims took me to their house. They snatched from me 6 finger rings and two bangles—all worth Rs. 1000/. I was raped by 9 men during the night. I stayed with them for four or five days. I was raped throughout by them. Then I was sent to the Gujrat camp where I passed 7 days with another female of Bannu side. I came to Gujranwala after that and staying there for one night was escorted to the D.A.V. college camp, Lahore by the military.[27]

Remaining faithful to standard documentary criteria, the statement enumerates her experience of violence and situates her sexual assault within a chronological narrative that makes specific note of the value of cash and jewelry lost. In this way, the statement performs a sort of accounting. As a way of establishing the facticity of the event, officials took statements from six other passengers on the same train. The statement of Amir Chand describes the same sequence:

At 11 A.M. the attackers ran towards the train and breaking open the window panes entered into the compartment. They robbed us of all our cash, ornaments and household effects. The precious clothes worn by females were stripped of them. The young females and children were abducted by them. I lost my wife in the attack. Covering myself beneath two corpses I saved my life. In the loot and murder, the Gujratis, National Guards armed with axes cut the dying persons into pieces. At 3 P.M. cease fire order was observed by them and we were taken to the camp near the railway station. I saw many dying out of thirst. I was sent with a batch of 200 injured to the Gujranwala camp, where I stayed for two days. On the 14th January, I was removed to the Sir Ganga Ram Hospital, Lahore with 6 truckloads of the wounded. Coming to the D.A.V. college camp on the 19th I was sent here with others for getting my statement recorded. Out of 3300 passengers, we reached about 1400 here including injured.[28]

What must have been an experience of horror—the violent death of his wife, the mutilation of the dead, the deprivation of hunger and thirst—becomes in this statement a form of state knowledge and a series of administrative facts. The information contained in these statements was collated into an official report that jettisoned the first-person perspective.[29] Some statements were taken entirely to confirm the validity of other statements: "I was also belong to the group of Ambalika Rani and the Statement of Ambalika Rani has been recorded within my hearing and I have only to endorse this statement almost in its entirety."[30] As information, these testimonial statements were integral to the functioning of a state suffering an epistemological crisis. Moreover, Indian officials frequently forwarded statements to their Pakistani counterparts as evidence to support their requests that they take certain actions.[31] These statements were even used as evidence to settle insurance claims.[32] It is in this instrumental functionality that they "bear witness" in the legalistic sense of the term.

The statements generally adhere to a standard temporal and narrative structure. They all share the same *telos*: a final arrival in an Indian refugee camp or in India itself. They are attentive to time and place, charting the individual's movement leading up to the moment of giving his or her statement in the camp. The narratives begin with the onset of the event: disturbances force individuals to flee their homes, they undergo a series of trials and tribulations, and they move to various places until they ultimately end up under the paternal protection of Indian officials. The Indian state is cast in the role of guarantor of life, Pakistan as a space of insecurity, Muslims as a threat, and India as a space of sanctuary. This structuring of the story of people displaced from their ancestral homelands seeks to naturalize India as their new homeland and frames the project of sovereignty as one of peace rather than betrayal. In the statements, the experience of the event is defined by a vulnerability to violence and a lack of rights. Consequently, the entrance into the nation as a sovereign territorial community was portrayed as characterized by peace, bodily security, and, ostensibly, individual rights vis-à-vis the state. Arrival at the refugee camp as the end point of these narratives also serves to signal a resumption of normative time, a closing of the event as a time of exception. The biopolitical project of refugee relief and rehabilitation, the management of displaced populations by the Indian state, was, in this respect, a process of converting the exceptional into the normal, the event into the everyday.

This narrative structure is linked to another feature of these statements: the speakers are always cast in the role of the victim. They are, without exception, the victims of violence rather than its perpetrators. This was of course true of most individual experiences of Partition, especially for non-Muslims in West Punjab or Muslims in East Punjab. Nevertheless, the Indian state made little effort to catalog the experiences of perpetrators of violence in the civil war. This was a foundational feature of Partition narratives, and it remains true of nearly all oral histories collected in the last few decades. The EPLA narratives reinforced the role of the Indian state as a sovereign protector of life against violent outsiders, namely Muslims and Pakistanis. The narrators' status as victims—that is, as essentially innocent—became the basis upon which individuals would make rights-based claims upon the state. Nationalist leaders and state officials courted this role of rectifying wrongs and ameliorating suffering as the rightful duty of the state.

This was the underlying premise for unprecedented state action and intervention during this period. It was true for state efforts to resettle and provide material welfare to displaced peoples, and for the project of "recovering" abducted women. The statements of "recovered" women portray them not simply as victims but as virtuous victims who never wavered in their resistance. This framing was linked to state-backed efforts to reintegrate abducted women into Indian society, itself part of the wider project of fostering a return to normative social life after an event marked by social chaos. This points to the ways in which the Partition experience was intrinsically gendered and the ways the nascent nation-state sought to reinstitute patriarchal power as a means of suturing the event and consolidating state sovereignty. Take, for example, the statement of fifteen-year-old Yashoda Bai of Multan district. On September 23, 1947, her family was forced to leave their village of Kacha Khu,[33] under threat of Muslim villagers led by a local schoolteacher:

> On the night of the 23rd Barkat Ali undertook to take us to Mian Channu. My father loaded the luggage in carts and we all went with him. In the way after walking for about 9 miles we were attacked by a

Muslim mob at the instance of Barkat Ali. Our property was looted and Barkat Ali caught hold of me. I resisted but my cries were of no avail. I jumped into the canal. I was very severely beaten and somehow or other Barkat Ali took me to the house in Chak No. 23 in a senseless condition. I was kept in that house for a month and 6 days. Every day Barkat Ali beat me mercilessly and threatened to kill me if I did not agree to marry him. I, however, persistently refused. I was once beaten with the blunt edge of dagger and with stones on my head and with shoes on other parts of the body. I was also beaten with sticks. There was not a day on which I was not beaten mercilessly and threatened with death. I was made to recite Quran and Namas. I was then taken to Chak No. 21/10-R in the house of Awal Khan the cousin of Barkat Ali. I was kept there for a month and 10 days. There also I was similarly beaten every day. On the 17th of October, a Maulvi was brought in the house and Nikah ceremony was forcibly performed. About 25 days later I was taken during night time to Chak No. 26/10-R in the house of Khan. From there I was taken to Tapisar district Mianwali in which place Awal Khan belonged. I was continued to be beaten as I refused to live with him as a wife but I was constantly raped during this period. I was then taken to Bahawalpur State Chak No. 94 Railway Station Bakshishan, Khan Chistian Nandi district.[34]

The main narrative theme is not simply Yashoda Bai's victimization but her steadfast resistance in the face of relentless violence. Such speech about sexual violence was taboo but also an invitation to the state to undo harm and social risk. Following the arrest of his father, Barkat Ali released her to the evacuee camp at Multan in the last few days of June 1948, over nine months from the date of her abduction.[35] It was speech, rather than silence, that aimed to facilitate the "descent into the ordinary."[36] The narrative of the virtuous victim, moreover, lent legitimacy and urgency to controversial state efforts of "recovery." It was on this basis as virtuous victims that nationalist leaders exhorted the public to offer "recovered" women social acceptance within their families and communities.[37]

Government officials became involved in arranging marriages of "recovered" women as a means of integrating them back into normative social life. The East Punjab government partnered with the Arya Samaj to arrange marriages for women rejected by their husbands or natal families.³⁸ Tara Devi, the maharani of Jammu and Kashmir, offered to arrange marriages for the "Hindu girls of Rajouri" who were staying at the Gandhi Vanita Ashram in Jalandhar because their marriages should be "celebrated."³⁹ In certain cases, victims' speech was the means by which the state's role as *parens patriae* was authorized. One remarkable example was that of a young woman from Jhang District who was abducted, forcibly married, and converted to Islam before she was "recovered" in mid-1948. According to the official report, she "expressed fear that she would not be well treated in Hindu society and therefore not willing to come into the Hindu fold."⁴⁰ The stenographer who was taking her statement, "a bachelor belonging to a highly respectable family," offered to marry her. "The girl," according to the report, "consented to return to the Hindu fold."⁴¹ This "happy event" demonstrated the stenographer's "exemplary spirit and remarkable courage." The marriage was "solemnized at Amritsar on the 7th August 1948 in the presence of the Deputy Commissioner and the elite of the town."⁴² The Indian state portrayed its efforts to restore patriarchal power as a narrative of a courageous man and a virtuous and victimized woman.

State "recovery" and evacuation efforts were ideologically grounded in the idea that the state was acting with the consent of the people. Testimonial statements became a means of staging consent. Yashoda Bai's statement burnished her nationalist credentials: "I told him that I would fight for India if my father did so." She concludes, "I have suffered terribly on account of my religion and I do not wish to remain any longer in Pakistan."⁴³ Other statements, even those of orphaned children as young as six, conclude with "We are willing to go to India" or "I am willing to go to India," and are marked with signatures or thumbprints.⁴⁴ Others frame "recovery" efforts as both essential and consensual: "I was approached by Bhai Jang Vir D.L.O with the A.S.I. [illegible] and hearing my kinsmen including my husband are alive I gave consent to be evacuated and I have now seen my relatives in the D.A.V. College Camp in Lahore and I thank God to have joined the family."⁴⁵ Another woman "recovered" nearly a year after her abduction concludes: "I now know that my parents and my husband are alive, and have gone over to India. I, therefore, want to go to India."[46] In such statements, the new social contract, grounded in a victim-protector relationship, is articulated as consensual.

These obsessions with virtue and consent also worked to convert perpetrators into victims and victims into martyrs, as in the case of Thoa Khalsa.[47] Take, for example, the December 1947 report sent by the EPLA's district liaison officer in Montgomery:

(1) In village Hujra Hindus and Sikhs killed their own women-folk with their own hands while they were being attacked by a furious Muslim mob armed with deadly weapons. In all about 150 women and children *were done to death in order to save the honour of ladies and girls.* 10 to 15 men were also murdered by the Muslim mob. This incident took place on the 27th August.

(2) In village Basirpur Hindus and Sikhs killed their kith and kin especially the women-folk when they were challenged to embrace Islam or die. *They preferred death and sacrificed their lives for the sake of conviction, honour and freedom of religion.* Number of casualties was about 250. Incident took place on the 27th August 1947.[48]

This report was made for internal rather than public consumption. Discourses of sacrifice permeated the ideological scaffolding of state sovereignty during this period. Perpetrators of violence against women became virtuous victims deserving of state support. The report holds the actions of the Hindu and Sikh men to be entirely determined by external force: "a furious Muslim mob" and a challenge to "embrace Islam or die." The men were left with no choice but to take the most extreme action in order to preserve their "honour." As a consensual sacrifice, the deaths of the women were imbued with larger meaning: "conviction, honour and the freedom of religion," all things that would be safeguarded by the nascent nation-state. In this way, the sovereign nation was instated as a "pure" and masculine space.[49]

Discourses of wounding, struggle, and sacrifice became essential aspects of the grammar of sovereignty surrounding Partition. Prime Minister Nehru, for example, framed the violence as a moral injunction:

> We have passed through grievous trials. We have survived them, but at a terrible cost; and the legacy they have left in tortured minds and stunted souls will pursue us for a long time. Our trials are not over. Let us prepare ourselves for them in the spirit of free and disciplined men and women—stout of heart and purpose—who will not stray from the right path or forget our ideals and objectives. We have to start this work of healing and we have to build and create. The wounded body and spirit of India call upon all of us to dedicate ourselves to this great task.[50]

Nehru wrote and spoke eloquently about Partition violence as a senseless tragedy. He thought the only way it could be given meaning was as a sacrifice to the project of freedom and nation building. As such, it called for peace, collective effort, and discipline, at a foundational moment. Indeed, the resilient Punjabi refugees—virile, disciplined, industrious—would in the years after 1947 come to stand in as the ideal national subjects, who overcame tragedy and committed themselves to the patient work of building the new nation.[51] The experience of Partition and its recounting were, in this way, appropriated by the Indian nation-state.

III. Testimony and Truth

In recent years, efforts to interview Partition survivors have resulted in a growing archive of testimonial narratives. Scholarly explorations of the rich archive of poetry, literature, and cinema have also illuminated the human experience of Partition and its lasting trauma. In light of such endeavors, how should we read the first-person testimonial statements found in the EPLA archive? So far, I have emphasized their functional and documentary aspects rather than their subjective or representative character. Does the factuality of the statements obscure the subjects they portend to represent? How do the statements help us think about the question of authorship? Gyanendra Pandey argues for approaching such forms of primary discourse as testimony inasmuch as they "constitute a form of remembrance, struggling as they do to preserve a memory of the dead, of the houses and sites they inhabited, and of communities that are crumbling."[52] I consider below statements that, in my reading, have a subjective character that cannot be reduced to the bureaucratic instrumentality of the state or the overriding imperatives of the national project. As a way of excavating subjectivity—of understanding these statements as forms of individual testimony—I want to focus our attention on the ways in which certain statements diverge from the standard documentary form. Such narrative divergences reveal something, if only momentarily and in a fragmented manner, of the individual who is credited as the statement's sole author. These glimpses into the uniqueness of individual experiences constitute a form of truth that was not, and is not, entirely appropriated or elided by the state. These narrative divergences are more resistant to being incorporated into standard historical narratives in the way that Khosla used the FFO interviews as evidence of a historical truth that could be corroborated and verified. The concealment of the FFO archive and the refusal to officially memorialize Partition violence can, from this perspective, be understood as a tacit recognition that these stories and experiences never fully belonged to the nation-state, not least because of the betrayal the statements sought to hide.

Almost every statement contains information regarding the speaker: name, son-of, daughter-of, village, caste, occupation, and so on. Yet this remains the entirety of what we know of them, aside from the content of the statement itself. The statements capture moments of individuation, when the statistical refugee is given name and speech. Yet this speech is mediated through the state, and ultimately it resides in the archive in English prose. In what way does this process of mediation erase the authorship of the individual speakers or preserve evidence of their authorship? Let us take the example of twenty-year-old Pushpa Kumari, who was abducted after her train carrying refugees from Pind Dadan Khan was attacked at Kamoke in Gujranwala district on September 24, 1947. The statement begins with her departure on the train and then proceeds to establish the complicity of the local police in the ensuing attack. A narrative of the attack on the train at Kamoke railway station follows:

> At about 12 p.m. a concerted attack was made on the train by the police and military and the armed mob. The attack continued until 5 p.m. The attackers had with them knives, spears and other lethal weapons. Military and police fired at those refugees who got down from the train and

tried to escape. No man was saved. Women and children were snatched away and taken to the neighbouring villages round Kamoki. A muslim resident of Ghakhar caught hold of me and dragged me out of the train and threw me on the railway platform. At this I became unconscious and when I regained my consciousness I found myself in the house of this Muslim's relation. When I was dragged from the train my baby girl was with my mother. When I was thrown at the platform I saw my father was still alive. Only 2-3 male refugees were on the platform and the remaining had been finished.[53]

The narrative picks up when she awakes in the home of her abductor and engages in a tussle over a *dupatta*: "The women of the household in the house of the Muslim asked me to remove my bloodstained clothes which I did. They gave me instead old and worn out clothes which I put on. The women left me and went upstairs. They also tried to dissuade me from crying. After they had gone I dozed off and was awakened by a girl who came to snatch away the 'Dopatta' which had been given to me and was slightly better than the other clothes."[54] This evocative incident diverges from the standard documentary narrative mode. The statement gives a sense of the devastation felt by Pushpa Kumari who, having lost her child and other family members, was subjected to further senseless cruelty and indignity. This incident also serves as turning point in her narrative:

After the girl had taken away the Dopatta I heard noise outside the house. The Muslims entered the house and shouted the women to take me upstairs and from there to take me to the other side of the village from where the men would take me in a tonga to Gakhar. I told him that I would jump off the roof as I was under the impression that Hindu military was there trying to rescue me. The neighbors told the Muslim that all the houses would be searched and as the authorities knew that I was in that house they would be able to recover me. I then myself came down and found the Muslim Leaguers blocking the door. They told me that in case I accompanied them to the camp of the girls from the train I shall be able to meet my kith and kin. I accompanied them to a flour mill where I found other women from the same train had been locked up. I was put in that room along with them. This was in the town of Kamoki. They told us that they had in their possession other children who would be delivered to us next morning but they contradicted each other as others denied this fact. Members of Muslim League told us that we shall be killed. They also said that we shall be married to Muslims and made to live with them.[55]

The rest of this statement follows the standard documentary format in identifying relevant individuals (including other abducted women and children), adhering to a chronological narrative, and tracing her movement from place to place until her ultimate arrival at the deputy high commissioner's residence in Lahore nearly two months later. For all that she went through, Pushpa Kumari includes the tussle over the *dupatta* as essential to the narrative of experience. This inclusion depended on the editorial power of the government stenographer but nevertheless offers a glimpse of Pushpa Kumari in the role of author.

The narrative of thirty-four-year-old Shanta's harrowing experience is marked by a similar divergence from the standard documentary form.[56] Her statement shifts between the documentary and more personal expressions of horror. A sense of confusion and desperation are able to filter through the dry English prose. The narrative begins, as usual, with the opening of the event and the onset of her flight: "In June when papar Mandi was burnt at Lahore I went to my parents along with my girl aged 15 years at Bhimber Poonch State. My inlaws were at Gujranwala. After the partition my son by name Mohan Ram who was employed in Punjab National Bank, Delhi came to fetch us from Bhimber. He reached Bhimber in the evening and the following morning two [groups] of Pathans raided Bhimber."[57] The statement then describes the siege of Bhimber: "For 7 days engagement between Pathans and state troops continued on the 7th day the Pathans succeeded in getting into the town and started incendiarism. The Tehsildar and Sub Inspector of police ran away. Pathans came into Tehsils and finding no escape the wives of four prominent men of Bhimber took poison. Their girls also took poison. One boy of by name Tripurdaman of Gujrat, and Anand Raj of

Bhimber and others killed their own womenfolk."⁵⁸ Clearly disturbed by the violence against women, Shanta sets a grim tone as the statement shifts to her own story of survival:

> We slunk out of tehsil and hid ourselves in Sri Dwara, myself my elder sister and my daughter. Later in the night some others also took refuge there. They went early in the morning to a village near Bhimber. My son joined the people in defending the town. My son however did not meet me thereafter. In the morning at about 3 a.m. we tried to get out to our house but there again we heard the noise of bombardment and therefore again went back to the Shri Dwara Temple. The Pathans who combed out every bush to find out non-muslims came to the temple and found us there. The door was knocked but we kept quiet. They swore that they will not molest us and that we should open the door. We therefore opened the door thinking that even otherwise the door would be broken open. On opening the door the three pathans captured us. One of them said that he would marry me, the other said he would marry my daughter. My elder sister was quite old. They snatched away all our valuables from us. I entrusted them to take me to the house to see if my boy had been killed or not. He is my only son. They took us to the house. We went through the town and met a horrible sight. The streets were littered with mutilated dead bodies, with the dogs sniffing around. We were eventually brought to Bhimber School. I was convinced that my son must have been killed and I implored the officer of the pathans to look round for the dead body of my son. I saw all the dead bodies but could not see the dead body of my son. While we were confined in the school we saw that the pathans brought non-muslim in batches of twenty and thirty. They were all arranged in a line and shot dead.⁵⁹

There is a palpable sense of desperation as the statement depicts the search for her son, dogs sniffing around streets strewn with bodies, and systematic ethnic cleansing. Rather than evacuate the horror from her experience, the stark and matter-of-fact English prose evokes a horror all of its own. This passage abandons much of the standard documentary criteria; the worth of the "valuables," for example, is not specified as in other statements. Yet this divergence is only temporary, as the statement then returns to a chronological narrative and documentary mode, although a palpable sense of suffering, hunger, and deprivation percolates through:

> At about 1 P.M. we were put into a lorry along with five others. We were taken to village Jokalian, Tehsil Phalia, Distt. Gujrat. About six hundred women and children all belonging to Bhimber were found there.... We were told that we will be married there and distributed and old women will be killed. For a little more than two months we all were kept at Jokalian. During this period of incarceration about hundred twenty five women and children died of hunger, cold and fear. From Jokalian in December we managed to go send out two hundred boys to Jammu. Muslims used to come from Gujrat to give us rations. They took about eight good looking young girls. At Jokalian we were given two very small chapaties in the morning and in the evening. The children were given only one chapaty. In the end of December we were taken to Kunjah. The pathans had left us at Gujrat.... From Gujrat the local muslims took us to Jokalian and from Jokalian again the local muslims took us to Kunjah and handed over to the police. We were taken to Kunjah after two months and some days. At Kunjah we remained for 2 months. At Kunjah we were given two big chapaties a day only. No salt or pepper was given. At Kunjah two camps were set up. The Sub Inspector in charge of our camp was a good man and we were not molested. Molestation took place in the other camp where police officials were rotten to the core.... In our camp there were 469 women and children and in the other camp there were about 700. Only 700 in all have been brought out, 350 from each camp were taken and brought here.[60]

This statement was recorded at the camp for recovered women at the Sir Ganga Ram Hospital in Lahore. Kamlaben Patel, the social worker in charge of the camp, described in her memoirs the arrival of the "skeletons" from Kunjah, their condition wavering between life and death.[61] The individual suffering evoked by this statement represents a historical truth that exceeds its existence as a form of state knowledge or as a compact between sovereign and subject.

The statement of seventeen-year-old Ambalika Rani describes the fall of Mirpur. After the garrison of the state forces fell, much of the civilian population fled to the military camp outside the city. The "marauders" then entered the city and "indulged in indiscriminate looting and incendiarism."[62] The state forces eventually abandoned their post and attempted to flee with the civilians toward Jammu. Ambalika Rani's statement details the fate of the civilians fleeing Mirpur:

> The pathans butchered every man they came across and from the place where we were . . . wherever my glance could go, I saw the grounds littered with corpses. The men were butchered most mercilessly and barbarously. Some of them were *actually* cut into pieces. Even the men who had fallen due to bullet wounds, were hacked into pieces. My approximate estimate of the dead is about 6 to 7 thousand. Most of the women, who were killed, died of bullets. *Actually* the women were sorted out for being carried away. They actually made them into groups and carried them away. Infants in arms were forcibly snatched away from the mothers. Near about me I *actually* saw about half a dozen of such groups being driven away like dumb cattle by the pathans. My father died of a bullet wound before my very eyes. I was also hit on my left foot by a bullet. The husband of my father's sister was done to death with spears. He was *actually* cut into pieces.[63]

Ambalika Rani's incredulity, her repeated use of the word *actually*, works to establish the truth of her experience while also marking it as exceptional. The narrative style of the statement shifts back and forth between a standard documentary form and stark passages of traumatic violence. "We were first searched. All our ornaments and valuables were taken away. We were concentrated in a room which was filled with smoke from the lighted fire and the doors of the room were locked from outside. There was no ventilation in the room. The room was filled with smoke in order to choke us. After locking us they again went off for looting. We were confined for four days. We were only allowed to go out of the rooms twice and that too in night time for answering call of nature etc." The statement ends with a chronological narrative of her odyssey that ultimately concluded with her "rescue" by Indian troops.

> From village Bandral we were taken to village Chechian where we were confined for the night. On the following morning we were taken to Jhelum and then to Chakwal, Talagang and eventually to Musakhel. We were transported to Musakhel in a civilian lorry. At Musakhel our group was distributed to the various pathans, our captors, who took us to their own respective villages. I was taken to a village whose name I forget now as it is difficult to pronounce but probably it is Hathikhel. I was taken to Mianwali by Alam Khan pathan for treatment of my bullet wound. At Mianwali I was made to stay in the house of Mohd Akbar Khan Tehsildar and thereafter I was taken back to village Hathikhel by Alam Khan pathan, where I remained for two days and one night when I was rescued by Captain Nolan of 3rd Marathas troops, accompanied by my father's sister. I was being constantly intimidated and kept under duress. I was told that I would be duly converted after my wounds had healed and then I would be married to some muslim.[64]

The statement's conclusion rehearses common themes regarding the efficacy of state-led "recovery" efforts, the threat of conversion, and Ambalika Rani's status as a victim (and specifically a vulnerable woman) requiring state protection. Indian territory was framed as a sanctuary and the government as a source of security and protection. Her speech, in this respect, wasn't subversive, transgressive, or disruptive; rather, it contributed to a legitimizing master narrative for the nascent nation-state. Yet these unique narrative divergences serve as reminders that despite the bureaucratic mediation these statements underwent, they originated in speech acts of real people describing their real experiences. However, the narratives of these individual experiences were at no point considered belonging to the public: they were intimate secrets. Such speech acts and their truth were sequestered away in the archive, to be neither disavowed nor proclaimed. Many survivors, and women in particular, spoke candidly—breaking social taboos and making themselves potentially even more vulnerable—on the assumption of privacy.⁶⁵ This vulnerability and exposure were at the heart of the new regime of state sovereignty and citizenship revolving around refugee relief and rehabilitation. The refusal of the Indian state to memorialize Partition violence as a foundational event or to make available the archive of Khosla's FFO appears in this respect as an act of fidelity, a tacit acknowledgment of the foundational betrayal of the Partition.

CHAPTER FIVE

AN INDIAN YAN'AN
Telangana, 1946–52

> Between two worlds, one dead
> And the other powerless to be born.[1]
> > Andhra Saraswatha Parishath of Hyderabad
> > (paraphrasing Matthew Arnold) describing Telangana
> > to President Rajendra Prasad, August 30, 1951

> So far as the communists are concerned, we
> are more or less at war with them.[2]
> > Nehru to B. C. Roy, May 7, 1950

ON THE FOURTH OF JULY 1946, a revolution began in the village of Kadivendi. A confrontation arose between villagers and the armed men of the *deshmukh*. The leader of the villagers, Doddi Komariah, was shot dead on the spot. The Telangana revolution had its first martyr. Komariah's death, the communist leader P. Sundarayya observed, "set ablaze the pent-up fury of the Telangana peasantry."[3] The revolution did indeed begin with a blaze, when Komariah's comrades set fire to the house of the *deshmukh*, Rapaka Ramachandra Reddy. The four thousand people attending Komariah's funeral proclaimed what they called the *sangham*, a sovereign community that restructured society by redistributing power and resources. Its members were *sanghapollu*, or "those who belonged to a new community of close relationship."⁴ Volunteers carrying sticks embarked on *jaitra yatras* (victory marches) carrying the red flag from village to village, singing folk songs, and rousing the people to rebel against the landlords. Landlords, *patels*, and *patwaris* fled the villages. By September, the *sangham* had spread to three hundred villages in Nalgonda, Warangal, and Khammam districts. The *sangham* promised equality: an end to *vetti* (caste-based forced labor), *bhagela* (debt bondage), and traditional gender hierarchies. The redistribution of land under the direction of elected *gram panchayats*—a democratic transformation of tenants into owners—held out the promise of a complete overhaul of agrarian power relations. Debts were forgiven, wages raised, and revenue and levy payments stopped altogether. A new society was being founded: *praja rajyam* (people's rule), a radical form of direct democracy that challenged the state's monopoly on violence.

In early September 1946, the police in Nalgonda were confronted by two to three thousand people after the arrest of a *sangham* leader. The Nizam's government decided to strike back, sending waves of additional police and army forces, who, meeting with "considerable opposition from the villagers," conducted mass arrests, resorted to violence, and opened fire on several occasions, killing five and wounding ten more.⁵ The revenue and police minister of the Nizam's executive council, W. V. Grigson, accused the police of employing "terrorist methods." Grigson went to meet the prisoners, whom he found to be "nearly all *decent villagers*, including cultivators, agricultural laborers, depressed classes and even Roman Catholic and Baptist converts." He noted in particular the prevalence among the prisoners of Malas and Madigas, the Dalit castes of Telangana. There was, Grigson deduced, "a lot more behind the disturbances than mere communist propaganda."⁶

He was right. And what Grigson was witnessing was just the beginning. The *sangham* would continue the struggle for five more years, achieving many triumphs and enduring much hardship. At the height of the movement in the months prior to the September 1948 Police Action, the *sangham* had established *praja rajyam* in somewhere between two and four thousand villages across Telangana. The *sangham* claimed to have redistributed upwards of a million acres of land, investing a whole swath of rural Telangana in the struggle. For the leaders of the Andhra Mahasabha (AMS) and the Communist Party of India (CPI), this revolutionary eruption was not only an expression of the righteous indignation of the rural masses but a culmination of years of patient organizing and disciplined leadership. For the communist leader D. V. Rao, the *gram panchayats* were the "embryonic form of new democratic state" initiated by the "revolutionary masses."[7]

Indian communists have since hailed Telangana as their most "glorious" and "heroic" chapter.[8] And yet, not *all* of the revolution is remembered approvingly. Virtually every account, by scholars and the CPI leadership alike, focuses on the events before the Police Action.[9] This was when an agrarian revolution against landlords and *deshmukhs* became an armed liberation struggle against the Nizam's state. The *sangham* in Telangana was, in this respect, part of a wider coalition of democratic forces, including the Congress and the government of India, opposing the Nizam's bid for independence. Indian communists would later frame the Telangana revolution as both a battle against feudal autocracy and an essential part of the struggle for national liberation. Indeed, the *sangham* did the bulk of the fighting against the Nizam's forces and the Razakars, which provided fodder for Congress propaganda about the victimization of Hindus in Hyderabad. It was in the context of the 1947–48 anti-Nizam struggle that guerrilla *dalams* were formed, firearms were taken up, and mass enthusiasm for the struggle was openly expressed. Those inducted into guerrilla *dalams*, village cells, and other *sangham*-related groups took a sacrificial oath as newly enfranchised "citizens of the glorious Telangana."[10]

The Police Action, in this respect, changed everything. The *sangham* was now pitted against the Indian Union rather than the Nizam. The question of continuing the armed struggle deeply divided the CPI. The Andhra comrades, in putting forth the first articulation of Indian Maoism, cast Telangana as an Indian Yan'an. The socialist writer Mulk Raj Anand observed of Telangana that in the "battle of ideas" over the future of democracy in India, the liberals and Gandhians were being most forcefully challenged by the "example of North China, the new democracy of Mao Tse Tung's conception."[11] Although the CPI leadership would later largely disavow the post–Police Action phase of the revolution, Indian

Maoists have been of a different opinion: the party's abandonment of the Telangana struggle in 1951 is considered the original sin of the Indian communist movement. For those who stayed in the CPI after the 1964 party schism, such as Ravi Narayan Reddy, the decision to continue the armed struggle was theoretically, practically, and morally unjustified: "People's role in struggle diminished after the police action. People stopped participation in these struggles and as a consequence the movement lost its character of a people's upsurge and degenerated into individual terrorism by a few squad members. The naxalite movement today has a similar character. The struggle till the police action is of a glorious character."[12] For those who later joined the CPI(M), such as Sundarayya, the period after the Police Action was a "partial partisan struggle" necessary for "defending the gains of the movement by every means at our disposal."[13] Historians too have largely concluded their narratives of the revolution in Telangana with the Police Action in September 1948.[14] And yet, the revolution continued all the way up to the end of 1951, when the CPI unilaterally withdrew its support for the armed struggle. The post–Police Action phase was significant: it represented a radical challenge to the twin projects of state sovereignty and liberal democracy at the very moment of independence. It was also the foundational event of Indian Maoism. It was consequential to the trajectory of communism in postcolonial India and, as such, to the development of Indian democracy. It also shaped the development of the security architecture of the postcolonial state.

In the first half of the twentieth century, revolutionary and antistatist democratic traditions in India coexisted alongside institutionalist ones in a fraught yet productive relationship. When the British left India, the contradictions in this relationship erupted into an open confrontation. Modern Indian political life, forged in the interwar crucible of anticolonial struggle, was violently reforged into a postcolonial political order. Transforming the Raj into the Republic involved domesticating or containing revolutionary and antistatist political traditions within an institutional order. Revolutionary Telangana was in this respect a culmination of a longer historical trajectory as much as it was the origin of another. At a founding moment of the Republic, a battle was fought over the very nature of Indian democracy.

I. The Making of Revolutionary Telangana

Telangana has an unusually high concentration of socially disadvantaged groups. Dalits, Adivasis, and Other Backward Classes make up nearly 90 percent of the population.[15] Agriculture in Telangana was difficult and not very productive: the region had rocky, sandy soils, poor irrigation, and unreliable rains. The Nizam's state squeezed taxes out of Telangana's 10,300 villages, invested very little back into them, and gave free rein to local landlords and officials to build their own fiefdoms.[16] From the late nineteenth century, most service, nonagricultural, and landowning cultivating castes had become landless agricultural or domestic laborers and tenants at will.[17] Some of these laborers were paid wages, while others were forced to work as *vettolu* and *bhagelas*. Between 1901 and 1941, the ranks of landless laborers increased by 473 percent in Nalgonda and by 234 percent in Warangal.[18] Indebtedness spread like an epidemic, and debt became an effective tool of social domination. Many peasants were deprived of their land, labor, and dignity. According to Inukonda Thirumali, by the 1940s these people were seen as one class, *chillarollu* (trivial people), despite the caste differences among them. Their social standing was determined by the fact that they lived by *rekkalammukoni brathikevallu* (selling their hands).[19] As a result, the *chillarollu* developed a cross-caste class consciousness that made them receptive to the principles of the communist-led AMS. The unifying factor was a loss of dignity and social respect connected to the erosion of land ownership and other rights.

In rural Telangana there were, according to Thirumali, three main socioeconomic classes. In addition to *chillarollu*, there were *kapus* (respectable agriculturalist castes who both owned and cultivated land), and *doras* (lords, generally referring to landlords, but also village officials and moneylenders). The term *kapu* is used here to refer to all non-Brahmin landed castes within the system of intercaste relations of Telangana's agrarian society, rather than specific castes as in coastal Andhra. *Kapu* means "protector" in a broad sense and refers to those who look after or protect the soil.[20] The leadership of the AMS and the CPI in Telangana was largely made up of *kapus* from the Reddy castes, although some, like D. V. Rao, were Brahmins. In the Andhra districts of Madras, landholding Kamma peasants came to lead the communist movement with the support of landless agricultural laborers from Dalit and other lower castes as part of their competition with Reddy and Brahman castes, who controlled the Andhra Congress Party.[21] The *sangham*, in certain important ways, had a caste-based division of labor: *kapus* generally occupied leadership positions both within the party and within the new *gram panchayats*, while *chillarollu*, and later Adivasis, filled the ranks of the fighting cadres and other *sangham* volunteers.

The *sangham* aimed to revolutionize the social, economic, and political structures of rural Telangana. The *sangham* promised equality, of sorts, among the castes, and, according to Chinnaiah Jangam, communist ideology inspired dreams of liberation among the oppressed castes throughout Telugu country.[22] The abolition of *vetti* and *bhagela*, and the transformation of landless laborers into landowners, sought to restore the dignity and livelihood that had been lost by multiple social groups, *kapus* and *chillarollu* alike, in preceding decades. An end to caste discrimination and caste-based labor, a cancellation of debts, and the restoration of land were the key planks of the *sangham* program. The attempt to harmonize the disparate interests of the *chillarollu* and the *kapus* profoundly shaped the way the revolution developed. In order to attract *kapu* support, for example, the CPI fixed a relatively high ceiling for land ownership. Initially, only those owning more than five hundred acres, then two hundred, and finally one hundred had their lands redistributed.

There were ideological, economic, and political factors behind *kapu* support for the *sangham*. The basic factor of the *kapu-chillarollu* alliance was their shared antagonism toward the *doras*. The removal of *dora* power would open up new possibilities to common benefit. While their parents and grandparents had largely been reliably conservative, a younger *kapu* generation, many of whom were educated, became influenced by socialism and nationalism. They had seen their land rights further eroded over the 1930s and into the 1940s. This generation developed a critique of the feudal nature of rural Telangana and, indeed, Hyderabad as a whole. Ravi Narayan Reddy, who turned to communism after the 1938 anti-Hyderabad *satyagraha* and who led the communist capture of the AMS in 1941, was representative of this ideological shift among *kapu* youth. The Great Depression and the Second

World War, especially the forcible collection of land revenue and the grain levy, further eroded the economic prospects of younger *kapus*, leading them to throw their lot in with the *sangham*. They were also animated by nationalist sentiments. The popularity of the *sangham* grew rapidly after the 1938–39 anti-Hyderabad *satyagraha* and then exponentially as a result of the Nizam's bid for independence and the rallying call of *Visalandhra*, a unification of the Telugu-speaking peoples of Hyderabad and Madras.[23]

Women were another important constituency of the *sangham* coalition and were, arguably, the crucial element of the *sangham*'s success.[24] Women provided the majority of everyday support for the *sangham*, from reporting on police movements, to acting as messengers, to feeding fighters and other volunteers. Some, such as Mallu Swarajyam, became *dalam* commanders and leaders within the party.[25] This important role played by women still holds for the Maoists today. The *sangham* promised emancipation from traditional gender roles and hierarchies. Sexual violence was a ubiquitous aspect of *dora rajyam*.[26] In practice, these emancipatory promises went largely unfulfilled, as party leaders saw the mobilization of women largely in terms of how it could benefit the party and the movement.[27] But because it promised to better their lives and those of their menfolk, women nevertheless became active and invested in the *sangham*. However, the *sangham*'s social base and multiclass alliance began to unravel after the Police Action, when *kapu* support for the armed struggle waned over the long years of revolution and counterrevolution. Ravi Narayan Reddy, for example, emerged from underground to publicly denounce the armed struggle in 1950. Yet the *sangham* retained mass support after the Police Action among the *chillarollu*. Nevertheless, the multicaste and multiclass coalition that powered the revolutionary surge from 1946 eroded gradually over time. Even though the CPI hierarchy, including the top ideologues and organizers, was entirely dominated by Telangana Reddys, Andhra Kammas, and Brahmins, it was the *chillarollu*, by and large, who carried on the fight after September 1948.

The *sangham* sought to overturn the hierarchical and feudal political economy of Telangana. The term *feudal* is understood here in its broadest sense. Indeed, the social and economic transformations brought about in rural Telangana from the late nineteenth century onwards had much to do with the commercialization of agriculture and colonial India's unequal integration in the world economy.[28] They were also due to the modernizing efforts of Hyderabad State administrators and the colonial political economy more broadly. In Telangana, reforms enacted by Salar Jung in the late nineteenth century allowed for *deshmukhs*, formerly local chiefs and revenue collectors, to lay claim to vast swathes of land as *pattadars*, or landowners. This gave birth to a new class of hereditary landlords, who set about consolidating their holdings into large estates. The *deshmukh* of Visnur, Rapaka Ramachandra Reddy, who was confronted by Doddi Komariah and his comrades in 1946, was believed to have owned between 40,000 and 150,000 acres of land.[29] These dominant landlords were able to bring entire villages under a new social and economic regime, which was referred to as *dora rajyam*.[30] *Doras* arrogated the land rights of a substantial portion of the peasantry. Customary, more reciprocal and fluid caste-based social relations were converted into a system of forced labor. Government officials in the villages, the *patels* and *patwaris*, largely functioned at the behest of *doras*. The *doras* exercised magisterial powers and also controlled credit in rural Telangana. Debt-bondage was an integral element of rural class and caste relations. *Doras* sought to legitimate their dominant position by sponsoring the construction and maintenance of temples and by performing religious ceremonies.[31] In this way the *doras* became the dominant class in rural Telangana and integral pillars of the Nizam's patrimonial state over the course of the first half of the twentieth century. And for this reason both large landlords and the *patwari* offices holding land records became the primary targets of *sangham* offensives from 1946. Land records were destroyed or altered everywhere the *sangham* spread.

In sum, the social basis of the revolution was grounded in long-standing conflicts over caste, land, and debt. These conflicts intensified over the 1930s and the war years. The AMS, under communist leadership from 1941, sought to address these concerns directly and from that time began to organize village-level groups that became known as the *sangham*. The communist takeover of the Mahasabha was connected to the outbreak of people's movements throughout the Indian states in the late 1930s, the fallout from the 1938 *satyagraha*, and Hyderabad's failed constitutional reforms discussed in chapters 1 and 2.

The AMS was originally founded in 1921 as the Andhra Jana Sangham. Early efforts were concerned with establishing libraries and promoting Telugu language, culture, and history.[32] From 1930, when it became the Mahasabha, it turned to social reform. Only in the late 1930s did the AMS become an explicitly political organization. In 1937, it called for a new constitution that provided for representative government and civil liberties under the aegis of the Nizam. The AMS was initially led by urban elites, although educated *kapus* from petty landlord families played an increasingly important role. Politically, the leadership was generally moderate and liberal, and wary of rocking the boat too much. Many of the prominent men of the AMS would go on to have successful local, regional, and national political careers after 1948, largely as members of the Congress.

In Telangana, a young generation of AMS leaders, including Ravi Narayan Reddy, Baddam Yella Reddy, D. V. Rao, and others, joined the communist movement in the late 1930s and early 1940s.[33] Their agenda was basically that of the "united front" strategy undertaken by communists throughout India and, indeed, elsewhere in the colonial world as per Comintern policy. The basic principle of the united front was for communists to join and support bourgeois nationalist organizations and, over time, to bring them under communist influence. Under the united front policy, the AMS was converted from a liberal cultural organization into a militant mass organization. The united front provided the ideological justification for the *kapu-chillarollu* alliance, that is, the unification of all classes of the peasantry in opposition to *dora rajyam*. When Ravi Narayan Reddy became president in 1941, the AMS adopted resolutions demanding the abolition of vetti, a halt to the eviction of tenants, the elimination of the tax on toddy tapping, and the end of the *jagirdari* system more broadly. They also demanded reduced land taxes, rents, and new legal protections for land claims.[34] Their agenda was not, in other words, concerned with the interests of labor alone, nor was it limited to cultural reform. It directly addressed the "land question" by offering a comprehensive agenda for the remaking of rural society that sought to harmonize disparate interests into a coherent vision of a just society.

The success of such a project required, of course, a certain amount of solidarity across caste and class lines. The AMS undertook efforts to spread deep into rural villages, where the *sangham* began to take root in the early 1940s. Their activities were connected to a wider flowering of Telugu literature and drama during this period, much of which was inspired by leftist politics.[35] The AMS spread their message through various folk art forms, most notably *burrakatha*, a performance art that incorporates narrative, music, dance, costume, and political satire.[36] The most popular among these, later made into a feature film, was *Maa Bhoomi* (Our Land), a story of the martyrdom of a poor peasant in his struggle against the *deshmukh*.[37] Village *gayaks* (singers) incorporated revolutionary themes and heroic deeds of local people into their songs. Maxim Gorky's *Mother*, first translated into Telugu in 1934, and other stories of the Russian Revolution, including a biography of Stalin, circulated widely.[38] In 1945, the communists established the Telangana Praja Natya Mandali (Cultural Front) to organize and train cultural squads, who were then dispatched to villages with scripts for the various folk art forms of rural Telangana.[39] The *sangham* also conducted night classes to teach villagers how to read and to educate them along revolutionary lines.[40] *Mahila sanghams* organized women volunteers. *Bala sanghams* were formed among young men and children, particularly shepherds, who became key cogs of the *sangham*'s intelligence and communications networks. Some of the earliest and most dedicated supporters of the *sangham* were the Lambada, a traditionally pastoral and itinerant community, whose mobility was perceived as particularly threatening by officials of the Nizam's government and, after the Police Action, by the government of India.[41]

The first agitations launched by the AMS in 1944 were directed against *vetti* and sought to directly confront caste-based inequality. The movement against *vetti* escalated into a wider fight against the entire socioeconomic basis of *dora rajyam*. From Komaraiah's martyrdom in mid-1946, the *sangham* further matured into an embryonic revolutionary state, and, after the Police Action, a classical guerrilla war. This trajectory was not part of some top-down master plan implemented by scheming communists. It was, rather, contingent on a number of factors, both deeply rooted in Telangana and bound up with all-India transformations. In 1946, for example,

Komaraiah and his comrades were engaged in a local struggle against their landlord, but they were also part of the revolutionary upsurge that swept across India after the war. All of the major leaders from the CPI and AMS report in their memoirs that mass actions in Telangana arose out of the grassroots. The masses were, initially, leading the leaders. The uprisings of 1946 were open public affairs, involving thousands of people. They had few weapons and little organization. To the credit of the disciplined work of party functionaries, by the time of the Police Action the *sangham* had a deep well of popular support, extensive village-level organization, a grassroots communications network, armed guerrilla *dalams*, and a coherent party structure. Revolutionary governments were set up in anywhere between two and four thousand villages across Telangana (primarily Nalgonda and Warangal). Sweeping changes were implemented, and a bulk of the population became invested in the ideal of a new society. This was a democratizing moment for Telangana: the *sangham*, as the State Congress leader Swami Tirtha put it, "made the peasant stand erect."[42]

The Nizam's bid for independence and the fight against state forces and the Razakars had a transformative impact on the *sangham*. The anti-Nizam struggle gave the *sangham* greater purpose and potential, and the crisis facing Hyderabad State provided an opportunity to expand its reach and organizational capacity. As the Nizam's rule collapsed under external and internal pressures, the *sangham* filled the void. According to one source, in June 1948 *sangham rajyam* had been established in 600 villages in Nalgonda, 400 villages in Atraf-i-Balda [Hyderabad district], 350 villages in Warangal, 300 villages in Karimnagar, 100 villages in Mahbubnagar, 80 villages in Medak, 50 villages in Adilabad, and 30 villages in Nizamabad, for a total of 1,910 villages.[43] The revolution was not, of course, entirely autochthonous to Telangana. The coastal Andhra districts had by the end of the 1930s become a bastion of the CPI, and the party's Andhra Provincial Committee provided much of the leadership and resources for the struggle in Telangana. *Sangham* leaders who hailed from Andhra included P. Sundarayya, Chandra Rajeswara Rao, and M. Basavapunnaiah. The latter two would later join with Telangana comrade D. V. Rao to push for a Maoist line within the national CPI. The party set up a hierarchical chain of command in Telangana. Below the Provincial Committee there were regional, area, *prantiya* (zonal), *kendra* (four or five villages), and, last, village committees. Yet despite this formal structure, in practice the *sangham* had what Sundarayya called "decentralized leadership at all places."[44] The *sangham* also received clandestine support, including arms, from a group in Hyderabad City that came together in 1940 as the Comrades Association and that included Makhdoom Mohuiddin and Raj Bahadur Gour. Student groups and labor unions based in the capital city and other urban areas of Hyderabad were also sympathetic to the *sangham*, although their capacity for actively aiding the struggle was limited.[45] After the Police Action, the military cordon around Telangana made it even more difficult.

At the very moment of independence, Telangana was of "decisive importance" for the development of communism in postcolonial India.[46] The CPI became deeply divided over whether to continue the armed struggle. This sapped the Telangana comrades of both resources and a reliable support structure that could link their struggle to those elsewhere in India. Yet Telangana also pushed the Andhra Provincial Committee and, for a time, the national party in a new direction, leading to the first articulation of Maoism in India and inaugurating Maoism's global trajectory. Pushing their Maoist line, the Andhra comrades would, in 1950, nearly two years after the Police Action, take over the national party. The liberal nation-state and Indian Maoism, in other words, were born out of the same historical moment. Telangana was cast in the historic and epochal role as India's Yan'an.[47]

II. An Indian Yan'an

On the eve of independence in August 1947, the CPI proclaimed that it would "join the day of national rejoicing" and would stand "shoulder to shoulder with the national movement for full independence."[48] This was the line of "loyal opposition" to the Congress that the party had been following under the leadership of P. C. Joshi since 1945. The postwar years were a period of the great "upsurge" in revolutionary activity in India, from the Indian National Army trials to the Royal Indian Navy insurrection and peasant and worker struggles across the breadth of India.

In each case, the desire for national liberation was an integral element. The CPI called off the Tebhaga movement in Bengal, arguing that the new Congress government "must be given an opportunity of fulfilling its promises through legal channels."⁴⁹ Joshi was seeking to rebuild the CPI's public standing after the communists supported the British war effort during the Quit India movement. The CPI was also concerned about the balance of power within the Congress itself: Nehru needed to be supported against the "reactionary bloc led by Sardar Vallabhbhai Patel."⁵⁰ The party praised Nehru as "the voice of the people" and hoped that he would strengthen progressives within the Congress and become "India's Premier No. 1 who set her on the road to Socialism and prosperity."⁵¹ In August 1947, Indian Union flags were raised alongside the red flag of the Communist Party in villages throughout Telangana.⁵²

Over the course of the preceding decades, an intimate and ambivalent relationship had developed between socialism and nationalism in India. The Indian National Congress was an ideological big tent. For some in the Congress, such as Jawaharlal Nehru, socialism was essential to visions of freedom and democracy. Although never a member, Nehru was crucial to the formation of the Congress Socialist Party as a caucus within the Congress and, more broadly, to the mainstreaming of socialist ideas and rhetoric throughout the 1930s. In 1936, the CSP began admitting communists. The communists were at this time following the "united front" line as per Comintern dictates.

This was the context in which the All India Kisan Sabha (Peasant Congress) was founded. Prior to 1947, the Congress had for decades followed a policy of what Ranajit Guha called "discipline and mobilize," in which the interests of the peasantry and working classes were subordinated to those of the national movement led by the nationalist bourgeoisie.⁵³ The thinking was that the Kisan Sabha would represent the interests of *all* classes of the peasantry, in order to further the interests of the rural sector as a whole and, as a result, the struggle for national liberation. Moreover, after 1935, the Congress, socialists, and communists alike were all committed to a program of popular sovereignty. They competed to see who could best claim to represent "the people." The mobilization of the peasantry was essential in this regard.⁵⁴ N. G. Ranga, a founding father of modern *kisan* politics, spoke of a "common front to be put up by both the landed and landless kisans" and the "common suffering of all classes of the rural public."⁵⁵ Socialists like Narendra Deva and Asoka Mehta agreed. This too was the approach of the Telangana comrades who took over the AMS. The "united front" line was the ideological basis of the *kapu-chillarollu* alliance that sought to harmonize the interests of all classes of the peasantry, including the small landlords.

Shortly after August 1947, Joshi's strategy of "loyal opposition" came under fire from within the CPI. It was seen as a compromise with imperialism and with bourgeois hegemony over the project of national liberation. B. T. Ranadive (BTR) replaced Joshi as general secretary in December. BTR set an insurrectionary course for the CPI, declaring that a socialist revolution was imminent. He argued that the urban proletariat organized under the CPI would serve as the revolutionary vanguard to depose the Nehru government. In his *Political Thesis*, BTR dismissed August 15 as "not real but fake independence."⁵⁶ At the Second Party Congress held in Calcutta in February 1948, the CPI officially committed itself to the revolutionary overthrow of the Congress government. The CPI was subsequently banned in many states throughout the Indian Union. In Andhra, the CPI was banned in January 1948, when Patel encouraged the Madras government to "take drastic action against them."⁵⁷ The Congress, now in control of the Raj's coercive institutions, began a concerted nationwide offensive against the CPI, with tens of thousands of communist leaders and activists ending up behind bars or forced underground.

The CPI under BTR launched armed struggles and strike actions across India. Between 1947 and 1949, there were 3,990 strikes.⁵⁸ These actions were supposed to culminate with a railway strike in March 1949 that aimed to paralyze the government and that set the stage for a general insurrection. Thousands of workers in Hyderabad City went on strike, chanting, "*Desh ki janata bhooki hai. Yeh azaadi jhooti hai.*" (The people are hungry. This freedom is a lie.)⁵⁹ Yet BTR's nationwide strike was a massive flop, and the general insurrection failed to develop. Strikes did, however, continue in Hyderabad throughout 1949 and 1950, climaxing in the January 1950 strike of over ten thousand workers led by the socialist Hyderabad State Mazdoor Sangh.[60] Yet in India as a whole, the government offensive left the party and its affiliates in tatters.[61] At the Second Party Congress, BTR declared that "Telengana today means Communists and Communists mean Telengana."[62] This slogan was carried across the country. Peasant partisans in Malabar, for example, raised the slogan of "Telangana way, our way."[63] Yet despite this elevation of Telangana, the Andhra comrades and BTR had fundamental disagreements regarding both the class composition of the revolution and the strategy used to bring about the revolution.[64] The Andhra Provincial Committee—Chandra Rajeswara Rao, D. V. Rao, M. Basavapunniah, Chandrasekhar Rao, and Hanumantha Rao—issued their Draft Note in April 1948. Sundarayya was the committee's lone dissenting voice.[65] Often referred to as the Andhra Thesis or Andhra Letter, the Draft Note consisted of eighteen pages, nearly five of which were filled with quotations of Mao.[66]

The Andhra comrades saw in Maoism a theoretical outline for what they believed to be responsible for their success in Telangana, and thus a blueprint for the Indian revolution. This included the alliance of all classes of peasantry, including the so-called rich peasant and even the cooperative petty landlord.[67] The slogan "Land to the tiller" had already been raised years earlier in Telangana, and the Andhra comrades turned to Mao to justify this: "All peasants with the exception of these rich farmers unable to shake off their tails of feudalism, are taken by the slogan of 'land to the tiller.'"[68] The peasantry, as in China, would be the driving force of the Indian revolution. The Andhra comrades disagreed with BTR's proposition of a general strike that would become a general insurrection and argued that India was more analogous to China than Russia: "Our revolution, in many respects, differs with the classical Russian Revolution; but to a great extent similar to that of Chinese Revolution. The perspective is likely not that of general strike and armed uprising, leading to the liberation of the rural side; but the dogged resistance and prolonged civil war in the form of agrarian revolution, culminating in the capture of political power by the Democratic Front in the process of a bitter struggle for the New Democracy."[69] The Andhra comrades saw Telangana as exemplary of India's revolutionary future and the spark that would light the prairie fire. They envisioned an agrarian revolt radiating from Telangana throughout the isolated and underdeveloped areas of the Indian countryside:

> The liberation struggle in the form of Telangana is almost a pointer in the possible direction of forming two governments, which in process, must lead to general uprising and capture of power by the people. There are many more territories such as Telangana with a similar social-political-economic and terrain conditions spread throughout the country. They can and must be utilised as guerrilla districts to begin with, which affords ample scope to develop them as liberation bases. For example, in Andhra alone areas like Rayalaseema, Telangana border areas like Munagala, Nuzvid, Chintalapudi and the agency belt, where agriculture is primitive and undeveloped, where landlordism is dominant, with poor peasant and wage labour forming overwhelming majority of population, where already there is sufficient stir in the direction of agrarian revolt, present before us huge reserves of revolutionary possibilities. Backward communication system, topographic and terrain conditions are exceptionally suited for prolonged guerrilla battles (Chinese way) which lead to establishment of liberation bases.[70]

The Andhra comrades' strategy was protracted people's war. The formation of "liberation bases" in the remote areas of the countryside would be the first step in a long "civil war" that would, eventually, lead to the capture of urban areas and the overthrow of the Congress government by an army of peasant revolutionaries. This state of civil war was not one of choice; it was forced upon the CPI by the government of India: "Armed resistance has been forced on the agenda of the revolution by this offensive of the bourgeoisie."[71] Nehru, referring to the communists at a rally in Madras in July 1948, declared that "if any group of people wants to declare war against the state, then the state is at war with them."[72] It was in this context that the Andhra comrades concluded: "The path is that of Chinese liberation struggle under the leadership of Comrade Mao Tse-Tung, the practical, political and theoretical leader of the mighty colonial and semi-colonial revolution."[73] Indian Maoism was thus born more than a year before Mao proclaimed the People's Republic in October 1949. Telangana was cast as

India's Yan'an.[74] In June 1950, nearly two years after the Police Action, the Andhra comrades took over the Politburo, and Chairman Mao became the lodestar of the Indian revolution.

III. Telangana after the Police Action

The Indian Army's victory over the Nizam was celebrated throughout Telangana. There was hope that the new government, as a democratic state, would recognize and affirm the revolutionary changes enacted throughout Telangana. Yet with the CPI in a declared state of insurrection against the government of India, the government offensive came swiftly on the heels of the Police Action. The *sangham*, however, was caught by surprise, not least because the struggle had from its inception been waged against the feudalism of the Nizam's state. Many activists returned home, and weapons were abandoned. The *sangham* up to that point had been an open mass movement. Army and police forces swept up sangham volunteers: ten thousand people were put behind bars.[75] D. V. Rao lamented that the *sangham* "lost a major part of our guerrilla army and leadership in the wake of the enemy offensive" in late 1948 and early 1949.[76] Most accounts of the revolution after the Police Action contend that the *sangham* collapsed under the weight of the Indian Army and with the loss of popular support. Yet the revolution actually spread to a greater geographical area and, as a result, affected more people. There is further evidence of considerable popular support for the *sangham* all the way up to 1951, not only in terms of clandestine everyday support, but also in terms of mass actions involving hundreds of people.

The Union government's offensive dramatically altered the spatial dimension of the revolution. The army and police made mass actions difficult on the plains, so *sangham* volunteers and guerrilla *dalams* were forced either to go underground or to gather in the forest and hill areas of Hyderabad State. The Andhra Provincial Committee ordered the reorganization of the *sangham* along Maoist principles of guerrilla warfare.[77] Communication between the CPI leadership and the *sangham* was, however, risky and unreliable.[78] As a result, the movement was propelled largely by autonomous, local initiatives. By March 1949, the police in Warangal were reporting that the forests and hills of the district were functioning as "Moscow centres."[79] The forest and hill areas that ran throughout Telangana were conduits for the spread of the *sangham* from its base in Nalgonda and Warangal to the other districts of Telangana. This has been true ever since; comrades hailing from Telangana have played a decisive role in the development of Indian Maoism over the last seventy years, especially in the establishment of base areas in the forests of central India. Indeed, in 1950 the Andhra Provincial Committee considered moving their base to Bastar. This prospect alarmed the director of the Intelligence Bureau, who presciently warned that it "will be difficult to dislodge them."[80]

It was at this juncture that Indian Maoism began its engagement with Adivasi politics. Northern Telangana was inhabited by an assortment of tribal groups, many of whom took up arms against the Nizam and continued the fight against the Indian state until late 1951.[81] Decades of declining autonomy and increasing indebtedness had fueled regular revolts by Adivasis in Telangana and the adjacent agency districts of the Madras presidency since the 1920s.[82] In 1940, Gonds of Adilabad district, under the leadership of Kumaram Bhimu, launched an armed struggle for a separate and independent Gond Raj.[83] Bhimu raised the slogan *Jal, jangal, jameen* (Water, forest, land), now widely used by Adivasi activists making claims to territory and self-determination.[84] When Bhimu and his supporters were killed by state forces, leaders from the AMS, including the communists B. Yella Reddy and Ravi Narayan Reddy, formed a fact-finding committee that voiced support for the Gonds' demands. Bhimu's demands for political recognition of Adivasi territorial claims were revived in 1949, as the *sangham* moved into the Adivasi areas of Telangana, especially Warangal, where the Koya claimed an autonomous "Koyasthan." The *sangham* also spread to the tribal areas of Karimnagar and Adilabad, the Nallamallai range bordering Madras, and the Chenchu homeland of the Amrabad Plateau in Mahbubnagar. By the time the CPI unilaterally withdrew the armed struggle in October 1951, Adivasis "formed the backbone of the Communist organisation" and provided the majority of recruits into the guerrilla *dalams*.[85]

Yet the *sangham* did not simply disappear on the plains, nor did it spread only among Adivasis. Despite the post–Police Action offensive, the government was unable to establish effective administration in most of the core *sangham* areas of Nalgonda and Warangal.[86] A special report on "Red Terror in Hyderabad" published in the *Times of India* noted that there "was no government worth the name in these two districts," and that "officials had abandoned their posts of duty and the Indian Union policing forces had not filled the vacuum."[87] Military Governor Chaudhuri noted that the *sangham* maintained the "full support of the peasantry": "The country is extremely difficult and the peasants who have been under Communist domination before the Police Action are not altogether co-operative in this matter. . . . Party funds were obtained through loot and plunder, but the victims were only the rich persons and in some cases, the party's opponents. In general, they did not oppress women."[88] In Warangal, an intelligence report noted, "Administration in the rural areas has been practically in the hands of villagers who have become Communists and no village patel or patwari dare visit the villages."[89] A group of Gandhian congressmen who made an extensive tour of Nalgonda, Karimnagar, Warangal, and Medak reported that "wherever we go we find that most of the village-folk are communists and their sympathisers." The *sangham*, they warned, was "strengthening day by day."[90]

In January 1950, at the founding moment of the Republic of India, the Ministry of States designated the districts of Nalgonda and Warangal as the "Telengana Special Area" under the direct jurisdiction of the government of India. India Civil Service officer V. Nanjappa began work as the special commissioner in the first week of February 1950.[91] The Special Area was a legal space of exception, where civil laws were suspended and all police and administrative powers were consolidated in the person of the special commissioner. Well over a year after the Police Action, the government of India created the Special Area in "appreciation of the danger and potentialities of the movement and the complications likely to spread over the whole country if this movement is not nipped in the bud."[92] From early 1949, the *sangham* spread to Mahbubnagar, Karimnagar, Atraf-e-Balda [Hyderabad] and Medak.[93] These districts were added to the Special

Area in August 1950. "The terrorists," Nanjappa lamented in February 1951, "are pushing forward from their bases in Nalgonda and Warangal districts to the north and trying to consolidate themselves in the dense forest areas."[94] *Sangham* organizers were also active in Nizamabad, Bidar, and, in particular, Adilabad.

The *sangham* spread to new areas in a methodical fashion. First, unarmed activists would go to a new village, recruit members for the formation of a village cell, determine nearby hideouts, and distribute propaganda literature. *Sangham* cultural squads would sing revolutionary songs, recite poetry, and perform *burrakatha*.[95] After unarmed activists and cultural squads gained the support of a suitable number of villagers, guerrilla *dalams* forced local *doras* to leave, burned land records and other documents, and abolished *vetti*.[96] Wages for agricultural labor were raised, and debts owed to landlords or moneylenders were forgiven.[97] While some *doras* were killed, most relocated to the nearest police station, town, or one of the 268 "civil centres" staffed by armed police units.[98] Their wives and children frequently remained in the village.

Land distribution by elected *gram panchayats* was not as methodically and extensively undertaken as before the Police Action. Instead, it often came in the form of the cessation of rent and levy payments, making tenants the de facto owners of the land they worked. A 1951 intelligence report noted that "the 'Malas' and 'Madigas' and other landless peasants tend to favour the hostiles innately since they are no longer under the clutches of the rich and tyrannical landlords who have all been scared away by the communists."[99] The *sangham*, rather than institute a new government in each village as they had done prior to the Police Action, simply destroyed the old power structures by banishing the *doras*: "The grazier is happy in having uncared-for lands of Deshmukhs to graze cattle, the toddy tappers can tap more toddy trees, there being none to check, the Harijan is happy that he has to do no 'begari.'"[100] It was in this sense that the post–Police Action revolution was anarchic. Yet the organizational machinery of the *sangham* still operated over significant parts of Telangana. Sovereignty in Telangana had temporal as well as spatial dimensions: "After the police action, our party men were known as 'Lords of the Night,'" wrote A. R.

Reddy in his memoirs, "whereas the Indian army was called 'Lords of the Day.'"[101] This temporal division continued in many areas of Telangana well into 1951. Landlords and village officials would spend their evenings "in the nearest armed outposts."[102] Even with an armed escort, it was "unsafe to stop in a village."[103]

Special Commissioner Nanjappa admired the *sangham*'s discipline and idealism: "They have got a very well set up organisations, and they work on certain definite principles." He rejected the notion that it was "pure and simple Goondaism." Nanjappa, who waged a bloody counterinsurgency against the *sangham*, was under no illusions about the extent of its popular support. He noted in May 1950:

> The Communist does not loot or rob or trouble the average villager, nor does he molest their women. They indulge in regular propaganda in the villages, collect their food from the villages, and subscriptions to their party funds. Many of them are highly educated, and are actuated by a high idealism—that they are suffering untold hardships to improve the lot of the poor villagers, though the latter does not appreciate this fully. They take drastic action against those who do not give them food, or subscribe to their funds. They don't hesitate to shoot the village official who does not help them, or one who gives information to Governmental authority against them. Land-holders, deshmukhs, money-lenders, etc. find no favour with the party, and all of them are ruthlessly liquidated. . . . The hold that the Communists have over the villagers—and one has to admit that it is strong in many cases—is almost entirely due to the terror the methods of the Communists have inspired in their hearts; there is also a certain amount of sympathy for them, if not for the ideals for which they are preaching, at least for the practical good they sometimes do to the average villager by way of distribution of land etc. During the Razakar Regime, these Communist Leaders, helped the villagers to defend themselves against Razakar Atrocities, and thus gained their affection also to a great extent. A large section of the rural population thus feel that the Communists are trying to help the poorer classes.[104]

Nanjappa further noted that the forced collection of grain levy by revenue officials accompanied by armed police units was "becoming increasing unpopular in the villages" because revenue officers "make all this collection from smaller cultivators whereas bigger producers with political influence manage to escape." He contrasted this with the methods of the *sangham*: "The communist dalams generally do not indulge in indiscriminate looting or molestation of women in villages. They take action only against big land-lords (deshmukhs) and other village officials who oppose them in their activities. When these *dalams* go to a new area, they try to win the affection of the people, and do not commit any atrocities but carry on subtle propaganda; and they pay for the supplies made to them unless the villagers offer it free."[105] More than two years after the Police Action, a December 1950 intelligence report noted that the *sangham* had "sympathizers and members in almost every village" and was still recruiting new members and collecting subscriptions from villagers. Government officers traveled only with an armed escort and even then did not stop in the villages for too long. Not only had "normal conditions" not been restored, but the *sangham* was extending its influence well beyond its bases in Warangal, Nalgonda, and Karimnagar: "There is no sign that there is any slackening in their efforts or that their field of activities is shrinking."[106]

Popular support for the *sangham* was also evident in the number of mass events after the Police Action. In January 1949, for example, five thousand landless agricultural laborers in the Bhongir Taluk of Nalgonda District staged a strike demanding higher wages.[107] As the *sangham* spread, it was common for peasants numbering in the hundreds to raid grain stocks and *patwari* offices. In May 1950, for example, three hundred villagers in Mahbubnagar District raided five villages and seized promissory notes, account books, and other documents from the landlords. A few weeks later in Karimnagar District, two hundred people attacked a police station and made off with rifles and ammunition. Officials reported an appetite for armed struggle well into 1950, with local youths continuing to join the guerrilla *dalams*.[108] Attacks on the police and military increased from 81 in 1949 to 328 the following year.[109] After initial setbacks following the Police Action, the *sangham* regrouped and reasserted itself to challenge the sovereignty of the Indian state.

IV. Making the State Salient: Telangana and Indian Counterinsurgency

"I will be quite frank with you," Prime Minister Nehru replied when asked whether communist victory in China would lead to the growth of communism in India. "I think the Communist Party in India is the stupidest party there is or has ever been anywhere."[110] Nehru was dismayed at what he considered an irresponsible and shortsighted course of action by the CPI. At the very moment of national liberation, after decades of hard struggle, and as the subcontinent reeled from the Partition, the CPI had embarked on a quest to overthrow the government of India by the force of arms. For Nehru, India's tryst with destiny demanded constructive collective effort. Discipline and cooperation were essential to building up the economic and institutional foundations of modern India. For Nehru, if an all-India democratic republic was to be built that would stand the test of time, that could deliver India to its future, politics needed to be institutionalized. Partition, war with Pakistan, economic crisis, and the conflict over Hyderabad created tremendous anxiety among India's new nationalist rulers. Nehru, as both a historian and a political practitioner, understood that his vision of an independent, sovereign, modern republic, of a free and democratic India, was by no means predestined. He was haunted by the prospect that India's hard-won freedom would be irresponsibly squandered and the potential of the historical moment lost. For Nehru and the Congress, democracy could succeed only by establishing a political life that was reproducible over time, routinized, and largely institutionalized. They urged workers to give up the strike, at least temporarily, as a tool of class struggle, and for *satyagraha* to be abandoned as a relic of the anticolonial freedom struggle.[111]

As such, the sovereignty of the state became from 1947 the immediate and overriding imperative. Independence, democracy, and development, all of these were contingent upon the sovereignty of the state. This was a considerable shift for Nehru, who in 1936 had founded the Indian Civil Liberties Union and had helped propagate a rhetoric of civil liberties that became central to the demands of the people's movements in the Indian states that erupted in the late 1930s. In *The Discovery of*

India, written during his wartime imprisonment, Nehru ruminated on the inherent "conflict" between "the idea of progress and that of security and stability."[112] However, amid the event of independence from 1947, Nehru argued that progress was contingent upon security. "There is often a conflict between the State's duty to maintain security, and the State's duty to maintain liberty. Both should be maintained, but in moments of crisis for a State security becomes the more basic thing, after which only can liberty come."[113] This relationship between security and liberty was inscribed into the Republic at a founding moment. Among the first major acts of Parliament after the enactment of the 1950 Constitution was the Preventive Detention Act. Introducing Article 22 of the Indian Constitution to the Constituent Assembly, B. R. Ambedkar, chairman of the Drafting Committee, was quite clear about the justness of preventive detention: "I do not think that the exigency of the liberty of the individual should be placed above the interests of the State."[114] The government of India consolidated and enlarged the Raj's coercive institutions. The Central Reserve Police Force was developed out of the Crown Representative's Police and the forces of various Indian states during the Police Action and the counterinsurgency that followed. The coercive power of the postcolonial nation-state and its capacity for violence exceeded that of its colonial predecessor.

For Nehru, Telangana represented "a degradation of the human spirit, murder, terrorism and violence."[115] He argued in the Constituent Assembly that it was not "the Government's conception of civil liberty to permit methods of coercion and terrorism to be practised against the general community. . . . It is the paramount duty of the Government to give security to the people."[116] State violence, now authorized by "the people," was necessary to demarcate the limits of appropriate political behavior. Nehru ordered the word *communist* dropped from all official communications regarding Telangana: "We must not make it appear that we are undertaking these special measures simply because these people are Communists."[117] Speaking about Telangana in March 1948, Nehru made it clear that there was space for communism and socialism within the confines of liberal democracy:

> It is open to any person to agitate against the Government for any theory or ideology which he or she chooses. It is also open to people to change that Government by democratic process. That is how it is done in a democracy.... If we do want a democratic form of government then there is no meaning in violence. Violence only comes if we discard the democratic form of government. You have to decide that and each of us has to decide that, because I stand for democracy in India, because I stand, if I may say so further, for *socialism allied with democracy* in India.

The discourse of security, and the ability to wield the institutions of the state against its opponents, shaped the conflicts between different ideological strands within the Indian national movement that burst into the open at independence. Nehru was dismayed at their turn to insurrection partly because he thought the communists had an important role to play as an integral part of the Left in India. Both Nehru and the CPI called for a democratic socialist state with an industrializing agenda. Yet the business community and the right wing of the Congress, led by Sardar Vallabhbhai Patel, moved quickly to push the socialists out of the Congress, to discipline striking labor, and to expand their power and influence over the state and economy.[118] CPI members and their comrades were thrown behind bars. Patel, as we have seen in the case of Hyderabad, was a key figure in the grafting of the Congress Party onto the institutions of the state. Yet despite their differences, both Nehru and Patel were committed to a project of state sovereignty and were equally convinced that the Congress Party was the necessary instrument in the development of an independent sovereign republic and the progress of the nation.

Of course, the establishment of the "Telengana Special Area" demarcating a space of sovereignty beyond the reach of the law was a key link between a colonial and postcolonial jurisprudence of emergency.[119] Police "encounters" became a routine part of the state's counterinsurgency program. In Hyderabad and Telangana, the coercive institutions inherited from the colonial state were repurposed for national security and national development. The initial state offensive against the *sangham* in the aftermath of the Police Action involved two brigades of the Indian Army and nearly ten thousand armed policemen brought from the Indian Union. A few battalions of the Hyderabad Army and two squadrons of cavalry were also made available.[120] The police and the military coordinated directly only from April 1949, when the local police, armed police units brought from the Indian Union, and the army were placed under the unified command of Military Governor Chaudhuri.[121]

One reason for the persistence of the *sangham* after the Police Action was that the initial state responses was heavy-handed, giving locals a sense of an occupation. At least 9,555 people were arrested in the first two years after the Police Action.[122] In 1950, the commander in chief of the Indian Army, K. M. Cariappa, observed that the "alleged communists" held at the Central Jail "looked a miserable specimen of humanity" who "appeared to be a lot of poor villagers who had just been made "scape-goats.""[123] In a two-part special report entitled "Red Atrocities in Hyderabad," the *Times of India* claimed that "somewhere in Telangana" was a place called "The Cage." The Cage was said to consist of two barbed wire enclosures extending over an area of ten acres. Upwards of four thousand men were detained there, with two to three hundred men arrested in Nalgonda and Warangal brought into the Cage on a daily basis for interrogation and detention.[124] Chaudhuri's successor and first civilian chief minister of Hyderabad, the Indian Civil Service officer M. K. Vellodi, later remarked that after the Police Action, "The majority of the population had resigned themselves to being alternatively beaten up by the Police, by the Army, or by the Communists."[125] Indeed, Vellodi would later push for the complete removal of the army in 1951, after yet another series of abusive incidents: "I doubt whether the army have to their credit any important achievement."[126]

In February 1950, military units were withdrawn from the countryside to *taluk* or district headquarters, where they were used as a "striking force" to aid the police units under command of the special commissioner.[127] Nanjappa's main strategy depended on the use of small, mobile police parties. "Small parties of police started combing the surrounding hills and hide-outs very systematically with the result that the hostiles were driven out of their shelters, and had to go out into the open, where they were arrested or shot in action. Couriers, sympathisers and informers were arrested and interrogated and information received from them was duly worked out, with the result that more and more hide-outs were found and raids organized. Relatives and friends of well-known Communists were also arrested and interrogated, and the properties of known Communists were confiscated."[128] Indian officials also adopted a strategy of reestablishing the power of the *doras*. While Nehru publicly declared that all peasants should retain redistributed lands, the opposite policy was actually policy implemented in Telangana. "The Deshmukhs, patwaris and patels should be given all the facilities to return to their villages. Lands unlawfully distributed by the Communists should be restored to their lawful owners so that they can return to the villages and help the administration by giving them information etc. whatever required of them at least in their won interest. This, of course, means that an atmosphere should be created for them by show of force and restoring Law and order so that they can breathe freely."[129] This policy of using state violence to restore the power of the *doras* only served to further alienate people from the state and to affirm support for the *sangham*.

Shortly after the Police Action, representatives of the Telangana rural elite and certain Hyderabad State Congressmen approached the Hyderabad government and the Ministry of States with requests for arms, arguing that the "guerilla menace can be only annihilated by armed parties belonging to the people of the area."[130] In January 1949 the Ministry of States took up their suggestion, acknowledging that the "help of local people is necessary to overcome the guerrilla tactics of Communists," and ordered that "civil guards should be organized" and "Wattandars and Zamindars should be armed."[131] The Ministry of Defense refused to aid these efforts on the grounds that it was dangerous to arm people not "subject to any strict disciplinary control."[132] The Hyderabad government and the Ministry of States nevertheless proceeded to organize units variously referred to as home guards, village defense squads, or *gram raksha dals*. These efforts were not regulated or legalized in any way; they proceeded instead on an informal ad hoc basis at minimal cost to the government.[133]

As with the anti-Hyderabad mobilizations of 1947–48, this dispersal of violence into the body politics sought to affirm the state's sovereignty. While organizing and arming of villagers and landlords in defense of the state was taken up in 1949, the strategy was given greater impetus only after the appointment of Special Commissioner Nanjappa in February 1950.[134] By April 1950 the Hyderabad government had distributed over 3,500 firearms to "Civic Guards" in the "Communist Areas" of Hyderabad, Karimnagar, Warangal, and Nalgonda districts. Recruitment picked up considerably in mid-1950, and by the end of the year the special commissioner was claiming to have units in over 1,800 villages, with upwards of twenty thousand villagers under arms by this time.[135] While thousands of firearms were distributed, many villagers were armed with spears, axes, and other rudimentary weapons. The responsibilities of the home guards included protecting their village from communist *dalams*, passing information to the police, and accompanying the police on raids and combing operations. Officials legitimated this dispersal of violence under the rubric of the "collective responsibility" of the villagers to defend the state.[136] The same logic applied to "collective fines" amounting to tens of thousands of rupees that were imposed on hundreds of villages across Telangana.[137]

Local units were organized under the auspices of *deshmukhs*, landlords, and other "influential men of the village" who were "persuaded to come forward to organise these Squads, which are being supplied with free arms and ammunition."[138] The home guard scheme placed severe demands on villagers and offered no compensation: "In some villages some young men are being trained as Home-Guards but no financial help is given to them. Most of the Home Guards are from poor class and they are passing their lives in great hardship. Home Guards are expected to work some hours in the day and whole nights. In some villages they are also following police in raids. Home-Guards depending upon cultivation cannot look to it properly. So their crops have yielded very little."[139] This exacerbated hunger at a time of grave food shortages in Telangana. Most services were rendered without payment, and home guard duty became made a new form of *vetti*. It was also risky to openly side with the *doras*.[140] By the middle of 1950, villagers enrolled in home guard and village defense units were regularly attacked by guerrilla *dalams*. An intelligence report noted that "there is no urge in most of the villagers to come forward voluntarily to join the above organisations."[141] Another put it more bluntly: "The poor classes, who form the bulk of the Home Guards, have little sympathy for the rich and cannot be expected to show the same determination to protect the properties of their rich neighbours as they would protect their own."[142] It was common for home guards to surrender their weapons to the *dalams* without a fight.[143] Nevertheless, these demands for villagers to kill and die for the state constituted foundational claims of sovereignty in Telangana.

In practice, the authority of the new state depended on local power brokers, who, in turn, manipulated access to state resources for their own ends. For example, a deshmukh in a village near Kallur in Warangal District was "having illicit connections with the wife of one Kumaraswamy of Kurlagudem, a nearby village." The deshmukh approached the sub-inspector at Kallur with "a request to remove the thorn in his way." The police, according to the official report, "took Kumaraswamy along with two other hostiles to Tallepenta Forest, made him run and while doing so shot him dead and announced that he was killed in an engagement with hostiles. The two other hostiles were also killed."[144] This practice of the "police encounter" has arguably been the signature form of state violence in postcolonial India.

After Telangana was designated a "Special Area" in 1950, the number of suspected communists killed became greater than the number captured. General Cariappa described the army's activities in Telangana as "communist-hunting."[145] In official reports of encounters, the number of individuals killed consistently outnumbered the quantity of firearms captured, often by a significant margin. In the month of April 1950, for example, forty-four communists were shot dead, four were arrested, and only six guns recovered in Warangal District.[146] A report from December 1950 showed that in Nalgonda there were eight encounters between the police and communists, resulting in the death of "21 terrorists and the recovery of some utensils, rice and an axe."[147] Indeed, the government of Hyderabad used the number of suspected communists killed and arrested as the primary metric of progress in Telangana. Official records routinely described encounter killings. Usually, a captured "hostile" was leading a police party in the forest for the purpose of locating a guerrilla camp or ammunition dump. In the process, the police party was ambushed by communist guerrillas, resulting in the death of the prisoner in their custody. Prisoners were also often shot while allegedly attempting to escape from police custody.[148] One prominent example was the death in police custody of the two men arrested with Hyderabadi CPI leader Raj Bahadur Gour in late April 1951.[149]

"I confess," Nehru admitted upon receiving reports of extrajudicial killings in Telengana, "it troubles me."[150] Noting that Nanjappa was "an efficient person, but also ruthless," Nehru was concerned that the government's violent methods in Telangana would become institutionalized elsewhere and that the state of exception would become the rule.[151] Gopalaswami Ayyangar, the minister for states following Patel's death in December 1950, responded that "ruthlessness is not entirely out of place in dealing with violent anti-social elements."[152] For Hyderabad Chief Minister Vellodi, such violence was a necessary form of political communication: "So far as the Communists are concerned, we are in a state of war, and nothing makes an impression on the Communist, whose terrorist activities are too well known to need any description, as fairly severe counter offensive. None of us desire violence, but in the world as it is constituted today, particularly in the Telengana area, I see no escape from it."[153] One intelligence officer, remarking on the recent killing of twenty-two individuals, "most of whom were active sympathisers and dhalam members," commented that "this has shattered the morale of the hostiles to a large extent and has also created a sense of seriousness in the minds of the villagers to come forward in informing the movements of the hostiles and catching them too at times."[154] The "encounter" is a curious if paradigmatic form of state violence. It is not a public act of awe-inspiring sovereign violence. It is, rather, clandestine and disavowed.

Raj Bahadur Gour, speaking in Parliament during a debate on the Preventive Detention Act, referred to the Telangana Special Area as the "law of the jungle": "Yes, we have broken the Constitution. We have challenged the Constitution. But was there the rule of the Constitution in Telengana after the police action?.... But your police just go to the villages, catch hold of peasants and simply shoot them dead on the pretext that the police had information that they had sheltered a patriot.... If we have broken that law, I say we have broken it because that was the law of the jungle; that was not the Constitution that was in operation in Telengana."[155] Developments within Hyderabad after the Police Action illuminate the ways in the Raj's legal and institutional apparatus was co-opted and converted in the making of the sovereign nation-state.

The legal inheritance of Hyderabad State and the continued role of the Nizam as a lawmaking figure also shaped the development of the security architecture of the early postcolonial state. In 1951 the Hyderabad government passed the Hyderabad Public Security Measures Bill, which replaced the Public Security Act and the Defence of Hyderabad Regulation, both passed as wartime measures in 1940. The new legislation normalized the state of emergency. It allowed for the imposition of collective fines, restricted press and speech freedoms, required individuals suspected of possessing certain information to divulge or acquire said information, gave government forces immunity against prosecution, and stated that "any police officer may arrest without warrant any person who is reasonably suspected of having committed an offence punishable under this Act."[156]

Shortly after the Police Action, the government of Hyderabad also created three "Special Tribunals," with one each in Bidar, Parbhani, and Nalgonda. The "Special Tribunal Ordinance" was drafted by civil servants and declared into law by way of a *firman* issued by the Nizam in October 1948.[157] The tribunals were initially set up to deal with the backlog caused by the trial of thousands of suspected Razakars and communists arrested by the police and military after the Police Action.[158] They were set up, the government of Hyderabad insisted, not to "debar the accused from privileges available under the ordinary law but solely to expedite decisions as the number of cases were very large." The "ordinary machinery of the Law Courts could not be expected to deal with them except in the usual *leisurely* manner."[159] Of the 15,642 alleged Razakars detained after the Police Action, 340 were convicted to various terms of imprisonment or death by the tribunals.[160] The vast majority of individuals tried and convicted by the Special Tribunals were suspected communists. Of the hundreds of suspected communists tried by the Special Tribunals, eighty-nine individuals were sentenced to death.[161] It is unclear how many executions were carried out, but it seems that at least a dozen were. Almost all of the convicted did not know English, were illiterate, had no defense counsel, could not cross-examine witnesses, did not call any defense witnesses, and did not submit any evidence on their own behalf.[162] Moreover, many of those sentenced to death were convicted of crimes committed before the Police Action, and, in many cases, their alleged victims were Razakars.[163]

With thousands languishing in prison awaiting their hearings, there was considerable public protest both in India and abroad over the death sentences passed by the Special Tribunals.[164] The Indian government received thousands of telegrams and letters from around the world denouncing this "judicial murder."[165] Paul Robeson, the American singer, actor, civil rights activist, and international communist, condemned the tribunals at a meeting in Prague in June 1949.[166] However, those tried by the tribunals did, from October 1949, have the right to appeal to the Hyderabad High Court, which overturned or ordered retrials for a number of the convictions.[167] Similar tribunals created elsewhere in India, such as West Bengal and Saurashtra, were declared unconstitutional after the adoption of a judiciable Bill of Rights in 1950. Hyderabad's tribunals were not considered unconstitutional, pointing to the way in which the fragmented juridical and jurisdictional landscape of the Raj continued to operate, not only leading up to the founding of the Republic, but *within* the Republic itself at this transitional moment. At India's frontiers, both internal and external, the juridical framework of the "Telangana Special Area"—the "law of the jungle"—became routinized and institutionalized after 1947.

At these frontiers we can also see the operation of the ideology of development within a new national regime of sovereignty in India. Security and development are, of course, the fundamental tenets of the "two-pronged" approach that has been the hallmark of counterinsurgency in India. After General Cariappa toured Warangal in September 1950, he concluded that "just shooting down 'leaders' and imprisoning hundreds of communists is **NOT** the answer."[168] That same year Special Commissioner Nanjappa outlined a series of "ameliorative measures in the villages whereby the villager would be made to feel that the Government were interested in him and his welfare, and that it would be better for him to work with the Government rather than against it."[169] The proposed "ameliorative measures" included the construction and repair of irrigation tanks, the opening up of roads and markets, the sinking of wells for drinking water, the provision of adequate medical aid, the opening of schools, the regular distribution of food and other essential commodities, and, most importantly, agrarian reforms.[170]

Yet the vast majority of the planned developmental schemes were not implemented by the time of the CPI's unilateral withdrawal of the armed struggle in October 1951. According to an intelligence report, "Welfare measures, which have been undertaken, are still in their initial stages and also lack in determination and aim."[171] The sinking of wells in Nalgonda and Warangal, for example, began only in July 1951, and by mid-August the government was reporting that the "progress of wells is not good." "Mobile Medical Units" began work in Nalgonda, Karimnagar, Warangal, and Medak the same month. At the end of September, it was reported that cholera was still "prevailing" in these districts.[172] Hundreds of miles of new roads were built, but primarily because they facilitated movement of police and army forces.[173] The chronic shortage of food, verging on crisis in Telangana and elsewhere in rural Hyderabad, was not remedied before October 1951.[174] The government continued, however, to confiscate the mandatory grain levy first implemented as a wartime measure by the Nizam's government. Armed police units accompanied revenue officials on their collection tours.[175] The most significant of the state's developmental interventions was aimed at the Adivasis of Telangana. Toward the end of 1949, the government of Hyderabad initiated the "Tribal Rehabilitation Scheme," also referred to as the "Tribal Reclamation Scheme." The basic premise was to remove Adivasis, primarily Koya and Lambada, from their villages in the hills and forests to roadside camps or "Rural Welfare Centres." This security strategy was authorized by an ideology of "tribal development" that sought to contain and control Adivasis within the Indian nation-state. These camps form the subject of the following chapter. Ultimately, however, it was politics, not development, that brought the Telangana revolution to its conclusion.

V. The Land Question and Liberal Democracy

Speaking in Parliament in 1951, Prime Minister Nehru referred to the "land question" as the "basic and primary problem," not only for India, but for the entirety of Asia.[176] As an overwhelmingly agrarian society, few questions were more crucial to the nature of Indian democracy than the land question. What would a free and democratic society look like for the Indian peasantry? What sort of rights to land would they have as citizens? And how should those rights be secured? These questions were not, of course, unique to India. They were central to debates over democracy around the world. In India, Telangana gave urgency to these questions at the very moment of independence. The *sangham* was exemplary of a potential revolutionary future, in which an old society would be destroyed and a new society created from below through mass collective action. The *sangham* did not collectivize property, it redistributed it for the common good. Its idea of socialism was one that democratized access to property ownership in pursuit of a more just society. The slogan of "Land to the tiller" was the fundamental demand of the revolutionary masses. The CPI has long claimed that the *sangham* redistributed upwards of one million acres. Government estimates were far more modest.[177]

In the wake of the Police Action, Nehru expressed support for the principles and ideals behind the *sangham*'s program of land redistribution. "The tiller of the soil should be made a free man," he said, and "Even if someone had usurped the land he should not be dispossessed."[178] He recognized the *sangham* on its own terms: an insistence that the land question was fundamental to the meaning of freedom itself. Indeed, this same ideal inspired the resettlement of Partition refugees in what was called the "biggest land resettlement operation in the world."[179] Nehru rejected, moreover, the right to private property as a fundamental right. He argued that one benefit of not dispossessing redistributed land in Telangana was that it would "help to create a good atmosphere."[180] "The poor cultivator" should be "particularly protected," he insisted, while the "landowner's right will be determined later."[181]

Nehru had long been of the opinion that some sort of land redistribution or common ownership of the means of production would be necessary for "socialism allied with democracy" in India.[182] Yet he insisted that the means of both democracy and socialism were more fundamental than the ends. For Nehru, Telangana represented a "degradation of the human spirit" not because of the goals and aspirations of the peasant revolutionaries but because of their violent methods. His greatest challenge, ultimately, was "to build a just society by just means."[183] As Sunil Khilnani has observed, for Nehru, particularly at this moment of crisis and transformation, this meant "to run a just state by just means."[184] Moreover, Nehru was convinced that revolutionary violence led to an expansion of the political domain that was more likely to lead to fascism than socialism: "It is absurd to imagine that out of conflict the social progressive forces are bound to win."[185] A liberal politics was needed to keep India's lurking illiberal forces at bay. This concern became all the more acute following the unprecedented violence of Partition and the assassination of the Mahatma.

For Nehru and the Congress, the land question had to be resolved through an institutional and deliberative democratic process: that is, through legislative efforts conducted by democratically elected representatives of the people. Yet the land question, in being submitted to electoral and legislative processes, became not a fundamental question about the meaning of democratic freedom but a competition between various interests. The conversion of anticolonial and revolutionary politics into an institutionalized politics of interest was a double-edged sword. It was, on the one hand, integral to the successful establishment of a liberal parliamentary democracy in India, one that was routinized and durable. On the other, it was a withdrawal from some common ideals and aspirations shared within India's fractious and heterogeneous movement for national liberation.

Nehru's comment that the "tiller of the soil should be made a free man" was not merely a rhetorical concession to the justness of the *sangham*'s program of land redistribution. It was, rather, a rearticulation of long-standing commitments by him, the Congress, and the Indian national movement more broadly. Antilandlord rhetoric had become part and parcel of the nationalist repertoire, and the Congress had promised policies to radically reshape rural society, land reform above all.[186] In 1946, the Congress election manifesto called for *zamindari* abolition. Shortly after independence, in November 1947, the All India Congress Committee resolved that land "must belong to and be regulated by the community" and recommended the elimination of all intermediary tenures, all forms of tenancy, and private moneylenders and traders. They suggested the formation of village cooperatives and a ceiling on personal ownership of land. In 1949, the *Report of the Congress Agrarian Reforms Committee*—what Francine Frankel called the "most threatening document ever drafted by an official committee of the Congress"—proposed even more radical reforms.[187] Nehru campaigned for the first general election on a platform of antilandlordism and communal harmony.

Such efforts, pushed by socialists and some Gandhians within the Congress, were met with fierce opposition by the Congress right wing, led by Vallabhbhai Patel. Immediately upon independence and all the way up to Patel's death in 1950, the Congress Right successfully put the brakes on radical economic reforms and, indeed, successfully pushed for policies to the benefit of industrial, commercial, and large agrarian interests and the former Indian princes.[188] Not only was government machinery deployed to discipline labor, but plans for land redistribution and the nationalization of industry were considerably compromised. The Industrial Policy Resolution of April 1948, for example, announced a public monopoly only over the manufacture of weapons, atomic energy, and the railways. Instead, the government pursued the "socialization of the vacuum" approach that sought to gradually build up industries that did not already exist and invest in areas of the economy free from public investment.[189]

Between 1947 and 1950, most major states of the Indian Union, including Hyderabad, passed major land reforms, highlighted by the abolition of *zamindari*. These reforms were intended to make good on the promises of the anticolonial struggle for national liberation. In practice, however, their successes were more modest, and their failures equally sobering. The political power of landlords was greater at the state level than at the national level, and they were able to dilute initially radical legislation and to subsequently influence the bureaucracy tasked with implementing the reforms. "The story of land reform in India," Hamza Alavi observed more than four decades ago, "is one of progressive attenuation of radical commitments."[190] Indeed, significant protections for propertied classes were incorporated into the legal and institutional framework of the new postcolonial political order.[191]

The Congress-led Constituent Assembly decided to list the right to property as a "fundamental right" in the 1950 Constitution.[192] There was, however, a consensus within the Constituent Assembly that the major land reform legislation should be treated differently, and clauses intending to secure the land reform measures passed between 1947 and 1950 were inserted into the Constitution.[193] Although the fundamental right to private property would be amended in 1951 and another nine times before it was ultimately abolished in 1978, it meant that many land reform measures became tangled up in the courts well into the 1950s. The Republic's judiciary played a key role in the dampening of more radical visions of land reform and the ability of Nehru's central government to implement sweeping top-down changes from the center. The Indian Constitution reserved the authority to implement land reforms to the state legislatures. The land question, an issue seen to be of paramount importance to the essence of Indian democracy, was delegated to the individual states, a hugely consequential fact of India's postcolonial federal system. Yet the land reforms implemented in the transformational period of the late 1940s differed in the Indian states and the former provinces of British India, where land reform legislation, while significant, was watered down in assemblies dominated by regional elites. The princely states, in contrast, were brought under the control of the Ministry of States, under the direction of Patel and Menon, and land reform measures were largely crafted by the government of India and implemented through royal decree, as in Hyderabad, rather than the legislative process.

Sundarayya and other communist leaders held up land reform and the dismantling of the feudal structures of Hyderabad's patrimonial state as accomplishments of the revolution in Telangana. The *sangham*, no doubt, made land reforms a necessity. It was in Telangana, after all, where Vinoba Bhave began the Bhoodan movement, which sought to grapple with the ethical significance of the land question. The leaders of India's counterinsurgency in Telangana recognized the land question as the fundamental issue. "In my considered view," Special Commissioner Nanjappa concluded, "it is necessary to destroy the economic and political power of the landed aristocracy in Telengana to create more contentment amongst the poorer sections."[194] When General Cariappa toured Telangana in 1950, he called for the "immediate implementation of the plans they have for agrarian reform." Otherwise, "I cannot see how we can possibly effectively deal with the communist problem in Telengana."[195] It was the land question that was at the heart of continued popular support for the *sangham* well into 1951. After the Police Action, the Hyderabad government, initially under military command, gradually took control over all the *jagirs*, *samasthans*, and other estates. In February 1949, the 1,961 villages of the Nizam's personal lands, known as the Sarf-e-Khas, were merged into the adjacent *diwani* areas. In September 1949, the 6,535 *jagirdari* villages followed suit upon the abolition of the *jagirdari* system.[196] On January 25, 1950, the day before the Republic of India was founded, the Hyderabad government paid *jagirdars* compensation amounting to Rs. 18 *crore*, a fact widely publicized by the CPI.[197]

The Hyderabad Tenancy and Agricultural Land Act came into effect in June 1950. Among other things, the act gave tenants significantly greater rights vis-à-vis landlords. There were, however, considerable problems with the implementation of the new legislation in Telangana and elsewhere in the state. The Revenue Department noted that "large scale eviction of tenants was apprehended immediately in the wake of the promulgation of the Act to deprive them of the benefits of the act."[198] A year later, Nanjappa noted that implementation of the act was "proceeding slowly" and that "a larger number of villagers still are landless whereas most of the land continues to be held by Deshmukhs." He called for reducing the size of the maximum holding and distributing the surplus land to the landless.[199] The government counted more than 60 percent of the total population of Nalgonda District, the historical center of the *sangham*, as landless agricultural laborers. In Telangana, the reforms secured the claims, by and large, of *kapu* landholders, while more modest gains were made by the *chillarollu*. This was typical of the impact of *zamindari* abolition and land reform around India. By 1960, after legislative reforms and a decade of planning, land inequality nationwide had improved only marginally.[200] The answer to the land question was both a victory in the development of India's liberal democracy and a demonstration of its limitations to effect the emancipatory promises of the Indian constitution.

VI. From Insurrection to Election

For the CPI, the big question was whether to participate in India's first universal franchise general election. Should an underground revolutionary party become a parliamentary one? After the Andhra comrades gained control of the Politburo and Central Committee in June 1950, the national CPI remained deeply fractured and dysfunctional. The CPI was illegal in many areas of the country, and most prominent communist leaders were either in prison or underground. With the party organization in tatters and elections looming, many communist leaders began questioning the wisdom of the CPI's revolutionary program and its support for the *sangham*. Telangana became the focal point of a contentious debate over the future of communism at a founding moment of the Republic.

The Andhra comrades came under attack from various directions. A rival party center was set up in Bombay. S. A. Dange, A. K. Ghosh, and S. V. Ghate in Bombay and Muzaffar Ahmed and Ranen Sen in Bengal criticized the Andhra leadership and called for the suspension of the armed struggle. Ravi Narayan Reddy, formerly head of the AMS and a hero of the pre–Police Action *sangham*, came out of hiding in late 1950 and called for an immediate withdrawal. R. P. Dutt, the Communist Party of Great Britain's longtime expert on Indian affairs, wrote a series of articles denouncing the Andhra leadership. Dutt advocated the adoption of nonviolent methods and the participation of the CPI in the electoral process. The former general secretary P. C. Joshi, earlier expelled from the party, launched a public campaign rejecting the "false independence" line, defending Nehru's foreign policy, and arguing that the CPI, as an integral part of the Indian Left, had a major role to play in a democratic India's mainstream political life. This involved recognizing the legitimate sovereignty of the state, conducting class struggle through legislative processes and state-led economic development, and growing the CPI into a mass party as an electoral rather than insurrectionary force.

This opposition within the national CPI paralyzed the Andhra leadership and deprived the *sangham* in Telangana of any sort of wider organizational support. In December 1950, General Secretary Rajeswara Rao was forced to concede to changes to the Central Committee and the Politburo. E. M. S Namboodiripad, Dange, Ghate, and S. S. Yusuf were added to the Politburo, and the Telangana Maoist D. V. Rao was dismissed. Yet the party remained formally committed to the *sangham*: "Every effort should be made to defend the cause of the Telengana fighters and no worker should issue slogans to the press for the withdrawal of the struggle." Disagreements over the question of violence continued to paralyze the party, reducing it "to a state of passivity during the period when mighty events were taking place."[201] In February 1951, a secret delegation consisting of Dange, Ghosh, and the Andhra Maoists Rajeswara Rao and Basavapunniah went to Moscow for talks with Stalin and other Soviet leaders.[202] "Once Comrade Stalin has said that it was not a liberation struggle," Sundarayya observed in his autobiography, "there was no question of arguing on it."[203] Rajeswara Rao, Sundarayya, D. V. Rao, and Basavapunniah all resigned from the Central Committee. Ghosh took over as general secretary, and Joshi was readmitted to the party.

The new CPI leadership sought a solution to the conflict in Telangana that would maintain their credibility with their party workers, guerrilla fighters, and wider social base of support, while allowing for their participation in the upcoming elections. In June 1951, the Central Committee of the CPI issued a press release declaring it was "prepared to solve the problem by negotiation and settlement intended to preserve and protect the interests of the peasantry and the people and to restore peaceful conditions in the area."[204] They denied that the armed struggle aimed to overthrow the Nehru government. It was, rather, a struggle by peasants for land and "against oppression of the feudal landlords and the Nizam."[205] The CPI issued a number of demands: land to the tiller, village administration by *panchayats* elected by all villagers including women, the right of tribal people to use and cultivate the forest under their own elected *panchayats*, immediate withdrawal of armed forces and disbanding of the home guards, release of political prisoners and cancellation of collective fines, lifting of the ban on AMS and the CPI, restoration of civil liberties, a constituent assembly elected by adult franchise to decide the future of the Asaf Jah dynasty, and the dissolution of Hyderabad State into linguistic provinces and autonomous tribal regions.[206]

In pursuance of these objectives, Jyoti Basu, Muzaffar Ahmed, and A. K. Gopalan went to Hyderabad to parley with state officials. They met Hyderabad's home minister and offered a complete withdrawal of the armed struggle in exchange for amnesty for CPI leaders and the Telangana cadres. The Hyderabad government was noncommittal. Basu then requested meetings with Nehru and C. Rajagopalachari, the Union home minister, to discuss "enabling them to take part in the elections."[207] Both refused, demanding that the CPI first withdraw from the Telangana struggle and disavow violence altogether. Unable to extract any conditions from either the Hyderabad or Central governments, the CPI leadership met in Calcutta in October 1951. After five years of struggle, an estimated four thousand members of the *sangham* had lost their lives. Without consulting local *sangham* leaders and *dalam* militants, the CPI unilaterally and unconditionally announced withdrawal from the Telangana struggle on October 23. That same month, the Hyderabad government reported over one hundred "incidents" in Telangana, most of which occurred in Warangal and Karimnagar.[208] Yet by the end of the year, most of the *dalams* had dumped their weapons and disbanded, although a few militants remained underground on account of pending criminal charges against them.[209] By the end of the year, the *doras* were back. Landlords and village officers returned to villages, sometimes after years of absence. The electoral rolls for the upcoming election were prepared.

Although various restrictions remained, Nehru and the Congress made good on their promise to allow the CPI to function openly within the limits of parliamentary democracy. Communist leaders in Hyderabad and around the country were released from prison and allowed to stand for election. In Hyderabad, however, the CPI remained banned. The communists joined together with disaffected State Congressmen and socialists to form the People's Democratic Front (PDF), a leftist party with a progressive agenda. In Hyderabad as a whole, the Congress put up 173 candidates, elected 93, and received 2,176,654 votes. The PDF put up 78 candidates, elected 42, and received 1,086,111 votes. The Socialist Party put up 97 candidates, elected 11, and received 591,215 votes.[210] The PDF did well in Telangana, winning all fourteen seats to the State Assembly in Nalgonda and eight of thirteen in Warangal. The PDF also sent seven representatives to the first Lok Sabha, including revolutionary leaders like Baddam Yella Reddy, who defeated future prime minister P. V. Narasimha Rao, and Ravi Narayan Reddy, who registered 309,162 votes, among the highest nationwide and 75,591 more than Nehru. Indian communism began a new trajectory as an integral part of India's liberal democracy.

The postcolonial state in India had what Kaviraj has called a double and contradictory inheritance: it was a successor to both the Raj and the national movement.[211] The triumph of the national bourgeoisie and their project of liberal democracy was a violent and contentious process, ultimately made possible by the commandeering of the bureaucratic and coercive structures of the colonial state. This "passive revolution," as Partha Chatterjee argued, depended on the bureaucratic power of the state to bring about a "molecular transformation" in Indian society in which the "old dominant classes" and the "popular masses" were both incorporated into a new democratic order.[212] Revolution was replaced by institutionalized democratic competition, on the one hand, and state-led "development" on the other, which sought to bring about social transformation through a progressive and managed process. In this highly contested transformation, a modernizing state project came to reconfigure relations between state and society and to mediate relations between groups within Indian society. The *sangham* and the dream of an Indian Yan'an were temporarily extinguished in 1951, only to be resurrected with the "Spring Thunder" of 1967. Ever since, revolutionary Maoism has existed as the shadow of India's liberal democracy and as a looking glass for its illiberal and authoritarian dimensions. It was in Telangana that Indian peasants and Adivasi revolutionaries first took to arms under the banner of Maoism. In this respect, the historical trajectory opened up by Telangana at the very moment of national independence has yet to be fully closed.

CHAPTER SIX

THE CAMP AND THE CITIZEN

IN THE LAST MONTHS OF 1949, the government of Hyderabad initiated what was variously referred to as the Tribal Rehabilitation Scheme or the Tribal Reclamation Scheme. Adivasis living in the hill and forest regions of the districts of Warangal, Karimnagar, and Adilabad were, by the thousands, forcibly relocated to roadside camps and settlements called Rural Welfare Centres. Koya predominated in Warangal and Karimnagar, and Gonds in Adilabad. By 1950, this area, and the Koya area of Warangal in particular, had become a base for the guerrillas of the revolutionary *sangham*. Many Koya had joined forces with the *sangham*, rallying behind the call for an autonomous Koyasthan, local self-government, and an end to the depredations of government officers, landlords, and moneylenders. Traditional *kula panchayats* (village councils) and the intervillage administrative mechanism known as *samuthu* were either reorganized by *sangham* militants or co-opted into the revolutionary struggle, thus creating a new political formation seeking accommodation and recognition in the postcolonial order.

Lambada, who had been at the forefront of the *sangham* since at least 1944, were also removed from their *tandas* and settled near state authorities. Also known as Banjaras, Lambada were a traditionally itinerant group, making them a resource as guides and messengers for the *sangham*, and a

225

great source of anxiety for the state. While it is unclear how many camps there were in Telangana, it is clear that thousands of tribal people were forcibly removed from their homes and detained elsewhere. Most commonly, they were settled in informal roadside camps in villages where the government had established armed police outposts, often referred to as Civil Centres. In one division of Warangal, for example, 200 of the 250 Koya villages were evacuated and their inhabitants moved into ninety such roadside camps.[1] A February 1951 intelligence report noted that seven thousand of the thirty thousand Koyas in the Warangal area had "been settled down in villages," in addition to an unspecified number of Lambada who had "now been brought from their Tandas in the interior forests and made to settle down in the villages."[2]

In addition to the more informal roadside camps, the government established Rural Welfare Centres, also known as Tribal Rehabilitation (or Reclamation) Colonies. These were run by the Revenue Department in conjunction with the Social Services Department, whose sole charge was tribal development and welfare. There were at least forty formal Welfare Centres of various sizes throughout Telangana. In one division of Warangal, the Koya of seventy villages were placed in four such centers, each having at least 1,000 to 1,200 residents.[3] While for officials the camps were projects of security and development, communist leaders called them "concentration camps." P. Sundarayya, a key organizer of the *sangham* and later member of Parliament, protested during a Rajya Sabha debate on the Preventive Detention Bill in 1952 that ten thousand people had died in these camps.[4] C. Rajeswara Rao, who became general secretary of the CPI for the first time in 1950, wrote that state forces "burned down about 2,000 tribal hamlets and herded the tribal people into concentration camps."[5] Many, Rao observed, "died in these camps because of semistarvation and undernourishment."[6]

The tribal camps of Telangana were created, first and foremost, in the context of the Indian state's efforts to defeat the revolutionary *sangham*. As security measures, the forced relocation and concentration of Adivasi populations in Telangana were part of a wider twentieth-century history of counterinsurgency. From Malaya and Vietnam to Kenya and Algeria, what was referred to as grouping, regrouping, villagization, strategic hamlets, or population removal formed a central aspect of state-led counterinsurgency campaigns. As Nandini Sundar has observed, the victims of internment have been either colonized populations, inhabitants of areas that challenge the sovereignty of postcolonial states, or "enemy races."[7] The Adivasis of Telangana were, in a sense, all three. At an internal frontier, the nascent postcolonial nation-state made sovereign claims over the lives and bodies of Adivasis at a foundational moment.

As the Raj developed into the Republic, the camps were sites of the violent transformation of the colonial ethnographic state into the postcolonial developmental state. The linking of the security of the state to the project of national development was integral to postcolonial counterinsurgency efforts.[8] Government officials justified the camps on the premise that they were protecting innocent Adivasis against coercive and illegitimate insurgents. The state needed to control Adivasi bodies in order to protect them. Adivasis did not, however, just need to be protected. They also needed to be improved. The camps were necessary, in this regard, for the state to provide the Adivasis with the welfare that they deserved as members of the nation and citizens of the Republic and, more specifically, as constitutionally designated Scheduled Tribes. The camps were thus thresholds to the nation and a national regime of sovereignty and citizenship. They aimed to induct the tribals into the nation as differentiated and developmental subjects. "In the republican conception of citizenship," Ornit Shani notes, "development was a condition for unity."[9] In the tribal camps of Telangana, the ideology of national development was linked to a new regime of sovereignty at a foundational moment of the Republic.

This chapter first examines the camps as a counterinsurgency tactic aimed at controlling tribal populations. Then the camps are interpreted as developmental projects, with a particular focus on the fraught relationship between the figure of the tribe and the nation. Next, the legal basis of the camps and the way in which the state sought to incorporate Telangana's Adivasis into a new regime of citizenship and sovereignty are explored. Their status as Scheduled Tribes inducted the Adivasis of Telangana into a state-led developmental regime that sought to convert Adivasi claims to land and autonomy into the state provision of welfare. The tribal camps of Telangana were, in many respects, paradigmatic of postcolonial tribal development efforts and, as such, of the trajectory of citizenship and sovereignty at the internal frontiers of the Indian state.

I. The Camp as Protection

In the last chapter we explored how the state as a source of violence was integral to counterinsurgency efforts in Telangana after the Police Action. This was true in terms of violence as spectacle and as spectral, as in the case of the police encounter. Officials sought to establish the state as an object of fear and awe, capable of withstanding and exercising greater violence than the *sangham*. The camp was, in this respect, a site where the citizen encountered the state in both its profane and sublime forms.[10] In the camps, state sovereignty was simultaneously articulated as the source of violence and the source of protection *from* violence.[11] Of course, state claims to provide protection from a perceived threat do not need to be true or even believed to be such. Indeed, the state itself could be the source of violence from which it offers protection, what Alpa Shah has referred to as a "double-edged sword."[12]

Responding to concerns voiced in Parliament about the internment policy, Hyderabad's chief secretary, L. C. Jain, argued that the forced removals and the camps were necessary for two reasons. First, "The Communists and other unsocial elements who infest the forest area were obtaining food and shelter in these villages." Second, the "Hill Tribes living in these far off places had been exploited by the Communists and also threatened with death or other punishment." The state, he argued, "could not give these Hill Tribes the protection that they needed so long as they continued to remain near the forests."[13] The camps had, officially, a dual function: to weaken the power of the *sangham* and to protect the Adivasis. Official discourse framed Adivasis as helpless, vulnerable, and without agency—that is, as essentially victims—while at the same time framing them as threats that needed to be controlled. The "Armed Police Centres" scattered throughout Telangana were also, from this perspective, "centres of rural uplift."[14] In this confusion of victim and enemy, the concept of "rehabilitation" represented the point at which the care for life became indistinguishable from the fight against the enemy.[15]

The government of India's commissioner for Scheduled Castes and Scheduled Tribes reported that the communists were using the "Scheduled Tribes as tools in their nefarious activities."[16] The director of the Intelligence Bureau noted that there was "no doubt that the primary motive in initiating this scheme was security by withdrawing the Koyas from areas under Communist influence."[17] Even the director of the Social Service Department, an agency dedicated to tribal development, cited numerous instances of the "desperadoes quitting the area covered by the Social Services Schemes" as evidence that they had achieved their desired results.[18] Yet government officials also perceived Adivasis as potentially subversive. The camps were necessary "in order to combat the spread of lawlessness among the Koyas."[19] Special Commissioner Nanjappa, the paramount official in charge of the state's counterinsurgency in the Telangana Special Area, noted approvingly that the camps were located in "central places where they could be well supervised."[20] K. M. Munshi, India's food minister, congratulated the Hyderabad government for "a great experiment" in weaning the Koya away from the communists.[21]

The camps marked a departure from late colonial state-building efforts by the Nizam's government, although they resembled, in certain respects, tribal internment policies in British India. Efforts to incorporate the Adivasis of Telangana into Hyderabad's patrimonial order were intensified in the last decade of the Nizam's rule.[22] During the Second World War, the Nizam conscripted the Austrian anthropologist Christoph von Fürer-Haimendorf into producing an extensive study of tribal Telangana.[23] This ethnographic work provided the basis for recommendations made by Fürer-Haimendorf to the Hyderabad government regarding tribal development.[24] The basis of the new policy was the granting of *patta*, or formal land titles, to Adivasis, so-called Haimendorf *patta*.[25] The Hyderabad government reached out to Fürer-Haimendorf again in mid-1949 as the *sangham* spread rapidly in the tribal areas of Telangana.[26] Indeed, officials in Hyderabad used the tribal development schemes initiated in the early 1940s as alibis for the camps, insisting that the "welfare schemes" suggested by Fürer-Haimendorf were being "fully implemented."²⁷ The postcolonial Indian state weaponized ethnographic knowledge in new ways and with lasting consequences. The camps were means for the Indian state to actualize its claims to sovereignty at an internal frontier on the basis of providing security and development to racialized groups.

When the Adivasis of Telangana joined forces with the *sangham*, they were continuing a longer history of tribal claims to political autonomy and territorial sovereignty.²⁸ The Gonds of Adilabad, under the leadership of Kumaram Bhim, had rebelled in the name of Gondi nationalism against the Nizam's state in the early 1940s.²⁹ The Koya of Warangal had also rebelled against the Nizam in the early 1940s and again in early 1948, months before *sangham* militants arrived in their villages.³⁰ They continued to claim an autonomous Koyasthan up to 1951.³¹ The CPI leadership and *sangham* militants took up the rallying call of Koyasthan and took measures to end forced labor, cancel debts, and remove restrictions on access to forest produce.³² By the time the CPI unilaterally withdrew the armed struggle in October 1951, Adivasis "formed the backbone of the Communist organisation" and provided the majority of recruits into the guerrilla *dalams*.³³ The revolution in Telangana after the Police Action had a distinctly tribal and telluric character and, as such, was an important moment in the history of tribal politics of territorial autonomy and revolutionary communism in postcolonial India.

While the camps were something new and specific to postcolonial India, as discussed below, they were also an inheritance of the disciplinary regime of the colonial "ethnographic state."³⁴ Tribal "reclamation" colonies had been a regular feature of the colonial landscape since the mid-nineteenth century.³⁵ The colonial language of "reclamation" and "rehabilitation" was redeployed as part of a postcolonial regime of sovereignty, citizenship, and national development. In Hyderabad, the Criminal Tribes Act No. 2 of 1307 Fasli (1897–98) created a system of policing of "criminal communities" along the lines of the British Indian Criminal Tribes Act of 1871.³⁶ While the Lambada of Hyderabad were listed as a Criminal Tribe, the Koya were not. Since the Criminal Tribes Act was not repealed until 1952, the schemes in Hyderabad were implemented under ambiguous and often contradictory legal premises.

The internment of Lambada in Hyderabad as part of the post–Police Action insurgency was, in this respect, built upon a preexisting legal-institutional structure. The colonial state developed surveillance and disciplinary mechanisms to control itinerant peoples or other populations deemed criminal or undesirable. Itinerant peoples were forcibly settled, often in the interest of capital-intensive projects seeking cheap and disciplined labor.[37] In Hyderabad, Lambada had been detained along with other tribes at the "Criminal Tribes Settlement" at Lingal, which had a total population of two hundred.[38] In 1950, there were a total of 3,037 registered male members of Criminal Tribes under surveillance in Hyderabad, not counting those detained as a result of the counterinsurgency. For both the colonial state and its successor, the settling of itinerant groups was part of larger projects of legibility, assimilation, and normalization.[39] Shifting cultivation and nomadism were seen as anachronistic and degrading, while settled agriculture was seen to have "humanizing tendencies."[40] The tribal camps of Telangana represented an exponential expansion of a colonial regime of discipline in which racial thinking targeted particular groups in Indian society as objects of special state action.

In the colonial ethnographic imagination, "hill tribes" such as the Koya were not usually considered inherently criminal or threatening. They occupied instead a distinct, and at times romantic, space. The romantic view was exemplified by the English anthropologist-administrator Verrier Elwin, who was a main proponent of keeping hill tribes separate from mainstream society, at one time proposing a "National Park" where nontribals would be barred from owning land, proselytizing, or otherwise interfering with traditional tribal life.[41] Nehru would later appoint Elwin as an administrator in the North-East Frontier Agency and endorsed his view that the state should actively take up a paternal role as the protector of tribals from the influence and exploitation of mainstream Indian society.[42] Central to this view was the idea that Adivasis were not only distinct but essentially vulnerable and, as such, in need of state protection.

In contrast to this isolationist and preservationist mode of ethnographic thinking was a more interventionist tendency, which saw the paternalistic state as an agent of civilization and modernization. Ajay Skaria has argued that an official discourse of "wildness" was "part of the effort to civilize" tribals. This civilizing mission involved "subordinating the tribes, making them take to settled cultivation," and, ultimately, "separating the wild forests and wild tribes."[43] In Telangana, upper-caste administrators considered the camps as mechanisms for "civilizing" or "modernizing" the tribals. The director of intelligence, B. N. Mullik, insisted that the camps were "the first constructive work which has been attempted during the last one century of civilizing the tribals who up till now . . . have been left as anthropological curiosities and allowed to live the life of jungle beasts."[44] He believed the purpose of the scheme was "to enable the Koyas to lead a civilised life. Driving them back to the jungle would mean the reversing of this process of civilisation and turning them again into wildlife."[45] The minister of home affairs of the Hyderabad government, N. N. Iengar, wrote to the Ministry of States that "these colonies were formed not only to wean away the Koyas from the influence of Communists but also to modernise their way of living."[46] The government of Hyderabad reported that "the aboriginal tribes and the Lambadas who had been the main source of succour and supply to the terrorists, were uprooted from their villages inside the forests and made to live nearer *human habitation*."[47] Echoing this language, Hyderabad's chief secretary described how tribals were "induced to leave their homes and to settle in and around villages nearer human habitation."[48] The camps, in other words, formed a link between the colonial civilizing mission and the project of national citizenship and development. As such, they were exemplary of the way in which the ideology of development was central to the forging of a new regime of sovereignty after 1947.

II. The Camp as Development

While officials readily admitted the disciplinary function of the camps, they also framed them as idealized projects of "tribal development." This discourse of development was crucial to attempts to justify and legitimize state action, including violence. In these camps, the sovereign responsibility to protect life was inseparable from the sovereign prerogative to control, improve, and, ultimately, dispose of life. Hyderabad's home secretary argued that it was "best to regroup all tribal villages" at "accessible places" in order to "rehabilitate them on well-planned Centres providing all their day-to-day necessities at the colonies." Such efforts should be conducted in "pursuance of the policy of uplift of aboriginals, safe-guarding their interests and protecting them from exploitation, worries and miseries." Frequent visits by government officers, moreover, "have helped to eradicate all their grievances." As a result, "Tribal Colonies have become model villages where all the necessities of life are made available to them." The ultimate goal was to "inculcate in them the spirit of cooperation."[49] The camps, then, were means for the state to take responsibility for the biological life and welfare of the tribals and, by doing so, to transform them into docile and productive subjects. The "spirit of cooperation" was not merely a side effect of development but the objective of it.

This connection between development and loyalty to the state was echoed by other administrators and is consistent with the idea of "hearts and minds" that has been an integral feature of global counterinsurgency doctrine. The director of the Social Services Department argued that "the aboriginals who have been given lands, agricultural loans, foodgrains and clothes as subsidy, medical and veterinary aid, education and better housing facilities have in more than one way shown their gratitude and loyalty towards the Government."[50] Hyderabad's Ministry of States–appointed chief minister, M. K. Vellodi, reported that "these hill tribes had to be brought away from their homes in the jungle and planted near the roadside." Starting them on their "new lives," he noted, "has been a difficult piece of work," but "the results have been wholly satisfactory." Most importantly, "Koyas have come over to us in large numbers."[51]

Officials envisioned the camps as the basis for providing welfare and development to Adivasis who were seen to previously lack access to such goods: "Adequate arrangements have been made for the re-settlement at selected centres of these villagers. They have been given suitable sites for construction of huts and have been supplied with free timber and other forest produce. Care has been taken to see that as far as possible villagers were not moved to places more than three miles from their original habitation. Every such new centre is being provided with a village hall, drinking water well and chawdi. Wherever possible monetary help is also being provided."⁵² A government pamphlet published in 1951 described the camps as "ideal villages" necessitated by administrative contingencies, yet ultimately desirable regardless of the immediate context of conflict:

> In spite of all the above ameliorative measures it was all the while felt that due to the lack of communications and accessibility to the far and wide scattered hamlets of the Koyas it was not easy to extend the welfare programme as extensively as it was deemed necessary. It was, therefore, considered best to regroup all tribal villages in such a way so as to bring in together all of them situated within a radius of 3 or at the most 5 miles and move them up to the road-side wherever possible or at least to the nearest accessible point. It was further envisaged that such newly formed villages shall be so planned as to be an *ideal village* with sufficient open spaces for community recreation, wide roads, open yards for kitchen gardens, suitable sites for manure pits, separate cattle-sheds and adequate arrangements for drinking water wells.... It was also decided that every settlement should be provided with a village school, suitable huts were, therefore, constructed for the accommodation of a school.⁵³

This vision of an "ideal village" was comprehensive and all-encompassing. It also prioritized state needs: rather than adapt and respond to society as it was, the state sought to create a new social order entirely. The state was proposing to completely refashion life for Adivasis who had hitherto lived on its margins and had, at times, actively worked to keep the state away. The camps were, in this respect, paradigmatic examples of the ideology behind economic planning and state-led development in a decolonizing India.

The camps were also mechanisms for the articulation and generation of state sovereignty at an internal frontier. They were sites of the production of biopolitical bodies, what Giorgio Agamben has called the "original activity of sovereign power."⁵⁴ On the one hand, they were intended to protect, foster, and improve life. On the other hand, they were intended to control life and, inadvertently or not, dispose of it. As it turned out, the vast majority of welfare services were undelivered in these "model villages." Most camps lacked basic necessities like potable water.⁵⁵ The director of the

Intelligence Bureau reported in December 1950 that "welfare measures, which have been undertaken, are still in their initial stages and also lack in determination and aim. If the people's minds are to be attracted by such measures, they must start feeling the benefit of such measures."[56] Another intelligence officer lamented in 1951 that it was "high time that the liberal promises made by the authorities" be "promptly fulfilled."[57] A military report similarly indicated a "paucity of food grains, water and other bare necessities of life at centres where they have been concentrated.... No medical aid is made available to the villagers. Consequently deaths due to various diseases are frequent. The places where locals have been concentrated are far away from their lands.... Generally, the welfare of the locals is neglected.... The local population should be properly rehabilitated. They should be supplied with the minimum necessities of life."[58] Special Commissioner Nanjappa conceded that services in the camps were not provided as quickly and effectively as desired.[59] Swami Tirtha, a leading congressman of Hyderabad and an ally of the government, argued that internment entailed "miseries" that were "too numerous to recount." Tirtha lamented that the "new habitations had none of the amenities of human life. Even drinking water was difficult to get. They contracted many diseases due to which hundreds of children and old folk died."[60] Noting that the Lambada in the camps were in a "pitiable condition," Tirtha warned the Hyderabad government that Telangana's tribals were "seething with unrest with no tangible advantage to the Government."[61]

In the extraordinary collection of oral histories put together by the Stree Shakti Sanghatana, Kamalamma, a woman from a lower-caste family of bonded laborers who joined a *sangham* cultural squad, later recalled that the police "gathered all the village folk from surrounding villages" into a camp and that "they did not allow the people to leave the camp which was guarded by home guards."[62] Official reports corroborate, to an extent, communist accusations of systematic torture and killing of suspected communists at the camps and police outposts in Telangana.[63] A delegation sent by the CPI reported that "facts of police oppression and torture could be multiplied ad infinitum" and that disease, rape, and murder were commonplace.[64] In one such camp, 480 of the 1,500 people brought from twenty-two villages were reported to have succumbed to disease.⁶⁵ Camps legitimated under the pretenses of protecting and improving life were, rather, spaces of death and of the provision of the "minimum necessities of life": that is, sites of the production and sustenance of bare life. The camps were attempts to capture Adivasis within the new political order founded in the years after 1947 while also excluding them from it.

III. The Camp and the Citizen

While having their roots in the colonial past, the tribal camps of Telangana also tell us something about the ambiguities and tensions in the relationship between Adivasis and the national project and, as an extension, Indian democracy. Nationalist thought incorporated key aspects of the colonial ethnographic imaginary, not least historicist notions of civilization and the idea that Adivasis lived outside of history and, as such, posed a threat to the potential of the nation to become fully modern.⁶⁶ As we have seen, officials likened Adivasis to "anthropological curiosities," "jungle beasts," and "wildlife." However, the context in which the camps were created was a distinctly national one, a foundational moment of the Republic and its emergent regime of sovereignty and citizenship that sought to transform *jungli* into citizens.

The official discourse deployed to legitimize the tribal camps in Telangana drew upon long-standing nationalist critiques of the isolationist approach of the colonial state to India's Adivasis. The sociologist G. S. Ghurye, for example, engaged in a contentious debate with Elwin, accusing him of seeking to thwart the natural path of Adivasi development. For Ghurye, the real threat posed by isolationists or protectionists like Elwin was the stabilization of old tribal cultures. He argued for a conception of India's history as a millennia-old teleological process of assimilation that would ultimately culminate in a homogeneous Indian nation. This process of assimilation had been rudely disrupted by British colonialism. Ghurye further questioned the distinction made between tribals and nontribals as a colonial myth, insisting that the "so-called Animists and Aborigines are best described as Backward Hindus."⁶⁷ More recent scholarship has confirmed that the "tribal" as a sociological and legal category was indeed a colonial invention. Adivasis, however, did not historically exist in splendid isolation from the rest of Indian society but had, rather, extensive engagements with "mainstream" society and state-based systems of political power.[68]

For Ghurye, as for the officials overseeing the tribal camps of Telangana, the solution to the tribal "problem" was the resumption and completion of the assimilation process that had been interrupted by colonialism. Ghurye argued that it was a "process that is natural" and that it was "beneficial to the tribal people and to the whole society."[69] He identified tribal practices of agriculture as an impediment to the national project of progressive development. Indeed, tribals needed to be assimilated because they "have hardly any thought of the morrow, and are therefore generally improvident."[70] This improvidence was seen to be incompatible with nationalist notions of historical progress, a key dimension of the legitimizing ideology of the postcolonial state. Improvidence was seen to inhibit the development of tribals into fully modern and economically productive members of the national community capable of bearing constitutional rights.

The term *Adivasi*, meaning "inhabitants from the earliest times,"[71] but often translated as "original" or "ancient inhabitant," entered the nationalist lexicon in the 1930s.[72] It is thought to have been coined by the Gandhian activist A. V. Thakkar, who criticized the "isolationism" of anthropologists and "British members of the I.C.S. and other Government officers" for aiming to keep "the aborigines in their areas untouched by the civilization of the plains." Thakkar, who headed the subcommittee on tribal rights in the Constituent Assembly and was hired by the Hyderabad government to consult on tribal affairs during the period of the camps, supported the "assimilation" policy advocated by Ghurye.[73] He explained in a 1941 lecture: "The aborigines should form part of the civilized communities of our country not for the purpose of swelling the figures of the followers of this religion or that, but to share with the advanced communities the privileges and duties on equal terms in the general social and political life of the country. Separatism and isolation seem to be dangerous theories, and they strike at the root of national solidarity."[74] There was thus anxiety among Indian nationalists surrounding Adivasis as both integral members of the nation and potential threats to national unity. Such anxieties were expressed by officials in Telangana who argued for the camps as necessary instruments not only of state sovereignty but of national integration and development. Dams, mines, and other developmental projects have since 1947 displaced tens of millions of Adivasis on the premise that they should sacrifice their territorial claims for the "greater common good."[75] Since 1947, in other words, Adivasis have been cast by the state and national press alike as obstacles to national development and unity.

In the context of counterinsurgency at an internal frontier, the camps point to the contested, incomplete, and ongoing project of national hegemony and to the tensions and contradictions in the way in which Adivasis were incorporated into a national citizenship regime. The camps are demonstrative of the coercive and violent means by which the sovereignty of nations is constructed and reproduced over time and space. The Indian nation-state exercises uneven forms of territoriality at its internal frontiers. That the camps were intended as thresholds to the nation was made clear by the names they were given: Ashoknagar, Vallabhnagar, Gandhinagar, Bapunagar, Jawaharnagar, Kakatiyanagar, and so on.[76] Yet the sovereignty of the nation-state in Telangana was not founded through a consensual social contract; indeed, there wasn't even a pretense of one. It was founded, rather, on the "will to prefer life to death."[77] In certain instances, suspected communist supporters were stripped naked, paraded in public, and forced to prostrate before images or statues of nationalist leaders such as Gandhi.[78]

As in the case of the home guards elsewhere in Telangana, Adivasis who had been interned in camps were asked to take up arms to fight the *sangham* and defend the state. That is, they were asked to kill and be killed in the name of the state. The army and police organized Koya from the camps into "Koya tiger squads" and "anti-hostile dalams," or appointed them as "Special Police Constables."[79] The state attempted to construct a regime of sovereignty, not by monopolizing violence, but by cohering a sacrificial community around the state in order to generate what Arjun Appadurai has called the "full attachment" of the people to the state.[80] Officials reported that the Koya detained in the camps had undergone a "fast change in mentality" and that "the hostiles are of late nervous to mix with the Koyas who have gone to the rehabilitation centres." The *sangham* was, instead, "instigating" the "unreformed Koyas" who had not been "rehabilitated."[81] The sign of rehabilitation, in other words, was that the Koya were willing to kill and be killed for the state rather than the *sangham*. They were rewarded, according to one official, with the "bare necessities of life, such as foodgrains, chilies, clothing and drugs, in return for the good work rendered or even promised."[82] This exchange—loyalty, "service," and sacrifice for the "bare necessities of life"—was the contract by which the Adivasis of Telangana were inducted into the nation and the national state made sovereign claims at an internal frontier.

If the forest and hills of Telangana were an internal frontier of state sovereignty, then the camps represented, in certain respects, the site of the border. As Paul Kahn has argued, the border is the "archetypal space of sovereignty." Its function is one of "symbolic transit" where people move from the "regime of sovereignty to that of law."[83] In this respect, the tribal camps of Telangana were similar to the archetypical camps of this period in India: the refugee camps of Punjab and elsewhere in North India that millions of people moved through in months and years after August 1947. Both types of camps were governmental mechanisms and biopolitical spaces where care for and control of life were irreducibly combined. The refugee camps of Punjab were crucial sites in the making of a postcolonial regime of sovereignty and citizenship. Partition violence was an essential ingredient to the historical context in which originary invocations of citizenship were made. As in the partitioned Punjab, in Telangana the camp emerged as part of a sequence of violence followed by "rehabilitation" that worked to forge new relationships between state and society at this foundational moment.

Yet there were crucial differences. The camps in Punjab were part of an effort to fix a displaced population to a new national territory. In Telangana, tribals were removed from territory over which they had an original claim. Officials, tapping into international counterinsurgency discourses, referred to Adivasis as "squatters," in essence denying them any property rights over their ancestral lands. One suggested that "these squatters can all be removed from forest areas":

> The same type of squatters' problem, which is present in Malaya, is also present in Telengana. The Koyas, the Chenchus and the Lambada hill tribes, who reside in deep jungles and the hilly areas and live on forest produce, have provided good many recruits to the Communist "dalams" and have been extremely useful to the latter as couriers, guides, procurers of food and generally for maintaining the lines of communication. The only way this squatters problem could be tackled was to withdraw the entire Koya population from the hills and resettle them in new villages near Civil Centres, so that their activities could be kept in check and they could be kept away from Communist influence.[84]

As we have seen with the claim to Koyasthan, tribal politics in India has largely been articulated in terms of territoriality, the restitution of property ownership, and the recovery of unpaid debt.[85] Put differently, the Adivasi articulation of democracy has been through the question of autonomy.[86] Tribal politics was, and in many ways remains, essentially telluric. What the tribal camps of Telangana illustrate is the attempt to convert a telluric tribal politics—the politics of *jal, jangal, jameen* (water, forest, land)—into a regime of citizenship rights and the provision of state-led welfare and development. In this process, tribal claims to territory were reinterpreted as claims to resources within a certain territory.[87] The postcolonial state, moreover, continued the colonial state's ownership of forests and tribal lands, along with its attendant legal architecture.[88] A significant difference, of course, was that this colonial legal-bureaucratic inheritance was, after 1947, authorized to intervene in tribal life and appropriate tribal territories on behalf of "the nation."

The *sangham* raised the land question not only for peasants on the plains, as discussed in the previous chapter, but also for the Adivasis in the forests. In 1951, seeking a peaceful settlement to the armed struggle, the CPI asked the government to recognize the "right of the tribal people to free use and sale of forest produce and freedom to cultivate the forest lands under their own elected panchayats." They coupled their demand for "complete regional autonomy to tribal areas" with a demand for the dissolution of Hyderabad State into linguistic states of Andhra, Maharashtra, and Karnatak.[89] They were demanding, in other words, a federal solution that treated tribal claims to land not alongside the welfare claims of the Scheduled Castes, as the Constitution does, but as legitimate claims to territory alongside those of linguistic groups within a federal India.

The relationship of the camps to the law was, as mentioned above, ambiguous and often contradictory. As discussed in the previous chapter, Telangana had been designated a "Special Area," a legal space of exception in which civil liberties were suspended. Central funding for relocation of the Lambada was withdrawn because they were not included in the Constitution (Scheduled Tribes) Order of 1950.[90] The relocation of the Lambada was thus consequently pursued according to their status as a Criminal Tribe according to the statutes of Hyderabad State.[91] The relocation of the Koya, however, was conducted according to their status as a constitutionally designated Scheduled Tribe, thus blurring the lines between criminalization and "schedulization." The Fifth Schedule of the Constitution gave juridical form to the category of Scheduled Tribe and contained specific provisions for the protection of tribal rights. Article 46 of the Directive Principles of the Constitution tasks the state with caring for the "educational and economic interests" of the Scheduled Tribes and Scheduled Castes. The inclusion of the Scheduled Tribes in the 1950 Constitution incorporated Adivasis into the nation as differentiated subjects marked as needing improvement by the developmental modalities of the postcolonial state. Officials perceived the tribal camps of Telangana as giving rather than depriving rights to tribals as Indian citizens. The government sought to convert claims for autonomy and territory into the provision of welfare and to transform *jungli* into what Rajendra Prasad, president of India, called "useful citizens."[92] Hyderabad's Social Services Department agreed: "In Hyderabad the tribes are rapidly becoming a settled community and it can be safely said that Hyderabad is ahead of most of the States in regard to aboriginals welfare and education. It is not the idea to submerge their ancient culture but to give all the facilities of modern civilization and to make them useful citizens."[93] In many respects, the Constitution placed Scheduled Tribes into a compensatory system designed for, and more suited to, Scheduled Castes. The new legal code established by the Constitution thus departed from colonial understandings of the tribal. By placing both Adivasis and Dalits within a similar compensatory logic, the Constitution failed to distinguish between difference-as-inequality and difference-as-not-sameness.[94] As is evident in the official discourse cited above, state welfare for Scheduled Tribes was based on an understanding of civilizational progress and of the modernity of the new nation, while restitution for Scheduled Castes was founded on an idea of historical discrimination and injustice that the state needed to reconcile. In the new constitutional order, the tribal became subsumed into the fundamentally hierarchical and inherently scalar category of caste.[95]

This partial or misrecognition of tribal difference produced a contradiction between tribal politics and the liberal democratic and developmental institutions of the Indian state. The first-past-the-post electoral system has led to the underrepresentation of Adivasis in legislative bodies and a near-complete exclusion from institutional political power, even in the "tribal" state of Jharkhand formed in 2000. In the Northeast, however, tribes have since 1947 negotiated differing levels of autonomy and self-rule within and through federal avenues. Yet the Northeast has also been heavily militarized by a nation-state making hegemonic claims to territorial sovereignty. Over the last few decades peninsular India too has become increasingly militarized in the name of a security operation aimed at revolutionary Maoists and at Adivasi communities portrayed as both victims and threats. As in Telangana in 1950, tribal claims to territory and property in peninsular India have been treated, not as legitimate articulations of their citizenship rights, but as challenges to the sovereignty of the territorial Indian nation-state.

IV. The Camp as Paradigm

The Koya and other Gonds, Lambada, Chenchu, and others who were interned in Telangana were not, of course, merely victims or enemies. They both resisted and engaged with the state. Some of the "Rural Development Centres" in Warangal were burned down. After one such blaze, the special commissioner wryly noted that the "Koyas who had been helping the hostiles have not taken kindly to the shifting of the sites of their Tandas." They set fire to the camp "in the fond hope" that they would be able to return home. "The Koyas," the special commissioner continued, "have definitely been made to understand that they will have to remain in the new centre."⁹⁶ Indeed, the relocation scheme itself was a primary grievance against the government. Many Lambada took to arms and joined the *dalams* only after the government attempted to move them from their *tandas*. Koya and other tribals also moved further into the forest to avoid being interned or relocated.⁹⁷

Most of the camps in Telangana were abandoned between 1952 and 1953, only to reappear in tribal areas elsewhere—Nagaland, Mizoram, Srikakulam, and, more recently, Chhattisgarh—when the sovereignty of the state was in crisis.⁹⁸ A few of the formal "Rural Welfare Centres" were, however, eventually provided with proper infrastructure and have remained occupied ever since. For example, Ashoknagar, located on the road between Narsampet and Pakhal Lake in Warangal District, has evolved into a town indistinguishable from others in Telangana, excepting the precise grid layout of certain neighborhoods. Monuments on the town's main road testify to the tradition of revolutionary communism and gesture to its origins in violent conflict.

Although most of the camps were ultimately abandoned, they were products of ideological and discursive frameworks that have had a lasting legacy in the decades since 1950. Most obviously, "rehabilitation colonies" and their equivalents have become a common feature of tribal development efforts throughout India. In 1974, the Andhra Pradesh Legislature went as far as recommending that the entire "tribal population in the State should be grouped in small numbers and colonization schemes implemented."⁹⁹ Indeed, since the early 1970s, government-led tribal development efforts in Andhra Pradesh were geared toward combating Maoist insurrection. In 1975, the AP government reported that vast increases in government expenditure on tribal development were "due to the unrest created by extremist elements in the tribal areas of the State and the consequent necessity for stepping up of tribal welfare activities with a positive growth oriented approach."¹⁰⁰ The "Scheme for Rehabilitation of Podu Cultivators," initiated by the Tribal Welfare Department in 1984, had, as its stated goal, "to wean the tribals from the influence of extremists" by settling them in villages and "providing housing, water supply, link roads, education and medical facilities."[101] India's postcolonial regime of sovereignty linked together development and security, especially at the internal frontiers of the state.

The idea of tribals as both victims and threats has remained a preoccupation of development planners since 1950. A 1988 evaluation of previous tribal development efforts in Andhra Pradesh noted, for example, that tribals remained both "open to exploitative force and prone to the potentially dangerous winds of extremism."[102] Colonial ideas of racial determinism also persisted long after 1947. As late as the mid-1980s, the Tribal Welfare Department was conducting anthropometric studies of tribal groups in Andhra Pradesh.[103] The 1976 "Plan for Development of Chenchus" described the Chenchus of Mahbubnagar district as having "criminal propensities" and as suffering from an inherited "recidivism" that could be solved only through a "scheme of re-socialisation involving preventive, reformative and productive measures." The first step in such a scheme was to build a police post in a Chenchu village.[104] There are clear echoes here of Special Commissioner Nanjappa's 1951 order that if the Chenchu "has to be taught and his habits of living and mental outlook have to be changed, he should be made to get mixed up with other classes."[105]

Tribal development was cast in terms of civilizational progress and the potential of Adivasis to be fully modern and productive members of the nation. One Tribal Welfare Department report noted that the "majority of the Chenchus inhabiting the project area continue to be in the lowest and primeval stage of development."[106] The government campaign against *podu* (shifting or slash-and-burn horticulture) was launched not only because it was "unremunerative for the tribals" but also because it was a "national loss."[107] Traditional Adivasi lifestyles, in other words, were a hindrance to national progress. The 1975 "Sub Plan for the Tribal Areas of Andhra Pradesh," for example, argued that it was "imperative to divert the man power in tribal areas to occupations mainly industrial labour, livestock rearing and dairying, mining, processing of forest and agricultural produce and certain traditional crafts."[108] Accordingly, the department sponsored an "Action Plan for Industrialisation of Tribal Areas in Warangal District," prepared by the Andhra Pradesh state subsidiary of the Industrial

Development Bank of India. The expansion of mining, in particular, was seen as the best way of "absorbing them as unskilled, semi-skilled and skilled labourers."[109] The displacement of Adivasis from their lands and their transformation into wage laborers in modern industries was an object of tribal development.

By the mid-1980s, officials in Andhra Pradesh began to reckon with the adverse impact of state-led tribal development efforts and the continued efforts by Adivasis to resist enclosure and assimilation. A 1984 report details that after a "large number of tribal settlements were submerged by reservoirs" and hydroelectric projects, the "displaced tribal families without any alternative source of livelihood have started migrating to the interior forest areas," where they resumed traditional practices of shifting cultivation. Moreover, with "the process of industrialisation and urbanization making strong inroads, the tribals had perceived a threat to their culture... They have decided to shift to interior areas."[110] A 1988 review noted that an "analysis of developmental programmes over the last three decades and the present tribal predicament reveals a skewed pattern of development" that further impoverished and alienated tribal communities. Yet, officials concluded, "In view of the special nature of the area marked by a sense of isolation, alienation and deprivation and the potential danger of being drawn into the vortex of extremism there is an imperative need to intensify the ongoing programmes."[111] Failed development programs needed to be intensified not because they provided desirable outcomes for Adivasis but because they furthered the security interests of the state.

Much, of course, has changed in the decades since 1950–51, and I do not wish to simplify a much more complex history of Adivasis in postcolonial India. Yet the tribal camps of Telangana were illustrative of wider ideological paradigms and institutional regimes of power. They were created in exceptional circumstances, but in this case the exception tells us something about the norm. The camps speak to the retrofitting of the colonial ethnographic state into the postcolonial developmental state, the uneven forms of state territoriality at India's internal frontiers, official anxieties regarding Adivasis as subversive subjects, ongoing ambiguities about the contested place of tribals as citizens of the nation, and the way in which violence has mediated relations between state and society in order to constitute the political domain. In this sense, the tribal camps of Telangana were foundational to various interconnected trajectories of democracy and sovereignty in postcolonial India.

EPILOGUE
From Raj to Republic, 1946–52

> It is always a rather dangerous thing to uproot deep historical
> and cultural forces. Or rather, it may not be difficult, but it is very
> difficult to replace them by something constructive and substantial.
> Nehru to Patel, October 19, 1950.
>
> Everything considered, it was nothing short of a revolution.
> Patel to Nehru, October 26, 1950.[1]

THIS BOOK has offered an account of the transformation of the British Raj into the Republic of India. This transformation entailed a radical reconstruction of India as a political space, a transformation that arose out of a multidimensional and highly contingent historical event. This book has narrated these developments as a story of sovereignty and democracy. It has traced the emergence of a new state formation and body politic out of a subcontinental and multicentric event of violence. An imperial regime of sovereignty with an uncodified constitution was reforged into a national regime of sovereignty with a republican constitution. I emphasize the importance of the Indian states to developments in the decades leading up to 1946 and the contested nature of the republican revolution from that time. Hyderabad, in this respect, was much more than a mere road bump in the Indian nation's tryst with destiny. It was a story about law and sovereignty, kingship and constituent power, majorities and minorities, and violence and territory at a foundational moment for modern India.

As an imperial space was refashioned into an international one, constitutional change was accompanied by a dramatic spatial reordering of the subcontinent. By connecting the Punjab to Hyderabad and Telangana, this book links processes of border making to internal territorializing processes. "These two things have gone on together," Nehru noted to the Constituent Assembly in early 1948, "a process of cutting away and a process of integration." The princely states were a factor in the grim calculations that resulted in the Partition, which, in turn, determined the subsequent fate of the princely states. "We see the sweep of history suddenly coming," Nehru declared, "the big broom of history, and changing this 130 years' old structure and putting something else in its place." Future historians, he predicted, "will no doubt consider this integration of the States into India as one of the dominant phases of India's history."[2] The distillation of the Raj's uncodified, fragmented, and plural regime of sovereignty into a new national sovereign formation with a republican constitution was the crucial phase of India's "integrative moment."[3] The crisis of the late 1940s as an event of violence was both destructive and productive, disintegrative and integrative. This process was grounded in a dialectic between constituting and constituted power, as a nationalist movement claiming to represent the *demos* occupied the Indian state and sought to endow governmental authority with democratic legitimacy.

In tracing these constitutional and territorial lineaments, this book has explored how a new sovereign formation and political community arose out of a subcontinental event of violence. The historical arrival of "the people" as the proper subject of the political was, as Shruti Kapila argues, founded in violence.[4] This process was neither uniform nor inevitable, and I have attended to the historically contingent ways in which violence was enacted, dispersed, absorbed, and routinized. Violence was both state making and people making. This book has connected processes of refugee evacuation, relief, and rehabilitation in Punjab to a diffusion and mobilization of violence in and around Hyderabad, and to counterinsurgency and tribal development in Telangana. I have sought to illuminate a contingent and conjunctural history of sovereignty at a foundational moment, while emphasizing the contested rather than the consensual dimensions of democratic transformations in India.

The Partition has come to be understood by many as constitutive and foundational, yet Hyderabad and Telangana, while not exactly obscure, have been largely relegated to the footnotes of most narratives of this period. Democratic ideas and practices in India developed within a context in which sovereign kingship was a central organizing principle of political life. Discourses of popular sovereignty and political demands for a constituent assembly—the basic ingredients of Indian republicanism—emerged directly out of debates over the legitimacy and future of kingship in India. By highlighting the centrality of Hyderabad and the princely states to interwar visions of an Indian federation, I emphasize the extent of the departure that occurred from 1947: postcolonial modalities of federalism developed along completely different lines. Hyderabad's bid for independence raised important questions relating to international and constitutional law, challenged nationalist projects of territorial sovereignty, and tested the potential for non-national and non-republican futures in the subcontinent.

The revolution in Telangana, which began as a struggle against the colonial feudalism of the Nizam's dominions, developed into a site of extraordinary political contestation at the very moment of independence. As the meaning and substance of freedom were negotiated in these crucial initial years, two competing democratic projects—one statist and liberal, the other revolutionary and socialist—proposed radically divergent ideas of the *demos*, sovereign subjectivity, and the future itself. Both projects spoke of revolution. India needed and wanted to bring about a revolution, but what type of revolution would it be? The communist leadership from Andhra named China as India's analogue and future: Telangana was the spark of a revolutionary blaze that would radiate throughout the subcontinent.

China also featured prominently in Nehru's contemplations on the nature of historical change and the right path for India. He felt a deep affinity for China as an ancient civilization and peasant society ravaged by imperialism that would, through great struggle, join India in reclaiming Asia's centrality to world history. During his wartime imprisonment, Nehru expressed envy of China's "mass experience" and a desire for an event in India that would provide for rupture, rebirth, and an animating energy for India's march into the future.[5] India's mass experience of the late 1940s, for Nehru, did indeed mark a new beginning. "The past is over," he declared in his tryst-with-destiny speech, "and it is the future that beckons to us now." Yet these ruptures also reminded Nehru of the destructive potentiality of politics, the mercilessness of the forces of history at work, and the futility of revolutionary violence. "It is absurd to imagine," he wrote of India's communists, "that out of conflict the social progressive forces are bound to win." This was especially true of India, he noted, because of its "inherent disruptive character."[6] For Vallabhbhai Patel, China was a warning rather than an exemplar. Yet he too spoke of an Indian revolution when referring to the popular violence in Hyderabad that destroyed the ancien régime and founded a new democratic state. In his desire to "wash away" the past and his belief in the unleashing of popular violence as a means of securing the primacy of the state, however, Patel's conception of the political shared affinities with Mao.

The Congress-controlled Constituent Assembly, who claimed to speak in the name of "We, the People," certainly conceived of its task in revolutionary terms. They were constituting India into something entirely new: a sovereign democratic republic committed to the universal principles of liberty, equality, and fraternity. The violent events examined in this book were part of a subcontinent event of political transformation: India was constituted anew as a political community and body politic. Independence, Partition, and the founding of the Republic marked a moment in time, an event of departure, that we continue to understand in terms of the before and the after.

To the revolutionary trinity of liberty, equality, and fraternity, the Constitution's preamble added justice—social, economic, and political. The "seamless web" created by the Indian Constitution sought to protect national unity, establish the institutions of democracy, and foster the "social revolution."[7] The political revolution was an event, and thus immediate and transcendent, while the social revolution was conceived as aspirational and as a process unfolding over time. The postcolonial trajectory of democracy in India would be one of gradual deepening rather than a revolutionary reconstitution of state and society.⁸ The social revolution emanated from the project of state sovereignty, which was seen as the necessary prerequisite for a nonviolent democratic life that was largely institutionalized and reproducible over time.⁹

From 1946, the Indian National Congress set about eliminating, subduing, and incorporating its rivals. For the Congress, sovereignty of the state was paramount, and they did not shy away from wielding state power against challenges to their government and party hegemony. This was the basis of the consensus between the duumvirate of Nehru and Patel: the Indian nation-state must first be made sovereign in order to be made democratic. Power must be built up before it could be redistributed. Nehru and Patel conceived this project as fully in line with a Gandhian ethos: only a sovereign state could serve as a means of nonviolent democratic competition and could bring about the social revolution without terror. Gandhian mass politics was thus a means to the founding of an institutional political life. The postcolonial state's dual inheritance as the successor to the British colonial state and as the instrument of Indian nationalism gave birth to the "simultaneous power of democracy and bureaucracy" in postcolonial India.¹⁰

In Telangana, the arbitrary and excessive exercise of sovereign violence provided for the emergence of a new liberal democratic order out of a revolutionary situation. The CPI was co-opted into electoral politics, the land question was subordinated to the legislative process, class struggle was linked to state-led economic development, and the Indian state's claim to embody "the people" was validated. The "passive revolution" was contingent upon the reanimation of colonial traditions of bureaucratic authoritarianism under a new regime of national sovereignty. India's liberal democracy was grafted onto an authoritarian state, creating a "disjuncture" between the "promise of the constitution" and the "functioning of India's administrative apparatus."¹¹ Indeed, because it acted in the name of the nation, the postcolonial Indian state was authorized to intervene in Indian society in unprecedented and hugely consequential ways. At the same time, the state's authoritarian tendencies and capacity for violence were also given new authorization and impetus after 1947. The subsequent development, accelerating with astonishing rapidity in recent years, of Indian democracy's majoritarian and illiberal dimensions, represents the metastasizing of certain congenital features of the Indian Republic described in this book.

The violent events of 1946–52 facilitated the conversion of long-standing contradictions into a settled institutional order. Out of this closing of the event, multiple trajectories of Indian democracy emerged. By 1952, mass displacement in Punjab had given way to refugee relief and rehabilitation and the resumption of a normative social and political life. The Indian states were integrated and dissolved into the Indian Union. The insurrection in Telangana had been exhausted, and revolutionary politics were pushed to India's margins or converted into parliamentarism. India's first general election was an unprecedented exercise in universal franchise. The Republic was founded, a new body politic formed, and a new regime of sovereignty and citizenship constituted. This book ultimately makes no claim to offer a comprehensive history of the complex conjunctures of midcentury India. My intention has been to tell three stories that are multifaceted and important in their own right, but that, read together, shed light on this highly consequential moment in world history.

ABBREVIATIONS USED IN NOTES

AISPC Papers	All India States Peoples' Conference Papers
CWMG	*Collected Works of Mahatma Gandhi*, e-book, 98 vols. (New Delhi: Publications Division, Government of India, 1999), www.gandhi-ashramsevagram.org/gandhi-literature/collected-works-of-mahatma-gandhi-volume-1-to-98.php
EPLA	East Punjab Liaison Agency
IOR	India Office Records, British Library, London
MoS	Ministry of States
NAI	National Archives of India, New Delhi
NMML	Nehru Memorial Museum and Library, New Delhi
PSA	Punjab State Archives, Chandigarh
SWJN-1	*Selected Works of Jawaharlal Nehru (First Series)*, ed. S. Gopal, 15 vols. (New Delhi: Jawaharlal Nehru Memorial Fund, 1972–82)
SWJN-2	*Selected Works of Jawaharlal Nehru (Second Series)*, ed. S. Gopal, 71 vols. (New Delhi: Jawaharlal Nehru Memorial Fund, 1984–2017)
TCRTI	Tribal Cultural Research and Training Institute Library, Hyderabad

NOTES

Introduction

1. William H. Sewell Jr., *Logics of History: Social Theory and Social Transformation* (Chicago: University of Chicago Press, 2005).

2. Brighupati Singh, *Poverty and the Quest for Life: Spiritual and Material Striving in Rural India* (Chicago: University of Chicago Press, 2015).

3. Thomas Blom Hansen and Finn Stepputat, eds., *Sovereign Bodies: Citizens, Migrants, and States in the Postcolonial World* (Princeton, NJ: Princeton University Press, 2005), 3. See also Thomas Blom Hansen and Finn Stepputat, eds., *States of Imagination: Ethnographic Explorations of the Postcolonial State* (Durham, NC: Duke University Press, 2001).

4. James Sheehan, "The Problem of Sovereignty in European History," *American Historical Review* 111, no. 1 (2006): 4; Natasha Wheatley, "The Mandate System as a Style of Reasoning: International Jurisdiction and the Parceling of Imperial Sovereignty in Petitions from Palestine," in *The Routledge Handbook of the History of the Middle East Mandates*, ed. Cyrus Schayegh and Andrew Arsan (London: Routledge, 2015), 106–22; Salhia Belmessous, ed., *Native Claims: Indigenous Law against Empire, 1500–1920* (New York: Oxford University Press, 2012); Aradhana Sharma and Akhil Gupta, eds., *The Anthropology of the State: A Reader* (Malden, MA: Blackwell, 2006); Jonathan Spencer, *Anthropology, Politics, and the State: Democracy and Violence in South Asia* (Cambridge: Cambridge University Press, 2007); Veena Das and Deborah Poole, eds., *Anthropology in the Margins of the State* (Santa Fe, NM: School of American Research Press, 2004).

5. Shruti Kapila, *Violent Fraternity: Global Political Thought in the Indian Age* (Princeton, NJ: Princeton University Press, forthcoming), "A History of Violence," *Modern Intellectual History* 7, no. 2 (2010): 437–57, and "Global Intellectual History and the Indian Political," in *Rethinking Modern European Intellectual History for the Twenty-First Century*, ed. Samuel Moyn and Darrin McMahon (New York: Oxford University Press, 2013), 425–63.

6. Madhav Khosla, *India's Founding Moment: The Constitution of a Most Surprising Democracy* (Cambridge, MA: Harvard University Press, 2020).

7. Eric Beverley, *Hyderabad, British India, and the World: Muslim Networks and Minor Sovereignty, c. 1850–1950* (Cambridge: Cambridge University Press, 2015); Michael Fisher, *Indirect Rule in India: Residents and the Residency System, 1764–1858* (Delhi: Oxford University Press, 1991); Sudipta Sen, "Unfinished Conquest: Residual Sovereignty and the Legal Foundations of the British Empire in India," *Law, Culture and the Humanities* 9, no. 2 (2012): 227–42; Kavita Saraswathi Datla, *The Language of Secular Islam: Urdu Nationalism*

and Colonial India (Honolulu: University of Hawai'i Press, 2013); Stephen Legg, "Dyarchy: Democracy, Autocracy, and the Scalar Sovereignty of Interwar India," *Comparative Studies of South Asia, Africa and the Middle East* 36, no. 1 (2016): 44–65; Manu Bhagavan, *Sovereign Spheres: Princes, Education and Empire in Colonial India* (New Delhi: Oxford University Press, 2003); Janaki Nair, *Mysore Modern: Rethinking the Region under Princely Rule* (Minneapolis: University of Minnesota Press, 2012); Julie E. Hughes, *Animal Kingdoms: Hunting, the Environment and Power in the Indian Princely States* (Cambridge, MA: Harvard University Press, 2013); Taylor Sherman, *Muslim Belonging in Secular India: Negotiating Citizenship in Postcolonial Hyderabad* (Cambridge: Cambridge University Press, 2015); Sarath Pillai, "Fragmenting the Nation: Divisible Sovereignty and Travancore's Quest for Federal Independence," *Law and History Review* 34, no. 3 (2016): 743–82; Yaqoob Khan Bangash, *A Princely Affair: The Accession and Integration of the Princely States of Pakistan, 1947–1955* (Karachi: Oxford University Press, 2015); Barbara Ramusack, *The Indian Princes and Their States* (Cambridge: Cambridge University Press, 2004); Ian Copland, Aya Ikegame, and Andrea Major, eds., "Princely Spaces and Domestic Voices: New Perspectives on the Indian Princely States," special issue, *Indian Economic and Social History Review* 46, no. 3 (2009); Aya Ikegame, *Princely India Re-imagined: A Historical Anthropology of Mysore from 1799 to the Present* (London: Routledge, 2012); Waltraud Ernst and Biswamoy Pati, eds., *India's Princely States: People, Princes and Colonialism* (London: Routledge, 2007); Milinda Banerjee, *The Mortal God: Imagining the Sovereign in Colonial India* (Cambridge: Cambridge University Press, 2018).

8. Lauren Benton, *A Search for Sovereignty: Law and Geography in European Empires, 1400–1900* (Cambridge: Cambridge University Press, 2010); Frederick Cooper, *Citizenship between Empire and Nation: Remaking France and French Africa, 1945–1960* (Princeton, NJ: Princeton University Press, 2014); Susan Pederson, *The Guardians: The League of Nations and the Crisis of Empire* (Oxford: Oxford University Press, 2015); Mark Mazower, *No Enchanted Palace: The End of Empire and the Ideological Origins of the United Nations* (Princeton, NJ: Princeton University Press, 2013); Antony Anghie, *Imperialism, Sovereignty and the Making of International Law* (Cambridge: Cambridge University Press, 2004); Natasha Wheatley, "Spectral Legal Personality in Interwar International Law: On New Ways of Not Being a State," *Law and History Review* 35, no. 3 (2017): 753–87, and "Mandatory Interpretation: Legal Hermeneutics and the New International Order in Arab and Jewish Petitions to the League of Nations," *Past and Present* 227 (2015): 205–48; Durba Ghosh and Dane Kennedy, eds., *Decentering Empire: Britain, India and the Transcolonial World* (New Delhi: Orient Longman, 2006); Manu Bhagavan, *India and the Quest for One World: The Peacemakers* (New York: Palgrave Macmillan, 2013); Stephen Legg, "An International Anomaly? Sovereignty, the League of Nations and India's Princely Geographies," *Journal of Historical Geography* 43 (2014): 96–110.

9. Karuna Mantena and Rama Sundari Mantena, "Political Imaginaries at the End of Empire," *Ab Imperio* 3 (2018): 31–35; Rama Sundari Mantena, "Anticolonialism and Federation in Colonial India," *Ab Imperio* 3 (2018): 36–62; Kavita Saraswathi Datla, "Sovereignty and the End of Empire: The Transition to Independence in Colonial Hyderabad," *Ab Imperio* 3 (2018): 63–88.

10. Faisal Devji, *Muslim Zion: Pakistan as a Political Idea* (Cambridge, MA: Harvard University Press, 2013); Manu Goswami, "Imaginary Futures and Colonial Internationalisms," *American Historical Review* 117, no. 5 (2012): 1461–85; Karuna Mantena, "Popular Sovereignty and Anti-colonialism," in *Popular Sovereignty in Historical Perspective*, ed. Richard Bourke and Quentin Skinner (Cambridge: Cambridge University Press, 2016), 297–319.

11. Jawaharlal Nehru, "Aims and Objects of the Constituent Assembly," December 13, 1946, in *SWJN-2*, vol. 1.

12. Veena Das, *Critical Events: An Anthropological Perspective on Contemporary India* (Delhi: Oxford University Press, 1996); Urvashi Butalia, *The Other Side of Silence: Voices from the Partition of India* (New Delhi: Penguin Books India, 1998); Ritu Menon and Kamla Bhasin, *Borders and Boundaries: Women in India's Partition* (Delhi: Kali for Women, 1998).

13. Uditi Sen, *Citizen Refugee: Forging the Indian Nation after Pakistan* (Cambridge: Cambridge University Press, 2018); Niraja Gopal Jayal, *Citizenship and Its Discontents: An Indian History* (Cambridge, MA: Harvard University Press, 2013); Anupama Roy, *Mapping Citizenship in India* (New Delhi: Oxford University Press, 2010); Vazira Fazila-Yacoobali Zamindar, *The Long Partition and the Making of Modern South Asia: Refugees, Boundaries, Histories* (New York: Columbia University Press, 2007); Joya Chatterji, *The Spoils of Partition: Bengal and India, 1947–1967* (Cambridge: Cambridge University Press, 2007); Willem Van Schendel and Mahbubar Rahman, "'I Am Not a Refugee': Rethinking Partition Migration," *Modern Asian Studies* 37, no. 3 (2003): 551–84; Haimanti Roy, *Partitioned Lives: Migrants, Refugees, Citizens in India and Pakistan, 1947–1965* (New York: Oxford University Press, 2012).

14. Ritu Menon, "Birth of Social Security Commitments: What Happened in the West," in *Refugees and the State: Practices of Asylum and Care in India, 1947–2000*, ed. Ranbir Samaddar (New Delhi: Manas Publications, 2003), 152–81.

15. Urvashi Butalia, ed., *Partition: The Long Shadow* (Delhi: Zubaan, 2015); Jisha Menon, *The Performance of Nationalism: India, Pakistan, and the Memory of Partition* (Cambridge: Cambridge University Press, 2013); Suvir Kaul, ed., *The Partitions of Memory: The Afterlife of the Division of India* (Delhi: Permanent Black, 2001); Ananya Jahanara Kabir, *Partition's Post-amnesias* (Dhaka: University Press, 2014); Ayesha Jalal, *The Pity of Partition: Manto's Life, Times and Work across the India-Pakistan Divide* (Princeton, NJ: Princeton University Press, 2013).

16. Veena Das, *Life and Words: Violence and the Descent into the Ordinary* (Berkeley: University of California Press, 2007); Gyanendra Pandey, *Remembering Partition: Violence, Nationalism and History in India* (Cambridge: Cambridge University Press, 2004) and "The Prose of Otherness," in *Subaltern Studies VIII*, ed. David Arnold and David Hardiman (Delhi: Oxford University Press, 1994), 188–221.

17. Yasmin Khan, *India at War: The Subcontinent and the Second World War* (Oxford: Oxford University Press, 2015); Sumit Sarkar, "Popular Movements and National Leadership, 1945–47," *Economic and Political Weekly* 17, nos. 14/16 (1982): 677–89; Leela Gandhi, *The Common Cause: Postcolonial Ethics and the Practice of Democracy, 1900–1955* (Chicago: University of Chicago Press, 2014); Shalini Sharma, "'Yeh Azaadi Jhooti Hai!':

The Shaping of the Opposition in the First Year of the Congress Raj," *Modern Asian Studies* 48, no. 5 (2014): 1358–88; Anirudh Deshpande, *Hope and Despair: Mutiny, Rebellion and Death in India, 1946* (Delhi: Primus Books, 2016); Kunal Chattopadhyay, "India, Post-World War II Upsurge," in *The International Encyclopedia of Revolution and Protest*, ed. Immanuel Ness (Malden, MA: Wiley-Blackwell, 2009).

18. Hamza Alavi, "Peasants and Revolution," *Socialist Register* 2 (1965): 268.

19. Sujit Choudhry, Madhav Khosla, and Pratap Bhanu Mehta, eds., *The Oxford Handbook of the Indian Constitution* (New Delhi: Oxford University Press, 2016); Udit Bhatia, ed., *The Indian Constituent Assembly: Deliberations on Democracy* (New York: Routledge, 2017); Rajeev Bhargava, ed., *Politics and Ethics of the Indian Constitution* (New Delhi: Oxford University Press, 2008); Ananya Vajpeyi, ed., "We the People: A Symposium on the Constitution of India after 60 Years, 1950–2010," *Seminar*, no. 615 (November 2010), www.india-seminar.com/2010/615.htm.

20. Partha Chatterjee, *Nationalist Thought and the Colonial World: A Derivative Discourse* (London: Zed Books, 1986); Sudipta Kaviraj, "A Critique of the Passive Revolution," *Economic and Political Weekly* 23, nos. 45/47 (1988): 2429–44, *The Trajectories of the Indian State: Politics and Ideas* (Ranikhet: Permanent Black, 2010), and *The Imaginary Institution of India: Politics and Ideas* (New York: Columbia University Press, 2010). See also Barrington Moore, *Social Origins of Dictatorship and Democracy: Lord and Peasant in the Making of the Modern World* (Boston: Beacon Press, 1966).

21. Ranajit Guha, "On Some Aspects of the Historiography of Colonial India," in *Subaltern Studies I: Writings on South Asian History and Society*, ed. Ranajit Guha (Delhi: Oxford University Press, 1982), 1–8.

22. Sunil Khilnani, *The Idea of India* (New York: Farrar, Straus, Giroux, 1999). See also Gyanesh Kudaisya, *A Republic in the Making: India in the 1950s* (Oxford: Oxford University Press, 2018), and Srinath Raghavan, *War and Peace in Modern India* (New York: Palgrave Macmillan, 2010).

23. Putchalapalli Sundarayya, *An Autobiography*, ed. and abr. Atlury Murali (Delhi: National Book Trust, 2009), 221.

24. On Indian liberalism, see C. A. Bayly, *Recovering Liberties: Indian Thought in the Age of Liberalism and Empire* (Cambridge: Cambridge University Press, 2011). See also Ranajit Guha, *Dominance without Hegemony: History and Power in Colonial India* (Cambridge, MA: Harvard University Press, 1997), and Khilnani, *Idea of India*. On revolutionaries in late colonial India, see Chris Moffat, *India's Revolutionary Inheritance: Politics and the Promise of Bhagat Singh* (Cambridge: Cambridge University Press, 2019); J. Daniel Elam, Kama Maclean, and Chris Moffat, eds., "Writing Revolution: Practice, History, Politics in Modern South Asia," *South Asia: Journal of South Asian Studies* 39, no. 3 (2016): 513–694; Kama Maclean, *A Revolutionary History of Interwar India: Violence, Image, Voice and Text* (New York: Oxford University Press, 2015); Maia Ramnath, *Haj to Utopia: How the Ghadar Movement Charted Global Radicalism and Attempted to Overthrow the British Empire* (Berkeley: University of California Press, 2011).

25. Rohit De, *A People's Constitution: The Everyday Life of Law in the Indian Republic* (Princeton, NJ: Princeton University Press, 2018); Benjamin Siegel, *Hungry Nation: Food,*

Famine, and the Making of Modern India (Cambridge: Cambridge University Press, 2018); Ornit Shani, *How India Became Democratic: Citizenship and the Making of the Universal Franchise* (Cambridge: Cambridge University Press, 2018).

26. Sumit Sarkar, "Indian Democracy: The Historical Inheritance," in *The Success of India's Democracy*, ed. Atul Kohli (Cambridge: Cambridge University Press, 2001), 34.

Chapter One

1. Nizam's *firman*, June 11, 1947, file no. 68, pt. II, AISPC Papers, NMML.

2. Government of Hyderabad, *Census of India, 1941*, vol. 21, H.E.H. the Nizam's Dominions (Hyderabad State), Part I Report (Hyderabad: Government Central Press, 1945), 1.

3. B. R. Ambedkar, statement, June 17, 1947, in *Documents and Speeches on the Indian Princely States*, ed. Adrian Sever, vol. 2 (New Delhi: B. R. Publishing, 1985), 628–34.

4. Nehru to Sheikh Abdullah, October 10, 1947, in *Nehru-Patel: Agreement within Differences. Select Documents and Correspondences, 1933–1950*, ed. Neerja Singh (New Delhi: National Book Trust, 2010), 142.

5. Speech at Panthic Conference, Patiala, October 22, 1947, in Vallabhbhai Patel, *For a United India: Speeches of Sardar Patel, 1947–1950* (New Delhi: Publications Division, Ministry of Information and Broadcasting, 1967), 11. In an October 30, 1948, speech in Bombay, Patel said, "The price of partition was worth paying for. *We suffered grievously as a result of partition. A limb was torn asunder and we bled profusely.* But it was nothing as compared to the troubles that would have been in store for us and with which we would have had to put up. I have, therefore, no regrets for accepting partition." In Vallabhbhai Patel, *Sardar Patel: In Tune with the Millions*, Birth Centenary ed., vol. 2, ed. G. M. Nadurkar (Ahmedabad: Sardar Vallabhbhai Patel Smarak Bhavan, 1975), 36–37.

6. Speech at Junagadh, November 13, 1947, in V. Patel, *For a United India*, 55–56.

7. Sumathi Ramaswamy, "Maps and Mother Goddesses in Modern India," *Imago Mundi* 53 (2001): 97–114.

8. Reginald Coupland, *The Future of India* (Oxford: Oxford University Press, 1943), 151–53.

9. V. P. Menon, *The Story of the Integration of the Indian States* (Calcutta, 1956), 373. The August 23, 1948, letter sent to Hyderabad made this clear: "The Government of India regards the differences between it and Hyderabad as a purely domestic issue and cannot admit that Hyderabad, considering its historic as well as its present position in relation to India, has any right in international law to seek the intervention of the United Nations or any other outside body for a settlement of the issue." *Manchester Guardian*, August 30, 1948. In a November 13, 1947, speech at Junagadh days after the state's accession, Patel stated, "The problem of Hyderabad is the affair of India and India alone." V. Patel, *For a United India*, 11.

10. Clyde Eagleton, "The Case of Hyderabad before the Security Council," *American Journal of International Law* 44, no. 2 (1950): 277–302.

11. September 13, 1948. In Maniben Patel, *Inside Story of Sardar Patel, The Diary of Maniben Patel: 1936–50*, ed. P. N. Chopra and P. Chopra (Delhi: Vision Books, 2001), 210.

12. Nizam's *firman*, June 11, 1947.

13. Indian Independence Act, sec. 2.

14. Indian Independence Act, sec. 7.

15. V. Menon, *Story of the Integration*, 95. Menon was constitutional adviser to Mountbatten before his appointment as secretary of the Ministry of States from July 1947. He was a key figure in the negotiations that brought the Indian states into the Indian Union.

16. "Memorandum on the Case of Hyderabad," in Hyderabad Delegation to the United Nations, *The Hyderabad Question before the United Nations (Documents and Other Materials)* (Karachi: Civil and Military Gazette, 1951), 16.

17. "Discussion in the Security Council, 16 September 1948," in Hyderabad Delegation, *Hyderabad Question*, 62.

18. Hyderabad Delegation, *Hyderabad Question*.

19. Beverley, *Hyderabad*, 5.

20. Emphasis in original. Fisher, *Indirect Rule*.

21. E. W. R. Lumby, "British Policy toward the Indian States, 1940–7," in *The Partition of India: Policies and Perspectives, 1935–1947*, ed. C. H. Philips and Mary Doreen Wainwright (Cambridge, MA: MIT Press, 1970), 95–103.

22. Edwin Montagu, *Report on Indian Constitutional Reforms* (London: HMSO, 1918), 242.

23. Ramusack, *Indian Princes*, 51–52, 255.

24. Gurmukh Nihal Singh, *Indian States and British India: Their Future Relations* (Benares: Nand Kishore and Bros., 1930), 347.

25. S. Sen, "Unfinished Conquest," 228.

26. Benton, *Search for Sovereignty*, 250.

27. Beverley, *Hyderabad*, 64.

28. Ibid., 65.

29. Karen Leonard, "Palmer and Company: An Indian Banking Firm in Hyderabad State," *Modern Asian Studies* 47, no. 4 (2013): 1159–60.

30. Standing Committee of the Chamber of Princes, *The British Crown and the Indian States: An Outline Sketch Presented to the Indian States Committee* (London: P. S. King, 1929), 25; Beverley, *Hyderabad*, 66.

31. Kavita Datla, "The Origins of Indirect Rule in India: Hyderabad and the British Imperial Order," *Law and History Review* 33, no. 2 (2015): 332.

32. Bernard Cohn, "Representing Authority in Victorian India," in *The Invention of Tradition*, ed. Eric Hobsbawm and Terence Ranger (Cambridge: Cambridge University Press, 1983), 165–210.

33. Dhananjay Keer, *Mahatma Jotirao Phooley: Father of Indian Social Revolution* (Mumbai: Popular Prakashan, 2002), 78.

34. Ibid.

35. Hastings Fraser, *Our Faithful Ally, the Nizam* (London: Smith, Elder, 1865).

36. Quoted in S. M. Mitra, *Indian Problems* (London: John Murray, 1908), 340–42.

37. Harcourt Butler, Sidney Peel, and W. S. Holdsworth, *Report of the Indian States Committee, 1928–1929* (London: HMSO, 1929), 20.

38. Datla, "Origins of Indirect Rule."
39. C. A. Bayly, *Indian Society and the Making of the British Empire* (Cambridge: Cambridge University Press, 1988).
40. Edward Thompson, *The Making of the Indian Princes* (London: Oxford University Press, 1943).
41. Taraknath Das, "The Status of Hyderabad during and after British Rule in India," *American Journal of International Law* 43, no. 1 (1949): 59–60.
42. Eric Beverley, "Frontier as Resource: Law, Crime, and Sovereignty on the Margins of Empire," *Comparative Studies in Society and History* 55, no. 2 (2013): 241–72.
43. Datla, "Origins of Indirect Rule."
44. V. K. Bawa, *The Nizam between Mughals and British: Hyderabad under Salar Jang I* (New Delhi: S. Chand, 1986), chap. 5.
45. Ibid., 153–65.
46. Ibid., 162–63.
47. Ibid., 168.
48. K. R. R. Sastry, *Indian States* (Allahabad: Kitabistan, 1941), 176–77.
49. Bawa, *Nizam between Mughals*, 172.
50. Erez Manela, *The Wilsonian Moment: Self-Determination and the International Origins of Anticolonial Nationalism* (Oxford: Oxford University Press, 2007).
51. Montagu, *Report*, 5.
52. Ibid., 249.
53. Ibid., 244.
54. Ibid., 243–44.
55. Ibid., 240.
56. John Simon et al., *Report of the Indian Statutory Commission* 1 (Calcutta: Central Publication Branch, 1930), 1:89.
57. Butler, Peel, and Holdsworth, *Report*, 5.
58. V. K. Bawa, *The Last Nizam: The Life and Times of Mir Osman Ali Khan* (New Delhi: Viking Penguin India, 1992).
59. MSS EUR F137/35, IOR.
60. Gandhi to Nizam, March 5, 1924, in *CWMG*, 27:33.
61. Reading to Nizam, March 27, 1926, MSS EUR F137/35, IOR.
62. Ibid.
63. Bawa, *Last Nizam*, 116, 129.
64. Standing Committee, *British Crown*, 140.
65. Ibid.
66. Butler, Peel, and Holdsworth, *Report*, 31.
67. Ibid., 13.
68. Ibid., 29.
69. Ibid., 23.
70. Ibid., 23.
71. Ibid., 31–32.

72. I borrow the term *veto* from R. J. Moore but differ on the origins; see his "The Making of India's Paper Federation, 1927–35," in *The Partition of India*, ed. C. H. Philips and M. D. Wainwright (London: Allen and Unwin, 1970), 62.

73. Arthur Berriedale Keith, *A Constitutional History of India, 1600–1935*, 2nd ed. (1937; repr., Allahabad: Central Book Depot, 1961), 451.

74. Simon et al., *Report*, 2:13.

75. Ibid., 2:197.

76. Ibid., 2:12.

77. Ian Copland, *The Princes of India in the Endgame of Empire, 1917–1947* (Cambridge: Cambridge University Press, 1997), chap. 3; Ramusack, *Indian Princes*, chap. 8.

78. Copland, *Princes of India*, 91.

79. *The Government of India Act, 1935*, pt. 3, chap. 1 (New Delhi, 1936).

80. Copland, *Princes of India*, 131–32.

81. N. Gangulee, *The Making of Federal India* (London: Nisbet, 1936), 258.

82. Shafa'at Ahmad Khan, *The Indian Federation: An Exposition and Critical Review* (London: Macmillan, 1937), 183.

83. October 27, 1936, letter, in Government of Hyderabad, *Census of India, 1941*, 21:2.

84. Keith, *Constitutional History*, 320.

85. Copland, *Princes of India*, chap. 5.

86. Muhammad Iqbal, "Iqbal's Presidential Address Delivered at the Annual Session of the All-India Muslim League at Allahabad on the 29th December, 1930," in *Iqbal, Jinnah, and Pakistan: The Vision and the Reality*, ed. C. M. Naim (Syracuse, NY: Syracuse University Press, 1979), 199.

87. Ayesha Jalal, *The Sole Spokesman: Jinnah, the Muslim League and the Demand for Pakistan* (Lahore: Sang-e-Meel Publications, 1999), 20.

88. Ian Copland, "The Princely States, the Muslim League, and the Partition of India in 1947," *International History Review* 13, no. 1 (February 1991): 48.

89. B. R. Ambedkar, *Federation versus Freedom* (Poona Gokhale Institute of Politics and Economics, 1939), www.ambedkar.org/ambcd/08.%20Federation%20vs%20Freedom.htm.

90. Ibid.

91. Ibid.

92. Ian Copland, "Congress Paternalism: The 'High Command' and the Struggle for Freedom in Princely India, c. 1920–1940," *South Asia* 1–2, no. 8 (1985): 121–40.

93. Barbara Ramusack, "Congress and the People's Movement in Princely India: Ambivalence in Strategy and Organization," in *Congress and Indian Nationalism, The Pre-Independence Phase*, ed. Richard Sisson and Stanley Wolpert (Berkeley: University of California Press, 1988).

94. *SWJN-1*, 8:761n2.

95. Presidential Address, December 29, 1929, in *SWJN-1*, 4:192.

96. *SWJN-1*, 4:193.

97. Granville Austin, *Working a Democratic Constitution: The Indian Experience* (New Delhi: Oxford University Press, 1999), 70–71.

98. The resolution adopted on the Indian states at the Haripura session of the Congress in February 1938 committed the Congress to working for *purna swaraj* for the entirety of India while upholding the policy of not directly organizing struggles in the states. Indian National Congress, *Report of the 51st Indian National Congress* (Ahmedabad, 1938), 206–8.

99. Presidential Address, December 27, 1936, in *SWJN-1*, 7:605.

100. Ibid., 606.

101. Ibid., 606–8.

102. R. Moore, "Making of India's Paper Federation," 82.

103. Gurmukh Nihal Singh, "Constitutional Reforms in Indian States: A Comparative Study," *Indian Journal of Political Science* 3, no. 1 (1941): 90.

104. *Harijan*, February 4, 1939, in *CWMG*, 75:1–3.

105. Ibid.

106. Statement to the press, February 7, 1939, in *SWJN-1*, 9:414.

107. Speech at Allahabad, February 9, 1939, in *SWJN-1*, 9:415.

108. Speech at subjects committee meeting, February 18, 1938, in *SWJN-1*, 8:762.

109. Presidential Address at the All India States Peoples' Conference, February 15, 1939, in *SWJN-1*, 9418.

110. Ibid., 420.

111. Ibid., 421.

112. Ibid., 427.

113. Ibid., 429.

114. Maurice Gwyer and A. Appadorai, *Speeches and Documents on the Indian Constitution, 1921–47*, 2 vols. (Bombay: Oxford University Press, 1957), 1:267.

115. *SWJN-1*, 7:605.

116. For the multidimensional nature of Indian politics, see Devji, *Muslim Zion*, chap. 5.

117. Aga Khan to Fazl-i-Husain, n.d., cited in Azim Husain, *Fazl-i-Husain, a Political Biography* (Bombay: Longmans Green, 1946), 300–301.

118. Bayly, *Recovering Liberties*, 323–25.

119. Rama Mantena, "Publicity, Civil Liberties and Political Life in Princely Hyderabad," *Modern Asian Studies* 53, no. 4 (2019): 1248–77.

120. Nair, *Mysore Modern*.

121. Datla, *Language of Secular Islam*.

122. Ibid., 10.

123. Nile Green, "The Trans-border Traffic of Afghan Modernism: Afghanistan and the Indian 'Urdusphere,'" *Comparative Studies in Society and History* 53, no. 3 (2011): 479–508; Kavita Saraswathi Datla, "Worldly Vernacular: Urdu at Osmania University," *Modern Asian Studies* 43, no. 5 (2009): 1117–48.

124. Beverley, *Hyderabad*, chaps. 7 and 8.

125. Ibid., 6–7.

126. See, for example, the pamphlet *Hyderabad State, A Souvenir* (by Ghulam Yasdani), originally published in 1922 on the occasion of the Prince of Wales' visit to Hyderabad

and rereleased in 1938 in connection with Viceroy Linlithgow's visit. See also *The Economic Life of Hyderabad* (Hyderabad: Government Central Press, 1937).

127. St. Nihal Singh, *The Nizam and the British Empire* (n.p.: Nihal Singh, 1923).

128. Hyderabad Labour Ministry, *Hyderabad (Deccan)* (Hyderabad, 1947), 37.

129. Ibid.

130. Ibid., v.

131. Ibid., vi.

132. M. Hanumanth Rao et al., *Constitutional Reforms in Hyderabad: A Report* (Hyderabad: Hyderabad People's Convention, 1938), 5.

133. Benjamin B. Cohen, *Kingship and Colonialism in India's Deccan: 1850–1948* (New York: Palgrave Macmillan, 2007).

134. Ibid., 157–68.

135. Karen Leonard, "Hyderabad: The Mulki–Non-Mulki Conflict," in *People, Princes and Paramount Power: Society and Politics in the Indian Princely States*, ed. Robin Jeffrey (Oxford, 1978), 65–106.

136. Ibid., 87–88.

137. Syed Abid Hasan, *Whither Hyderabad?* (Hyderabad, 1935).

138. R. Mantena, "Publicity."

139. Ibid.

140. Lord Irwin, *Indian Problems* (London: Allen and Unwin, 1932), 174–75.

141. Speech by Gandhiji at the second plenary meeting of the second session of the Indian Round Table Conference, November 30, 1931, in Gwyer and Appadorai, *Speeches and Documents*, 236.

142. Bawa, *Last Nizam*, 91–92.

143. H. K. Sherwani, "The Evolution of the Legislature in Hyderabad," *Indian Journal of Political Science* 1, no. 4 (1940): 429–30.

144. Nizam to Reading, October 25, 1923, Digital Repository of Gokhale Institute of Politics and Economics, http://dspace.gipe.ac.in/xmlui/handle/10973/21660.

145. S. Aravamudu Aiyangar et al., *Report of the Reforms Committee 1938 1347F* (Hyderabad: Government Central Pressa, 1938), v–vi.

146. Ibid., 7–8.

147. Ibid., 8.

148. The exception was the petty western Indian state of Aundh, whose ruler established a remarkable democratic federation of villages. G. Singh, "Constitutional Reforms," 90–107.

149. Aiyangar et al., *Report*.

150. M. Venkatarangaiya, "The Reformed Constitution of the Hyderabad State," *Indian Journal of Political Science* 3, no. 1 (1941): 29.

151. Nizam's June 11, 1947, *firman*, file no. 68, pt. II, AISPC Papers, NMML; B. R. Ambedkar, *Pakistan, or the Partition of India* (Bombay: Thackers, 1945).

152. Ian Copland, "'Communalism' in Princely India: The Case of Hyderabad, 1930–1940," *Modern Asian Studies* 22, no. 4 (1998): 783–814. See also Lucien Benichou, *From*

Autocracy to Integration: Political Developments in Hyderabad State, 1938–48 (Hyderabad: Orient Longman, 2000), 8–29.

153. M. A. Moid and A. Suneetha, "Rethinking Majlis' Politics: Pre-1948 Muslim Concerns in Hyderabad State," *Indian Economic and Social History Review* 55, no. 1 (2018): 33.

154. H. Sherwani, "Evolution," 431.

155. Emphasis added. Ibid., 432.

156. Ambedkar, *Pakistan*, chap. 8.

157. Venkatarangaiya, "Reformed Constitution," 39.

158. Ambedkar, *Pakistan*, chap. 8.

159. Moid and Suneetha, "Rethinking Majlis' Politics."

160. He was bestowed his title after reducing the Nizam to tears with his oratory at a meeting in 1930. Benichou, *From Autocracy to Integration*, 92.

161. Rasheeduddin Khan, "Muslim Leadership and Electoral Politics in Hyderabad: A Pattern of Minority Articulation—I," *Economic and Political Weekly* 6, no. 15 (1971): 787.

162. Moid and Suneetha, "Rethinking Majlis' Politics," 33.

163. Ibid., 44–45.

164. *Ana'l-malik* could be translated as "I am king" or "We are rulers."

165. Benichou, *From Autocracy to Integration*, 108–9.

166. Moid and Suneetha, "Rethinking Majlis' Politics," 45–46.

167. Benichou, *From Autocracy to Integration*, 99.

168. Ibid., 163.

169. Nizam's June 11, 1947 *firman*, file no. 68, pt. II, AISPC Papers, NMML.

170. Copland, "'Communalism'"; Dick Kooiman, *Communalism and Indian Princely States: Travancore, Baroda and Hyderabad in the 1930s* (New Delhi: Manohar, 2002).

171. Sudhir Kakar, *The Colors of Violence: Cultural Identities, Religion, and Conflict* (Chicago: University of Chicago Press, 1996); Ashutosh Varshney, *Ethnic Conflict and Civic Life: Hindus and Muslims in India* (New Haven, CT: Yale University Press, 2002).

172. Beverley, *Hyderabad*, chap. 3.

173. Ibid., chap. 4.

174. Server ul-Mulk, *My Life: Being the Autobiography of Nawab Server-ul-Mulk Bahadur*, trans. Nawab Jiwan Yar Jung Bahadur (London, 1903), 230. Amir al Mu'minin can be translated as "Commander of the Faithful" or "Leader of the Faithful."

175. Syed Vali Reza Nasr, *Vanguard of the Islamic Revolution: The Jama'at-I Islami of Pakistan* (Berkeley: University of California Press, 1994), 225.

176. J. P. Slight, "The British Empire and the Hajj, 1865–1956" (PhD diss., University of Cambridge, 2011), 98–107.

177. David Lelyveld, *Aligarh's First Generation: Muslim Solidarity in British India* (Princeton, NJ: Princeton University Press, 1978), 141, 184.

178. Green, "Trans-border Traffic"; Datla, "Worldly Vernacular" and *Language of Secular Islam*.

179. Faisal Devji, "Britain's Muslim Empire and Its Indian Future," *Seminar*, no. 601

(September 2009), www.indiaseminar.com/2009/601/601_faisal_devji.htm. See also Syed Ahmed Khan, *An Account of the Loyal Mahomedans of India* (London, 1860).

180. Beverley, *Muslim Modern*, 95.

181. W. W. Hunter, *The Indian Mussulmans: Are They Bound in Conscience to Rebel against the Queen?* (London: Trübner, 1871).

182. Margrit Pernau-Reifeld, "Reaping the Whirlwind: Nizam and the Khilafat Movement," *Economic and Political Weekly* 34, no. 38 (1999): 2746–47.

183. Beverley, *Hyderabad*, 130; M. A. Sherif, "Pickthall's Islamic Politics," in *Marmaduke Pickthall: Islam and the Modern World*, ed. Geoffrey Nash (Boston: Leiden, 2017), 106–36.

184. Bawa, *Last Nizam*.

185. Devji, "Britain's Muslim Empire."

186. Jalal, *Sole Spokesman*, 52.

187. Ibid., 152.

188. Choudhry Rahmat Ali, *The Millat and the Mission* (Cambridge: Pakistan National Movement, 1944), 5, and *Osmanistan: The Fatherland of the Osman Nation* (Cambridge: Osmanistan National Movement, 1946).

189. Syed Abdul Latif, *The Muslim Problem in India: Together with an Alternative Constitution for India* (Bombay: Times of India, 1939). See also Nawab Dr. Nazir Yar Jung, ed., *The Pakistan Issue* (Lahore: M. Ashraf, 1943).

190. M. Rafique Afzal, ed., *The Case for Pakistan* (Islamabad: National Commission on Historical and Cultural Research, 1979), xvii.

191. Rajendra Prasad, *India Divided* (Bombay, 1947), 194–99.

192. "A Punjabi" [pseud.], *Confederacy of India* (Lahore: Nawab Sir Muhammad Shah Nawaz Khan, 1939).

193. Ibid., 14.

194. Afzal, *Case for Pakistan*, xvii.

195. Syed Zafarul Hasan and Muhammad Afzal Husain Qadri, *The Problem of Indian Muslims and Its Solution* (Aligarh: Aligarh Muslim University Press, 1939).

196. R. Prasad, *India Divided*, 183.

197. Ayesha Jalal, *Self and Sovereignty: Individual and Community in South Asian Islam since 1850* (Delhi: Oxford University Press, 2001), 412.

198. Haroon to President, All-India Muslim League, February 11, 1941, in Yar Jung, *Pakistan Issue*, 73–80.

199. Ibid.

200. Ibid.

201. Copland, "Princely States."

202. M. Patel, *Inside Story*, 210.

203. Devji, *Muslim Zion*, 103.

204. Copland, *Princes of India*, 255.

205. R. J. Moore, "India in 1947: The Limits of Unity," in *The States of South Asia: Problems of National Integration*, ed. A. Jeyaratnam Wilson and Dennis Dalton (London: Hurst, 1982), 45–76.

206. "Cripps' Proposals," in *A Guide to Constituent Assembly*, ed. Moti Ram (Delhi, 1947), 179–81.

207. Yaqoob Khan Bangash, "Betrayal of Trust: Princely States of India and the Transfer of Power," *South Asia Research* 26, no. 2 (2006): 185.

208. Resolution of the Congress Working Committee, April 2, 1942, in Moti Ram, *Guide to Constituent Assembly*, 182.

209. Ibid., 182.

210. Jawaharlal Nehru, *The Discovery of India* (London: Meridian, 1960), 464.

211. Ibid., 465–66.

212. Swami Ramananda Tirtha, *Memoirs of Hyderabad Freedom Struggle* (Bombay: Popular Prakashan, 1967), 133.

213. Archibald Percival Wavell, *Wavell: the Viceroy's Journal*, ed. Penderel Moon (London: Oxford University Press, 1973), 120.

214. Copland, *Princes of India*, 234.

215. Sketch of a Possible Proposal, December 17, 1945, Papers of Walter Turner Monckton, Dep. Monckton Trustees 26, Balliol College, Oxford.

216. Note by Constitutional Advisor, December 21, 1945, Papers of Walter Turner Monckton, Dep. Monckton Trustees 26.

217. Viceroy's Broadcast, June 14, 1945, in Moti Ram, *Guide to Constituent Assembly*, 193.

218. Statement by the Cabinet Delegation and the Viceroy, May 16, 1946, in Moti Ram, *Guide to Constituent Assembly*, 16.

219. Ibid.

220. Mission's Memorandum on States' Future Position, May 22, 1946, in Moti Ram, *Guide to Constituent Assembly*, 71.

221. D. R. Gadgil, *The Federal Problem in India* (Poona: Gokhale Institute of Politics and Economics, 1947), 61, 178–79.

222. Nizam to Lothian, May 6, 1946, R/1/4913, IOR.

223. See V. P. Menon's account of Cabinet Mission's interview with Hyderabad's *diwan*, the *nawab* of Chhatari, in *Story of the Integration*, 63–64.

224. Memorandum for the consideration of the Executive Council of HEH the Nizam of Hyderabad, February 1946, Papers of Walter Turner Monckton.

226. Nehru to Mountbatten, April 9, 1947, R/1/1/4628, IOR.

227. Nehru, "Aims and Objects," in *SWJN-2*, vol. 1.

228. The Second Resolution passed by the All-India Muslim League Council meeting at Bombay on July 29, 1946, commonly known as the "Direct Action" resolution, R/3/1/35, IOR. See also Jinnah's statement on the Cabinet Mission Plan published in *Dawn* on May 22, 1946, in *Pakistan Resolution to Pakistan, 1940–1947: A Selection of Documents Presenting the Case for Pakistan*, ed. Latif Ahmed Sherwani (Karachi: National Publishing House, 1969), 118–21.

229. Ibid.

230. D. V. Tahmankar, *Sardar Patel* (London: Allen and Unwin, 1970), 209.

231. R. J. Moore, *Escape from Empire: The Attlee Government and the Indian Problem* (Oxford: Clarendon Press, 1983), 295–96.

232. Nehru to Mountbatten, May 11, 1947, ff. 234–40, L/P&J/10/79, IOR.

233. Ibid.

234. R. J. Moore, "India in 1947" and "Mountbatten, India, and the Commonwealth," *Journal of Commonwealth and Comparative Politics* 19, no. 1 (1981): 5–43.

235. For policy on refusing international status to states, see Listowel to Attlee, July 9, 1947, in *The Transfer of Power, 1942–7*, ed. Nicholas Mansergh (London: HMSO, 1983), 12:39–42.

236. Copland, *Princes of India*, 255.

237. Minutes of All India Congress Meeting, June 14, 1947, in *Partition of India*, vol. 6 of *The Making of India and Pakistan, Select Documents*, ed. S. R. Bakshi (New Delhi: Deep and Deep, 1997), 90.

238. Bakshi, *Partition of India*, 97.

239. C. Rajagopalachari to Stafford Cripps, June 8, 1947, in R. Moore, *Escape from Empire*, 299.

240. Speech at the All India Congress Committee meeting, June 15, 1947, in *SWJN-2*, 3:217–20.

241. Maulana Abul Kalam Azad, *India Wins Freedom: The Complete Version* (1959; repr., Madras: Orient Longman, 1988), 204.

242. "By the partition India had lost an area of 364,737 square miles and a population of 81? millions. By the integration of the States, we brought in an area of nearly 500,000 square miles with a population of 86? millions (not including Jammu and Kashmir)." V. Menon, *Story of the Integration*, 490.

243. Speech at Calcutta, January 3, 1948, in V. Patel, *For a United India*, 132.

244. Speech at Shillong, January 2, 1948, in V. Patel, *For a United India*, 132, 134–42.

245. August 11, 1947, in V. Patel, *For a United India*, 126.

246. The six states were Hyderabad, Mysore, Bhopal, Tripura, Manipur, and Cooch-Behar. In December 1947, the states of the Eastern and Chhattisgarh political agencies were integrated into Orissa. The following month the states of the Kathiawar peninsula were united into the single unit of Saurashtra. This was followed by the merging of the smaller states of the Deccan and Gujarat into Bombay Province and the merger of the Punjab hill states into the centrally administered Himachal Pradesh. Indore, Gwalior, and around twenty smaller states were combined in April 1948 into the Union of Madhya Bharat. The states of Rajputana were similarly incorporated into Rajasthan, the Punjab states into PEPSU, and Baroda into Bombay Province. Copland, *Princes of India*, 262–63.

247. Ashutosh Varshney, "How Has Indian Federalism Done?," in *Battles Half Won: India's Improbable Democracy* (New Delhi: Penguin, 2013), 169–203; Harshan Kumarasingham, *A Political Legacy of the British Empire: Power and the Parliamentary System in Post-colonial India and Sri Lanka* (London: Tauris, 2013), especially chap. 4; Jyotirindra Dasgupta, "India's Federal Design and Multicultural National Construction," in *The Success of India's Democracy*, ed. Atul Kohli (Cambridge: Cambridge University Press, 2001), 49–77; Louise Tillin, *Remapping India: New States and Their Political Origins* (London: Oxford University Press, 2013) and "India's Democracy at 70: The Federalist Compromise," *Journal of Democracy* 28, no. 3 (2017): 64–75.

248. For the Instrument of Accession, see Menon to Patrick, August 2, 1947, in Mansergh, *Transfer of Power*, 12:467–73.
249. V. Menon, *Story of the Integration*.
250. Statement of Policy Governing the Princely States, New Delhi, July 5, 1947, in V. Patel, *For a United India*, 3–5.
251. Ibid., 5.
252. Ibid., 4.
253. V. Menon, *Story of the Integration,* 108.
254. Address by Rear-Admiral Viscount Mountbatten of Burma to a Conference of the Rulers and Representatives of Indian States, July 25, 1947, in Mansergh, *Transfer of Power*, 12:348.
255. Ibid., 351.
256. Menon to Abell, July 1947, in Mansergh, *Transfer of Power*, 12:275.
257. Mountbatten, July 25, 1947, in Mansergh, *Transfer of Power*, 12:350.
258. Ibid., 350.
259. Ibid., 351.
260. Bangash, "Betrayal of Trust."
261. Bhopal to Mountbatten, July 22, 1947, in Mansergh, *Transfer of Power*, 12:293.
262. Nizam to Mountbatten, July 9, 1947, in Mansergh, *Transfer of Power*, 12:31.
263. Ibid., 31–32.
264. Nizam to Mountbatten, August 8, 1947, in Mansergh, *Transfer of Power*, 12:575–78.
265. Mountbatten meeting with Hyderabad Delegation, July 11, 1947, in Mansergh, *Transfer of Power*, 12:82.
266. Gandhi interview with Mountbatten, July 9, 1947, in Mansergh, *Transfer of Power*, 51.
267. Nizam to Mountbatten, August 8, 1947, in Mansergh, *Transfer of Power*, 12:578.
268. Nizam to Jinnah, August 2, 1947, in Mohamad Ali Jinnah, *Quaid-i-Azam Mohammad Ali Jinnah Papers*, vol. 9, *The States: Hyderabad, Jammu and Kashmir*, ed. Z. H. Zaidi, (Islamabad: Quaid-i-Azam Papers Project, National Archives of Pakistan, 2003), 158.
269. Ibid., 161.
270. Nizam to Mountbatten, August 8, 1947, in Mansergh, *Transfer of Power*, 12:575.
271. Nizam to Mountbatten, August 8, 1947, in Mansergh, *Transfer of Power*, 12:575–76.
272. Minutes of Viceroy Meeting with Hyderabad Delegation, July 11, 1947, in Mansergh, *Transfer of Power*, 12:87.
273. Notes of Meeting of Viceroy with Chhatari and Monckton, August 3, 1947, in Mansergh, *Transfer of Power*, 12:497.
274. Mountbatten's Record of Interview with Nehru, Patel and Kripalani, June 10, 1947, in *SWJN-2*, 3:221.
275. Nizam to Jinnah, July 15, 1947, in Mohammad Ali Jinnah, *Quaid-i-Azam Mohammad Ali Jinnah Papers*, vol. 3, *On the Threshold of Pakistan, 1 July–25 July 1947*, ed. Z. H.

Zaidi (Islamabad: Quaid-i-Azam Papers Project, National Archives of Pakistan, 1996), 415.

276. June 18, 1947, Statement, in Jinnah, *Quaid-i-Azam Mohammad Ali Jinnah Papers*, 9:ix.

277. Interview between Mountbatten and Jinnah, July 12, 1947, in Mansergh, *Transfer of Power*, 12:121.

278. Nizam to Jinnah, July 28, 1947, in Mohammad Ali Jinnah, *Quaid-i-Azam Mohammad Ali Jinnah Papers*, vol. 4, *Pakistan at Last, 26 July–14 August 1947*, ed. Z. H. Zaidi (Islamabad: Quaid-i-Azam Papers Project, National Archives of Pakistan, 1999), 42.

279. Ibid., 44.

280. Note by Nawab Ali Yavar Jung about Interview with M. A. Jinnah, August 4, 1947, in Jinnah, *Quaid-i-Azam Mohammad Ali Jinnah Papers*, 4:196A.

281. Ibid., 196.

282. V. Menon, *Story of the Integration*, 334–35.

283. Raghavan, *War and Peace*.

284. Syed Ahmed El Edroos and L. R. Naik, *Hyderabad of "The Seven Loaves"* (Hyderabad: Laser Prints, 1994), 135.

285. Press Note Issued by the Government of Pakistan, June 1, 1948, in Mohammad Ali Jinnah, *Selected Speeches and Statements of the Quaid-i-Azam Mohammad Ali Jinnah (1911–34 and 1947–48)*, ed. M. Rafique Afzal (Lahore: Research Society of Pakistan, University of the Punjab, 1966), 465.

286. Ibid.

287. *New York Times*, September 10, 1948.

288. In a June 29, 1948, speech at Dehra Dun, Sardar Patel approved of Attlee's position: "I am glad to know that His Majesty's Government have not fallen a prey to these machinations of Mr. Churchill and his henchmen and have refused to treat the Hyderabad issue otherwise than as one of domestic concern of the Indian Dominion." V. Patel, *For a United India*, 181.

289. Churchill cited in *Manchester Guardian*, July 31, 1948.

290. Intelligence report dated August 3, 1948, file no. LVI/15/23–G, pt. I, PSA.

291. Eagleton, "Case of Hyderabad"; Clyde Eagleton, "Hyderabad as UN Issue," letter to *New York Times*, May 15, 1949.

292. T. Das, "Status of Hyderabad."

293. Copland, *Princes of India*, 262–63.

Chapter Two

1. S. N. Prasad, *Operation Polo: The Police Action against Hyderabad, 1948* (New Delhi: Historical Section, Ministry of Defence, 1972).

2. A British intelligence report from March 1948 put the total strength of the Hyderabad Army at twenty-four thousand, but only five thousand "fully equipped" troops, without tanks or aircraft. "The Hyderabad army commander, Major-General El Edroos . . . said that . . . India . . . 'can walk into Hyderabad whenever she wants to.'" Benichou, *From Autocracy to Integration*, 229.

3. The official casualty statistics were, for the Razakars, 1,373 killed, 42 wounded, and 1,911 captured, and for the Hyderabad Army, 807 killed, 64 wounded, and 1,647 captured; an additional 43 Hyderabadi combatants were killed. On the Indian side, only 10 were killed. Benichou, *From Autocracy to Integration*, 243.

4. El Edroos and Naik, *Hyderabad of "The Seven Loaves,"* 140.

5. Mir Laik Ali, *Tragedy of Hyderabad* (Karachi: Pakistan Co-operative Book Society, 1962).

6. V. Menon, *Story of the Integration*, 380.

7. A. G. Noorani, *The Destruction of Hyderabad* (Delhi: Tulika Books, 2013), 286.

8. Ibid., 286.

9. Note on Hyderabad, August 1951, file no. 16(3)-H/51, MoS, NAI.

10. Noorani, *Destruction of Hyderabad*, 287–89.

11. Hyderabad Delegation, *Hyderabad Question*, 65.

12. Ibid.

13. Ibid., 68.

14. September 13, 1948, cited in M. Patel, *Inside Story*, 210.

15. Nehru to Ministers, September 17, 1948, in *SWJN-2*, 7:252.

16. Swami Ramananda Tirtha, *Indian National Congress: Fifty-Eight Session* (Hyderabad, 1953), 2.

17. V. Menon, *Story of the Integration*, 378.

18. *Times of India*, September 18, 1948.

19. Emphasis added. Speech commemorating Gandhi's birthday, October 2, 1948, in *SWJN-2*, 7:143.

20. "Standing Threat to India," *Manchester Guardian*, August 11, 1948.

21. Arjun Appadurai, *Fear of Small Numbers: An Essay on the Geography of Anger* (Durham, NC: Duke University Press, 2006).

22. K. L. Gauba, *Hyderabad or India* (Delhi: Rajkamal Publications, 1948), 146–47.

23. Ian Talbot, "A Tale of Two Cities: The Aftermath of Partition for Lahore and Amritsar, 1947–1957," *Modern Asian Studies* 41, no. 1 (2007): 179.

24. The newspaper *Inqilab*, it appears, was the first to make claims of widespread violence on September 24, 1948. The following day *Zamindar* claimed that "such atrocities are being committed on Deccan Muslims as would melt the heart of the most callous. Aurangabad is totally destroyed. . . . It is a city of the dead." Both *Safeena* and *Imrooz* published Zafrullah Khan's comments that the United Nations observers should be sent to Hyderabad on September 29. *Maghrabi Pakistan* made claims of "atrocities" on October 9. The same day *Jung* wrote of wholesale massacres in Hyderabad that made the events in East Punjab and Delhi pale in significance. On October 17 *Ehsan* published letters said to be received from Hyderabad and claimed that "Muslims are being butchered 'en bloc.'" Translations from Urdu from Press Bureau Reports, LVI/15/23–G, pt. I, PSA.

25. "Note to the Ministry of States," November 14, 1948, in *SWJN-2*, 8:103.

26. "Note to Ministry of States," November 26, 1948, in *SWJN-2*, 8:106–7.

27. Azad to Nehru, November 23, 1948, file no. 1(11)-H/48, MoS, NAI; Bawa, *Last Nizam*, 288.

28. November 29, 1948, diary entry, in M. Patel, *Inside Story*, 234.
29. Omar Khalidi, ed., *Hyderabad: After the Fall* (Wichita, KS: Hyderabad Historical Society, 1988), 95.
30. A. G. Noorani, "Of a Massacre Untold," *Frontline* magazine (Chennai), March 3–16, 2001.
31. "Communal Frenzy in Hyderabad, 1948. Reports of the Goodwill Mission Which Visited Hyderabad to Find Out the Damages Done in Hyderabad Owing to the Communal Frenzy and the Possible Remedies for Overriding Future Outbreaks," Pandit Sunder Lal Papers, 2, NMML. See also Noorani, *Destruction of Hyderabad*, 361–75.
32. "Communal Frenzy."
33. K. M. Panikkar, *The Foundations of New India* (London: Allen and Unwin, 1963), 150.
34. Patel to Nehru, October 26, 1950, file no. 1(44)-H/50, MoS, NAI.
35. File nos. 260-H/48 and 5(5)-H/50, 1(15)-H/49, 19(12)-H/50, 6(17)-H/51, 1(44)-H/50, MoS, NAI.
36. Patel to K. M. Abdul Gaffar, January 4, 1949, in Vallabhbhai Patel, *Sardar's Letters: Mostly Unknown*, ed. G. M. Nandurkar (Ahmedabad: Sardar Vallabhbhai Patel Smarak Bhavan, 1981), 3:69–70.
37. Military Governor J. N. Chaudhuri to V. P. Menon, Secretary, Ministry of States, December 21, 1948, file no. 12(6)-H/49, MoS, NAI.
38. Chaudhuri to Ministry of States, "A Report on Certain Aspects of the Situation in Hyderabad as on 19 Nov 48," file no. 1(11)-H/48, MoS, NAI.
39. Nehru to Patel, October 19, 1950, file no. 1(44)-H/50, MoS, NAI.
40. "Note on the Situation in Hyderabad State," Central Intelligence Officer, Madras, forwarded to Ministry of States by B. N. Mullick, Deputy Director, Intelligence Bureau, October 20, 1948, file no. 260–H/48, MoS, NAI.
41. Government of Hyderabad, *Hyderabad Reborn: First Six Months of Freedom (September 18, 1948–March 17, 1949)* (Hyderabad: Government of Hyderabad, 1949), 30.
42. This number, however, was a fixed government quota and not representative of the total number of widows in Hyderabad. Nagendra Bahadur, Home Secretary, Government of Hyderabad, to S. Narayanaswamy, January 4, 1952, file no. 17(1)-H/52, MoS, NAI.
43. "Communal Frenzy."
44. Gyanendra Pandey, *The Construction of Communalism in Colonial North India* (New Delhi: Oxford University Press, 1990); Taylor Sherman, "Moral Economies of Violence in Hyderabad State, 1948," *Deccan Studies* 8, no. 2 (2010): 65–90.
45. Nagendra Bahadur, Revenue Department Circular, n.d., file no. 1(71)-H/49, MoS, NAI.
46. D. S. Bakhle, Chief Civil Administrator, Government of Hyderabad, November 28, 1948, file no. 112–H/48, vol. 1, MoS, NAI.
47. "A Report on Certain Aspects of the Situation in Hyderabad as on 19 Nov 48," file no. 1(11)-H/48, MoS, NAI.
48. Nehru to Dr. Paul Ruegger, International Red Cross, Geneva, July 30, 1949, file no. 1(15)-H/49, MoS, NAI.

49. Vellodi, June 16, 1949, file no. 1(50)-H/49, MoS, NAI.
50. N. M. Buch, Ministry of States, October 8, 1948, file no. 327-H/48, MoS, NAI.
51. Chaudhuri to Ministry of States, June 17, 1949, file no. 1(50)-H/49, MoS, NAI. At the time of the amnesty, the "number of cases arising out of retaliation of Police action" was 875, including 114 murders and involving 3,031 accused.
52. Patel to Nehru, June 5, 1949, in Vallabhbhai Patel, *Sardar Patel's Correspondence, 1945–50*, ed. Durga Das (Ahmedabad: Navajivan Publishing House, 1973), 7:321.
53. D. S. Bakhle to V. P. Menon, October 3, 1948, file no. 327-H/48, MoS, NAI.
54. Chaudhuri to States Ministry, May 31, 1949, file no. 1(50)-H/49, MoS, NAI.
55. Government of Hyderabad, *Hyderabad Reborn*.
56. S. Prasad, *Operation Polo*, 37.
57. Government of Hyderabad, *Hyderabad Reborn*, 101.
58. Ibid., 106.
59. Ibid., 107.
60. "Communal Frenzy."
61. Government of Hyderabad, *Hyderabad Reborn*, 119–20.
62. "Complaints against the Workers of the Hyderabad State Congress and Certain Officials of the State Administration," file no. 1(61)-H/49, MoS, NAI.
63. "Confidential Report of the Rehabilitation Committee Appointed by the Government of Hyderabad," file no. 17(1)-H/52, MoS, NAI.
64. Rahman to Nehru, January 9, 1950, file no. 1(71)-H/49, MoS, NAI.
65. Government of Hyderabad, *Hyderabad Reborn*, 112.
66. Ibid., 124.
67. Ibid., 128.
68. Rahman to Nehru, January 1, 1950, file no. 1(71)-H/49, MoS, NAI.
69. Puccalapali Sundarayya, *Telengana People's Struggle and Its Lessons* (New Delhi: Foundation Books, 1972), 188–89.
70. Ravi Narayan Reddy, "The Naked Truth about Telengana," March 15, 1951, file 1951/94, Archive of Contemporary History, Jawaharlal Nehru University.
71. Vellodi to Buch, Joint Secretary, Ministry of States, June 13, 1951, file no. 6(17)-H/51, MoS, NAI.
72. Vellodi to S. Narayanaswamy, Deputy Secretary, Ministry of States, February 20, 1950, file no. 1(71)-H/49, MoS, NAI.
73. Fortnightly Report for Second Half of January 1950, L. C. Jain, Chief Secretary, Government of Hyderabad, to Buch, February 20, 1950, file no. 19(12)-H/50, MoS, NAI.
74. See also Bakhle to Patel, November 6, 1948, in V. Patel, *Sardar Patel's Correspondence*, 7:275; Nagendra Bahadur to Ministry of States, January 4, 1952, file no. 17(1)-H/52, MoS, NAI.
75. Ministry of States' telegram to Military Governor, file no. 103-H/48, MoS, NAI.
76. "Communal Frenzy."
77. Chaudhuri to Ministry of States, "A Report on Certain Aspects of the Situation in Hyderabad as on 19 Nov 48," file no. 1(11)-H/48, MoS, NAI.

78. Tirtha to Menon, cited by Chaudhuri to Vellodi, May 31, 1949, file no. 1(50)-H/49, MoS, NAI.

79. Tirtha to Patel, May 10, 1949, file no. 1(50)-H/49, MoS, NAI.

80. M. Narsing Rao et al. to President, Indian National Congress, November 11, 1948, file no. 72, AISPC Papers, NMML.

81. Chaudhuri to Ministry of States, June 17, 1949, file no. 1(50)-H/49, MoS, NAI.

82. "Note on the Situation in Hyderabad State," Central Intelligence Officer, Madras, forwarded to Ministry of States by B. N. Mullick, Deputy Director, Intelligence Bureau, October 20, 1948, file no. 260-H/48, MoS, NAI.

83. *Times of India*, September 30, 1948.

84. Chaudhuri to Ministry of States, June 17, 1949, file no. 1(50)-H/49, MoS, NAI.

85. Mohammed Hyder, *October Coup: A Memoir of the Struggle for Hyderabad* (New Delhi: Lotus Collection, 2012), 79.

86. "Communal Frenzy."

87. Chaudhuri to Vellodi, May 29, 1949, and "Supplementary Note on Visit to Osmanabad," May 29, 1949, file no. 1(61)-H/49, MoS, NAI. See also file no. 1(11)-H/48.

88. Bindu to Nehru, December 21, 1950, and Bindu to Patel, May 21, 1950, both in file no. 1(5)-H/51, MoS, NAI. See also Hyderabad State Congress to President, Indian National Congress, November 11, 1948, file no. 72, AISPC Papers, NMML.

89. Rahman to Nehru, January 1, 1950, file no. 1(71)-H/49, MoS, NAI.

90. "Report of the Rehabilitation Committee Appointed by the Government of Hyderabad," file no. 17(1)-H/52, MoS, NAI.

91. Gail Omvedt, *Dalits and the Democratic Revolution: Dr. Ambedkar and the Dalit Movement in Colonial India* (New Delhi: Sage, 1994), 298.

92. Ibid., 313.

93. "Communal Frenzy."

94. "Note on the Situation in Hyderabad State," Central Intelligence Officer, Madras, forwarded to Ministry of States by B. N. Mullick, Deputy Director, Intelligence Bureau, October 20, 1948, file no. 260-H/48, MoS, NAI.

95. Inner C.C. No. 6, 1949/56, Archive of Contemporary History, Jawaharlal Nehru University, New Delhi.

96. *Zamindar*, *Safeena*, *Ehsan*, and *Mahgrabi Pakistan* all made such claims. Press Intelligence Reports, October 28 and November 6, 1948, file no. LVI/16/23–G, pt. II, EPLA, PSA.

97. Chaudhuri to Vellodi, May 31, 1948, file no. 1(50)-H/49, MoS, NAI.

98. "A Report on Certain Aspects of the Situation in Hyderabad as on 19 Nov 48," file no. 1(11)-H/48, MoS, NAI.

99. Moid and Suneetha, "Rethinking Majlis' Politics"; Benichou, *From Autocracy to Integration*; Margrit Pernau, *The Passing of Patrimonialism: Politics and Political Culture in Hyderabad, 1911–1948* (New Delhi: Manohar, 2000); Bawa, *Last Nizam*; Noorani, *Destruction of Hyderabad*.

100. Vinay Sitapati, *Half-Lion: How P. V. Narasimha Rao Transformed India* (Gurgaon:

Penguin/Viking, 2016), 32. On *Vande Mataram* in Hyderabad, see Datla, *Language of Secular Islam*, chap. 5.

101. Sitapati, *Half-Lion*, 37.

102. Benichou, *From Autocracy to Integration*, chap. 3.

103. Cited in Ian Copland, "'Communalism,'" 803.

104. Copland, "'Communalism,'" 802.

105. International Aryan League, *The Case of Arya Samaj in Hyderabad State* (Delhi: International Aryan League, 1938).

106. P. V. Kate, *Marathwada under the Nizams, 1724–1948* (Delhi: Mittal Publications, 1987), 66–67.

107. Benichou, *From Autocracy to Integration*, 35–37.

108. Copland, "'Communalism,'" 783–814; Kooiman, *Communalism*.

109. Benichou, *From Autocracy to Integration*, 59.

110. Manu Bhagavan, "Princely States and the Hindu Imaginary: Exploring the Cartography of Hindu Nationalism in Colonial India," *Journal of Asian Studies* 67, no. 3 (2008): 881–915.

111. Ibid.

112. Datla, *Language of Secular Islam*, 146.

113. *Times of India*, November 21, 1938.

114. Gopal Godse, *May It Please Your Honour: Statement of Nathuram Godse* (Delhi: Surya-Prakashan, 1989), 135.

115. N. Ramesan, ed., *The Freedom Struggle in Hyderabad*, vol. 4, *1921–1947* (Hyderabad: Government of Andhra Pradesh, 1997), 98. See also T. Uma Joseph, *Accession of Hyderabad: The Inside Story* (Delhi: Sundeep Prakashan, 2006), 134.

116. The Samajists in the border areas were led by "Field Marshal" Swami Swathantra Nandji and Mahatma Narayan Swamiji. Narayan Rao Pawar, a Samajist known as the "Daredevil of Hyderabad," threw a bomb at the Nizam's car but missed his mark and injured five bystanders. Joseph, *Accession*, 127, 131–33, 138.

117. The Mahasabha leader B. S. Moonje was also a leader of the RSS and had been organizing and training Hindu youths in CP and Berar since the early 1920s. As late as 1943, approximately half of the seventy-six thousand members of the RSS lived in CP and Berar. Kanchanmoy Mojumdar, *Saffron versus Green: Communal Politics in the Central Provinces and Berar, 1919–1947* (New Delhi: Manohar, 2003), 102–3, 187.

118. Ibid.

119. Benichou, *From Autocracy to Integration*, 60.

120. Fortnightly Report for Second Half of January, 1950 from Chief Secretary, Government of Hyderabad, to Joint Secretary, file no. 19(12)-H/50, MoS, NAI.

121. Extract from the CIO Nagpur's review of the political situation for the first half of September 1947, file no. 2(5)-PR/47, MoS, NAI.

122. See, for example, the report of the Shankaracharya of Jyotimath, Badrinath, sent to Hyderabad as an emissary of the Hindu Mahasabha in 1939, in Benichou, *From Autocracy to Integration*, 80.

123. "Hindu-Muslim Tension: Its Causes and Cure," in *CWMG*, 28:57–58.

124. Government of India, *White Paper on Hyderabad* (Delhi: Manager of Publications, 1948), 2–3.

125. Ibid., 4.

126. Ibid., 5, 6, 30.

127. Ibid., 6.

128. K. M. Munshi, *Report on the Razakars of Hyderabad* (Hyderabad, 1948), 2.

129. A report dated October 30, 1947, observed that Hindu refugees from Hyderabad generally "said that the Hyderabad State officials did not trouble them in any way. But they are afraid on account of rumours they hear that Hindu subjects might be terrorized later on." Likewise, the Hindus along the Hyderabad border "were feeling panicky on account of rumours filtering owing to the fact that Nizam was making preparations for an attack on the border." Government of CP and Berar to Ministry of States, December 20, 1947, file no. 106–PR/47, MoS, NAI.

130. Munshi, *Report on the Razakars*, 4.

131. Nagendra Bahadur, "A Short Note on the Refugee Problem of Hyderabad," December 1, 1948, file no. 103-H/48, MoS, NAI.

132. The Nizam's government started a Refugee Department to manage the influx of people into the state. At one point, there were 125,000 refugees in eighteen camps being supplied with rations. About 8,000 to 10,000 refugees were given employment in the government, mostly in the police, customs, and excise departments. Others were settled on forest and agricultural lands, in small cottage industries, or in larger industrial projects. Overall, it was estimated that "more than 1 lakh refugees have thus been absorbed in various occupations agricultural and non-agricultural." Ibid.

133. Foreign Ministry to the Ministry of States, October 16, 1947, file no. 2(5)-PR/47, MoS, NAI.

134. Kher to Patel, October 10, 1947, file no. 2(5)-PR/47, MoS, NAI.

135. *Indian Express*, Madras ed., October 4, 1947, file no. 2(5)-PR/47, pt. II, MoS, NAI.

136. Vaidya to Patel, November 24, 1947, file no. 2(5)-PR/47, pt. II, MoS, NAI.

137. Mookerjee to Patel, December 11, 1947, file no. 2(5)-PR/47, pt. II, MoS, NAI.

138. *Hindustan Times*, October 19, 1947, file no. 2(5)-PR/47, pt. II, MoS, NAI.

139. *Times of India*, May 21, 1948. As a result of these suspicions, governments kept a close watch on the movement of Hyderabadi Muslims in the Indian Union and prevented Indian Muslims from moving to Hyderabad. See *Times of India*, June 5, 1948.

140. Interview between Mountbatten and Jinnah, July 12, 1947, in Mansergh, *Transfer of Power*, 12:121.

141. Gyanendra Pandey, "Can a Muslim Be an Indian?" *Comparative Studies in Society and History* 41, no. 4 (1999): 608–29.

142. Speech at a public meeting, Lucknow, January 6, 1948 cited in V. Patel, *For a United India*, 64–70.

143. Diary entry of August 16, 1949, in M. Patel, *Inside Story*, 300–301.

144. *Times of India*, April 22, 1948.

145. Speech at Shillong, January 2, 1948, in V. Patel, *For a United India*, 132, 134–42;

K. M. Munshi, *End of an Era* (Bombay: Bharatiya Vidya Bhavan, 1957), 1. See also Patel, speech, October 30, 1948, in V. Patel, *Sardar Patel: In Tune*, 37.

146. Patel, speech, September 16, 1948, in V. Patel, *Sardar Patel: In Tune*, 115.

147. R. S. Shukla to Patel, July 21, 1947, in S. Patel, *Sardar Patel's Correspondence*, 7:36–37.

148. *New York Times*, September 16, 1948; Taylor C. Sherman, "The Integration of the Princely State of Hyderabad and the Making of the Postcolonial State in India, 1948–1956," *Indian Economic and Social History Review* 44, no. 4 (2007): 489–516.

149. Nagendra Bahadur, "A Short Note on the Refugee Problem of Hyderabad," December 1, 1948, file no. 103-H/48, MoS, NAI; see also Ministry of States Note, October 30, 1948, file no. 226-H/48, MoS, NAI.

150. DM, Krishna District to Chief Secretary, Govt of Madras, September 27, 1947, file no. 2(5)-PR/47, pt. II, MoS, NAI.

151. For example, see *Times of India*, March 22, 1948, and *New York Times*, August 20, 1948.

152. Chaudhuri to Vellodi, May 31, 1949, file no. 1(50)-H/49, MoS, NAI.

153. *Times of India*, January 14, 1948.

154. Government of India, *White Paper on Hyderabad*, 5–6.

155. Raghavan, *War and Peace*, 77–79, 81.

156. Government of India, *White Paper on Hyderabad*.

157. V. Patel, *Sardar Patel's Correspondence*, 7:236–37.

158. Statement in the Constituent Assembly, September 7, 1948, in *SWJN-2*, 7:231.

159. *Times of India*, September 11, 1948.

160. Supplement to Government of India, *White Paper on Hyderabad*, 27.

161. Ibid.

162. In a March 1948 meeting with Mountbatten and the Hyderabad delegation, Patel was reported to have informed the Hyderabadis that if they introduced "fully responsible government" then "all difficulties would certainly be speedily resolved and all bloodshed and sabotage would be stopped." Meeting of the Governor-General with the Hyderabad Delegation (Mir Laik Ali, Nawab Moin Nawaz Jung, Walter Monckton), March 4, 1948, Papers of Walter Turner Monckton, Dep. Monckton Trustees 26, Balliol College, Oxford.

163. Socialist Party Hyderabad Struggle Committee, *The Hyderabad Problem: The Next Step* (Bombay: Hyderabad Struggle Committee, 1948).

164. M. Narsing Rao et al. to President, Indian National Congress, November 11, 1948, file no. 72, AISPC Papers, NMML.

165. Michael Witmer, "The 1947–1948 India-Hyderabad Conflict: Realpolitik and the Formation of the Modern Indian State" (PhD diss., Temple University, 1996), 232.

166. Emphasis added. D. P. Mishra to Patel, June 29, 1947, in V. Patel, *Sardar Patel's Correspondence*, 7:34. Morarji Desai was home minister of the government of Bombay. Swami Ramananda Tirtha was president of the Hyderabad State Congress. Dr. P. Subbarayan was minister for home and police, government of Madras. Gupta was speaker of the CP and Berar Legislative Assembly and president of the International Aryan League (Arya Samaj).

167. Joseph, *Accession*, 131.

168. Tirtha, *Memoirs*, 192.

169. Ibid., 176–77, 196.

170. John Roosa, "Passive Revolution Meets Peasant Revolution: Indian Nationalism and the Telangana Revolt," *Journal of Peasant Studies* 28, no. 4 (2001): 57–94.

171. "List of Camps of the Hyderabad State Congress," n.d. (ca. late 1947 or early 1948). John Roosa kindly provided a copy of this document.

172. "Note by Deputy Inspector General of Police, CID," file no. 2(5)-PR/47, pt. II, MoS, NAI.

173. Roosa, "Passive Revolution," 20. See also, for example, file no. 3(20)-H/48, MoS, NAI.

174. September 5, 1947, report, file no. 2(5)-PR/47, pt. II, MoS, NAI.

175. The Hyderabad State Congress offices in Bombay and Madras issued press releases on a regular basis. While the Razakars were always portrayed as bloodthirsty tyrants, the press releases also glorified the violence of the State Congress "Kisan Dals." See file no. 69, AISPC Papers, NMML.

176. In the pamphlet, the State Congress claimed to have destroyed 182 customs *nakas* (posts), forty-seven police stations, and sixty Razakar centers. Further, they distributed the grain of twenty-three government-owned *godowns* (storehouses), damaged railway lines at thirty-five different places, derailed two train wagons, set two government buses on fire, blew up four bridges, destroyed four government buildings and six railway stations, and exploded five bombs near police stations. They claimed to have killed 42 police officials, 205 constables, 361 Razakars, and 36 "Rohilas & Arabs," for a total of 844, while seventeen "martyrs" were "killed in actions." Moreover, they said they had organized 214 "Village Kisan Dals" and had "liberated" the people of 250 villages by August 1948. Hyderabad State Congress, *Thus Fought Marathwada*, Maharashtra Provincial Office, Bombay, 1948, file no. 337-H/48, MoS, NAI.

177. V. T. Dehejia, Secretary, Home Department, Government of Bombay, to Ministry of States, November 5 and 20, 1947, file no. 111-PR/47, MoS, NAI.

178. Socialist Party's Hyderabad Struggle Committee, *Hyderabad Problem*; V. H. Desai and Pretti Kumar, eds., *The Democrat: Saga of a Jail Journal of Hyderabad Freedom Struggle, 1947–1948* (Mumbai: Bharatiya Vidya Bhavan, 1998). The Special Branch reported in June 1948 that "the Socialist party is dominating for the present all the oppositionists on the borders. All the camps of resisters are busily working and take anti-Hyderabad steps." B. M. Shukul, Assistant I.G. of Police, Special Branch, CP and Berar, June 30, 1948, file no. 3(2)-H/48, MoS, NAI.

179. "Statement on Hyderabad Affairs," Madras, June 12, 1948, in Jayaprakash Narayan, *Selected Works*, ed. B. Prasad, vol. 5 (Delhi: Manohar, 2005), 28.

180. *Times of India*, June 12, 1948.

181. *Times of India*, April 30, 1948.

182. *Times of India*, June 11, 1948.

183. S. M. Jawad Razvi, *Political Awakening in Hyderabad: Role of Youth and Students*

(1938–1956) (Hyderabad: Visalandhra, 1985), 84–85; Raj Bahadur Gour et al., *Glorious Telengana Armed Struggle* (New Delhi: Communist Party of India, 1973), 8.

184. Desai and Kumar, *Democrat*, 147–48.

185. *Times of India*, June 3, 1948.

186. The Ahmadnagar District Magistrate complained that "some persons under the garb of State Congress workers collect grains, money, etc. by use of threat or even by dacoities in the Nizam's territory. All this confirms the goondas in the border villages in our area under the garb of political workers are exploiting the situation created by the activities of the State Congress workers." District Magistrate, Ahmednagar, to Secretary to the Government of Bombay, Home Department, December 29, 1947, file no. 3(20)-H/48, MoS, NAI.

187. Roosa, "Passive Revolution," 75.

188. V. T. Dehejia to Ministry of States, December 5, 1947, file no. 111-PR/47, MoS, NAI.

189. Dehejia to Ministry of States, December 8, 1947, file no. 111-PR/47, MoS, NAI.

190. Laik Ali, *Tragedy of Hyderabad*, 110.

191. See K. M. Munshi, *Akhand Hindustan* (Bombay: New Book Company, 1942).

192. Pernau, *Passing of Patrimonialism*, 331.

193. Manjiri N. Kamat, "Border Incidents, Internal Disorder and the *Nizam's* Claim for an Independent Hyderabad," in Ernst and Pati, *India's Princely States*, 214. See also Kooiman, *Communalism*, 199.

194. Bhagavan, "Princely States," 909.

195. Ibid.

196. Ibid., 910.

197. Ibid.

198. Munshi to Patel, May 21, 1948, in V. Patel, *Sardar Patel's Correspondence*, 7:156.

199. Nehru to Chief Minister of CP and Berar, July 4, 1948, in *SWJN-2*, 7:189.

200. Nehru to Chief Ministers, July 1, 1948, in Jawaharlal Nehru, *Letters to Chief Ministers*, vol. 1, *1947–1949*, ed. G. Parthasarathi (New Delhi: Publications Division, Ministry of Information and Broadcasting, 1985), 147.

201. Munshi, *Report on the Razakars*.

202. *Hindu*, October 4, 1948; Joseph, *Accession*, 42–43.

203. *Times of India*, September 22, 1948.

204. Nehru to Patel, June 6, 1948, in V. Patel, *Sardar's Letters*, 2:110–11. See also Raghavan, *War and Peace*, 88.

205. Bombay was the first province to pass a Home Guards Act in 1947.

206. Colonel Ganguly, General Officer Commanding the Home Guards in CP and Berar, paraphrased in *Times of India*, July 14, 1949.

207. Nehru to Chief Ministers, November 2, 1947, and December 19, 1947, cited in Nehru, *Letters to Chief Ministers*, 1:7, 10, 41.

208. Andrew Whitehead, "The People's Militia: Communists and Kashmiri Nationalism in the 1940s," in Butalia, *Partition*, 128–54.

209. Nehru to Chief Ministers, February 5, 1948, in Nehru, *Letters to Chief Ministers*, 1:64–65.

210. Ranajit Guha, "Discipline and Mobilize," in *Subaltern Studies VII: Writings on South Asian History and Society*, ed. Partha Chatterjee and Gyanendra Pandey (Delhi: Oxford University Press, 1993), 69–120.

211. Nehru to Chief Ministers, January 17, 1948, in Nehru, *Letters to Chief Ministers*, 1:53–54.

212. Nehru to Chief Ministers, May 20, 1948, in Nehru, *Letters to Chief Ministers*, 1:131–32.

213. Baldev Singh to Ravi Shankar Shukla, April 13, 1948, file no. 10/37/48–Police, Ministry of Home Affairs, NAI.

214. D. S. Bakhle, Secretary to the Government of Bombay, Home Department to Secretary to the Ministry of Home Affairs, May 31, 1948, file no. 19/8/48–Police, Ministry of Home Affairs, NAI.

215. Ibid.

216. *Times of India*, August 9, 1948.

217. V. T. Dehejia to Ministry of States, December 5, 1947, file no. 111-PR/47, MoS, NAI. See also *Times of India*, August 9, 1948.

218. *Times of India*, May 24, 1948.

219. Kamat, "Border Incidents," 217.

220. *Times of India*, May 16, 1948, and August 4, 1948.

221. *Times of India*, February 14, 1948.

222. Ravi Shankar Shukla speech, April 27, 1946, in Y. Khan, *Great Partition*, 53; Fortnightly Report for First Half of April 1948, Government of CP and Berar, file no. 3(21)-H/48, MoS, NAI. See also *Times of India*, July 24, 1948, and June 15, 1948.

223. Chief Secretary to Government, CP and Berar, Political and Military Department, to the Secretary to Ministry of States, July 1, 1948, file no. 3(2)-H/48, MoS, NAI.

224. *Times of India*, August 3, 1948. Patel approvingly inspected the uniformed and fully armed C. Home Guards at Nagpur in December 1947. V. Patel, *For a United India*, 145.

225. *Times of India*, May 17, 1948.

226. Shukla to Ministry of States, July 1, 1948, file no. 3(2)-H/48, MoS, NAI.

227. Y. Khan, *Great Partition*, 100–101.

228. Nehru to S. A. Brelvi, June 26, 1947, in SWJN-2, 3:161.

229. Minutes of Governors' Conference, February 2, 1948, file no. 24/1/48–Police, Ministry of Home Affairs, NAI.

2eo. *Hindustan Times*, June 7, 1947, file no. 2(5)-PR/47, pt. II, MoS, NAI.

231. Shukla to Nehru, July 11, 1948, file no. 3(22)-H/48, MoS, NAI.

232. S. Prasad, *Operation Polo*, 25.

233. Nehru to Ministry of States, June 20, 1948, file no. 3(2)-H/48, MoS, NAI.

234. The Hyderabad government protested the deployment of troops along the border, arguing that "detachments of Indian Army personnel comprising of 25 sepoys and a Jamadar have been posted at each of the Congress Camps set up on the border to assist the

'goondas' in their subversive activities, against the State." Hyderabad Govt to Ministry of States, July 27, 1948, file no. 7.3(18)-H/48, MoS, NAI.

235. See, for example, *Manchester Guardian*, July 29 and August 10, 1948.

236. Nehru to Ministry of States, 20 June 1948. NAI, MoS, 3(2)-H/48.

237. Shukla to Nehru, July 11, 1948, file no. 3(22)-H/48, MoS, NAI. In Bombay, the district collector of Bijapur district issued an order "prohibiting the export of all goods to Hyderabad." *Times of India*, June 5, 1948. The Madras government too was working to prevent any smuggling into the state. *Times of India*, July 11, 1948.

238. *Times of India*, November 24, 1948.

239. Munshi to Patel, May 21, 1948, in V. Patel, *Sardar Patel's Correspondence*, 7:155.

240. Nehru to Chief Ministers, July 1, 1948, in Nehru, *Letters to Chief Ministers*, 1:146–47.

241. Minutes of Meeting in Defense Secretary's Room, June 19, 1948, file no. 3(22)-H/48, MoS, NAI.

242. Pandey, "Can a Muslim."

243. Tuft of hair left unshaven by Hindu men to signify their twice-born status.

244. "Communal Frenzy," 2.

245. Extract from Civil Intelligence Report, November 11, 1948, file no. 112-H/48, vol. 1, MoS, NAI.

246. Paul W. Kahn, *Sacred Violence: Torture, Terror, and Sovereignty* (Ann Arbor: University of Michigan, 2008), 164.

247. Appadurai, *Fear of Small Numbers*. On tattooing and Partition violence, see R. Menon and Bhasin, *Borders and Boundaries*, 43.

248. "Communal Frenzy." See also Abstract of Intelligence, Hyderabad Police, March 24, 1949, file no. 11(9)-H/49, MoS, NAI.

249. Lunje to Chaudhuri and Nehru, December 6, 1948, file no. 112–H/48, vol. 1, MoS, NAI.

250. See statements by All-India Jamiat-ul-Ulema-i-Hind, Aligarh students, the *nawab* of Rampur, Sir Sultan Ahmed, Sheikh Abdullah, and others, *Times of India*, September 19 and 20, 1948.

251. S. C. Dube, *Indian Village* (1955; repr., London: Routledge, 1998), 161–62.

252. M. A. Shakir to Chaudhuri and Nehru, March 9, 1949, file no. 112–H/48, vol. 1, MoS, NAI.

253. Maulana Azad address at Jama Masjid, Delhi, October 23, 1947, in Maulana Abdul Kalam Azad, *Selected Speeches and Writings*, ed. Syed Shahabuddin (Gurgaon: Hope India Publications, 2007), 109–14.

254. Azad, *India Wins Freedom*, 246–47.

255. Emphasis added. Maulana Abdul Kalam Azad, address at All India Muslim Conference, August 1948, in *Selected Speeches and Writings*, 117.

256. Nehru to Provincial Congress Committee Presidents, August 5, 1954, in Prakash Chandra Upadhyaya, "The Politics of Indian Secularism," *Modern Asian Studies* 26, no. 4 (1992): 828. See also S. Gopal, "Nehru and Minorities," *Economic and Political Weekly* 23, nos. 45/47 (1988): 2463–66.

257. Gopal, "Nehru and Minorities," 2466.

258. Nehru to Mohanlal Saxena, September 10, 1949, N. Gopalaswamy Ayyangar Papers, subject 23, NMML.

259. At the time of writing, Nehru was in Paris and reflecting upon India's standing as a secular state in the international arena. "Our world position, which is high at present, would suffer irretrievably. Every action that we have taken in the past, every declaration that we have made will be judged from a new standpoint and we shall be condemned and isolated. Our enemies would of course say that they were right throughout, our friends will remain silent in a shame-faced way. All kinds of new problems and difficulties would arise and the consequences in every direction will be bad." Nehru to Gopalaswamy Ayyangar, October 27, 1948, N. Gopalaswamy Ayyangar Papers, Correspondence with Jawaharlal Nehru, NMML.

260. Nehru to Mohanlal Saxena, Minister for Relief and Rehabilitation, September 10, 1949, N. Gopalaswamy Ayyangar Papers, subject 23, NMML.

261. Jawaharlal Nehru, *Before and after Independence: A Collection of the Most Important and Soul-Stirring Speeches Delivered by Jawaharlal Nehru during the Most Important and Soul-Stirring Years in India's History, 1922–1950*, ed. J. S. Bright (New Delhi: Indian Printing Works, n.d.), 467.

262. Nehru to S. A. Brelvi, June 26, 1947, in *SWJN-2*, 3:161.

263. For example, a group of Hyderabadi Muslims traveled to Dehra Dun to see Nehru at the meeting of the All India Congress Committee. Nehru consequently took up their case with the government of Bombay, as their families had taken refuge in Sholapur after fleeing from Osmanabad and Gulbarga. A. V. Pai to Chaudhuri, May 26, 1949, file no. 10(27)-H/49, MoS, NAI.

264. Nehru to Ministry of States, November 14, 1948, file no. 112–H/48, vol. 1, MoS, NAI.

265. They agreed to a method in which "Muslim officers with less than 5 years service should preferably be retired unless they are of exceptional utility or technical ability. In the case of non-Muslim officers, only those who have proved inefficient should be asked to go." File no. 10(38)-H/49, MoS, NAI.

266. File no. 1(46)-H/50, MoS, NAI.

267. Ibid.

268. Vellodi to Jamiat-ul-Ulema, April 19, 1951, file no. 1(15)-H/51, MoS, NAI.

269. Taylor Sherman, "Migration, Citizenship and Belonging in Hyderabad (Deccan), 1946–1956," *Modern Asian Studies* 45, no. 1 (2011): 81–107, and *Muslim Belonging*.

270. Vellodi to A. V. Pai, June 2, 1949, file no. 1(15)-H/49, MoS, NAI.

271. Rahman to Nehru, January 1, 1950, file no. 1(71)-H/49, MoS, NAI.

272. Nehru to Patel, October 19, 1950, file no. 1(44)-H/50, MoS, NAI.

273. Sunil Purushotham, "World History in the Atomic Age: Past, Present and Future in the Political Thought of Jawaharlal Nehru," *Modern Intellectual History* 14, no. 3 (2017): 837–67.

274. Nehru to Patel, October 19, 1950, file no. 1(44)-H/50, MoS, NAI.

275. Ibid.

276. Sunil Khilnani, "Nehru's Judgement," in *Political Judgement: Essays for John Dunn*, ed. Richard Bourke and Raymond Geuss (Cambridge: Cambridge University Press, 2009), 274.

277. Nehru to Patel, October 19, 1950, file no. 1(44)-H/50, MoS, NAI.

278. Patel to Nehru, October 13, 1950, file no. 1(44)-H/50, MoS, NAI.

279. Patel to Nehru, October 26, 1950, file no. 1(44)-H/50, MoS, NAI.

280. Ibid.

281. Ibid.

282. Ibid.

283. *Times of India*, February 28, 1949.

284. M. A. Moid, "Muslim Perceptions and Responses in Post-Police Action Contexts in Hyderabad," *Deccan Studies* 6, no. 2 (2008): 52–74.

285. R. Khan, "Muslim Leadership," 786.

286. Karen Leonard, *Locating Home: India's Hyderabadis Abroad* (Stanford, CA: Stanford University Press, 2007), 56–83.

287. S. Sharma, "'Yeh Azaadi Jhooti Hai!,'" 1386; *Times of India*, February 28, 1949.

288. Munshi to Patel, August 3, 1948, in V. Patel, *Sardar Patel's Correspondence*, 7:201.

289. *New York Times*, August 16, 1948.

290. Chaudhuri, "A Report on Certain Aspects of the Situation in Hyderabad as on 19 Nov 48," file no. 1(11)-H/48, MoS, NAI.

291. Notes on Meeting between Officers of Government of India, Government of Madras, and Government of Hyderabad, April 26, 1950, file no. 17(1)-H/50, MoS, NAI. A brigade in the Indian Army is generally made up of three thousand or more men.

292. He also set up a "high-level committee" to identify and purge "Communist cells inside Government itself." Patel to Chief Ministers, October 15, 1948, in V. Patel, *Sardar Patel's Correspondence*, 7: 444–45.

293. R. J. Moore, *Making the New Commonwealth* (Oxford: Clarendon Press, 1987), 141.

294. G. D. Adhikari, *What Is Happening in Hyderabad?* (Bombay: V. M. Kaul, 1949).

Chapter Three

1. Coupland, *Future of India*, 86.

2. S. M. Gokhale, *India's Refugee Problem: Causes and Cures* (Baroda: Prakash Publications, 1948), 73.

3. Yasmin Khan, *The Great Partition: The Making of India and Pakistan* (New Haven, CT: Yale University Press, 2007), 4.

4. Ibid., 4–5.

5. Ibid., 133.

6. Tony Judt, *Postwar: A History of Europe since 1945* (New York: Penguin, 2005).

7. Willem van Schendel, *The Bengal Borderland: Beyond State and Nation in South Asia* (London: Anthem Press, 2005); Delwar Hussain, *Boundaries Undermined: The Ruins of Progress on the Bangladesh/India Border* (London: Hurst, 2013); David N. Gellner, ed., *Borderland Lives in Northern South Asia* (Durham, NC: Duke University Press, 2013).

8. Wheatley, "Spectral Legal Personality," 762.

9. Zamindar, *Long Partition*.

10. The government of India passed the Influx from Pakistan (Control) Ordinance in July 1948. File no. XVI/32/231, EPLA, PSA.

11. S. Kapila, *Violent Fraternity*.

12. Shail Mayaram, *Resisting Regimes: Myth, Memory and the Shaping of a Muslim Identity* (Delhi: Oxford University Press, 1997); Ian Copland, "The Further Shores of Partition: Ethnic Cleansing in Rajasthan 1947," *Past and Present* 160, no. 1 (1998) 203–39.

13. Uday S. Mehta, "Violence," in *Political Concepts: A Critical Lexicon*, 2012, www.politicalconcepts.org/violence-uday-s-mehta/.

14. Paul Brass, "The Partition of India and Retributive Genocide in the Punjab, 1946–47: Means, Methods, and Purposes," *Journal of Genocide Research* 5, no. 3 (2003): 71–101.

15. Arafaat Valiani, *Militant Publics in India: Physical Culture and Violence in the Making of a Modern Polity* (New York: Palgrave Macmillan, 2011).

16. Robert Gerwarth and John Horne, eds., *War in Peace: Paramilitary Violence in Europe after the Great War* (Oxford: Oxford University Press, 2012).

17. Valiani, *Militant Publics*.

18. Y. Khan, *Great Partition*.

19. Penderel Moon, *Divide and Quit* (London: Chatto and Windus, 1962).

20. Brass, "Partition of India."

21. Resolution of Partition Council, July 17, 1947, in Kirpal Singh, *The Partition of the Punjab* (Patiala: Punjabi University, 1972), 102.

22. Robin Jeffrey, "The Punjab Boundary Force and the Problem of Order, August 1947," *Modern Asian Studies* 8, no. 4 (1974): 498–500. The number of PBF members as given in the Constituent Assembly of India debates was 25,818 total personnel. This included 13,638 Hindus, 9,777 Muslims, 1,900 Sikhs, 307 British, and 196 "Others." Kirpal Singh, *Select Documents on Partition of Punjab-1947: India and Pakistan* (Delhi: National Book Shop, 2006), 107–8, 561.

23. November 26, 1947, press conference in Amritsar by Brigadier Mohite, head of the MEO, file no. V/36/16, EPLA, PSA.

24. By November 22 the estimates of the total number of non-Muslims moved from West to East Punjab by military transport lorries was 349,834, by rail 849,500, and by foot convoy 1,014,000, for an estimated total of 2,213,334 people. The estimated number of Muslims moved from East to West Punjab by military transport lorries was 215,690, by rail 943,720, and by foot convoy 2,385,165, for an estimated total of 3,544,575 people. In total, the Indian and Pakistani MEOs claimed to have moved 5,757,909 people during this period. File no. LVII/26/45, EPLA, PSA.

25. Five million of the approximately 8,085,000 persons who came into India from Pakistan by the end of January 1951 were from West Pakistan. R. Menon, "Birth of Social Security Commitments."

26. Official estimates of abducted women were fifty thousand Muslim women in India and thirty-three thousand non-Muslims in Pakistan. R. Menon and Bhasin, *Borders and Boundaries*, 70.

27. The chief liaison officer from September 1947 to January 1948 was R. B. Nathu Ram. In January 1948, Nathu Ram was replaced by the deputy chief liaison officer, the Punjab Civil Service officer Ram Rattan. File no. LVIII/15/180, EPLA, PSA.

28. Chief Secretary to Government, West Punjab, H. A. Majid, Esq., to All Deputy Commissioners in West Punjab, September 4, 1947, file no. LII/29/I, EPLA, PSA.

29. H. A. Majid to Deputy Commissioners, September 4, 1947, file no. LII/29/I, EPLA, PSA.

30. This was to be done in consultation with a "Priority Board" consisting of the deputy refugee commissioner and the Information Office at Amritsar, as well as a senior military officer stationed in Lahore. Chief Liaison Officer Nathu Ram, "Determination of Priorities for the Movement of Evacuees," September 10, 1947, file no. XIV/16/14, pt. I, EPLA, PSA.

31. Gokhale, *India's Refugee Problem*, 31.

32. CLO to Major General B. S. Chimni, Amritsar, September 10, 1947, file no. XIV/16/14, pt. I, EPLA, PSA.

33. Rajendra Singh, *The Military Evacuation Organisation, 1947–48* (New Delhi: Manager Press, 1961), 106.

34. Brigadier Mohite, Commander, MEO "Weekly Report," November 30, 1947, file no. V/36/16, EPLA, PSA.

35. This number was the estimate given by the MEO(I) on November 14, 1947. File no. LVII/26/45, EPLA, PSA. These numbers were estimates and varied widely, testifying to the instability of the state's information order. For instance, on November 29 the MEO estimated that the total number of non-Muslims in "pockets" in West Punjab and NWFP was 133,630. File no. V/35/16, EPLA, PSA.

36. "Monthly Report on the Work of East Punjab Liaison Agency for the Month of July, 1948," file no. LV/24/17-EV, EPLA, PSA.

37. R. Menon, "Birth of Social Security Commitments." See also Gyanesh Kudaisya, "From Displacement to 'Development': East Punjab Countryside after Partition, 1947–67," in *Freedom, Trauma, Continuities: Northern India and Independence*, ed. D. A. Low and Howard Brasted (New Delhi: Sage, 1998), 73–90; Satya M. Rai, *Partition of the Punjab: A Study of Its Effects on the Politics and Administration of the Punjab*, vol. 1, *1947–56* (London: Asia Publishing House, 1965); Ian Talbot, "Punjabi Refugees' Rehabilitation and the Indian State: Discourses, Denials and Dissonances," *Modern Asian Studies* 25, no. 1 (2011); 109–30. For official accounts, see Mohanlal Saksena, *Some Reflections on the Problems of Rehabilitation* (New Delhi: Caxton Press, 1950); M. S. Randhawa, *Out of the Ashes: An Account of the Rehabilitation of Refugees from West Pakistan in Rural Areas of East Punjab* (Chandigarh: Public Relations Department, 1954); Government of India, *Millions on the Move: The Aftermath of Partition* (New Delhi: Ministry of Information and Broadcasting, 1948).

38. V. K. R. V. Rao, *An Economic Review of Refugee Rehabilitation in India: A Study of Faridabad Township* (Delhi: University Press, 1955).

39. Randhawa, *Out of the Ashes*, 219.

40. R. Menon, "Birth of Social Security Commitments," 162.

41. *Times of India*, July 5, 1948.

42. Mridula Sarabhai to Ajit Prasad Jain, Ministry of Rehabilitation, November 19, 1950, file no. 7(55)-K/50, MoS, NAI. See also Aparna Basu, *Mridula Sarabhai: Rebel with a Cause* (New Delhi: Oxford University Press, 2003).

43. Nehru to John Matthai, August 18, 1949, in *SWJN-2*, 13:113.

44. Ibid.

45. Speech at United Council for Relief and Welfare, New Delhi, October 3, 1949, in *SWJN-2*, 13:115.

46. Ibid., 13:116.

47. Statement to the press, New Delhi, January 23, 1948, in *SWJN-2*, 5:147–49.

48. Nehru to Rajendra Prasad (at the time chairman of Faridabad Township Development Board), January 7, 1950, in *SWJN-2*, 14(pt. 1):211.

49. S. Gopal, *Jawaharlal Nehru: A Biography*, vol. 2, *1947–1956* (Delhi: Oxford University Press, 1979), 199.

50. Nehru to Prasad, January 7, 1950, in *SWJN-2*, 14(pt. 1): 212.

51. Gopal, *Jawaharlal Nehru*, 2:199–200.

52. Nehru to Chief Ministers, September 28, 1953, in Jawaharlal Nehru, *Letters to Chief Ministers*, vol. 3, *1952–1954* (New Delhi: Publications Division, Ministry of Information and Broadcasting, 1987), 394.

53. Navyug Gill, "Limits of Conversion: Caste, Labor, and the Question of Emancipation in Colonial Panjab," *Journal of Asian Studies* 78, no. 1 (2018): 1–20.

54. Jesús F. Cháirez-Garza, "'Bound Hand and Foot and Handed Over to the Caste Hindus': Ambedkar, Untouchability and the Politics of Partition," *Indian Economic and Social History Review* 55 (2018): 1–28; Dwaipayan Sen, *The Decline of the Caste Question: Jogendranath Mandal and the Defeat of Dalit Politics in Bengal* (Cambridge: Cambridge University Press, 2018) and "'No Matter How, Jogendranath Had to Be Defeated': The Scheduled Castes Federation and the Making of Partition in Bengal, 1945–1947," *Indian Economic Social History Review* 49, no. 3 (2012): 321–64; Ravinder Kaur, *Since 1947: Partition Narratives among Punjab Migrants of Delhi* (New Delhi: Oxford University Press, 2007), "Distinctive Citizenship: Refugees, Subjects and Postcolonial State in India's Partition," *Cultural and Social History* 6, no. 4 (2009): 429–46, and "Narrative Absence: An 'Untouchable' Account of Partition Migration," *Contributions to Indian Sociology* 42, no. 2 (2008): 281–306; Sekhar Bandyopadhyay, "Transfer of Power and the Crisis of Dalit Politics in India, 1945–47," *Modern Asian Studies* 34 (2000): 893–942.

55. Jesús F. Cháirez-Garza, "Nationalizing Untouchability: The Political Thought of B. R. Ambedkar, ca. 1917–1956" (PhD diss., University of Cambridge, 2014).

56. Devji, *Muslim Zion*.

57. Ambedkar, *Pakistan*.

58. Omvedt, *Dalits*, 281–314; Chinna Rao Yagati, *Dalits' Struggle for Identity: Andhra and Hyderabad, 1900–1950* (New Delhi: Kanishka, 2003).

59. Ramnarayan Rawat, "Partition Politics and Achhut Identity: A Study of the Scheduled Castes Federation and Dalit Politics in UP, 1946–48," in Kaul, *Partitions of Memory*, 111–39.

60. Joya Chatterji, *Bengal Divided: Hindu Communalism and Partition, 1932–1947* (Cambridge: Cambridge University Press, 1994).

61. D. Sen, "No Matter How."

62. Vijay Prashad, *Untouchable Freedom: A Social History of a Dalit Community* (Delhi: Oxford University Press, 2000); Christopher Harding, *Religious Transformation in South Asia: The Meanings of Conversion in Colonial Punjab* (Oxford: Oxford University Press, 2008).

63. Mian Muhammad Sadullah, ed., *The Partition of the Punjab, 1947: A Compilation of Official Documents* (Lahore: Sang-e-Meel Publications, 1983), 2:193, 196.

64. Lajpat Rai, *The Arya Samaj* (London: Longmans, Green, 1915); Gill, "Limits of Conversion."

65. The following two paragraphs are largely drawn from Mark Juergensmeyer, *Religion as Social Vision: The Movement against Untouchability in 20th-Century Punjab* (Berkeley: University of California Press, 1982). See also Ronki Ram, "Untouchability in India with a Difference: Ad Dharm, Dalit Assertion, and Caste Conflicts in Punjab," *Asian Survey* 44, no. 6 (2004): 895–912, and "Untouchability, Dalit Consciousness, and the Ad Dharm Movement in Punjab," *Contributions to Indian Sociology* 38, no. 3 (2004): 323–49.

66. For South India, see M. S. Pandian, *Brahmin and Non-Brahmin: Genealogies of the Tamil Political Present* (New Delhi: Permanent Black, 2007), and Rupa Viswanath, *The Pariah Problem: Caste, Religion, and the Social in Modern India* (New York: Columbia University Press, 2014).

67. See also Surinder Jodhka, "Prejudice without Pollution? Scheduled Castes in Contemporary Punjab," *Journal of Indian School of Political Economy* 12, nos. 3–4 (2000): 381–403; Harish Puri, "Scheduled Castes in Sikh Community: A Historical Perspective," *Economic and Political Weekly* 38, no. 26 (2003): 2693–2701.

68. Gill, "Limits of Conversion," 8.

69. Julia Leslie, *Authority and Meaning in Indian Religions: Hinduism and the Case of Valmiki* (Burlington, VT: Ashgate, 2003); Paramjit S. Judge, "Hierarchical Differentiation among Dalits," *Economic and Political Weekly* 38, no. 28 (2003): 2990–91.

70. Jalal, *Self and Sovereignty*. 436. Juergensmeyer, *Religion as Social Vision*, 144–45.

71. Pakistan Refugees and Evacuees Commissioner to Deputy High Commissioner for India, November 7, 1947, file no. LV/23/46-A, EPLA, PSA.

72. Note by Chief Liaison Officer, April 1948, file no. LVII/14/2-E, pt. II, EPLA, PSA.

73. Note by Deputy Chief Liaison Officer, November 13, 1947, file no. LVII/22/8-B, EPLA, PSA.

74. DLO Montgomery, Nand Lal Soni, to CLO, September 9, 1948, file no. X/5/20-EV, EPLA, PSA.

75. Ramnarayan Rawat, *Reconsidering Untouchability: Chamars and Dalit History in North India* (Bloomington: Indiana University Press, 2011).

76. The term *kamin* was used to describe groups of landless laborers who provided services to landowners known as *jajmans*. The *kamin-jajman* relationship was often hereditary, and many of the *kamins* in Panjab were of the Chamar and Chuhra castes.

77. Gill, "Limits of Conversion," 11–15.

78. Report by Deputy Chief Liaison Officer, July 10, 1948, file no. LV/29/226, EPLA, PSA. The DLO, Gujranwala, reported on November 21, 1947: "All kind of subterfuge are being invented, one being the issue of warrants for non-payment of collected revenue by the lambardars." Bundle No. II+II, file no. 3, EPLA, PSA. See also Bundle No. I, file no. 3.

79. Bundle No. I, file no. 5, EPLA, PSA.

80. DLO report regarding Montgomery District, March 26, 1948, file no. X/3/168, EPLA, PSA.

81. Note by Major-General Commander Pakistan MEO regarding "Evacuation—Non-Muslim Pockets—Rawalpindi Division," November 8, 1947, file no. XIV/16/14, pt. I, EPLA, PSA. The DLO at Gujranwala similarly reported that the "local authorities are also raising trouble about converted men brought from pockets. All kind of subterfuges are being invented, one being the issue of warrants for non-payment of collected revenue by the lambardars." Bundle No. II+III, file no. 3, EPLA, PSA.

82. DLO, "Report on the Progress of Evacuation of Non-Muslim from Narowal (West Punjab)," October 11, 1947, Bundle No. I, file no. 5, EPLA, PSA.

83. Report Regarding Montgomery District, DLO Nand Lal Soni, East Punjab Government, Montgomery, September 25, 1948, file no. LIX/2, EPLA, PSA.

84. Chief Liaison Officer to K. L. Punjabi, Officer on Special Duty, Government of India, August 9, 1948, Bundle No. I, file no. 6, EPLA, PSA.

85. K. L. Panjabi to V. D. Dantyagi, Joint Secretary to the Government of India, Ministry without Portfolio, August 4, 1948, Bundle No. I, file no. 3, EPLA, PSA.

86. Home Secretary, Government of West Punjab to All District Magistrates, West Punjab, June 22, 1948, file no. X/5/20-EV, EPLA, PSA.

87. K. L. Panjabi to V. D. Dantyagi, Joint Secretary to the Government of India, Ministry without Portfolio, August 4, 1948, Bundle No. I, file no. 3, EPLA, PSA.

88. Kaur, "Distinctive Citizenship" and "Narrative Absence."

89. There were also instances of conflict between Sikhs and Hindus during evacuation. For example, the DLO at Lyallpur was dismissed from his post for allegedly having prioritized the evacuation of Sikhs over Hindus. Om Prakash Bhankari, Charanji Lal, et al. to Chandu Lall Travedi, September 22, 1947, Bundle No. II+III, file no. 3, EPLA, PSA.

90. Officer on Special Duty R. L. Jadhav, "Visit to Lyallpur Refugee Camp, 12.11.1947," file no. LV/22/198, EPLA, PSA.

91. Deputy CLO, December 1948, file no. LV/23/46-A, EPLA, PSA.

92. The district liaison officer at Gujranwala reported in October 1947, "I have evacuated about 20 Sweepers from different localities into the camp and they have promised to keep the camp clean till the Refugees are evacuated." File no. X/3/168, EPLA, PSA.

93. Mufakharul Islam, "The Punjab Land Alienation Act and the Professional Moneylenders," *Modern Asian Studies* 29, no. 2 (1995): 271–91; Pervaiz Nazir, "Origins of Debt, Mortgage and Alienation of Land in Early Modern Punjab," *Journal of Peasant Studies* 27, no. 3 (2000): 55–91.

94. Kaur, *Since 1947*.

95. Gyanendra Pandey, "'Nobody's People': The Dalits of Punjab in the Forced Re-

moval of 1947," in *Removing Peoples: Forced Removal in the Modern World*, ed. Richard Bessel and Claudia Haake (Oxford: Oxford University Press, 2009), 297–320.

96. Ambedkar to Nehru, December 18, 1947, in Babasaheb Ambedkar, *Dr. Babasaheb Ambedkar Writings and Speeches*, ed. Hari Narke, vol. 21 (Mumbai: Government of Maharashtra, 2006), 253–59.

97. Ibid.

98. B. G. Rao, Ministry of Relief and Rehabilitation, to Rai Bahadur Nathu Ram, Chief Liaison Officer, November 22, 1947, EPLA, PSA.

99. EPLA, LV/23/46-A and LV/22/198.

100. Randhawa, *Out of the Ashes*; U. Bhaskar Rao, *The Story of Rehabilitation* (New Delhi: Dept. of Rehabilitation, Ministry of Labour, Employment and Rehabilitation, 1967). See also Talbot, "Punjabi Refugees' Rehabilitation."

101. R. L. Jadhav to Deputy High Commissioner for India in Pakistan, December 18, 1947, file no. LV/23/46-A, EPLA, PSA.

102. Ibid.

103. Chief Liaison Officer, Ram Rattan, to Chief Secretary, East Punjab, M. R. Sachdev, January 25, 1948, Bundle No. I, file no. 1, EPLA, PSA.

104. CLO to Sachdev, February 4, 1948, Bundle No. I, file no. 1, EPLA, PSA.

105. On prisoners, see file nos. XVI/2/151, LV/31/18-EV, pt. II, LV/4/25, and LXV/2, EPLA, PSA.

106. Deputy Commissioner for Criminal Tribes East Punjab, Jullundur, Mulkh Raj Mehra, to Chief Liaison Officer, East Punjab Government, Lahore, July 31, 1948, Bundle No. I, file no. 6, EPLA, PSA.

107. "The Progress of the Recovery of Abducted Girls during the Week Ending the 16th June 1948," file no. VI/3/1-EV, EPLA, PSA.

108. "Statement of Shri Surrender Kumar," February 21, 1948, Bundle No. II+III, file no. 7, EPLA, PSA.

109. V. Das, *Critical Events* and *Life and Words*; Butalia, *Other Side of Silence*; R. Menon and Bhasin, *Borders and Boundaries*; Pandey, *Remembering Partition*.

110. V. Das, *Critical Events*, 83.

111. R. Menon and Bhasin, *Borders and Boundaries*.

112. V. Das, *Life and Words*, 33.

113. Ibid., 21.

114. Ibid., 19.

115. The DLO at Montgomery reported in April 1948 that 440 local guides and 870 guides from India had stayed in the camp at Montgomery. File no. LV/9/25, EPLA, PSA. For statements of guides working in Mianwali District, see file no. XVI/30/225.

116. For example, Bachan Singh to CLO, received June 16, 1948, file no. VII/27, EPLA, PSA. Or the January 1948 letter from a man desperately requesting the CLO to locate his wife and other relations after they were abducted from Bhimber and were reported to be at the camp at Kunjah in Gujrat. Bundle No. I, file no. 4, EPLA, PSA. See also file no. 7(47)-K/50, MoS, NAI, and Bundle No. I, file no. 10; Bundle No. II+III, file no. 3; Bundle No. II+III, file no. 7; and Bundle No. II, file no. 2, all in EPLA, PSA.

117. Bundle No. II, file no. 2, EPLA, PSA. See also letter from Santosh Kumari, detained at the camp at Dadyal, near Mirpur in Azad Kashmir, file no. 7(17)-K/48, MoS, NAI.

118. "Statement of Mt. Sarjit Kaur Wife of Jaswant Singh, Khatri, Aged about 19 Years of Lahore Now Residing at Mahalpur, Hoshiarpur District," file no. LV/1/52, EPLA, PSA.

119. CLO to K. B. Sardar Ghulam Hassan Khan Leghari, Deputy Commissioner, Sargodha District, November 29, 1947, file no. LVI/5/52-P.I., pt. II, EPLA, PSA.

120. "Decisions Reached at the Conference between the Government of India and the Pakistan Government Held on the 6th December, 1947," file no. LVIII/11/134, EPLA, PSA.

121. "Minutes of the Propaganda Sub-Committee Meeting held on 9th Jan. '48," file no. LVIII/11/134, EPLA, PSA.

122. Deputy High Commissioner, Lahore to Ministry of Foreign Affairs, New Delhi, January 9, 1948, file no. LVI/5/52-P.I., pt. II, EPLA, PSA.

123. "Decisions Regarding Recovery of Abducted Girls, Reached between the Government of Pakistan and the Government of India at a Conference on the 6th December 1947, and Subsequent Dates," Lahore, January 14, 1948, file no. LVI/5/52-P.I., pt. II, EPLA, PSA.

124. R. Menon and Bhasin, *Borders and Boundaries*, 125.

125. "Decisions Regarding Recovery of Abducted Girls," January 14, 1948, file no. LVI/5/52-P.I., pt. II, EPLA, PSA.

126. Note by CLO, February 25, 1948, file no. LV/25/52-P.II, EPLA, PSA.

127. See, for example, "Statement of Sobha Singh Son of Uttam Singh Aged 30 Years" and the statement of Ram Piari of Gujrat District, file nos. LV/28 and LV/5/25, EPLA, PSA.

128. See, for example, "Nihal Chand Son of L. Ram," file no. LV/13/25, pt. II, EPLA, PSA. For more on the role of local police, see file nos. LV/26/41-EV and LV/1/52-VII, EPLA, PSA.

129. Kamla Patel, *Torn from the Roots: A Partition Memoir*, trans. Uma Randeria (New Delhi: Women Unlimited, 2006), 138.

130. DLO, "Report on the Progress of Evacuation of Non-Muslim from Narowal (West Punjab)," October 11, 1947, Bundle No. I, file no. 5, EPLA, PSA.

131. Note by Nathu Ram, Officer on Special Duty, Government of India, January 29, 1948, file no. LV/4/25, EPLA, PSA. See also the statements in file no. LV/27/2/4/R, EPLA, PSA.

132. K. L Panjabi, Deputy High Commissioner, to CLO, April 23, 1948, file no. LVI/5/52-P.I., pt. II, EPLA, PSA.

133. File no. VII/20/52–XVIII, EPLA, PSA. See also file nos. LVIII/12/164, VII/20/52–XVIII, VII/33/2J, LV/27/2/4/R, and LVIII/17/208.

134. K. Patel, *Torn from the Roots*.

135. "Notes on the Refugee Situation in the East Punjab, September and October 1948," file no. LVII/2/25-G, EPLA, PSA.

136. Report on Gujranwala District, file no. LIX/3, EPLA, PSA.

137. See record of interview with Ray Rani in file no. LV/27/2/4/R, EPLA, PSA.

138. "List of Hindu Recovered Girls and Their Particulars," file no. VII/20/52-XVIII, EPLA, PSA.

139. Note on the Refugee Situation in the East Punjab, September 30, 1948, file no. LVII/2/25-G, EPLA, PSA.

140. Anupama Roy, *Mapping Citizenship*, 40.

141. Ornit Shani, "Conceptions of Citizenship in India and the 'Muslim Question,'" *Modern Asian Studies* 44, no. 1 (2010): 145–73.

142. V. Das, *Life and Words*, 7.

Chapter Four

1. Gopal Das Khosla, *Stern Reckoning: A Survey Leading Up to and Following the Partition of India* (New Delhi: Bhawnani, 1949).

2. Ibid., viii.

3. Ibid., 119.

4. Butalia, *Other Side of Silence*; Pandey, *Remembering Partition*. See also Ashis Nandy, *An Ambiguous Journey to the City: The Village and Other Odd Ruins of the Self in the Indian Imagination* (New Delhi: Oxford University Press, 2007), 104–5, 135; Dipesh Chakrabarty, "Remembered Villages: Representations of Hindu-Bengali Memories in the Aftermath of the Partition," in Low and Brasted, *Freedom, Trauma, Continuities*, 133–52; Sukeshi Kamra, *Bearing Witness: Partition, Independence, End of the Raj* (Calgary: University of Calgary Press, 2002); Jonathan D. Greenberg, "Against Silence and Forgetting," in *Partitioned Lives: Narratives of Home, Displacement, and Resettlement*, ed. Anjali Gera Roy and Nandi Bhatia (Delhi, 2008).

5. V. Das, *Critical Events* and *Life and Words*.

6. See, for example, the 1947 Partition Archive at www.1947partitionarchive.org.

7. Butalia, *Partition*.

8. Tarun Saint, *Witnessing Partition: Memory, History, Fiction* (New Delhi: Routledge, 2010), 24–25.

9. Ann Laura Stoler, *Along the Archival Grain: Epistemic Anxieties and Colonial Commonsense* (Princeton, NJ: Princeton University Press, 2009), 32.

10. Anupama Roy, *Mapping Citizenship*, 34.

11. H. Roy, *Partitioned Lives*.

12. CLO notes on Jhang District, October 21, 1947, file no. LV/6/25, EPLA, PSA.

13. Note by CLO Regarding Visit to Sargodha on November 15, 1947, dated November 17, 1947, file no. LV/13/25, EPLA, PSA.

14. Deputy Chief Liaison Officer to the Vice President, All-India Dayanand Salvation Mission, Hoshiarpur, July 1948, file nos. VII/20/52-XVIII, EPLA, PSA.

15. Nehru, national broadcast, August 19, 1947, in *Jawaharlal Nehru's Speeches*, vol. 1, *September 1946–May 1949* (1949; repr., New Delhi: Publications Division, Ministry of Information and Broadcasting, 1963), 68.

16. Kirpal Singh Ahluwalia to Isher Singh Majhail, Minister for the Rehabilitation of

Refugees, East Punjab Government, October 4, 1947, file no. VIII/47/15-B/Rawalpindi, EPLA, PSA.

17. File no. LV/3/25, EPLA, PSA.

18. Fort Refugees Relief Committee to Deputy High Commissioner, Peshawar, file no. LV/2/25, EPLA, PSA. See also petition sent by "Representatives of the refugees" in the Multan evacuation camp in November 1947, Bundle No. 2, I[sic], EPLA, PSA, and also petitions from September 1947, Bundle I, 9/13-A, pt. I.

19. Ram Lal Juneja to Governor of East Punjab, September 17, 1947, Bundle No. II+III, file no. 3, EPLA, PSA.

20. Kaur, *Since 1947*.

21. Sohag Wanti to the Commissioner, Julundur Division, December 4, 1947, Bundle No. II, file no. 2, EPLA, PSA.

22. Bundle No. II+III, file no. 7, EPLA, PSA.

23. "Statement of Mr. Ram Nath Kapur," file no. LVIII/4/91, EPLA, PSA.

24. I have taken the liberty of changing certain names.

25. File no. LV/26/41-EV, EPLA, PSA.

26. Shahid Amin, *Event, Metaphor, Memory: Chauri Chaura 1922–1992* (Berkeley: University of California Press, 1995), 118.

27. File no. LVIII/6/94-A, EPLA, PSA.

28. Ibid.

29. M. R. Sachdev, Chief Secretary, Government of East Punjab, January 14, 1948, file no. LVIII/5/94, EPLA, PSA; A. Basu, *Mridula Sarabhai*, 114–15.

30. File no. LV/1/52–VII, EPLA, PSA.

31. For example, Nathu Ram, CLO to Hafiz Abdul Majid, Chief Secretary, Government of West Punjab, October 6, 1947, file no. LVII/24/35, pt. II, EPLA, PSA.

32. Bundle I, file no. 10, EPLA, PSA.

33. For more on Kacha Khu, currently in Khanewal District, see K. Singh, *Select Documents on Partition*, 651–52.

34. File no. LV/26/41-EV, EPLA, PSA.

35. File no. LV/26/41-EV, EPLA, PSA.

36. V. Das, *Life and Words*.

37. V. Das, *Critical Events*.

38. President, Arya Samaj, Darshanpurva, Cawnpore, to Chief Secretary, Government of East Punjab, October 18, 1947, file no. LVII/14/2-E, pt. II, EPLA, PSA.

39. Tara Devi to Vallabhbhai Patel, November 22, 1948, file no. 7(17)-K/48, MoS, NAI.

40. File no. LV/29/226, EPLA, PSA.

41. Ibid.

42. Monthly report on the work of EPLA for the month of August 1948, CLO to Chief Secretary, Government of East Punjab, September 11, 1948, file no. LV/24/17-EV, EPLA, PSA.

43. File no. LV/26/41-EV, EPLA, PSA. The village of Kacha Khu is currently in Khanewal District.

44. File no. LV/27/2/4/R, EPLA, PSA.
45. File no. LVII/23/35, pt. I, EPLA, PSA.
46. File no. LV/1/52-VII, EPLA, PSA.
47. Urvashi Butalia, "Community, State and Gender: On Women's Agency during Partition," *Economic and Political Weekly* 28, no. 17 (1993): WS12–WS21+WS24; Pandey, *Remembering Partition*, 84–88.
48. Emphasis added. Appendix to Report submitted by DLO on December 22, 1947, file no. X/3/168, EPLA, PSA.
49. V. Das, *Life and Words*, 19.
50. Nehru, speech at Allahabad University, December 13, 1947, in *SWJN-2*, 4:208.
51. Randhawa, *Out of the Ashes*; U. Rao, *Story of Rehabilitation*. See also Ian Talbot, "Punjabi Refugees' Rehabilitation."
52. Pandey, *Remembering Partition*, 88.
53. File no. LV/1/52-VII, EPLA, PSA. For official reports and correspondence regarding the attack on the train at Kamoke, see file nos. XIV/16/14, pt. I, and LVII/14/2-E, pt. II, EPLA, PSA.
54. File no. LV/1/52-VII, EPLA, PSA.
55. Ibid.
56. File no. LV/26/41-EV, EPLA, PSA.
57. Ibid.
58. Ibid. (names removed).
59. Ibid.
60. Ibid.
61. K. Patel, *Torn from the Roots*, 83–88.
62. File no. LV/1/52-VII, EPLA, PSA.
63. Ibid.
64. Ibid.
65. Urvashi Butalia, "Confronting the Past: Thoughts on a Partition Museum," *Context: Built, Living and Natural* 8, no. 2 (2011): 21–26.

Chapter Five

1. File no. 15(3)-H/51, MoS, NAI.
2. In *SWJN-2*, 14(pt. 2):167.
3. Sundarayya, *Telangana People's Struggle*, 38.
4. Inukonda Thirumali, *Against Dora and Nizam: People's Movement in Telangana, 1939–1948* (Delhi: Kanishka, 2003), 149.
5. C. G. Herbert, Resident in Hyderabad, to L. C. L. Griffin, Secretary to His Excellency the Crown Representative, New Delhi, December 23, 1946, file no. 15-P(S)/47, MoS, NAI.
6. W. V. Grigson, "Report to H.E.H. the Nizam's Government on Communist Agitation in Hyderabad State," December 5, 1946, L/PS/13/1203, no. 22, file 1/5, IOR.
7. D. V. Rao, *Refutation of Wrong Trends Advocating Withdrawal of Telengana Armed Struggle* (1949; repr., Hyderabad: Proletarian Line Publications, 1982), 100–101.

8. The authoritative account remains Sundarayya, *Telangana People's Struggle*. See also Arutla Ramachandra Reddy, *Telengana Struggle: Memoirs*, trans. B. Narsing Rao (Delhi: People's Publishing House, 1984); Ravi Narayan Reddy, *Heroic Telengana: Reminiscences and Experiences* (Delhi, 2010); Gour et al., *Glorious Telangana Armed Struggle*; Chandra Rajeswara Rao, *The Historic Telengana Struggle: Some Useful Lessons from Its Rich Experience* (Delhi: Communist Party of India, 1971); Devulapalli Venkateswara Rao, *Telangana Armed Struggle and the Path of Indian Revolution* (Calcutta: Proletarian Path Publications, 1974) and *Refutation of Wrong Trends*; Chandra Pulla Reddy, *The Great Heroic Telengana Struggle*, (Hyderabad, 1981).

9. D. N. Dhanagare, "Social Origins of the Peasant Insurrection in Telangana," *Contributions to Indian Sociology* 8 (1974): 109–34; Barry Pavier, *The Telengana Movement, 1944–51* (Delhi: Vikas, 1981); Amit Kumar Gupta, *The Agrarian Drama: The Leftists and the Rural Poor in India, 1934–1951* (Delhi: Manohar, 1996); Ramesh Panneeru, *Telangana Armed Struggle in Nalgonda District: A Case Study of Kadavendi Village, 1930–52 A.D.* (Hyderabad: Prajasakti Book House, 2010); Stree Shakti Sanghatana, *We Were Making History: Women and the Telangana Uprising* (London: Zed Books, 1989); Roosa, "Passive Revolution"; Carolyn M. Elliot, "Decline of a Patrimonial Regime: The Telangana Rebellion in India, 1946–51," *Journal of Asian Studies* 34, no. 1 (1974): 27–47; Akhil Gupta, "Revolution in Telengana, 1946–1951 (Part One)," *South Asia Bulletin* 4, no. 1 (1984): 1–26, and "Revolution in Telengana, 1946–1951 (Part Two)," *South Asia Bulletin* 4, no. 2 (1984): 22–32; Mohan Ram, "The Telengana Peasant Armed Struggle, 1946–51," *Economic and Political Weekly* 8, no. 23 (1973): 1025–32, and *Indian Communism: Split within a Split* (New Delhi: Vikas, 1969); Alavi, "Peasants and Revolution"; Kathleen Gough, "Indian Peasant Uprisings," *Economic and Political Weekly* 9, nos. 32–34 (1974): 1391–1412; Javeed Alam, "Communist Politics in Search of Hegemony," in *Wages of Freedom: Fifty Years of the Indian Nation-State*, ed. Partha Chatterjee (Delhi: Oxford University Press, 1998), 179–206.

10. According to Raj Bahadur Gour, the pledge was: "I, a citizen of the glorious Telengana and a son of the great Andhra people, pledge myself not to lay down my arms till the destruction of the Nizam's rule over my motherland is achieved. I promise to carry out the orders of my commanders unconditionally and to submit myself completely to the discipline of my squad. I will revenge myself against the Nizam's hordes, mercilessly and without hesitation for the pillage and destruction of our towns and villages, for the murder of our children, for the dishonour suffered by our women and the tortures inflicted on our people. I will shed blood for blood and take life for life. I promise that I am prepared to die in battle against the enemy rather than live while my people and I are slaves under the blood-thirsty tyranny of the Nizam. If, through cowardice or weakness, I violate this pledge in any way and act against the interests of my people, I am ready to die the death of a traitor at the hands of my comrades." Gour et al., *Glorious Telangana Armed Struggle*, 91–92.

11. Mulk Raj Anand, "India: Republic or Dominion?," *World Review*, October 1948, 28.

12. R. Reddy, *Heroic Telengana*, 80.

13. Sundarayya, *Telangana People's Struggle*.

14. Pavier, *Telengana Movement*; Thirumali, *Against Dora and Nizam*; Roosa, "Passive Revolution."

15. Dalel Benbabaali, "From the Peasant Armed Struggle to the Telangana State: Changes and Continuities in a South India Region's Uprisings," *Contemporary South Asia* 24, no. 2 (2016): 184. See also K. Purushotham et al., eds., *The Oxford India Anthology of Telugu Dalit Writing* (New Delhi: Oxford University Press, 2016).

16. Roosa, "Passive Revolution," 58.

17. Thirumali, *Against Dora and Nizam*.

18. Ibid., 48.

19. Ibid., chap. 3.

20. I. M. L. Kantha Rao, "A Study of the Socio Political Mobility of the Kapu Caste in Modern Andhra" (PhD diss., University of Hyderabad, 1999), 66–68.

21. Chinnaiah Jangam, "Recast-(e)-ing Class: Dalit Chronicles of Communist Organizing in Telugu Country," paper presented at Global Ambedkar workshop, Columbia University, October 19, 2018. See also Selig S. Harrison, "Caste and the Andhra Communists," *American Political Science Review* 50, no. 2 (1956): 378–404.

22. Jangam, "Recast-(e)-ing Class."

23. Sundarayya, *Telangana People's Struggle*; Roosa, "Passive Revolution."

24. Stree Shakta Sanghatana, *We Were Making History*.

25. Swarajyam was the chairperson of the Manukota Area Committee and directed all *sangham* activities in the area. Hailing from a petty landlord family, she became a revolutionary while still a child and was a top *sangham* leader and propagandist by the time she was sixteen. Stree Shakta Sanghatana, *We Were Making History*. See also file no. 6(7)-H/51, MoS, NAI.

26. Stree Shakta Sanghatana, *We Were Making History*.

27. Ibid.; Ranajit Guha, "The Small Voice of History," in *Subaltern Studies IX*, ed. Shahid Amin and Dipesh Chakrabarty (Delhi: Oxford University Press, 1996), 1–12.

28. Pavier, *Telengana Movement*.

29. Thirumali, *Against Dora and Nizam*, 139.

30. Ibid., 30.

31. Inukonda Thirumali, "Dora and Gadi: Manifestation of Landlord Domination in Telengana," *Economic and Political Weekly* 27, no. 9 (1992): 477–82.

32. Rama Mantena, "The Andhra Movement, Hyderabad State, and the Historical Origins of the Telangana Demand: Public Life and Political Aspirations in India, 1900–56," *India Review* 13, no. 4 (2014): 337–57.

33. Inukonda Thirumali, "The Political Pragmatism of the Communists in Telangana, 1938–48," *Social Scientist* 24, nos. 4/6 (1996): 164–83.

34. Akhil Gupta, "Revolution in Telengana (Part One)," 12.

35. V. Ramakrishna, "Left Cultural Movement in Andhra Pradesh: 1930s to 1950s," *Social Scientist* 40, nos. 1/2 (2012): 21–30; D. Anjaneyulu, "Impact of Socialist Ideology on Telugu Literature between the Wars," in *Socialism in India*, ed. B. R. Nanda (New York: Barnes and Noble, 1972), 244–60.

36. Vulli Dhanaraju, "The Telangana Movement (1946–1951): Folklore Perspective," *International Journal of Social Science Tomorrow* 8 (2012): 1–7, "Making Peoples History in Telangana Movement: Remembering Voyya Raja Ram," *International Research Journal of Social Sciences* 3, no. 6 (2014): 37–43, and "Voice of the Subaltern Poet: Contribution of Suddala Hanumanthu in Telangana Peoples' Movement," *Research Journal of Language, Literature and Humanities* 2, no. 7 (2015): 1–7.

37. Goutam Ghose, director, *Maa Bhoomi* (1980). *Maa Bhoomi* was written by Sunkara Satyanaryana and Vasireddi Bhaskara Rao. R. Reddy, *Heroic Telengana*, 63. See also Shyam Benegal, director, *Nishant* (1975).

38. Jangam, "Recast-(e)-ing Class."

39. Ramakrishna, "Left Cultural Movement," 26.

40. B. N. Mullick, "Communist Activities in Hyderabad during the Month of December, 1949," file no. 5(8)-H/50-(II), MoS, NAI. See also Thirumali, *Against Dora and Nizam*.

41. Bhangya Bhukya, *Subjugated Nomads: The Lambadas under the Rule of the Nizams* (Hyderabad: Orient Blackswan, 2010).

42. Tirtha to M. K. Vellodi, Chief Minister, Hyderabad, December 22, 1950, file no. 1(5)-H/51, MoS, NAI.

43. Thirumali, *Against Dora and Nizam*, 191. Other government sources put the figure at 2,500 villages. Ravi Narayan Reddy (*Heroic Telengana*, 70) claimed 4,000 villages under *sangham rajyam*, and Sundarayya (*Telangana People's Struggle*, 2) estimated 3,000.

44. Sundarayya, *Autobiography*, 226.

45. Razvi, *Political Awakening in Hyderabad*.

46. Alam, "Communist Politics," 181.

47. Sundarayya, *Autobiography*, 221.

48. *People's Age* 6 (August 3, 1947); Gene D. Overstreet and Marshall Windmiller, *Communism in India* (Berkeley: University of California Press, 1959), 263.

49. *People's Age* 6 (November 30, 1947); Overstreet and Windmiller, *Communism in India*, 264.

50. Overstreet and Windmiller, *Communism in India*, 264.

51. *People's Age* 6 (October 12, 1947, and November 9, 1947); Overstreet and Windmiller, *Communism in India*, 264.

52. Stree Shakti Sanghatana, *We Were Making History*, 81; A. Reddy, *Telengana Struggle*, 83; Sundarayya, *Telengana People's Struggle*, 56.

53. Ranajit Guha, "Discipline and Mobilize."

54. Chatterjee, *Nationalist Thought*.

55. Alavi, "Peasants and the Revolution," 263.

56. John H. Kautsky, *Moscow and the Communist Party of India: A Study in the Postwar Evolution of International Communist Strategy* (Cambridge, MA: MIT Press, 1956), 48.

57. Vallabhbhai Patel to O. P. Ramaswamy Reddy, January 19, 1948, in V. Patel, *Sardar Patel's Correspondence*, 7:131.

58. S. Sharma, "'Yeh Azaadi Jhooti Hai!'"

59. Abstract of Intelligence, Hyderabad Police, March 24, 1949, file 11(9)-H/49, MoS, NAI.
60. File nos. 11(4)-H/49, 11(9)-H/49, and 19(12)-H/50, all in MoS, NAI.
61. S. Sharma, "'Yeh Azaadi Jhooti Hai!'"
62. Kautsky, *Moscow*, 49.
63. P. Radhakrishnan, *Peasant Struggles, Land Reforms, and Social Change: Malabar, 1836–1982* (New Delhi: Sage, 1989), 64.
64. For Ranadive's agrarian policy and response to the Andhra comrades, see Communist Party of India, *On the Agrarian Question in India* (Bombay: People's Publishing House, 1949).
65. M. Basavapunniah has claimed that he was the principal author. A. G. Noorani, "Of Stalin, Telangana and Indian Revolution," *Frontline* magazine (Chennai), December 16, 2011.
66. Central Committee, Communist Party of India, "Report on the Left Deviation inside the Communist Party of India: Draft Critique Submitted by the Members of the Central Committee from Andhra and Amended and Approved by the Central Committee in Its Recent Meeting," May 1950, 47, Ajoy Bhavan Library, New Delhi.
67. Ibid., 50.
68. Ibid., 46–48.
69. Ibid., 106.
70. Ibid.
71. Ibid.
72. *New York Times*, July 27, 1948.
73. Central Committee, "Report on the Left Deviation," 106.
74. Sundarayya, *Autobiography*, 221.
75. An October 5, 1950, memo from Hyderabad's Home Department puts the number of communists "detained" since the Police Action as 9,555. File no. 1(44)-H/50, MoS, NAI.
76. D. Rao, *Refutation of Wrong Trends*, 139.
77. Ibid.
78. Special Commissioner's Fortnightly Report for Period Ending July 15, 1951, file no. 6(5)-H/51, MoS, NAI.
79. Daily Summary of Intelligence, CID Special Branch, Hyderabad, March 21, 1949, file no. 260-H/48, MoS, NAI.
80. Mullick notes of tour of Krishna, Guntur, and Kurnool in March 1951, file no. 6(7)-H/51, MoS, NAI.
81. Kodanda Ramaiah, President, All India Excluded Areas and Tribal Peoples Association, to K. M. Munshi, Agent-General of Indian Union, Hyderabad, January 19, 1948, file no. 19(2)-H/50, MoS, NAI.
82. David Arnold, "Rebellious Hillmen: the Gudem-Rampa Risings, 1839–1924," in Ranajit Guha, *Subaltern Studies I*, 88–142; J. Mangamma, *Alluri Sitarama Raju* (Hyderabad: A.P. State Archives, 1983).

83. Bhangya Bhukya, *The Roots of the Periphery: A History of the Gonds of Deccan India* (New Delhi: Oxford University Press, 2017), chap. 5.

84. Akash Poyam, "Gondwana Movement in Post-colonial India: Exploring Paradigms of Assertion, Self-Determination and Statehood," in *Social Work in India*, ed. S. R. Bodhi (Kolkata: Adivaani, 2016), 131–66.

85. "Note on Communist Activities during the Fortnight Ending 14th December 1950," Chief Secretary to Government of Hyderabad to the Joint Secretary of the Ministry of States, file no. 19(12)-H/50, MoS, NAI. See also file no. 6(7)-H/51, MoS, NAI. Sundarayya wrote that the "hard core" that remained in the Palvancha area of Warangal at the time of the withdrawal of the armed movement were 150 party members and many sympathizers in the plains, and 50 Koya Party members and 500 Koya militants in the forest area. *Telangana People's Struggle*, 246.

86. Report by M. Srinivasan, May 14, 1949, file no. 3(4)-H/49, MoS, NAI.

87. Sudhakar Bhat, "Ordeal of Nalgonda and Warangal," *Times of India*, February 27, 1949.

88. Chaudhuri, "A Report on Certain Aspects of the Situation in Hyderabad as on 19 November 48," file no. 1(11)-H/48, MoS, NAI.

89. Tour Notes, November 12, 1948, Central Intelligence Officer, Nagpur, file no. 260-H/48, MoS, NAI.

90. Y. Venkatishwara Rao to Military Governor, December 18, 1948, file no. 169-H/48, MoS, NAI.

91. Nanjappa had previously acted as the district collector of Nashik district and had been instrumental in aiding the government of India in the integration of the princely states.

92. Special Commissioner's Report for Period Ending May 14, 1950, file no. 5(32)-H/50, MoS, NAI.

93. See fortnightly reports from Government of Hyderabad, file no. 11(3)-H/49, MoS, NAI.

94. Special Commissioner's Report for Period Ending February 28, 1951, file no. 6(5)-H/51, MoS, NAI.

95. .R. Reddy, *Heroic Telengana*, 63.

96. Thirumali, *Against Dora and Nizam*, 238, 243.

97. Special Commissioner's Report for the Period up to May 14, 1950, file no. 5(32)-H/50, MoS, NAI.

98. Each outpost was "manned by armed police in strength varying between one section to one platoon." B. N. Mullick, "Report on Telengana," December 5, 1950, file no. 5(8)-H/50, MoS, NAI.

99. Intelligence report, March 15, 1951, file no. 6(7)-H/51, MoS, NAI.

100. Report by Mullick, January 4, 1950, file no. 6(7)-H/51, MoS, NAI.

101. A. Reddy, *Telengana Struggle*, 68.

102. Special Commissioner's Report for the Period Ending March 15, 1951, file no. 6(5)-H/51, MoS, NAI.

103. Communist Survey #18, Period Ending December 31, 1950, file no. 6(7)-H/51, MoS, NAI.

104. Special Commissioner's Report for the Period up to May 14, 1950, file no. 5(32)-H/50, MoS, NAI.

105. Fortnightly Report for the Period Ending June 15, 1950, file no. 5(32)-H/50, MoS, NAI.

106. Mullick, "Report on Telengana," to Ministry of Home Affairs, Ministry of States, and Chief Minister of Hyderabad, December 5, 1950, file no. 5(8)-H/50, MoS, NAI.

107. Intelligence Bureau, Daily Summary of Information, January 17, 1949, file no. 9(5)-P/49, MoS, NAI.

108. Note on Communist Activity for Fortnight Ending November 14, 1950, file no. 19(12)-H/50, MoS, NAI.

109. V. P. Menon, Secretary, Ministry of States to H. V. R. Iengar, Secretary, Ministry of Home Affairs, January 20, 1951, file no. 6(4)-H/51, MoS, NAI.

110. *Times of India*, November 13, 1949.

111. Dipesh Chakrabarty, "'In the Name of Politics': Democracy and the Power of the Multitude in India," *Public Culture* 19, no. 1 (2007): 35–57.

112. Nehru, *Discovery of India*, 133.

113. Nehru, statement to press, telegram from UK High Commissioner in India to Commonwealth Relations Office, August 8, 1949, IOR/L/WS/1/1198, IOR.

114. Constituent Assembly Debate, September 15, 1949, http://indiankanoon.org/doc/1278245/.

115. Cited in *Hindustan Times*, December 28, 1948, file no. 11(1)-H/49, pt. II, MoS, NAI.

116. Nehru, statement in Constituent Assembly, February 28, 1949, cited in *Communist Violence in India* (Ministry of Home Affairs, September 1949), 6.

117. Nehru to Military Governor J. N. Chaudhuri, May 22, 1949, file no. 11(1)-H/49-I, MoS, NAI.

118. S. Sharma, "'Yeh Azaadi Jhooti Hai!'"

119. Nasser Husain, *The Jurisprudence of Emergency: Colonialism and the Rule of Law* (Ann Arbor: University of Michigan Press, 2003).

120. Notes on Meeting between Officers of Government of India, Government of Madras, and Government of Hyderabad, April 26, 1950, file no. 17(1)-H/50, MoS, NAI. A brigade in the Indian Army is generally made up of three thousand or more men.

121. Chaudhuri to Ministry of States, September 29, 1949, file no. 1(80)-H/49, MoS, NAI. Most of the armed police units were supplied by other provinces and former princely states, though a few companies were provided directly by the Government of India. For example, in December 1950 there were eight companies of the U.P. Provincial Armed Constabulary, ten companies of the Madras Special Armed Police, eighteen companies of the Madhya Pradesh Special Armed Forces and Special Armed Constabulary, three companies of the Bombay Special Reserve Constabulary, two companies of the Mysore Armed Reserve Police, and two companies of the Government of India's Central Reserve Police. Mullick, "Report on Telengana," December 5, 1950, file no. 5(8)-H/50, MoS, NAI.

122. An October 5, 1950, memo from Hyderabad's Home Department puts the num-

ber of communists "detained" since the Police Action as 9,555. File no. 1(44)-H/50, MoS, NAI.

123. K.M. Cariappa to Ministry of Defence, September 8, 1950, file no. 5(8)-H/50, MoS, NAI.

124. Sudhakar Bhat, "Fiendish Ravages in Nalgonda and Warangal," *Times of India*, March 6, 1949.

125. Vellodi to Menon, April 13, 1950, file no. 17(1)-H/50, MoS, NAI.

126. Vellodi to Menon, April 14, 1951, file no. 6(11)-H/51, MoS, NAI.

127. Special Commissioner's Report for Period up to May 14, 1950, file no. 5(32)-H/50, MoS, NAI.

128. Special Commissioner's Report for Period up to May 14, 1950, file no. 5(32)-H/50, MoS, NAI.

129. Report by B. N. Mullick, Director, Intelligence Bureau, January 1951, file no. 6(7)-H/51, MoS, NAI.

130. Dr. Upender Rao to Patel, December 16, 1948, and Watandars and Pattadars of Nalgunda and Atrafbalda Districts to Patel, November 14, 1948, file no. 169-H/48, MoS, NAI.

131. Ministry of States Note, January 12, 1949, file no. 169-H/48, MoS, NAI.

132. B. B. Ghosh to Menon, April 11, 1950, file no. 5(24)-H/50, MoS, NAI.

133. S. Seshadri, Home Minister, Government of Hyderabad, to Buch, September 3, 1951, file no. 6(7)-H/51, MoS, NAI.

134. B. N. Mullick, "Communist Activities in Hyderabad during the Month of December, 1949," file no. 5(8)-H/50–II, MoS, NAI.

135. Special Commissioner's fortnightly reports, file no. 5(32)-H/50, MoS, NAI.

136. B. N. Mullick, "Communist Activities in Hyderabad during the Month of December, 1949," file no. 5(8)-H/50–II, and Special Commissioner's Report for fortnight ending May 31, 1950, file no. 5(32)-H/50, both in MoS, NAI.

137. File nos. 6(5)-H/51, 1(5)-H/51, 5(32)-H/50, and 6(7)-H/51, all in MoS, NAI.

138. Nanjappa to Ministry of States, May 14, 1950, file no. 5(32)-H/50, MoS, NAI. See also R. Venkatavaradhan to Bhaskaran, September 25, 1950, file no. 5(8)-H/50, MoS, NAI.

139. Note by Swami Ramananda Tirtha, December 22, 1950, file no. 1(5)-H/51, MoS, NAI.

140. R. Venkatavaradhan to P. V. Bhaskaran, September 25, 1950, file no. 5(8)-H/50-(I), MoS, NAI.

141. Ibid. See also file nos. 1(5)-H/51 and 19(12)-H/50 MoS, NAI.

142. A "Report on Telengana," Mullick to Iengar, December 12, 1950, and Menon and Vellodi, December 5, 1950, file no. 5(8)-H/50–(I), MoS, NAI. See also file no. 6(7)-H/51.

143. R. Venkatavaradhan to P. V. Bhaskaran, September 25, 1950, file no. 5(8)-H/50-(I), MoS, NAI.

144. Mullick report, July 7, 1950, file no. 1(30)-H/50, MoS, NAI.

145. General K. M. Cariappa, Commander in Chief, to Minister of Defence, September 8, 1950, file no. 5(8)-H/50, MoS, NAI.

146. Special Commissioner's fortnightly reports and Vellodi to Buch, May 14, 1950, file no. 5(32)-H/50, MoS, NAI.

147. Note on Communist Activity during Fortnight Ending December 14, 1950, file no. 19(12)-H/50, MoS, NAI. See also file nos. 1(30)-H/50, 11(3)-H/49, and especially 6(13)-H/51.

148. For example, the case of P. Rangachari, whose brother filed a habeas corpus petition after he was disappeared in Telangana. File no. 6(13)-H/51, MoS, NAI.

149. Note by P. V. Bhaskaran, Deputy Director, Intelligence Bureau, June 7, 1951, file no. 6(9)-H/51, MoS, NAI.

150. Nehru to Ayyangar, September 23, 1951, file no. 6(13)-H/51, MoS, NAI.

151. Ibid.

152. Ayyangar to Nehru, September 26, 1951, file no. 6(13)-H/51, MoS, NAI.

153. Vellodi to Menon, April 14, 1951, file no. 6(11)-H/51, MoS, NAI.

154. Tour Notes, January 25, 1951, file no. 6(7)-H/51 MoS, NAI.

155. Debates in the Council of States over the Preventive Detention Bill, August 9, 1952, file no. 6(16)-H/52, MoS, NAI.

156. File no. 3(25)-H/51, MoS, NAI.

157. File no. 100-H/48, MoS, NAI.

158. Sherman, "Integration."

159. Emphasis added. Government of Hyderabad, *Report on the Administration of Hyderabad State, September 1948–March 1950* (Hyderabad, 1950), 52.

160. Patel to Nehru, October 13, 1950, file no. 1(44)-H/50, MoS, NAI.

161. File no. 6(2)-H/52, MoS, NAI.

162. File no. 5(6)-H/50, MoS, NAI.

163. File no. 11(1)-H/49, MoS, NAI.

164. File no. 5(31)-H/50, MoS, NAI.

165. File no. 5(6)-H/50, MoS, NAI.

166. File no. 11(3)-H/49, MoS, NAI.

167. File no. 6(2)-H/52, MoS, NAI.

168. Emphasis in original. K. M. Cariappa to Ministry of Defence, September 8, 1950, file no. 5(8)-H/50, MoS, NAI.

169. Special Commissioner's Report for the Fortnight Ending May 14, 1950, file no. 5(32)-H/50, MoS, NAI.

170. Ibid. Chief Minister Vellodi supported this approach, insisting that "in this matter of suppressing terrorist activities, the Government as government cannot do very much more than police action plus ameliorative measures." Vellodi to V. P Menon, December 31, 1950, file no. 1(5)-H/51, MoS, NAI.

171. Mullick to Iengar, Menon, and Vellodi, December 5, 1950, file no. 5(8)-H/50, MoS, NAI.

172. Fortnightly Report for Period Ending September 30, 1951, file no. 6(5)-H/51, MoS, NAI.

173. By the end of September 1951, 595 miles of fair-weather roads had been con-

structed. Fortnightly Report for Period Ending September 30, 1951, file no. 6(5)-H/51, MoS, NAI.

174. File nos. 5(2)-H/50, 19(12)-H/50 and 6(7)-H/52, all in MoS, NAI.

175. Mullick to Iengar, Menon, and Vellodi, December 5, 1950, file no. 5(8)-H/50, MoS, NAI.

176. Nehru, statement in Parliament, May 16, 1951, in Mohan Lall Shrimal, *Land Reforms: Promise and Performance* (New Delhi, 1985).

177. The Hyderabad government claimed that less than ten thousand acres actually changed hands. This figure counted only land for which the landowner had lodged a formal complaint with proper paperwork. L. G. Rajwade to S. Narayanswamy, February 12, 1952, file no. 6(5)-H/52, MoS, NAI.

178. President, Agriculturalists' Association to Nehru, December 27, 1948, file no. 3(4)-H/49, MoS, NAI.

179. Ramachandra Guha, *India after Gandhi: The History of the World's Largest Democracy* (London: Macmillan, 2007), 98.

180. President, Agriculturalists' Association to Nehru, December 27, 1948, file no. 3(4)-H/49, MoS, NAI.

181. Ibid.

182. Nehru, March 14, 1948, in *SWJN-2*, 5:278–79.

183. Sunil Khilnani, "Nehru's Faith," *Economic and Political Weekly* 37, no. 48 (2002): 4797.

184. Ibid.

185. Jawaharlal Nehru, "The Basic Approach," *All India Congress Committee Economic Review: Fortnightly Journal of the Economic and Political Research Department of the All India Congress Committee* 10, nos. 8–9 (August 15, 1958): 3–6.

186. Hamza Alavi, "India and the Colonial Mode of Production," *Socialist Register* 12 (1975): 160–97.

187. Francine Frankel, *India's Political Economy, 1947–2004* (Delhi: Oxford University Press, 2005), 68–70.

188. Ibid., 76–77; Michael Brecher, *Nehru: A Political Biography* (London: Oxford University Press, 1959).

189. Brecher, *Nehru*, 195.

190. Alavi, "India," 162.

191. Frankel, *India's Political Economy*, 77.

192. Articles 19 and 31 being the key provisions.

193. Namita Wahi, "The Fundamental Right to Property in the Indian Constitution," *Social Science Research Network* (August 10, 2015).

194. Special Commissioner's Fortnightly Report for Period Ending April 30, 1951, and October 31, 1951, file no. 6(5)-H/51, MoS, NAI.

195. K. M. Cariappa to Ministry of Defence, September 8, 1950, file no. 5(8)-H/50, MoS, NAI.

196. Jagir Administrator's Office, *The Hyderabad Jagirs Commutation Manual* (Hyderabad, 1951).

197. "A Note on the Progress Achieved in the Departments under Revenue since 1–10–1948 to 1–3–1951," file no. 1(5)-H/51, MoS, NAI.

198. Ibid.

199. Special Commissioner's Fortnightly Report for Period Ending April 30, 1951, file no. 6(5)-H/51, MoS, NAI.

200. Ramachandra Guha, *India after Gandhi*, 227–28.

201. Communist Survey No. 18 for Period Ending December 31, 1950, file no. 6(7)-H/51 MoS, NAI.

202. Mohan Ram, *Indian Communism*, 50. See also Sundarayya, *Autobiography*, 231.

203. Sundarayya, *Autobiography*, 243.

204. Press Statement on the Telengana Question, June 8, 1951, file no. 6(7)-H/51, MoS, NAI.

205. Ibid.

206. Ibid.

207. Nehru to Home Minister, Ministry of States, and Chief Election Commissioner, July 24, 1951, file no. 6(15)-H/51, MoS, NAI.

208. Intelligence Bureau note, October 24, 1951, file no. 6(7)-H/51, MoS, NAI.

209. Vellodi to Ayyangar, January 4, 1952, file no. 6(4)-H/52, MoS, NAI.

210. "Hyderabad State Assembly Elections," Press Information Bureau, March 1, 1952, file no. 1(5)-H/52, MoS, NAI.

211. Sudipta Kaviraj, "A State of Contradictions: The Post-colonial State in India," in *Imaginary Institution*, 222.

212. Chatterjee, *Nationalist Thought*, 30.

Chapter Six

1. Report submitted by R. Venkatavaradhan, March 3, 1951, file no. 6(7)-H/51, MoS, NAI.

2. Tour note of S. Balakrishna Shetty, February 14, 1951, file no. 6(7)-H/51, MoS, NAI.

3. Report submitted by R. Venkatavaradhan, DCIO, Hyderabad, March 3, 1951, file no. 6(7)-H/51, MoS, NAI.

4. Sundarayya statement, Debates in Council of States over the Preventive Detention Bill, August 8, 1952, file no. 6(16)-H/52, MoS, NAI; Sundarayya, *Telangana People's Struggle*, 251–54.

5. C. Rao, *Historic Telengana Struggle*, 27.

6. Ibid.

7. Nandini Sundar, "Interning Insurgent Populations: The Buried Histories of Indian Democracy," *Economic and Political Weekly* 46, no. 6 (2011): 47–57.

8. Manoranjan Mohanty, "Adivasi Swaraj Is the Answer to Violence," *Economic and Political Weekly* 52, no. 21 (2017): 66–70.

9. Shani, "Conceptions of Citizenship."

10. Thomas Blom Hansen, *Wages of Violence: Naming and Identity in Postcolonial Bombay* (Princeton, NJ: Princeton University Press, 2002) and "Governance and Myths of

State in Mumbai," in *The Everyday State and Society in Modern India*, ed. Chris Fuller and Veronique Harris (London: Hurst, 2001), 31–67.

11. Charles Tilly, "War Making and State Making as Organized Crime," in *Bringing the State Back In*, ed. Peter Evans, Dietrich Rueschemeyer, and Theda Skocpol (Cambridge: Cambridge University Press, 1985), 169–91.

12. Alpa Shah, "A Double-Edged Sword: Protection and State Violence," *Critique of Anthropology* 26, no. 3 (2006): 251–57.

13. L. C. Jain, Chief Secretary to the Government of Hyderabad, to Secretary, Ministry of States, July 31, 1950, file no. 18(37)-H/50, MoS, NAI.

14. Chief Minister Vellodi to Ministry of States, August 10, 1950, file no. 5(8)-H/50-(I), MoS, NAI.

15. Giorgio Agamben, *Homo Sacer: Sovereign Power and Bare Life*, trans. Daniel Heller-Roazen (Stanford, CA: Stanford University Press, 1998), 147.

16. "Tour Report of the Commissioner for Scheduled Castes and Scheduled Tribes in Hyderabad (Deccan) from 15.12.1951 to 21.12.1951," file no. 17(17)-H/51, MoS, NAI.

17. Mullik, "The Situation in Telengana," August 22, 1952, file no. 6(18)-H/52, MoS, NAI.

18. Director, Social Services Department, Hyderabad to Ministry of States, June 8, 1951, file no. 4(17)-H/51, MoS, NAI.

19. Ibid. Gonds in Adilabad and Chenchu in Mahabubnagar were also relocated, or "rehabilitated." For example, the Hyderabad government reported in July 1951 that "terrorists are reported to be trying to enlist the sympathies of Gonds living in the forest villages of Asifabad (Adilabad district). To counter act this move, the local Police is rehabilitating the Gonds in big villages situated in the vicinity of Armed Police Outposts." L. G. Rajwade, Chief Secretary, Government of Hyderabad, to N. M. Buch, Secretary, Ministry of States, June 23, 1951, file no. 17(7)-H/51, MoS, NAI.

20. Special Commissioner's Report for Period Ending May 14, 1950, file no. 5(32)-H/50, MoS, NAI.

21. Munshi, July 12, 1951, file no. 6(5)-H/51, MoS, NAI.

22. Beverley, *Hyderabad*, chap. 5.

23. Christoph von Führer-Haimendorf, "Tribal Populations of Hyderabad: Yesterday and Today," in Government of India, *Census of India, 1941*. See also *The Aboriginal Tribes of Hyderabad*, vol. 1, *The Chenchus: Jungle Folk of the Deccan* (Bombay: Macmillan, 1943), *The Aboriginal Tribes of Hyderabad*, vol. 2, *The Reddis of the Bison Hills: A Study in Acculturation* (Bombay: Macmillan, 1945), and *The Aboriginal Tribes of Hyderabad*, vol. 3, *The Raj Gonds of Adilabad: Myth and Ritual* (London: Macmillan, 1948).

24. Christoph von Fuhrer-Haimendorf, *Tribal Hyderabad; Four Reports* (Hyderabad: Revenue Department, 1945).

25. Beverley, *Hyderabad*, 181–83.

26. Haimendorf to B. K. Nehru, Secretary, Ministry of Finance, July 6, 1949, file no. 10(34)-H/49, MoS, NAI.

27. Jain to Ministry of States, December 8, 1950, file no. 18(66)-H/50, MoS, NAI.

28. James C. Scott, *The Art of Not Being Governed: An Anarchist History of Upland Southeast Asia* (New Haven, CT: Yale University Press, 2009).

29. Bhangya Bhukya, "Colonisation of Forest and Emergence of Gond Nationalism in Hyderabad State," *Itihasa* 30, nos. 1 and 2 (2004): 59–79.

30. Kodanda Ramaiah, President, All India Excluded Areas and Tribal Peoples Association, to K. M. Munshi, Agent-General of Indian Union, Hyderabad, January 19, 1948, file no. 19(2)-H/50, MoS, NAI.

31. Special Commissioner's Report for Period Ending January 15, 1951, file no. 6(5)-H/51, MoS, NAI; Government of Hyderabad, Fortnightly Report for First Half of January 1951, file no. 17(7)-H/51, MoS, NAI.

32. Sundarayya, *Telengana People's Struggle*, 90–91, 248–51.

33. "Note on Communist Activities during the Fortnight Ending 14th December 1950," Chief Secretary to Government of Hyderabad to the Joint Secretary of the Ministry of States, file no. 19(12)-H/50, MoS, NAI. Sundarayya, *Telangana People's Struggle*, 246, maintains that the "hard core" that remained in the Palvancha area of Warangal at the time of the withdrawal of the armed movement were 150 party members and many sympathizers in the plains, with 50 Koya party members and 500 Koya militants in the forest area. See also file no. 6(7)-H/51, MoS, NAI.

34. Nicholas Dirks, *Castes of Mind: Colonialism and the Making of Modern India* (Princeton, NJ: Princeton University Press, 2001).

35. Sanjay Nigam, "Disciplining and Policing the 'Criminals by Birth,' Part 2: The Development of a Disciplinary System, 1871–1900," *Indian Economic and Social History Review* 21, no. 3 (1990): 131–64; Sandria B. Freitag, "Crime in the Social Order of Colonial North India," *Modern Asian Studies* 25, no. 2 (1991): 227–61.

36. Bhukya, *Subjugated Nomads*, 141.

37. Meena Radhakrishna, "The Criminal Tribes Act in Madras Presidency: Implications for Itinerant Trading Communities," *Indian Economic and Social History Review* 26, no. 3 (1989): 269–95.

38. Government of Hyderabad, *Report on the Administration*.

39. For example, Government of Andhra Pradesh, *Nomadism: Its Causes and Cure* (Hyderabad: Tribal Cultural Research and Training Institute, 1965).

40. Ajay Skaria, "Shades of Wilderness: Tribe, Caste, and Gender in Western India," *Journal of Asian Studies* 56, no. 3 (2007): 731.

41. Ramachandra Guha, *Savaging the Civilized: Verrier Elwin, His Tribals, and India* (Chicago: University of Chicago Press, 1999).

42. Verrier Elwin, *A Philosophy for NEFA* (Delhi, 1957).

43. Skaria, "Shades of Wilderness," 739, and *Hybrid Histories: Forests, Frontiers and Wildness in Western India* (Delhi: Oxford University Press, 1999); Nandini Sundar, *Subalterns and Sovereigns: An Anthropological History of Bastar (1854–2006)* (Delhi: Oxford University Press, 2007); Mahesh Rangarajan, *Fencing the Forest: Conservation and Ecological Change in India's Central Provinces* (New Delhi: Oxford University Press, 1996); Ramachandra Guha and Madhav Gadgil, "State Forestry and Social Conflict in British India," *Past and Present* 123, no. 1 (1989): 141–77.

44. Mullik, August 16, 1951, file no. 6(7)-H/51, MoS, NAI.
45. Mullik, August 22, 1952, file no. 6(18)-H/52, MoS, NAI.
46. N. N. Iengar to S. Narayanswamy, Deputy Secretary, Ministry of States, April 29, 1953, file no. 6(18)-H/52, MoS, NAI.
47. Emphasis added. Government of Hyderabad, *Report on the Administration*, 69.
48. L. C. Jain, Chief Secretary to the Government of Hyderabad to Secretary, Ministry of States, July 31, 1950, file no. 18(37)-H/50, MoS, NAI.
49. Nagendra Bahadur, Home Secretary, Government of Hyderabad to Ministry of States, June 20, 1952, file no. 18(11)-H/52 MoS, NAI.
50. Director, Social Services Department, Hyderabad, to Ministry of States, June 8, 1951, file no. 4(17)-H/51, MoS, NAI.
51. Vellodi to Menon, April 14, 1951, file no. 6(11)-H/51, MoS, NAI.
52. L. C. Jain, Chief Secretary to the Government of Hyderabad to Secretary, Ministry of States, July 31, 1950, file no. 18(37)-H/50, MoS, NAI.
53. K. A. Gafoor, "Koyas and Their Rehabilitation in Warangal," Director of Information and Public Relations, Hyderabad, July 15, 1951, file no. 4(17)-H/51, MoS, NAI.
54. Agamben, *Homo Sacer*, 6.
55. Fortnightly reports for 1951, file no. 6(5)-H/51, MoS, NAI.
56. Mullick, "Report on Telengana," December 5, 1950, file no. 5(8)-H/50, MoS, NAI.
57. Report submitted by R. Venkatavaradhan, March 3, 1951, file no. 6(7)-H/51, MoS, NAI.
58. Military Intelligence Directorate, "Communist Situation in Hyderabad," to Ministry of States, March 30, 1951, file no. 6(9)-H/51, MoS, NAI.
59. Special Commissioner's reports in file nos. 5(32)-H/50 and 6(5)-H/51, MoS, NAI.
60. Tirtha, *Memoirs*, 214.
61. Tirtha to Vellodi, December 22, 1950, file no. 1(5)-H/51, MoS, NAI.
62. Stree Shakti Sanghatana, *We Were Making History*, 48–52.
63. "Enquiries into the Death of Some Terrorists While in Police Custody in Hyderabad," file no. 6(13)-H/51, MoS, NAI. See the case of one T. Janardhanachari in file no. 6(14)-H/52, MoS, NAI; Stree Shakti Sanghatana, *We Were Making History*, 120.
64. "Report of the CKC Commission on Telangana," in *Documents of the Communist Movement in India*, vol. 6, *1949–1951*, ed. Jyoti Basu et al. (Calcutta: National Book Agency, 1997), 806.
65. Ibid., 809.
66. Prathama Banerjee, *Politics of Time: "Primitives" and History-Writing in a Colonial Society* (New York, 2006).
67. G. S. Ghurye, *The Aborigines—"So-Called"—and Their Future* (Poona: Gadgil, 1943), 24.
68. Sumit Guha, *Beyond Caste: Identity and Power in South Asia, Past and Present* (Leiden: Brill, 2013) and "States, Tribes, Castes: A Historical Re-exploration in Comparative Perspective," *Economic and Political Weekly* 50, nos. 46–47 (2015): 50–57.
69. Ghurye, *Aborigines*, 216.
70. Ibid., 155.

71. Skaria, "Shades of Wilderness," 704.
72. Aishwary Kumar, "The Idea of the 'Tribal' in British India: Law, Archive and Memory in Santal Parganas" (PhD diss., University of Cambridge, 2007).
73. Ramachandra Guha, *India after Gandhi*, 128.
74. Ghurye, *Aborigines*, 172–73.
75. Arundhati Roy, "The Greater Common Good," *Outlook*, May 24, 1999.
76. Sundarayya, *Telangana People's Struggle*, 253. See also "Tour Report of the Commissioner for Scheduled Castes and Scheduled Tribes in Hyderabad (Deccan) from 15.12.1951 to 21.12.1951," file no. 17(17)-H/52, MoS, NAI.
77. Michel Foucault, *"Society Must Be Defended": Lectures at the Coll?ge de France, 1975–76*, trans. David Macey (New York: Picador, 2003), 95.
78. Stree Shakti Sanghatana, *We Were Making History*, 144; Confidential Memorandum from Office of the Deputy Inspector General of Police, Northern Range, Waltair, May 19, 1949, Andhra Pradesh State Archives, Home Department, Government of Madras, 1949, Ms Series, G.O. #2568; Sundarayya, *Telangana People's Struggle*, 155; C. Rao, *Historic Telengana Struggle*, 21.
79. The special commissioner reported at the end of June 1951 that "15 Tiger squads are functioning in Warangal south and 2 in Warangal North." An additional 317 Koya had been enlisted in the police force in the two decades and another 97 "formed into antihostile dalams" were "being sent into the forests of Mulug and Narsampet to find out the hostile hide-outs." File no. 6(5)-H/51, MoS, NAI. See also file no. 6(7)-H/51.
80. Arjun Appadurai, "Full Attachment," *Public Culture* 10, no. 2 (1998): 443–49.
81. Report by R. Venkatavaradhan, March 3, 1951, file no. 6(7)-H/51, MoS, NAI.
82. Report by R. Venkatavaradhan, March 3, 1951, file no. 6(7)-H/51, MoS, NAI.
83. Kahn, *Sacred Violence*, 142–43.
84. B. N. Mullick to Ministry of Home Affairs, Ministry of States, and Vellodi, December 5, 1950, file no. 5(8)-H/50–(I), MoS, NAI.
85. Kriti Kapila, "Old Differences and New Hierarchies: The Trouble with Tribes in Contemporary India," in *Interrogating India's Modernity: Democracy, Identity, and Citizenship*, ed. Surinder Jodhka (New Delhi: Oxford University Press, 2013), 99–116.
86. Prathama Banerjee, "Writing the Adivasi: Some Historiographical Notes," *Indian Economic and Social History Review* 53, no. 1 (2016): 131–53.
87. K. Kapila, "Old Differences," 110.
88. Sundar, *Subalterns and Sovereigns*; K. Sivaramakrishnan, "Colonialism and Forestry in India: Imagining the Past in Present Politics," *Comparative Studies in Society and History* 37, no. 1 (1995): 3–40.
89. Press Statement on the Telengana Question, 8, June 1951, file no. 6(7)-H/51, MoS, NAI.
90. Note by S. Narayanaswamy, May 23, 1952, file no. 17(17)-H/52, MoS, NAI.
91. Andhra Pradesh would list Lambada as a Scheduled Tribe in 1976, while other states such as Karnataka list them as a Scheduled Caste. In Maharashtra they are included as part of the Other Backward Classes.
92. Rajendra Prasad in a press release entitled "Koyas and Their Rehabilitation in Wa-

rangal," written by the director of the Social Services Department, K. A. Gafoor, and issued by the director of information and public relations in Hyderabad on July 15, 1951, file no. 4(17)-H/51, MoS, NAI.

93. History of Social Services Department (1951), file no. 1(5)-H/51, MoS, NAI.

94. K. Kapila, "Old Differences."

95. Ibid.

96. Special Commissioner's Report for Period Ending June 30, 1950, file no. 5(32)-H/50, MoS, NAI.

97. Bhukya, *Subjugated Nomads*, 198.

98. Sundar, "Interning Insurgent Populations," 47–57.

99. Estimates Committee, "Third Report on Tribal Welfare," Fifth Legislative Assembly, Andhra Pradesh Legislature, August 1974, TCRTI.

100. "Sub Plan for the Tribal Areas of Andhra Pradesh," Tribal Welfare Department, Government of Andhra Pradesh, Hyderabad, 1975, TCRTI.

101. "Scheme for Rehabilitation of Podu Cultivators," Social Welfare Department, Government of Andhra Pradesh, Hyderabad, July 1984, TCRTI.

102. "Evaluation Study Report of Tribal Development Programmes: I.T.D.A. Paloncha-Khammam Dist.," Tribal Welfare Department, Bhadrachalam, Khammam District, Government of Andhra Pradesh, 1988, TCRTI.

103. V. Nagendra Kumar and K. V. Satyanarayana Rao, "Anthropometry of Konda Reddys East Godavari District (A.P.)," Tribal Welfare Department, Government of Andhra Pradesh, Hyderabad, 1983, TCRTI.

104. "Plan for Development of Chenchus," Tribal Welfare Department, Government of Andhra Pradesh, Hyderabad, 1976, TCRTI.

105. File no. 4(17)-H/51, MoS, NAI.

106. "Evaluating Chenchu Development Programmes," Tribal Welfare Department, Government of Andhra Pradesh, 1980, TCRTI.

107. "Scheme for Rehabilitation."

108. "Sub Plan for the Tribal Areas."

109. Ibid.

110. "Scheme for Rehabilitation."

111. "Evaluation Study Report."

Epilogue

1. File no. 1(44)-H/50, MoS, NAI.
2. Statement in Constituent Assembly, March 5, 1948, *SWJN-2*, 5:239–50.
3. Kudaisya, *Republic in the Making*, viii.
4. S. Kapila, *Violent Fraternity*.
5. S. Purushotham, "World History."
6. Nehru, "Basic Approach," 4.
7. Austin, *Working a Democratic Constitution*.
8. Rajni Kothari, *Politics in India* (Boston: Little, Brown, 1970). See also Christophe

Jaffrelot, *India's Silent Revolution: The Rise of the Lower Castes in North India* (New York, 2003).

9. Uday S. Mehta, "The Social Question and the Absolutism of Politics," *Seminar*, no. 615 (November 2010), www.india-seminar.com/2010/615/615_uday_s_mehta.htm.

10. Sudpta Kaviraj, "A State of Contradictions: The Post-colonial State in India," in *Imaginary Institution*, 210–33.

11. Thomas Blom Hansen, "Democracy against the Law: Reflections on India's Illiberal Democracy," in *Majoritarian State: How Hindu Nationalism Is Changing India*, ed. Angana P. Chatterji, Thomas Blom Hansen, and Christophe Jaffrelot (Oxford: Oxford University Press, 2019), 19–40.

BIBLIOGRAPHY

I. Archives
Ajoy Bhavan Library, New Delhi
Andhra Pradesh State Archives, Hyderabad Home Department, Government of Madras
Archive of Contemporary History, Jawaharlal Nehru University, New Delhi
Balliol College, Oxford
    Papers of Walter Turner Monckton, Dep. Monckton Trustees
The British Library, London
    India Office Records
National Archives of India, New Delhi
    Ministry of Home Affairs
    Ministry of States
Nehru Memorial Museum and Library, New Delhi
    All India States Peoples' Conference Papers
    Gopalaswamy Ayyangar Papers
    Pandit Sunderlal Papers
Punjab State Archives, Chandigarh
    East Punjab Liaison Agency
Tribal Cultural Research and Training Institute Library, Hyderabad
    Tribal Welfare Department Records, Government of Andhra Pradesh, Hyderabad

II. Published Sources
Adhikari, G. D. *What Is Happening in Hyderabad?* Bombay: V. M. Kaul, 1949.
Afzal, M. Rafique, ed. *The Case for Pakistan*. Islamabad: National Commission on Historical and Cultural Research, 1979.
Agamben, Giorgio. *Homo Sacer: Sovereign Power and Bare Life*. Translated by Daniel Heller-Roazen. Stanford, CA: Stanford University Press, 1998.
Aiyangar, S. Aravamudu, et al. *Report of the Reforms Committee, 1938 (1347F)*. Hyderabad: Government Central Press, 1938.
Alam, Javeed. "Communist Politics in Search of Hegemony." In *Wages of Freedom: Fifty Years of the Indian Nation-State*, edited by Partha Chatterjee, 179–206. Delhi: Oxford University Press, 1998.
Alavi, Hamza. "India and the Colonial Mode of Production." *Socialist Register* 12 (1975): 160–97.
———. "Peasants and Revolution." *Socialist Register* 2 (1965): 241–77.

Ambedkar, Babasaheb. *Dr. Babasaheb Ambedkar: Writings and Speeches*. Edited by Hari Narke. Vol. 21. Mumbai: Government of Maharashtra, 2006.

———. *Federation versus Freedom*. Poona: Gokhale Institute of Politics and Economics, 1939. www.ambedkar.org/ambcd/08.%20Federation%20vs%20Freedom.htm.

———. *Pakistan, or the Partition of India*. Bombay: Thackers, 1945.

Amin, Shahid. *Event, Metaphor, Memory: Chauri Chaura, 1922–1992*. Berkeley: University of California Press, 1995.

Anand, Mulk Raj. "India: Republic or Dominion?" *World Review*, October 1948, 24–28.

Anghie, Antony. *Imperialism, Sovereignty and the Making of International Law*. Cambridge: Cambridge University Press, 2004.

Anjaneyulu, D. "Impact of Socialist Ideology on Telugu Literature between the Wars." In *Socialism in India*, edited by B. R. Nanda, 244–60. New York: Barnes and Novle, 1972.

Appadurai, Arjun. *Fear of Small Numbers: An Essay on the Geography of Anger*. Durham, NC: Duke University Press, 2006.

———. "Full Attachment." *Public Culture* 10, no. 2 (1998): 443–49.

Arnold, David. "Rebellious Hillmen: The Gudem-Rampa Risings, 1839–1924." In *Subaltern Studies I: Writings on South Asian History and Society*, edited by Ranajit Guha, 88–142. Delhi: Oxford University Press, 1982.

Austin, Granville. *Working a Democratic Constitution: The Indian Experience*. New Delhi: Oxford University Press, 1999.

Azad, Maulana Abul Kalam. *India Wins Freedom: The Complete Version*. 1959. Reprint, Madras: Orient Longman, 1988.

———. *Selected Speeches and Writings*. Edited by Syed Shahabuddin. Gurgaon: Hope India Publications, 2007.

Bakshi, S. R., ed. *Partition of India*. Vol. 6 of *The Making of India and Pakistan, Select Documents*. New Delhi: Deep and Deep, 1997.

Bandyopadhyay, Sekhar. "Transfer of Power and the Crisis of Dalit Politics in India, 1945–47." *Modern Asian Studies* 34 (2000): 893–942.

Banerjee, Milinda. *The Mortal God: Imagining the Sovereign in Colonial India*. Cambridge: Cambridge University Press, 2018.

Banerjee, Prathama. *Politics of Time: "Primitives" and History-Writing in a Colonial Society*. New York: Oxford University Press, 2006.

———. "Writing the Adivasi: Some Historiographical Notes." *Indian Economic and Social History Review* 53, no. 1 (2016): 131–53.

Bangash, Yaqoob Khan. "Betrayal of Trust: Princely States of India and the Transfer of Power." *South Asia Research* 26, no. 2 (2006): 181–99.

———. *A Princely Affair: The Accession and Integration of the Princely States of Pakistan, 1947–1955*. Karachi: Oxford University Press, 2015.

Basu, Aparna. *Mridula Sarabhai: Rebel with a Cause*. New Delhi: Oxford University Press, 2003.

Basu, Jyoti, et al., eds. *Documents of the Communist Movement in India*. Vol. 6. *1949–1951*. Calcutta: National Book Agency, 1997.

Bawa, V. K. *The Last Nizam: The Life and Times of Mir Osman Ali Khan.* New Delhi: Viking Penguin India, 1992.

———. *The Nizam between Mughals and British: Hyderabad under Salar Jang I.* New Delhi: S. Chand, 1986.

Bayly, C. A. *Indian Society and the Making of the British Empire.* Cambridge: Cambridge University Press, 1988.

———. *Recovering Liberties: Indian Thought in the Age of Liberalism and Empire.* Cambridge: Cambridge University Press, 2011.

Belmessous, Salhia, ed. *Native Claims: Indigenous Law against Empire, 1500–1920.* New York: Oxford University Press, 2012.

Benbabaali, Dalel. "From the Peasant Armed Struggle to the Telangana State: Changes and Continuities in a South India Region's Uprisings." *Contemporary South Asia* 24, no. 2 (2016): 184–96.

Benichou, Lucien. *From Autocracy to Integration: Political Developments in Hyderabad State, 1938–48.* Hyderabad: Orient Longman, 2000.

Benton, Lauren. *A Search for Sovereignty: Law and Geography in European Empires, 1400–1900.* Cambridge: Cambridge University Press, 2010.

Beverley, Eric. "Frontier as Resource: Law, Crime, and Sovereignty on the Margins of Empire." *Comparative Studies in Society and History* 55, no. 2 (2013): 241–72.

———. *Hyderabad, British India, and the World: Muslim Networks and Minor Sovereignty, c. 1850–1950.* Cambridge: Cambridge University Press, 2015.

Bhagavan, Manu. *India and the Quest for One World: The Peacemakers.* New York: Palgrave Macmillan, 2013.

———. "Princely States and the Hindu Imaginary: Exploring the Cartography of Hindu Nationalism in Colonial India." *Journal of Asian Studies* 67, no. 3 (2008): 881–915.

———. *Sovereign Spheres: Princes, Education and Empire in Colonial India.* New Delhi: Oxford University Press, 2003.

Bhargava, Rajeev, ed. *Politics and Ethics of the Indian Constitution.* New Delhi: Oxford University Press, 2008.

Bhat, Sudhakar. "Ordeal of Nalgonda and Warangal." *Times of India*, February 27, 1949.

Bhatia, Udit, ed. *The Indian Constituent Assembly: Deliberations on Democracy.* New York: Routledge, 2017.

Bhukya, Bhangya. "Colonisation of Forest and Emergence of Gond Nationalism in Hyderabad State." *Itihasa* 30, nos. 1–2 (2004): 59–79.

———. *The Roots of the Periphery: A History of the Gonds of Deccan India.* New Delhi: Oxford University Press, 2017.

———. *Subjugated Nomads: The Lambadas under the Rule of the Nizams.* Hyderabad: Orient Blackswan, 2010.

Brass, Paul. "The Partition of India and Retributive Genocide in the Punjab, 1946–47: Means, Methods, and Purposes." *Journal of Genocide Research* 5, no. 3 (2003): 71–101.

Brecher, Michael. *Nehru: A Political Biography.* London: Oxford University Press, 1959.

Butalia, Urvashi. "Community, State and Gender: On Women's Agency during Partition." *Economic and Political Weekly* 28, no. 17 (1993): WS12–WS21 + WS24.

———. "Confronting the Past: Thoughts on a Partition Museum." *Context: Built, Living and Natural* 8, no. 2 (2011): 21–26.

———. *The Other Side of Silence: Voices from the Partition of India.* New Delhi: Penguin Books India, 1998.

———. *Partition: The Long Shadow.* Delhi: Zubaan, 2015.

Butler, Harcourt, Sidney Peel, and W. S. Holdsworth. *Report of the Indian States Committee, 1928–1929.* London: HMSO, 1929.

Cháirez-Garza, Jesús F. "'Bound Hand and Foot and Handed Over to the Caste Hindus': Ambedkar, Untouchability and the Politics of Partition." *Indian Economic and Social History Review* 55 (2018): 1–28.

———. "Nationalizing Untouchability: The Political Thought of B. R. Ambedkar, ca. 1917–1956." PhD diss., University of Cambridge, 2014.

Chakrabarty, Dipesh. "'In the Name of Politics': Democracy and the Power of the Multitude in India." *Public Culture* 19, no. 1 (2007); 35–57.

———. "Remembered Villages: Representations of Hindu-Bengali Memories in the Aftermath of the Partition." In *Freedom, Trauma, Continuities: Northern India and Independence,* edited by D. A. Low and Howard Brasted, 133–52. New Delhi: Sage, 1998.

Chatterjee, Partha. *Nationalist Thought and the Colonial World: A Derivative Discourse.* London: Zed Books, 1986.

Chatterji, Joya. *Bengal Divided: Hindu Communalism and Partition, 1932–1947.* Cambridge: Cambridge University Press, 1994.

———. *The Spoils of Partition: Bengal and India, 1947–1967.* Cambridge: Cambridge University Press, 2007.

Chattopadhyay, Kunal. "India, Post-World War II Upsurge." In *The International Encyclopedia of Revolution and Protest,* edited by Immanuel Ness. Malden, MA: Wiley-Blackwell, 2009.

Choudhry, Sujit, Madhav Khosla, and Pratap Bhanu Mehta, eds. *The Oxford Handbook of the Indian Constitution.* New Delhi: Oxford University Press, 2016.

Cohen, Benjamin B. *Kingship and Colonialism in India's Deccan: 1850–1948.* New York: Palgrave Macmillan, 2007.

Cohn, Bernard. "Representing Authority in Victorian India." In *The Invention of Tradition,* edited by Eric Hobsbawm and Terence Ranger, 165–210. Cambridge: Cambridge University Press, 1983.

Communist Party of India. *On the Agrarian Question in India.* Bombay: People's Publishing House, 1949.

Cooper, Frederick. *Citizenship between Empire and Nation: Remaking France and French Africa, 1945–1960.* Princeton, NJ: Princeton University Press, 2014.

Copland, Ian. "'Communalism' in Princely India: The Case of Hyderabad, 1930–1940." *Modern Asian Studies* 22, no. 4 (1998): 783–814.

———. "Congress Paternalism: The 'High Command' and the Struggle for Freedom in Princely India, c. 1920–1940." *South Asia* 1–2, no. 8 (1985): 121–40.

———. "The Further Shores of Partition: Ethnic Cleansing in Rajasthan 1947." *Past and Present* 160, no. 1 (1998): 203–39.

———. "The Princely States, the Muslim League, and the Partition of India in 1947." *International History Review* 13, no. 1 (February 1991): 38–69.

———. *The Princes of India in the Endgame of Empire, 1917–1947*. Cambridge: Cambridge University Press, 1997.

Copland, Ian, Aya Ikegame, and Andrea Major, eds. "Princely Spaces and Domestic Voices: New Perspectives on the Indian Princely States." Special issue, *Indian Economic and Social History Review* 46, no. 3 (2009).

Coupland, Reginald. *The Future of India*. Oxford: Oxford University Press, 1943.

Das, Taraknath. "The Status of Hyderabad during and after British Rule in India." *American Journal of International Law* 43, no. 1 (1949): 57–72.

Das, Veena. *Critical Events: An Anthropological Perspective on Contemporary India*. Delhi: Oxford University Press, 1996.

———. *Life and Words: Violence and the Descent into the Ordinary*. Berkeley: University of California Press, 2007.

Das, Veena, and Deborah Poole, eds. *Anthropology in the Margins of the State*. Santa Fe, NM: School of American Research Press, 2004.

Dasgupta, Jyotirindra. "India's Federal Design and Multicultural National Construction." In *The Success of India's Democracy*, edited by Atul Kohli, 49–77. Cambridge: Cambridge University Press, 2001.

Datla, Kavita Saraswathi. *The Language of Secular Islam: Urdu Nationalism and Colonial India*. Honolulu: University of Hawai'i Press, 2013.

———. "The Origins of Indirect Rule in India: Hyderabad and the British Imperial Order." *Law and History Review* 33, no. 2 (2015): 321–50.

———. "Sovereignty and the End of Empire: The Transition to Independence in Colonial Hyderabad." *Ab Imperio* 3 (2018): 63–88.

———. "Worldly Vernacular: Urdu at Osmania University." *Modern Asian Studies* 43, no. 5 (2009): 1117–48.

De, Rohit. *A People's Constitution: The Everyday Life of Law in the Indian Republic*. Princeton, NJ: Princeton University Press, 2018.

Desai, V. H., and Pretti Kumar, eds. *The Democrat: Saga of a Jail Journal of Hyderabad Freedom Struggle, 1947–1948*. Mumbai: Bharatiya Vidya Bhavan, 1998.

Deshpande, Anirudh. *Hope and Despair: Mutiny, Rebellion and Death in India, 1946*. Delhi: Primus Books, 2016.

Devji, Faisal. "Britain's Muslim Empire and Its Indian Future." *Seminar*, no. 601 (September 2009). www.indiaseminar.com/2009/601/601_faisal_devji.htm.

———. *Muslim Zion: Pakistan as a Political Idea*. Cambridge, MA: Harvard University Press, 2013.

Dhanagare, D. N. "Social Origins of the Peasant Insurrection in Telangana." *Contributions to Indian Sociology* 8 (1974): 109–34.

Dhanaraju, Vulli. "Making Peoples History in Telangana Movement: Remembering Voyya Raja Ram." *International Research Journal of Social Sciences* 3, no. 6 (2014): 37–43.

———. "The Telangana Movement (1946–1951): Folklore Perspective." *International Journal of Social Science Tomorrow* 8 (2012): 1–7.

———. "Voice of the Subaltern Poet: Contribution of Suddala Hanumanthu in Telangana Peoples' Movement." *Research Journal of Language, Literature and Humanities* 2, no. 7 (2015): 1–7.

Dhulipala, Venkat. *Creating a New Medina: State Power, Islam, and the Quest for Pakistan in Late Colonial North India.* Cambridge: Cambridge University Press, 2015.

Dirks, Nicholas. *Castes of Mind: Colonialism and the Making of Modern India.* Princeton, NJ: Princeton University Press, 2001.

Dube, S. C. *Indian Village.* 1955. Reprint, London: Routledge, 1998.

Eagleton, Clyde. "The Case of Hyderabad before the Security Council." *American Journal of International Law* 44, no. 2 (1950): 277–302.

———. *The Economic Life of Hyderabad.* Hyderabad: Government Central Press, 1937.

Elam, J. Daniel, Kama Maclean, and Chris Moffat, eds. "Writing Revolution: Practice, History, Politics in Modern South Asia." *South Asia: Journal of South Asian Studies* 39, no. 3 (2016): 513–694.

El Edroos, Syed Ahmed, and L. R. Naik. *Hyderabad of "The Seven Loaves."* Hyderabad: Laser Prints, 1994.

Elliot, Carolyn M. "Decline of a Patrimonial Regime: The Telangana Rebellion in India, 1946–51." *Journal of Asian Studies* 34, no. 1 (1974): 27–47.

Elwin, Verrier. *A Philosophy for NEFA.* Delhi, 1957.

Ernst, Waltraud, and Biswamoy Pati, eds. *India's Princely States: People, Princes and Colonialism.* London: Routledge, 2007.

Fisher, Michael. *Indirect Rule in India: Residents and the Residency System, 1764–1858.* Delhi: Oxford University Press, 1991.

Foucault, Michel. *"Society Must Be Defended": Lectures at the Collège de France, 1975–76.* Translated by David Macey. New York: Picador, 2003.

Frankel, Francine. *India's Political Economy, 1947–2004.* Delhi: Oxford University Press, 2005.

Fraser, Hastings. *Our Faithful Ally, the Nizam.* London: Smith, Elder, 1865.

Freitag, Sandria B. "Crime in the Social Order of Colonial North India." *Modern Asian Studies* 25, no. 2 (1991): 227–61.

Gadgil, D. R. *The Federal Problem in India.* Poona: Gokhale Institute of Politics and Economics, 1947.

Gandhi, Leela. *The Common Cause: Postcolonial Ethics and the Practice of Democracy, 1900–1955.* Chicago: University of Chicago Press, 2014.

Gandhi, Mahatma. *Collected Works of Mahatma Gandhi.* E-book. 98 vols. New Delhi: Publications Division, Government of India, 1999. www.gandhiashramsevagram.org/gandhi-literature/collected-works-of-mahatma-gandhi-volume-1-to-98.php.

Gangulee, N. *The Making of Federal India.* London: Nisbet, 1936.

Gauba, K. L. *Hyderabad or India.* Delhi: Rajkamal Publications, 1948.

Gellner, David, ed. *Borderland Lives in Northern South Asia.* Durham, NC: Duke University Press, 2013.

Gerwarth, Robert, and John Horne, eds. *War in Peace: Paramilitary Violence in Europe after the Great War.* Oxford: Oxford University Press, 2012.

Ghosh, Durba, and Dane Kennedy, eds. *Decentering Empire: Britain, India and the Transcolonial World.* New Delhi: Orient, Longman, 2006.

Ghurye, G. S. *The Aborigines—"So-Called"—and Their Future.* Poona: Gadgil, 1943.

Gill, Navyug. "Limits of Conversion: Caste, Labor, and the Question of Emancipation in Colonial Panjab." *Journal of Asian Studies* 78, no. 1 (2018): 1–20.

Godse, Gopal. *May It Please Your Honour: Statement of Nathuram Godse.* Delhi: Surya-Prakashan, 1989.

Gokhale, S. M. *India's Refugee Problem: Causes and Cures.* Baroda: Prakash Publications, 1948.

Gopal, S. *Jawaharlal Nehru: A Biography.* Vol. 2. *1947–1956.* Delhi: Oxford University Press, 1979.

———. "Nehru and Minorities." *Economic and Political Weekly* 23, nos. 45/47 (1988): 2463–66.

Gopal Jayal, Niraja. *Citizenship and Its Discontents: An Indian History.* Cambridge, MA: Harvard University Press, 2013.

Goswami, Manu. "Imaginary Futures and Colonial Internationalisms." *American Historical Review* 117, no. 5 (2012): 1461–85.

Gough, Kathleen. "Indian Peasant Uprisings." *Economic and Political Weekly* 9, nos. 32–34 (1974): 1391–1412.

Gour, Raj Bahadur, et al. *Glorious Telengana Armed Struggle.* New Delhi: Communist Party of India, 1973.

Government of Andhra Pradesh. *Nomadism: Its Causes and Cure.* Hyderabad: Tribal Cultural Research and Training Institute, 1965.

Government of Hyderabad. *Census of India, 1941.* Vol. 21. *H.E.H. The Nizam's Dominions (Hyderabad State), Part I Report.* Hyderabad: Government Central Press, 1945.

———. *Hyderabad Reborn: First Six Months of Freedom (September 18, 1948–March 17, 1949).* Hyderabad: Government of Hyderabad, 1949.

———. *Report on the Administration of Hyderabad State: September 1948–March 1950.* Hyderabad, 1950.

Government of India. *Millions on the Move: The Aftermath of Partition.* New Delhi: Ministry of Information and Broadcasting, 1948.

———. *White Paper on Hyderabad.* Delhi: Manager of Publications, 1948.

Green, Nile. "The Trans-border Traffic of Afghan Modernism: Afghanistan and the Indian 'Urdusphere.'" *Comparative Studies in Society and History* 53, no. 3 (2011): 479–508.

Greenberg, Jonathan D. "Against Silence and Forgetting." In *Partitioned Lives: Narratives of Home, Displacement, and Resettlement,* edited by Anjali Gera Roy and Nandi Bhatia, 255–73. Delhi: Pearson Longman, 2008.

Guha, Ramachandra. *India after Gandhi: The History of the World's Largest Democracy.* London: Macmillan, 2007.

———. *Savaging the Civilized: Verrier Elwin, His Tribals, and India.* Chicago: University of Chicago Press, 1999.

Guha, Ramachandra, and Madhav Gadgil. "State Forestry and Social Conflict in British India." *Past and Present* 123, no. 1 (1989): 141–77.

Guha, Ranajit. "Discipline and Mobilize." In *Subaltern Studies VII: Writings on South Asian History and Society*, edited by Partha Chatterjee and Gyanendra Pandey, 69–120. Delhi: Oxford University Press, 1993.

———. *Dominance without Hegemony: History and Power in Colonial India*. Cambridge, MA: Harvard University Press, 1997.

———. "On Some Aspects of the Historiography of Colonial India." In *Subaltern Studies I: Writings on South Asian History and Society*, edited by Ranajit Guha, 1–8. Delhi: Oxford University Press, 1982.

———. "The Small Voice of History." In *Subaltern Studies IX*, edited by Shahid Amin and Dipesh Chakrabarty, 1–12. Delhi: Oxford University Press, 1996.

———, ed. *Subaltern Studies I: Writings on South Asian History and Society*. Delhi: Oxford University Press, 1982.

Guha, Sumit. *Beyond Caste: Identity and Power in South Asia, Past and Present*. Leiden: Brill, 2013.

———. "States, Tribes, Castes: A Historical Re-exploration in Comparative Perspective." *Economic and Political Weekly* 50, nos. 46–47 (2015): 50–57.

Gupta, Akhil. "Revolution in Telengana, 1946–1951 (Part One)." *South Asia Bulletin* 4, no. 1 (1984): 1–26.

———. "Revolution in Telengana, 1946–1951 (Part Two)." *South Asia Bulletin* 4, no. 2 (1984): 22–32.

Gupta, Amit Kumar. *The Agrarian Drama: The Leftists and the Rural Poor in India, 1934–1951*. Delhi: Manohar, 1996.

Gwyer, Maurice, and A. Appadorai. *Speeches and Documents on the Indian Constitution, 1921–47*. Vol. 1. Bombay: Oxford University Press, 1957.

Haimendorf, Christoph von Führer. *The Aboriginal Tribes of Hyderabad. Vol. 1. The Chenchus: Jungle Folk of the Deccan*. Bombay: Macmillan, 1943.

———. *The Aboriginal Tribes of Hyderabad. Vol. 2. The Reddis of the Bison Hills: A Study in Acculturation*. Bombay: Macmillan, 1945.

———. *The Aboriginal Tribes of Hyderabad. Vol. 3. The Raj Gonds of Adilabad: Myth and Ritual*. London: Macmillan, 1948.

———. *Tribal Hyderabad: Four Reports*. Hyderabad: Revenue Department, 1945.

———. "Tribal Populations of Hyderabad: Yesterday and Today." In *Census of India, 1941*, vol. 21. New Delhi: Government Central Press, 1945, I-LII.

Hansen, Thomas Blom. "Democracy against the Law: Reflections on India's Illiberal Democracy." In *Majoritarian State: How Hindu Nationalism Is Changing India*, edited by Angana P. Chatterji, Thomas Blom Hansen, and Christophe Jaffrelot, 19–40. Oxford: Oxford University Press, 2019.

———. "Governance and Myths of State in Mumbai." In *The Everyday State and Society in Modern India*, edited by Chris Fuller and Veronique Harris, 31–67. London: Hurst, 2001.

———. *Wages of Violence: Naming and Identity in Postcolonial Bombay*. Princeton, NJ: Princeton University Press, 2002.

Hansen, Thomas Blom, and Finn Stepputat, eds. *Sovereign Bodies: Citizens, Migrants, and States in the Postcolonial World*. Princeton, NJ: Princeton University Press, 2005.

———. *States of Imagination: Ethnographic Explorations of the Postcolonial State*. Durham, NC: Duke University Press, 2001.

Harding, Christopher. *Religious Transformation in South Asia: The Meanings of Conversion in Colonial Punjab*. Oxford: Oxford University Press, 2008.

Harrison, Selig S. "Caste and the Andhra Communists." *American Political Science Review* 50, no. 2 (1956): 378–404.

Hasan, Syed Abid. *Whither Hyderabad?* Hyderabad, 1935.

Hasan, Syed Zafarul, and Muhammad Afzal Husain Qadri. *The Problem of Indian Muslims and Its Solution*. Aligarh: Aligarh Muslim University Press, 1939.

Hughes, Julie E. *Animal Kingdoms: Hunting, the Environment and Power in the Indian Princely States*. Cambridge, MA: Harvard University Press, 2013.

Hunter, W. W. *The Indian Mussulmans: Are They Bound in Conscience to Rebel against the Queen?* London: Trübner, 1871.

Husain, Azim. *Fazl-i-Husain, a Political Biography*. Bombay: Longmans Green, 1946.

Husain, Nasser. *The Jurisprudence of Emergency: Colonialism and the Rule of Law*. Ann Arbor: University of Michigan Press, 2003.

Hussain, Delwar. *Boundaries Undermined: The Ruins of Progress on the Bangladesh/India Border*. London: Hurst, 2013.

Hyder, Mohammed. *October Coup: A Memoir of the Struggle for Hyderabad*. New Delhi: Lotus Collection, 2012.

Hyderabad Delegation to the United Nations. *The Hyderabad Question before the United Nations (Documents and Other Materials)*. Karachi: Civil and Military Gazette, 1951.

Hyderabad Labour Ministry. *Hyderabad (Deccan)*. Hyderabad, 1947.

Ikegame, Aya. *Princely India Re-imagined: A Historical Anthropology of Mysore from 1799 to the Present*. London: Routledge, 2012.

Indian National Congress. *Report of the 51st Indian National Congress*. Ahmedabad, 1938.

International Aryan League. *The Case of Arya Samaj in Hyderabad State*. Delhi: International Aryan League, 1938.

Iqbal, Muhammad. "Iqbal's Presidential Address Delivered at the Annual Session of the All-India Muslim League at Allahabad on the 29th December, 1930." In *Iqbal, Jinnah, and Pakistan: The Vision and the Reality*, edited by C. M. Naim. Syracuse, NY: Syracuse University Press, 1979.

Islam, Mufakharul. "The Punjab Land Alienation Act and the Professional Moneylenders." *Modern Asian Studies* 29, no. 2 (1995): 271–91.

Jaffrelot, Christophe. *India's Silent Revolution: The Rise of the Lower Castes in North India*. New York: Columbia University Press, 2003.

Jagir Administrator's Office. *The Hyderabad Jagirs Commutation Manual*. Hyderabad, 1951.

Jalal, Ayesha. *The Pity of Partition: Manto's Life, Times and Work across the India-Pakistan Divide*. Princeton, NJ: Princeton University Press, 2013.

———. *Self and Sovereignty: Individual and Community in South Asian Islam since 1850*. Delhi: Oxford University Press, 2001.

———. *The Sole Spokesman: Jinnah, the Muslim League and the Demand for Pakistan*. Lahore: Sang-e-Meel Publications, 1999.

Jangam, Chinnaiah. "Recast-(e)-ing Class: Dalit Chronicles of Communist Organizing in Telugu Country." Paper presented at Global Ambedkar workshop, Columbia University, October 19, 2018.

Jeffrey, Robin. "The Punjab Boundary Force and the Problem of Order, August 1947." *Modern Asian Studies* 8, no. 4 (1974): 491–520.

Jinnah, Mohammad Ali. *Quaid-i-Azam Mohammad Ali Jinnah Papers*. Vol. 3. *On the Threshold of Pakistan, 1 July–25 July 1947*. Edited by Z. H. Zaidi. Islamabad: Quaid-i-Azam Papers Project, National Archives of Pakistan, 1996.

———. *Quaid-i-Azam Mohammad Ali Jinnah Papers*. Vol. 4. *Pakistan at Last, 26 July–14 August 1947*. Edited by Z. H. Zaidi. Islamabad: Quaid-i-Azam Papers Project, National Archives of Pakistan, 1999.

———. *Quaid-i-Azam Mohammad Ali Jinnah Papers*. Vol. 9. *The States: Hyderabad, Jammu and Kashmir*. Edited by Z. H. Zaidi. Islamabad: Quaid-i-Azam Papers Project, National Archives of Pakistan, 2003.

———. *Selected Speeches and Statements of the Quaid-i-Azam Mohammad Ali Jinnah (1911–34 and 1947–48)*. Edited by M. Rafique Afzal. Lahore: Research Society of Pakistan, University of the Punjab, 1966.

Jodhka, Surinder. "Prejudice without Pollution? Scheduled Castes in Contemporary Punjab." *Journal of Indian School of Political Economy* 12, nos. 3–4 (2000): 381–403.

Joseph, T. Uma. *Accession of Hyderabad: The Inside Story*. Delhi: Sundeep Prakashan, 2006).

Judge, Paramjit S. "Hierarchical Differentiation among Dalits." *Economic and Political Weekly* 38, no. 28 (2003): 2990–91.

Judt, Tony. *Postwar: A History of Europe since 1945*. New York: Penguin, 2005.

Juergensmeyer, Mark. *Religion as Social Vision: The Movement against Untouchability in 20th-Century Punjab*. Berkeley: University of California Press, 1982.

Kabir, Ananya Jahanara. *Partition's Post-amnesias*. Dhaka: University Press, 2014.

Kahn, Paul W. *Sacred Violence: Torture, Terror, and Sovereignty*. Ann Arbor: University of Michigan Press, 2008.

Kakar, Sudhir. *The Colors of Violence: Cultural Identities, Religion, and Conflict*. Chicago: University of Chicago Press, 1996.

Kamat, Manjiri N. "Border Incidents, Internal Disorder and the *Nizam's* Claim for an Independent Hyderabad." In *India's Princely States: People, Princes and Colonialism*, edited by Ernst Waltraud and Biswamoy Pati, 212–24. London: Routledge, 2007.

Kamra, Sukeshi. *Bearing Witness: Partition, Independence, End of the Raj*. Calgary: University of Calgary Press, 2002.

Kapila, Kriti. "Old Differences and New Hierarchies: The Trouble with Tribes in Contemporary India." In *Interrogating India's Modernity: Democracy, Identity, and Citizenship*, edited by Surinder Jodhka, 99–116. New Delhi: Oxford University Press, 2013.

Kapila, Shruti. "Global Intellectual History and the Indian Political." In *Rethinking Mod-*

ern European Intellectual History for the Twenty-First Century, edited by Samuel Moyn and Darrin McMahon, 425–63. New York: Oxford University Press, 2013.

———. "A History of Violence." *Modern Intellectual History* 7, no. 2 (2010): 437–57.

———. *Violent Fraternity: Global Political Thought in the Indian Age*. Princeton, NJ: Princeton University Press, forthcoming.

Kate, P. V. *Marathwada under the Nizams, 1724–1948*. Delhi: Mittal Publications, 1987.

Kaul, Suvir, ed. *The Partitions of Memory: The Afterlife of the Division of India*. Delhi: Permanent Black, 2001.

Kautsky, John H. *Moscow and the Communist Party of India: A Study in the Postwar Evolution of International Communist Strategy*. Cambridge, MA: MIT Press, 1956.

Kaviraj, Sudipta. "A Critique of the Passive Revolution." *Economic and Political Weekly* 23, nos. 45/47 (1988): 2429–44.

———. *The Enchantment of Democracy and India*. Ranikhet: Permanent Black, 2011.

———. *The Imaginary Institution of India: Politics and Ideas*. New York: Columbia University Press, 2010.

———. *The Trajectories of the Indian State: Politics and Ideas*. Ranikhet: Permanent Black, 2010.

Kaur, Ravinder. "Distinctive Citizenship: Refugees, Subjects and Post-colonial State in India's Partition." *Cultural and Social History* 6, no. 4 (2009): 429–46.

———. "Narrative Absence: An 'Untouchable' Account of Partition Migration." *Contributions to Indian Sociology* 42, no. 2 (2008): 281–306.

———. *Since 1947: Partition Narratives among Punjab Migrants of Delhi*. New Delhi: Oxford University Press, 2007.

Keith, Arthur Berriedale. *A Constitutional History of India, 1600–1935*. 2nd ed. 1937. Reprint, Allahabad: Central Book Depot, 1961.

Keer, Dhananjay. *Mahatma Jotirao Phooley: Father of Indian Social Revolution*. Mumbai: Popular Prakashan, 2002.

Khalidi, Omar. *Hyderabad: After the Fall*. Wichita, KS: Hyderabad Historical Society, 1988.

Khan, Rasheeduddin. "Muslim Leadership and Electoral Politics in Hyderabad: A Pattern of Minority Articulation—I." *Economic and Political Weekly* 6, no. 15 (1971): 833–40.

Khan, Shafa'at Ahmad. *The Indian Federation: An Exposition and Critical Review*. London: Macmillan, 1937.

Khan, Syed Ahmed. *An Account of the Loyal Mahomedans of India*. London, 1860.

Khan, Yasmin. *The Great Partition: The Making of India and Pakistan*. New Haven, CT: Yale University Press, 2007.

———. *India at War: The Subcontinent and the Second World War*. Oxford: Oxford University Press, 2015.

Khilnani, Sunil. *The Idea of India*. New York: Farrar, Straus, Giroux, 1999.

———. "Nehru's Faith." *Economic and Political Weekly* 37, no. 48 (2002): 4793–99.

———. "Nehru's Judgement." In *Political Judgement: Essays for John Dunn*, edited by Richard Bourke and Raymond Geuss, 254–78. Cambridge: Cambridge University Press, 2009.

Khosla, Gopal Das. *Stern Reckoning: A Survey Leading up to and following the Partition of India.* New Delhi: Bhawnani, 1949.
Khosla, Madhav. *India's Founding Moment: The Constitution of a Most Surprising Democracy.* Cambridge, MA: Harvard University Press, 2020.
Kooiman, Dick. *Communalism and Indian Princely States: Travancore, Baroda and Hyderabad in the 1930s.* New Delhi: Manohar, 2002.
Kothari, Rajni. *Politics in India.* Boston: Little, Brown, 1970.
Kudaisya, Gyanesh. "From Displacement to 'Development': East Punjab Countryside after Partition, 1947–67." In *Freedom, Trauma, Continuities: Northern India and Independence,* edited by D. A. Low and Howard Brasted, 73–90. New Delhi: Sage, 1998.
———. *A Republic in the Making: India in the 1950s.* Oxford: Oxford University Press, 2018.
Kumar, Aishwary. "The Idea of the 'Tribal' in British India: Law, Archive and Memory in Santal Parganas." PhD diss., University of Cambridge, 2007.
Kumarasingham, Harshan. *A Political Legacy of the British Empire: Power and the Parliamentary System in Post-colonial India and Sri Lanka.* London: Tauris, 2013.
Laik Ali, Mir. *Tragedy of Hyderabad.* Karachi: Pakistan Co-operative Book Society, 1962.
Latif, Syed Abdul. *The Muslim Problem in India: Together with an Alternative Constitution for India.* Bombay: Times of India, 1939.
Legg, Stephen. "Dyarchy: Democracy, Autocracy, and the Scalar Sovereignty of Interwar India." *Comparative Studies of South Asia, Africa and the Middle East* 36, no. 1 (2016): 44–65.
———. "An International Anomaly? Sovereignty, the League of Nations and India's Princely Geographies." *Journal of Historical Geography* 43 (2014): 96–110.
Lelyveld, David. *Aligarh's First Generation: Muslim Solidarity in British India.* Princeton, NJ: Princeton University Press, 1978.
Leonard, Karen. "Hyderabad: The Mulki–Non-Mulki Conflict." In *People, Princes and Paramount Power: Society and Politics in the Indian Princely States,* edited by Robin Jeffrey, 65–106. Oxford: Oxford University Press, 1978.
———. *Locating Home: India's Hyderabadis Abroad.* Stanford, CA: Stanford University Press, 2007.
———. "Palmer and Company: An Indian Banking Firm in Hyderabad State." *Modern Asian Studies* 47, no. 4 (2013): 1157–84.
Leslie, Julia. *Authority and Meaning in Indian Religions: Hinduism and the Case of Valmiki.* Burlington, VT: Ashgate, 2003.
Low, D. A., and Howard Brasted, eds. *Freedom, Trauma, Continuities: Northern India and Independence.* New Delhi: Sage, 1998.
Lumby, E. W. R. "British Policy toward the Indian States, 1940–7." In *The Partition of India: Policies and Perspectives, 1935–1947,* edited by C. H. Philips and Mary Doreen Wainwright, 95–103. Cambridge, MA: MIT Press, 1970.
Maclean, Kama. *A Revolutionary History of Interwar India: Violence, Image, Voice and Text.* New York: Oxford University Press, 2015.

Manela, Erez. *The Wilsonian Moment: Self-Determination and the International Origins of Anticolonial Nationalism.* Oxford: Oxford University Press, 2007.
Mangamma, J. *Alluri Sitarama Raju.* Hyderabad: A.P. State Archives, 1983.
Mansergh, Nicholas. *The Transfer of Power, 1942–7.* Vol. 12. London: HMSO, 1983.
Mantena, Karuna. "Popular Sovereignty and Anti-colonialism." In *Popular Sovereignty in Historical Perspective,* edited by Richard Bourke and Quentin Skinner, 297–319. Cambridge: Cambridge University Press, 2016.
Mantena, Karuna, and Rama Sundari Mantena. "Political Imaginaries at the End of Empire." *Ab Imperio* 3 (2018): 31–35.
Mantena, Rama Sundari. "The Andhra Movement, Hyderabad State, and the Historical Origins of the Telangana Demand: Public Life and Political Aspirations in India, 1900–56." *India Review* 13, no. 4 (2014): 337–57.
———. "Anticolonialism and Federation in Colonial India." *Ab Imperio* 3 (2018): 36–62.
———. "Publicity, Civil Liberties and Political Life in Princely Hyderabad." *Modern Asian Studies* 53, no. 4 (2019): 1248–77.
Mayaram, Shail. *Resisting Regimes: Myth, Memory and the Shaping of a Muslim Identity.* Delhi: Oxford University Press, 1997.
Mazower, Mark. *No Enchanted Palace: The End of Empire and the Ideological Origins of the United Nations.* Princeton, NJ: Princeton University Press, 2013.
Mehta, Uday S. "The Social Question and the Absolutism of Politics." *Seminar,* no. 615 (November 2010). www.india-seminar.com/2010/615/615_uday_s_mehta.htm.
———. "Violence." In *Political Concepts: A Critical Lexicon,* 2012. www.politicalconcepts.org/violence-uday-s-mehta/.
Menon, Jisha. *The Performance of Nationalism: India, Pakistan, and the Memory of Partition.* Cambridge: Cambridge University Press, 2013.
Menon, Ritu. "Birth of Social Security Commitments: What Happened in the West." In *Refugees and the State: Practices of Asylum and Care in India, 1947–2000,* edited by Ranbir Samaddar, 152–81. New Delhi: Manas Publications, 2003.
Menon, Ritu, and Kamla Bhasin. *Borders and Boundaries: Women in India's Partition.* Delhi: Kali for Women, 1998.
Menon, V. P. *The Story of the Integration of the Indian States.* Calcutta, 1956.
———. *The Transfer of Power in India.* Princeton, NJ: Princeton University Press, 1957.
Mitra, S. M. *Indian Problems.* London: John Murray, 1908.
Moffat, Chris. *India's Revolutionary Inheritance: Politics and the Promise of Bhagat Singh.* Cambridge: Cambridge University Press, 2019.
Mohanty, Manoranjan. "Adivasi Swaraj Is the Answer to Violence." *Economic and Political Weekly* 52, no. 21 (2017): 66–70.
Moid, M. A. "Muslim Perceptions and Responses in Post-Police Action Contexts in Hyderabad." *Deccan Studies* 6, no. 2 (2008): 52–74.
Moid, M. A., and A. Suneetha. "Rethinking Majlis' Politics: Pre-1948 Muslim Concerns in Hyderabad State." *Indian Economic and Social History Review* 55, no. 1 (2018): 29–52.
Mojumdar, Kanchanmoy. *Saffron versus Green: Communal Politics in the Central Provinces and Berar, 1919–1947.* New Delhi: Manohar, 2003.

Montagu, Edwin. *Report on Indian Constitutional Reforms.* London: HMSO 1918.
Moon, Penderel. *Divide and Quit.* London: Chatto and Windus, 1962.
Moore, Barrington. *Social Origins of Dictatorship and Democracy: Lord and Peasant in the Making of the Modern World.* Boston: Beacon Press, 1966.
Moore, R. J. *Escape from Empire: The Attlee Government and the Indian Problem.* Oxford: Clarendon Press, 1983.
———. "India in 1947: The Limits of Unity." In *The States of South Asia: Problems of National Integration,* edited by A. Jeyaratnam Wilson and Dennis Dalton, 45–76. London: Hurst, 1982.
———. "The Making of India's Paper Federation, 1927–35." In *The Partition of India,* edited by C. H. Philips and M. D. Wainwright, 54-78. London: Allen and Unwin, 1970.
———. *Making the New Commonwealth.* Oxford: Clarendon Press, 1987.
———. "Mountbatten, India, and the Commonwealth." *Journal of Commonwealth and Comparative Politics* 19, no. 1 (1981): 5–43.
Munshi, K. M. *Akhand Hindustan.* Bombay: New Book Company, 1942.
———. *End of an Era.* Bombay: Bharatiya Vidya Bhavan, 1957.
———. *Report on the Razakars of Hyderabad.* Hyderabad, 1948.
Nair, Janaki. *Mysore Modern: Rethinking the Region under Princely Rule.* Minneapolis: University of Minnesota Press, 2012.
Nandy, Ashis. *An Ambiguous Journey to the City: The Village and Other Odd Ruins of the Self in the Indian Imagination.* New Delhi: Oxford University Press, 2007.
Narayan, Jayaprakash. *Selected Works.* Edited by B. Prasad. Vol. 5. Delhi: Manohar, 2005.
Nasr, Syed Vali Reza. *Vanguard of the Islamic Revolution: The Jama'at-I Islami of Pakistan.* Berkeley: University of California Press, 1994.
Nazir, Pervaiz. "Origins of Debt, Mortgage and Alienation of Land in Early Modern Punjab." *Journal of Peasant Studies* 27, no. 3 (2000): 55–91.
Nehru, Jawaharlal. "The Basic Approach." *A.I.C.C. Economic Review: Fortnightly Journal of the Economic and Political Research Department of the All India Congress Committee* 10, nos. 8–9 (15 August 1958): 3–6.
———. *Before and after Independence: A Collection of the Most Important and Soul-Stirring Speeches Delivered by Jawaharlal Nehru during the Most Important and Soul-Stirring Years in India's History, 1922–1950.* Edited by J. S. Bright. New Delhi: Indian Printing Works, n.d.
———. *The Discovery of India.* London: Meridian, 1960.
———. *Jawaharlal Nehru's Speeches.* Vol. 1. *September 1946–May 1949.* 1949. Reprint, New Delhi: Publications Division, Ministry of Information and Broadcasting, 1963.
———. *Letters to Chief Ministers, 1947–1964.* Vol. 1. *1947–1949.* Edited by G. Parthasarathi. New Delhi: Publications Division, Ministry of Information and Broadcasting, 1985.
———. *Letters to Chief Ministers, 1947–1964.* Vol. 3. *1952–1954.* Edited by G. Parthasarathi. New Delhi: Publications Division, Ministry of Information and Broadcasting, 1987.
———. *Selected Works of Jawaharlal Nehru (First Series).* Edited by S. Gopal. 15 vols. New Delhi: Jawaharlal Nehru Memorial Fund, 1972–82.
———. *Selected Works of Jawaharlal Nehru (Second Series).* Edited by S. Gopal. 71 vols. New Delhi: Jawaharlal Nehru Memorial Fund, 1984–2017.

Nigam, Sanjay. "Disciplining and Policing the 'Criminals by Birth,' Part 2: The Development of a Disciplinary System, 1871–1900." *Indian Economic and Social History Review* 21, no. 3 (1990): 131–64.

Noorani, A. G. *The Destruction of Hyderabad.* Delhi: Tulika Books, 2013.

———. "Of a Massacre Untold." *Frontline* magazine (Chennai), March 3–16, 2001.

———. "Of Stalin, Telangana and Indian Revolution." *Frontline* magazine (Chennai), December 16, 2011.

Omvedt, Gail. *Dalits and the Democratic Revolution: Dr. Ambedkar and the Dalit Movement in Colonial India.* New Delhi: Sage, 1994.

Overstreet, Gene D., and Marshall Windmiller. *Communism in India.* Berkeley: University of California Press, 1959.

Pandey, Gyanendra. "Can a Muslim Be an Indian?" *Comparative Studies in Society and History* 41, no. 4 (1999): 608–29.

———. *The Construction of Communalism in Colonial North India.* New Delhi: Oxford University Press, 1990.

———. "'Nobody's People': The Dalits of Punjab in the Forced Removal of 1947." In *Removing Peoples: Forced Removal in the Modern World,* edited by Richard Bessel and Claudia Haake, 297–319. Oxford: Oxford University Press, 2009.

———. "The Prose of Otherness." In *Subaltern Studies VIII,* edited by David Arnold and David Hardiman, 188–221. Delhi: Oxford University Press, 1994.

———. *Remembering Partition: Violence, Nationalism and History in India.* Cambridge: Cambridge University Press, 2004.

Pandian, M. S. *Brahmin and Non-Brahmin: Genealogies of the Tamil Political Present.* New Delhi: Permanent Black, 2007.

Panikkar, K. M. *The Foundations of New India.* London: Allen and Unwin, 1963.

Panneeru, Ramesh. *Telangana Armed Struggle in Nalgonda District: A Case Study of Kadavendi Village, 1930–52 A.D.* Hyderabad: Prajasakti Book House, 2010.

Patel, Kamla. *Torn from the Roots: A Partition Memoir.* Translated by Uma Randeria. New Delhi: Women Unlimited, 2006.

Patel, Maniben. *Inside Story of Sardar Patel: The Diary of Maniben Patel, 1936–50.* Edited by P. N. Chopra and P. Chopra. Delhi: Vision Books, 2001.

Patel, Vallabhbhai. *For a United India: Speeches of Sardar Patel, 1947–1950.* New Delhi: Publications Division, Ministry of Information and Broadcasting, 1967.

———. *In Tune with the Millions.* Birth Centenary ed. Vol. 2. Edited by G. M. Nandurkar. Ahmedabad: Sardar Vallabhbhai Patel Smarak Bhavan, 1975.

———. *Sardar Patel's Correspondence, 1945–50.* 10 vols. Edited by Durga Das. Ahmedabad: Navajivan Publishing House, 1971–74.

———. *Sardar's Letters: Mostly Unknown.* Edited by G. M. Nandurkar. Ahmedabad: Sardar Vallabhbhai Patel Smarak Bhavan, 1981.

Pavier, Barry. *The Telengana Movement, 1944–51.* Delhi: Vikas, 1981.

Pederson, Susan. *The Guardians: The League of Nations and the Crisis of Empire.* Oxford: Oxford University Press, 2015.

Pernau, Margrit[-Reifeld]. *The Passing of Patrimonialism: Politics and Political Culture in Hyderabad, 1911–1948*. New Delhi: Manohar, 2000.

———. "Reaping the Whirlwind: Nizam and the Khilafat Movement." *Economic and Political Weekly* 34, no. 38 (1999): 2745–51.

Pillai, Sarath. "Fragmenting the Nation: Divisible Sovereignty and Travancore's Quest for Federal Independence." *Law and History Review* 34, no. 3 (2016): 743–82.

Poyam, Akash. "Gondwana Movement in Post-colonial India: Exploring Paradigms of Assertion, Self-Determination and Statehood." In *Social Work in India*, edited by S. R. Bodhi, 131–66. Kolkata: Adivaani, 2016.

Prasad, Rajendra. *India Divided*. Bombay, 1947.

Prasad, S. N. *Operation Polo: The Police Action against Hyderabad, 1948*. New Delhi: Historical Section, Ministry of Defence, 1972.

Prashad, Vijay. *Untouchable Freedom: A Social History of a Dalit Community*. Delhi: Oxford University Press, 2000.

"A Punjabi" [pseud.]. *Confederacy of India*. Lahore: Nawab Sir Muhammad Shah Nawaz Khan, 1939.

Puri, Harish. "Scheduled Castes in Sikh Community: A Historical Perspective." *Economic and Political Weekly* 38, no. 26 (2003): 2693–2701.

Purushotham, K., et al. *The Oxford India Anthology of Telugu Dalit Writing*. New Delhi: Oxford University Press, 2016.

Purushotham, Sunil. "World History in the Atomic Age: Past, Present and Future in the Political Thought of Jawaharlal Nehru." *Modern Intellectual History* 14, no. 3 (2017): 837–67.

Radhakrishna, Meena. "The Criminal Tribes Act in Madras Presidency: Implications for Itinerant Trading Communities." *Indian Economic and Social History Review* 26, no. 3 (1989): 269–95.

Radhakrishnan, P. *Peasant Struggles, Land Reforms, and Social Change: Malabar, 1836–1982*. New Delhi: Sage, 1989.

Raghavan, Srinath. *War and Peace in Modern India*. New York: Palgrave Macmillan, 2010.

Rahman, Mahbubar, and Willem Van Schendel. "'I Am Not a Refugee': Rethinking Partition Migration." *Modern Asian Studies* 37, no. 3 (2003): 551–84.

Rahmat Ali, Choudhry. *The Millat and the Mission*. Cambridge: Pakistan National Movement, 1944.

———. *Osmanistan: The Fatherland of the Osman Nation*. Cambridge: Osmanistan National Movement, 1946.

Rai, Lajpat. *The Arya Samaj*. London: Longmans, Green, 1915.

Rai, Satya M. *Partition of the Punjab: A Study of Its Effects on the Politics and Administration of the Punjab*. Vol. 1. *1947–56*. London: Asia Publishing House, 1965.

Ram, Mohan. *Indian Communism: Split within a Split*. New Delhi: Vikas, 1969.

———. "The Telengana Peasant Armed Struggle, 1946–51." *Economic and Political Weekly* 8, no. 23 (1973): 1025–32.

Ram, Moti. *A Guide to Constituent Assembly*. Delhi, 1947.

Ram, Ronki. "Untouchability, Dalit Consciousness, and the Ad Dharm Movement in Punjab." *Contributions to Indian Sociology* 38, no. 3 (2004): 323–49.

———. "Untouchability in India with a Difference: Ad Dharm, Dalit Assertion, and Caste Conflicts in Punjab." *Asian Survey* 44, no. 6 (2004): 895–912.

Ramakrishna, V. "Left Cultural Movement in Andhra Pradesh: 1930s to 1950s." *Social Scientist* 40, nos. 1/2 (2012): 21–30.

Ramaswamy, Sumathi. "Maps and Mother Goddesses in Modern India." *Imago Mundi* 53 (2001): 97–114.

Ramesan, N., ed. *The Freedom Struggle in Hyderabad*. Vol. 4. *1921–1947*. Hyderabad: Government of Andhra Pradesh, 1997.

Ramnath, Maia. *Haj to Utopia: How the Ghadar Movement Charted Global Radicalism and Attempted to Overthrow the British Empire*. Berkeley: University of California Press, 2011.

Ramusack, Barbara. "Congress and the People's Movement in Princely India: Ambivalence in Strategy and Organization." In *Congress and Indian Nationalism, The Pre-Independence Phase*, edited by Richard Sisson and Stanley Wolpert, 377–404. Berkeley: University of California Press, 1988.

———. *The Indian Princes and Their States*. Cambridge: Cambridge University Press, 2004.

Randhawa, M. S. *Out of the Ashes: An Account of the Rehabilitation of Refugees from West Pakistan in Rural Areas of East Punjab*. Chandigarh: Public Relations Department, 1954.

Rangarajan, Mahesh. *Fencing the Forest: Conservation and Ecological Change in India's Central Provinces*. New Delhi: Oxford University Press, 1996.

Rao, Chandra Rajeswara. *The Historic Telengana Struggle: Some Useful Lessons from Its Rich Experience*. Delhi: Communist Party of India, 1971.

Rao, Devulapalli Venkateswara. *Refutation of Wrong Trends Advocating Withdrawal of Telengana Armed Struggle*. 1949. Reprint, Hyderabad: Proletarian Line Publications, 1982.

———. *Telangana Armed Struggle and the Path of Indian Revolution*. Calcutta: Proletarian Path Publications, 1974.

Rao, I. M. L. Kantha. "A Study of the Socio Political Mobility of the Kapu Caste in Modern Andhra." PhD diss., University of Hyderabad, 1999.

Rao, M. Hanumanth, et al. *Constitutional Reforms in Hyderabad: A Report*. Hyderabad: Hyderabad People's Convention, 1938.

Rao, U. Baskhar. *The Story of Rehabilitation*. New Delhi: Dept. of Rehabilitation, Ministry of Labour, Employment and Rehabilitation, 1967.

Rao, V. K. R. V. *An Economic Review of Refugee Rehabilitation in India: A Study of Faridabad Township*. Delhi: University Press, 1955.

Rawat, Ramnarayan. "Partition Politics and Achhut Identity: A Study of the Scheduled Castes Federation and Dalit Politics in UP, 1946–48." In *The Partitions of Memory: The Afterlife of the Division of India*, edited by Suvir Kaul, 111–39. Delhi: Permanent Black, 2001.

———. *Reconsidering Untouchability: Chamars and Dalit History in North India*. Bloomington: Indiana University Press, 2011.

Razvi, S. M. Jawad. *Political Awakening in Hyderabad: Role of Youth and Students (1938–1956)*. Hyderabad: Visalandhra, 1985.
Reddy, Arutla Ramachandra. *Telengana Struggle: Memoirs*. Translated by B. Narsing Rao. Delhi: People's Publishing House, 1984.
Reddy, Chandra Pulla. *The Great Heroic Telengana Struggle*. Hyderabad, 1981.
Reddy, Ravi Narayan. *Heroic Telengana: Reminiscences and Experiences*. Delhi, 2010.
Roosa, John. "Passive Revolution Meets Peasant Revolution: Indian Nationalism and the Telangana Revolt." *Journal of Peasant Studies* 28, no. 4 (2001): 57–94.
Roy, Anupama. *Mapping Citizenship in India*. New Delhi: Oxford University Press, 2010.
Roy, Arundhati. "The Greater Common Good." *Outlook*, May 24, 1999.
Roy, Haimanti. *Partitioned Lives: Migrants, Refugees, Citizens in India and Pakistan, 1947–1965*. New York: Oxford University Press, 2012.
Sadullah, Mian Muhammad, ed. *The Partition of the Punjab 1947: A Compilation of Official Documents*. Vol. 2. Lahore: Sang-e-Meel Publications, 1983.
Saint, Tarun. *Witnessing Partition: Memory, History, Fiction*. New Delhi: Routledge, 2010.
Saksena, Mohanlal. *Some Reflections on the Problems of Rehabilitation*. New Delhi: Caxton Press, 1950.
Sarkar, Sumit. "Indian Democracy: The Historical Inheritance." In *The Success of India's Democracy*, edited by Atul Kohli, 23–46. Cambridge: Cambridge University Press, 2001.
———. "Popular Movements and National Leadership, 1945–47." *Economic and Political Weekly* 17, nos. 14/16 (1982): 677–89.
Sastry, K. R. R. *Indian States*. Allahabad: Kitabistan, 1941.
Server ul-Mulk. *My Life: Being the Autobiography of Nawab Server-ul-Mulk Bahadur*. Translated by Nawab Jiwan Yar Jung Bahadur. London, 1903.
Scott, James C. *The Art of Not Being Governed: An Anarchist History of Upland Southeast Asia*. New Haven, CT: Yale University Press, 2009.
Sen, Dwaipayan. *The Decline of the Caste Question: Jogendranath Mandal and the Defeat of Dalit Politics in Bengal*. Cambridge: Cambridge University Press, 2018.
———. "'No Matter How, Jogendranath Had to Be Defeated': The Scheduled Castes Federation and the Making of Partition in Bengal, 1945–1947." *Indian Economic Social History Review* 49, no. 3 (2012): 321–64.
Sen, Sudipta. "Unfinished Conquest: Residual Sovereignty and the Legal Foundations of the British Empire in India." *Law, Culture and the Humanities* 9, no. 2 (2012): 227–42.
Sen, Uditi. *Citizen Refugee: Forging the Indian Nation after Pakistan*. Cambridge: Cambridge University Press, 2018.
Sever, Adrian, ed. *Documents and Speeches on the Indian Princely States*. Vol. 2. New Delhi: B. R. Publishing, 1985.
Sewell, William H. *Logics of History: Social Theory and Social Transformation*. Chicago: University of Chicago Press, 2005.
Shah, Alpa. "A Double-Edged Sword: Protection and State Violence." *Critique of Anthropology* 26, no. 3 (2006): 251–57.
Shani, Ornit. "Conceptions of Citizenship in India and the 'Muslim Question.'" *Modern Asian Studies* 44, no. 1 (2010): 145–73.

———. *How India Became Democratic: Citizenship and the Making of the Universal Franchise*. Cambridge: Cambridge University Press, 2018.

Shankar, V. *My Reminiscences of Sardar Patel*. Vol. 1. Delhi: Macmillan Company of India, 1974.

Sharma, Aradhana, and Akhil Gupta, eds. *The Anthropology of the State: A Reader*. Malden, MA: Blackwell, 2006.

Sharma, Shalini. "'Yeh Azaadi Jhooti Hai!': The Shaping of the Opposition in the First Year of the Congress Raj." *Modern Asian Studies* 48, no. 5 (2014): 1358–88.

Sheehan, James. "The Problem of Sovereignty in European History." *American Historical Review* 111, no. 1 (2006): 1–15.

Sherif, M. A. "Pickthall's Islamic Politics." In *Marmaduke Pickthall: Islam and the Modern World*, edited by Geoffrey Nash, 106–36. Boston: Leiden, 2017.

Sherman, Taylor. "The Integration of the Princely State of Hyderabad and the Making of the Postcolonial State in India, 1948–1956." *Indian Economic and Social History Review* 44, no. 4 (2007): 489–516.

———. "Migration, Citizenship and Belonging in Hyderabad (Deccan), 1946–1956." *Modern Asian Studies* 45, no. 1 (2011): 81–107.

———. "Moral Economies of Violence in Hyderabad State, 1948." *Deccan Studies* 8, no. 2 (2010): 65–90.

———. *Muslim Belonging in Secular India: Negotiating Citizenship in Postcolonial Hyderabad*. Cambridge: Cambridge University Press, 2015.

Sherwani, H. K. "The Evolution of the Legislature in Hyderabad." *Indian Journal of Political Science* 1, no. 4 (1940): 424–38.

Sherwani, Latif Ahmed, ed. *Pakistan Resolution to Pakistan, 1940–1947: A Selection of Documents Presenting the Case for Pakistan*. Karachi: National Publishing House, 1969.

Siegel, Benjamin. *Hungry Nation: Food, Famine, and the Making of Modern India*. Cambridge: Cambridge University Press, 2018.

Simon, John, et al. *Report of the Indian Statutory Commission*. 2 vols. 1. Survey. Calcutta: Central Publication Branch, 1930.

Singh, Brighupati. *Poverty and the Quest for Life: Spiritual and Material Striving in Rural India*. Chicago: University of Chicago Press, 2015.

Singh, Gurmukh Nihal. "Constitutional Reforms in Indian States: A Comparative Study." *Indian Journal of Political Science* 3, no. 1 (1941): 90–107.

———. *Indian States and British India: Their Future Relations*. Benares: Nand Kishore and Bros., 1930.

Singh, Kirpal. *The Partition of the Punjab*. Patiala: Punjabi University, 1972.

———. *Select Documents on Partition of Punjab-1947: India and Pakistan*. Delhi: National Book Shop, 2006.

Singh, Neerja, ed. *Nehru-Patel: Agreement within Differences. Select Documents and Correspondences, 1933–1950*. New Delhi: National Book Trust, 2010.

Singh, Rajendra. *The Military Evacuation Organisation, 1947–48*. New Delhi: Manager Press, 1961.

Singh, St. Nihal. *The Nizam and the British Empire.* n.p.: Nihal Singh, 1923.
Sitapati, Vinay. *Half-Lion: How P. V. Narasimha Rao Transformed India.* Gurgaon: Penguin/Viking, 2016.
Sivaramakrishnan, K. "Colonialism and Forestry in India: Imagining the Past in Present Politics." *Comparative Studies in Society and History* 37, no. 1 (1995): 3–40.
Skaria, Ajay. *Hybrid Histories: Forests, Frontiers and Wildness in Western India.* Delhi: Oxford University Press, 1999.
———. "Shades of Wilderness: Tribe, Caste, and Gender in Western India." *Journal of Asian Studies* 56, no. 3 (2007): 726–45.
Slight, J. P. "The British Empire and the Hajj, 1865–1956." PhD diss, University of Cambridge, 2011.
Socialist Party Hyderabad Struggle Committee. *The Hyderabad Problem: The Next Step.* Bombay: Hyderabad Struggle Committee, 1948.
Spencer, Jonathan. *Anthropology, Politics, and the State: Democracy and Violence in South Asia.* Cambridge: Cambridge University Press, 2007.
Standing Committee of the Chamber of Princes. *The British Crown and the Indian States: An Outline Sketch Presented to the Indian States Committee.* London: P. S. King, 1929.
Stoler, Ann Laura. *Along the Archival Grain: Epistemic Anxieties and Colonial Commonsense.* Princeton, NJ: Princeton University Press, 2009.
Stree Shakti Sanghatana. *We Were Making History: Women and the Telangana Uprising.* London: Zed Books, 1989.
Sundar, Nandini. "Interning Insurgent Populations: The Buried Histories of Indian Democracy." *Economic and Political Weekly* 46, no. 6 (2011): 47–57.
———. *Subalterns and Sovereigns: An Anthropological History of Bastar (1854–2006).* Delhi: Oxford University Press, 2007.
Sundarayya, Putchalapalli. *An Autobiography.* Edited and abridged by Atlury Murali. Delhi: National Book Trust, 2009.
———. *Telengana People's Struggle and Its Lessons.* New Delhi: Foundation Books, 1972.
Tahmankar, D. V. *Sardar Patel.* London: Allen and Unwin, 1970.
Talbot, Ian. "Punjabi Refugees' Rehabilitation and the Indian State: Discourses, Denials and Dissonances." *Modern Asian Studies* 45, no. 1 (2011): 109–30.
———. "A Tale of Two Cities: The Aftermath of Partition for Lahore and Amritsar, 1947–1957." *Modern Asian Studies* 41, no. 1 (2007): 151–86.
Thirumali, Inukonda. *Against Dora and Nizam: People's Movement in Telengana, 1939–1948.* Delhi: Kanishka, 2003.
———. "Dora and Gadi: Manifestation of Landlord Domination in Telengana." *Economic and Political Weekly* 27, no. 9 (1992): 477–82.
———. "The Political Pragmatism of the Communists in Telengana, 1938–48." *Social Scientist* 24, nos. 4/6 (1996): 164–83.
Thompson, Edward. *The Making of the Indian Princes.* London: Oxford University Press, 1943.

Tillin, Louise. "India's Democracy at 70: The Federalist Compromise." *Journal of Democracy* 28, no. 3 (2017): 64–75.

———. *Remapping India: New States and Their Political Origins*. London: Oxford University Press, 2013.

Tilly, Charles. "War Making and State Making as Organized Crime." In *Bringing the State Back In*, edited by Peter Evans, Dietrich Rueschemeyer and Theda Skocpol, 169–91. Cambridge: Cambridge University Press, 1985.

Tirtha, Swami Ramananda. *Indian National Congress: Fifty-Eight Session*. Hyderabad, 1953.

———. *Memoirs of Hyderabad Freedom Struggle*. Bombay: Popular Prakashan, 1967.

Upadhyaya, Prakash Chandra. "The Politics of Indian Secularism." *Modern Asian Studies* 26, no. 4 (1992): 815–53.

Vajpeyi, Ananya, ed. "We the People: A Symposium on the Constitution of India after 60 Years, 1950–2010." *Seminar*, no. 615 (November 2010). www.india-seminar.com/2010/615.htm.

Valiani, Arafaat. *Militant Publics in India: Physical Culture and Violence in the Making of a Modern Polity*. New York: Palgrave Macmillan, 2011.

Van Schendel, Willem. *The Bengal Borderland: Beyond State and Nation in South Asia*. London: Anthem Press, 2005.

Varshney, Ashutosh. *Battles Half Won: India's Improbable Democracy*. New Delhi: Penguin, 2013.

———. *Ethnic Conflict and Civic Life: Hindus and Muslims in India*. New Haven, CT: Yale University Press, 2002.

Venkatarangaiya, M. "The Reformed Constitution of the Hyderabad State." *Indian Journal of Political Science* 3, no. 1 (1941): 27–40.

Viswanath, Rupa. *The Pariah Problem: Caste, Religion, and the Social in Modern India*. New York: Columbia University Press, 2014.

Wahi, Namita. "The Fundamental Right to Property in the Indian Constitution." *Social Science Research Network*, August 10, 2015.

Wavell, Archibald Percival. *Wavell: the Viceroy's Journal*. Edited by Penderel Moon. London: Oxford University Press, 1973.

Wheatley, Natasha. "The Mandate System as a Style of Reasoning: International Jurisdiction and the Parceling of Imperial Sovereignty in Petitions from Palestine." In *The Routledge Handbook of the History of the Middle East Mandates*, edited by Cyrus Schayegh and Andrew Arsan, 106–22. London: Routledge, 2015.

———. "Mandatory Interpretation: Legal Hermeneutics and the New International Order in Arab and Jewish Petitions to the League of Nations." *Past and Present* 227 (2015): 205–48.

———. "Spectral Legal Personality in Interwar International Law: On New Ways of Not Being a State." *Law and History Review* 35, no. 3 (2017): 753–87.

Witmer, Michael. "The 1947–1948 India-Hyderabad Conflict: Realpolitik and the Formation of the Modern Indian State." PhD diss., Temple University, 1996.

Yagati, Chinna Rao. *Dalits' Struggle for Identity: Andhra and Hyderabad, 1900–1950*. New Delhi: Kanishka, 2003.
Yar Jung, Nawab Dr. Nazir, ed. *The Pakistan Issue*. Lahore, M. Ashraf, 1943.
Yazdani, Ghulam. *Hyderabad State: A Souvenir. 1922*. Reprint, Hyderabad-Deccan, 1944.
Zamindar, Vazira Fazila-Yacoobali. *The Long Partition and the Making of Modern South Asia: Refugees, Boundaries, Histories*. New York: Columbia University Press, 2007.

INDEX

abducted and recovered women, 151–57; agency of, 152, 153–56; arranging marriages for, 156, 170–71; conversions of, 133, 155–56, 171, 180; national status of, as subaltern group, 130, 133–35, 150; number of abducted women, 153, 284n26; public pressure for recovery, 151–52, 289n116; testimonial narratives of, 161, 166–67, 169–72, 174–80
Abducted Persons Restoration and Recovery Act (1949), 152
Abdul Ghaffar, Qazi, 81, 82
Ad Dharmis, 139, 141–42, 144
Adi Dravida movement, 141
Adi Hindu movement, 151
Adivasi communities in Telangana: democracy as articulated by, 240; in popular revolution, 7, 8, 186, 187, 199–200, 214, 224; as Scheduled Tribe, 227; as "squatters," 239–40; as term, 237; in tribal camps, 225–31, 233, 234, 236–42, 244–45
Al-Afghani, Jamal al-Din, 47
Aga Khan, 34
Agamben, Giorgio, 234
Ahmadiyya, 140
Ahmed, Muzaffar, 220, 222
Ahrars, 131
AISPC (All India States Peoples Conference), 33, 62, 95
Aiyangar, S. Aravamudu, and Aiyangar proposals, 40–44, 96
Akali Dal, 131

Akali Fauj, 131
Akalis, 142
Akhand Hindustan movement, 109
Alavi, Hamza, 6–7, 217–18
Ali, Mir Laik, 76, 104, 109, 277n162
Aligarh Muslim University, 47, 50, 120
All India Congress Committee, 63, 87, 117, 217
All India States Peoples Conference (AISPC), 33, 62, 95
Ambedkar, B. R., 11, 30, 43, 138–39, 146–47, 148, 205
Amin, Shahid, 166
AMS. *See* Andhra Mahasabha
Anand, Mulk Raj, 184
Andhra Congress Party, 187
Andhra Mahasabha (AMS): founding and origins of, 190; sovereignty claims of Nizam of Hyderabad and, 4, 38, 42, 45, 60, 97; Telangana revolution and, 184, 186, 187, 189–92, 195, 199, 220, 222
Andhra Provincial Committee, CPI, 7, 192, 193, 196, 198, 199
Andhra Thesis/Andhra Letter, 196
Appadurai, Arjun, 79, 238
Arnold, Matthew, 182
Aruna Asaf Ali, 108
Arya Samaj (International Aryan League): Hyderabad State Congress compared, 95; Police Action against Hyderabad and, 82, 88, 91–92, 93, 96–98, 105, 109, 275n116; in Punjab, 140–41, 171; sovereignty claims of Hyderabad and, 4, 33, 45, 46, 60

Asaf Jah dynasty, Hyderabad, 10, 27, 37–38, 42, 44, 46, 49, 222
Attlee, Clement, 61, 72, 270n288
Aundh, democratic federation of villages in, 264n148
Ayyangar, Gopalaswami, 211
Azad, Maulana, 62, 80–81, 118–19, 125
Azad Hyderabad, 66–70, 71, 73, 93, 115, 117

Balmikis, 142, 143, 144
Basavapunnaiah, M., 192, 196, 221, 297n65
Basu, Jyoti, 222
Battle of Hyderabad (1948). *See* Police Action against Hyderabad
Bayly, C. A., 34
Bazigar, 148–49
Bengal: Dalits and Muslims *versus* caste Hindus in, 139–40; Partition in Punjab compared, 162; population exchanges in, 120; Tebhaga movement in, 193
Berar, Nizam of Hyderabad's contention over, 19–21, 23–24, 27, 29, 40, 44, 50, 59–60, 67–68
Beverley, Eric, 15, 35–36, 46
Bhagavan, Manu, 97, 110
Bhave, Vinoba, 218
Bhim, Kumaram, 199, 230
Bhonsle military school, Nasik, 98
Bhoodan movement, 218
Bhopal: contemplating independent sovereignty, 11; *nawab* of, 66–67
Bindu, D. G., 106
blockade, economic, on Hyderabad, 4, 45, 68, 93, 104, 110, 114–15, 281n237
Blunt, Wilfred Scawen, 47
border camps, in Police Action against Hyderabad, 88, 90, 94, 106–7
Boundary Commission, 128
Brass, Paul, 131, 132
BTR. *See* Ranadive, B. T.
burrakatha, 191

Butalia, Urvashi, *The Other Side of Silence*, 160
Butler (Indian States) Committee, 25–26

Cabinet Mission Plan (1946), 54, 56–58, 60–61, 66, 67, 267n228
Cariappa, K. M., 207, 210, 213, 219
castes and caste system: criminal convicts, tribes, and castes, 134, 148–50, 230–31, 241; division of Punjab and, 130, 134, 138–47; Scheduled Castes and Scheduled Tribes, 130, 134, 139–50, 227, 229, 241–42, 307n91; Telangana revolution and, 183, 186–87. *See also specific castes and outcastes*
Central Hindu Military Education Society, 98
Chamar community, 138, 141, 142, 144, 287n76
Chamber of Princes, 23, 24–25, 56, 66–67
Chand, Amir, 167
Chatterjee, Partha, 223
Chaudhuri, J. N., 76, 77, 82–84, 88–90, 92, 117, 121, 126, 200, 207
Cheesewright, Maurice, 110
Chelmsford, Viceroy, 22, 40
Chenchus, 199, 240, 242, 244, 304n19
chillarollu in Telangana, 186, 187, 188, 190, 195, 219
Christianity: converts to, 130, 140, 144–45, 150, 183; national status of Christians in division of Punjab, 130, 134, 139, 140, 141, 144–45
Chuhra community, 138, 141, 142, 143, 287n76
Churchill, Winston, 56, 72, 270n288
Cold War, 72
"communalism" in India, 42, 46, 97, 119
communism and communists in India: first universal franchise election and, 220–23; Nehru and, 182, 194, 197, 204, 220, 222, 250; Patel's concerns over, 125–26, 194, 195, 283n292;

Police Action against Hyderabad and, 85, 88; Telangana revolution and, 7, 85, 125–26, 184–85, 187, 189–200, 203–5, 208–12, 219, 220, 222–23, 238; tribal camps of Telangana and, 228, 230, 232, 305n33. *See also* Communist Party of India; Maoism, Indian

Communist Party of India (CPI), 251; Andhra Provincial Committee, 7, 192, 193, 196, 198, 199; first universal franchise election and, 220–23; sovereignty in Hyderabad and, 4, 45, 88, 92, 94, 126; Telangana revolution and, 7, 8, 184–85, 186–88, 192–95, 197–99, 204, 206, 211, 214, 215, 219, 220–23; tribal camps of Telangana and, 226, 230, 235, 240; unilateral withdrawal from Telangana revolution, 8, 185, 199, 214, 222, 230

Comrades Association, 193

Constituent Assembly: independence resolution (1946), 61; juridical and institutional basis of Indian democracy developed by, 7; on "land question," 218; Nehru on princely states failing to join, 62; origins and establishment of, 33–34, 53, 60, 75; Police Action against Hyderabad and, 87; princely states and republican turn of, 4, 33–34, 53, 75; in provincial elections of 1946, 61; Scheduled Castes of Punjab and, 146; Telangana revolution and, 205; on transformation of Raj into Republic, 250

Constitution of 1919, 26

Constitution of 1935, 28, 33, 58, 64, 95

Constitution of 1950, 13, 73, 77, 205, 211–12, 218, 241

conversion: of abducted women, 133, 155–56, 171, 180; to Christianity, 130, 140, 144–45, 150; of Dalits to Sikhism, Christianity, or Islam, 140, 144–45; honor killings/suicides in Punjab, 172, 176–77; Hyderabad, forced conversion to Islam under Nizam of, 99, 114, 116, 118; national status of converts to Islam in Punjab, 134, 135, 140, 141, 144, 149, 150, 288n81; Scheduled Castes in Punjab, forced conversions to Islam of, 144; to Sikhism, 140, 142, 145

Coupland, Reginald, 11, 127

CPI. *See* Communist Party of India

criminal convicts, tribes, and castes, 134, 148–50, 230–31, 241

Criminal Tribes Act (1871), 230

Cripps proposals (1942), 54, 55–56, 67

Curzon, Lord, 18, 21

dalams, in Telangana revolution, 184, 188, 192, 198, 199, 201, 203, 209–10, 222, 230, 238, 240, 243, 307n79

Dalits: in Bengal, 139–40; in Constitution of 1950, 242; conversion to Sikhism, Christianity, or Islam by, 140, 144–45; division of Punjab and, 138–47, 148, 153, 157; in Hyderabad, 91, 139; resettlement of, 145–50; Telangana revolution and, 183, 186, 187; treatment of abducted women compared, 153

Dange, S. A., 220, 221

Das, Taraknath, 72

Das, Veena, 151, 155, 156, 160

Datla, Kavita, 18, 35

Deccani nationalism, in Hyderabad, 37–38

democracy: Adivasi articulation of, 240; majoritarianism and, 34, 43; Maoism in India and, 8; Partition and, 2; princely states and republican turn, 3–4, 27, 29–34, 53, 75; Telangana revolution and, 6–7, 8, 183, 185, 196, 198, 204–6, 215–20, 223–24; violence shaping historical development of, 1, 2, 7, 185, 223–24

Democrat (newspaper), 108

Desai, Morarji, 106, 277n166

Deva, Narendra, 195

development, ideology of: Punjab evacuees and nation-building projects, 130, 136–38; Telangana counterinsurgency and, 213–14; tribal camps of Telangana and, 214, 227–28, 232–36; tribal people in modern India and, 243–44
Devji, Faisal, 48
Direct Action Resolution/Direct Action Day (1946), 61, 267n228
doras/dora rajyam in Telangana, 186–91, 201, 208, 209, 222
Dube, S. C., 117–18
Dutt, R. P., 220

Eagleton, Clyde, 72
East India Company, 15, 17, 18
East Punjab Liaison Agency (EPLA): division of Punjab and, 5, 6, 133–35, 144, 145, 147, 150, 153; testimonial narratives collected by, 161, 166, 169, 172, 173
economic blockade on Hyderabad, 4, 45, 68, 93, 104, 110, 114–15, 281n237
Edward VII (King of England), 21
Edward VIII (Prince of Wales/King of England), 23, 27, 263–64n126
El Edroos, Syed Ahmed, 76, 270n2
elections in India and Telangana revolution, 220–23
Elwin, Verrier, 231, 236
EPLA. *See* East Punjab Liaison Agency
ethnic cleansing, 5, 61, 127, 132, 177

Fact Finding Organization (FFO), 159, 160, 161, 174, 181
Federation of India: as codification/institutionalization of imperial regime of sovereignty, 52–53, 74; from "distant ideal" to immediate practical concern, 26–27; ethno-religious proposals for reorganization of, 48–51; failure of (1935–39), 28–35, 64–65, 74; in interwar political imaginaries, 3–4, 22, 26; Partition and, 64–65; princely states and, 24–27, 29–31
FFO (Fact Finding Organization), 159, 160, 161, 174, 181
Frankel, Francine, 217
Fürer-Haimendorf, Christoph von, 229

Gandhi, Mahatma: accusing Nizam of Hyderabad of trying to convert Hindus, 99; assassination of, 98, 111, 114, 123; Berar, contention over, 24, 68; evacuees and refugees writing to, 165; fast unto death of, 139; first India-wide mobilization and boycott (1922), 23; home guard concept and, 111; on Hyderabad State Congress, 95; Indian National Congress, influence on, 30; Munshi expelled from Congress by, 110; Nehru and, 119–20; on princely states, 39
Gandhians, 119, 154, 184, 200, 217, 237, 251
gender issues: honor killings/suicides in Punjab, 172, 176–77; Maoism in India and, 188; Police Action against Hyderabad, effects on women of, 83, 87, 90, 116, 117; Telangana's *sangham*, women's participation in, 188, 191; village administration and, 221. *See also* abducted and recovered women
George V (King of England), 39
George VI (King of England), 72
Ghate, S. V., 220, 221
Ghosh, A. K., 220, 221
Ghurye, G. S., 236–37
Godse, Nathuram, 97–98
Goldwalkar, M. S., 101–2
Gonds, 230, 242, 304n19
Gopalan, A. K., 222
Gorky, Maxim, *Mother*, 191
Gour, Raj Bahadur, 193, 211–12, 294n10
Government of India Act (1919), 21–22

Government of India Act (1935), 3, 22, 27, 29, 30, 31, 39, 52, 74, 139
Great Calcutta Killings (1946), 132
Grigson, W. V., 183
guerrilla *dalams*, in Telangana revolution, 184, 188, 192, 198, 199, 201, 203, 209–10, 222, 230, 238, 240, 243, 307n79
Guha, Ranajit, 7, 194
Gupta, G. S., 97, 106, 277n166

Haksar, K. N., 27
Hardinge, Lord, 18
Haripura Resolution (1938), 95
Haroon, Sir Abdullah, 51, 58
Hasan, Syed Abid, *Whither Hyderabad?*, 38
Hassan, Sayyid Zafarul, and Muhammad Afzal Husain Qadri, *The Problem of Indian Muslims and Its Solution*, 50
Hindu (newspaper), 110
Hindu Mahasabha: in Bengal, 140; Police Action against Hyderabad and, 93, 96–98, 101, 105, 109, 110, 113; Ram Sena, 131; sovereignty claims of Hyderabad and, 4, 33, 45, 46, 60
Hindu Outlook (newspaper), 97
Hindustan Times, 101
Hobbes, Thomas, 130, 131, 151
home guards: in Police Action against Hyderabad, 111–15; in Telangana counterinsurgency, 208–10, 222, 238
honor killings/suicides in Punjab, 172, 176–77
Imam Hussain, 70
Hyderabad, Partition, and Hindu-Muslim question, 3–4, 46–66; modernization in Hyderabad and, 42–46; Muslim state, Hyderabad viewed as, 46–52, 69, 75; Nizam's declaration of sovereignty and, 11, 46; Partition and the princely states, 52–66; Police Action against Hyderabad and, 4, 52, 53, 63, 75, 99–104, 114; relations between India and Pakistan and, 68–69; security concerns, Police Action justified by, 99–104
Hyderabad, sovereignty of, 2–5, 10–75, 249; after WWI, 18, 19, 21–27; Azad Hyderabad, Nizam's quest for, 66–70, 71, 73, 93, 115, 117; Berar, contention over, 19–21, 23–24, 27, 29, 40, 44, 50, 59–60, 67–68; "communalism" of British India, viewed as free from, 42, 46; Deccani nationalism and, 37–38; failure of federation and, 28–35; geopolitics of, 10, 11, 19–21, 20, 23–24, 27, 85–93, *86*, *91*; incorporation/ dissolution into India, 70–75, *74*, 268n246; landholding elites and, 37, 41; modernization efforts, 23, 35–46; Nizam's declaration of sovereignty, 2–3, 10–12, 14, 63, 69, 106; paramountcy, concept of, 3, 12–14, 17–18, 21, 24–26, 28, 32, 37, 56–58, 63, 65–66, 71; popular sovereignty in, 4–5, 27, 44, 46, 49, 123–25; population exchange proposals of 1930s in, 100; Punjab compared, 82, 100, 128; under Raj and imperial constitution (to 1935), 12–27, *13*, *16*, 20; *satyagraha* (1938–39) against, 3, 33, 37, 43–44, 46, 75, 92, 94–98, 109, 187–88; United Nations, appeal to, 4, 12, 14, 63, 68, 72–73, 76, 77–78, 259n9. *See also* Nizam of Hyderabad; Police Action against Hyderabad; Telangana revolution
Hyderabad Army, 76, 121, 207, 270–71nn2–3
Hyderabad Commercial Treaty (1802), 27, 68
Hyderabad People's Convention, 37
Hyderabad Reborn (publication), 83, 85–87
Hyderabad Special Tribunals, 211–12
Hyderabad State Congress: Police Action against Hyderabad and, 82, 85, 87, 89–91, 93, 94–97, 105–10, 278nn175–76, 279n186; sovereignty claims of

Hyderabad and, 4, 33, 45, 46, 60; *Thus Fought Marathwada*, 108, 278n176

Iengar, N. N., 232
Imam, Sir Ali, 40
Indian Army: home guard units and, 112; Muslims in, 47; in Police Action against Hyderabad, 4, 76–78, 88, 89, 92, 93, 110, 114, 198, 280–81n234; postwar trials involving, 193; Sikh units in, 92; Telangana revolution and, 126, 198, 202, 206
Indian Express, 100
Indian Independence Act (1947), 12, 53, 63, 66, 67
Indian National Congress: abducted women and, 156–57; Azad Hyderabad and, 67–69; castes/caste system and, 139; division of Punjab and, 128, 131, 132, 156–57; failure of federation and, 31–32, 52–53; Hyderabad State Congress and, 93, 94, 95, 96; on "land question," 216–17; Munshi expelled by Gandhi from, 110; Muslim state, Hyderabad regarded as, 52; on Partition and the princely states, 52–57, 60–66; Police Action against Hyderabad and, 82, 93, 94, 95, 97, 104–5; princely states and republican turn of, 3–4, 27, 29–34, 53, 75; provincial elections of 1937 and, 33, 39; provincial elections of 1946 and, 60–61; *purna swaraj* resolution (1929), 31, 263n98; Quit India Movement (1942) and, 55; sovereignty of state and, 251; Telangana revolution and, 7, 184, 194, 222
Indian States (Protection) Act (1934), 26
Indian States (Butler) Committee, 25–26
Indian Statutory Commission, 26
Instruments of Accession, 13, 28, 37, 65, 67
Inter-Dominion Agreement, 135, 143, 144, 150, 152

International Aryan League. *See* Arya Samaj
Iqbal, Muhammad, 29
Irwin, Lord, 35, 39

Jadhav, R. L., 147, 148
Jain, L. C., 88, 228
Jamiat-Ulama-i-Hind, 51, 87
Jangam, Chinnaiah, 187
Jinnah, Quaid-i-Azam Mohammad Ali: Hyderabad and, 29, 44, 51–52, 58, 61, 64, 69–71, 101, 267n228; Punjab and, 128, 139
Joshi, P. C., 193, 194, 195, 220, 221
Junadagh, 108, 109
June 3 Plan (1947), 53–54, 62–66, 67, 128, 132
Jung, Ali Yavar, 56
Jung, Bahadur Yar (Qaid-e-Millat), 44–45, 97, 99, 265n160
Jung, Nawab Moin Nawaz, 277n162
Jung, Sir Salar, 18, 20, 189

Kabir *(sant)*, 142
Kahn, Paul, 239
Kamalamma (tribal camp resident), 235
kamins, 143, 144, 145, 146, 287n76
Kammas/Andhra Kammas in Telangana, 186–87, 188
Kapila, Shruti, 2, 130, 248
kapus in Telangana, 186, 187–88, 190, 195, 219
Karachi resolution (1931), 31
Kashmir, 11, 70–72, 111, 120, 163
Kaur, Ravinder, 145
Khaksars, 131
Khan, Raja Ghazanfar Ali, 144, 149
Khan, Sikandar Hayar, 58; *The Outlines of a Scheme of Indian Federation*, 49–50
Khan, Sir Shaw Nawaz (*nawab* of Mamdot), 51; *The Confederacy of India*, 50
Khan, Yasmin, 128, 129
Khare, N. B., 113

Kher, B. G., 100, 112–13
Khilafatists, 48
Khilnani, Sunil, 123, 216
Khosla, G. D., 159–60, 161, 174
Kisan Dals, 108, 278n175
Kisan Sabha, 194–95
Komariah, Doddi, 182, 189, 192
Koya, 214, 225, 226, 229–34, 238–43, 298n85, 305n33, 307n79
Koya "tiger squads," 238, 307n79
Kripalani, Acharya, 102

Lahore Resolution (1940), 34, 52
Lambada (Banjaras), 191, 214, 225–26, 230–32, 235, 240–43, 307n91
land question: Telangana revolution and, 183, 186–90, 196–97, 208, 215–20, 221–22, 302n177; tribal people and, 221–22, 239–41
Latif, Syed Abdul, 51, 100; *The Muslim Problem in India*, 49
Leonard, Karen, 37–38
Linlithgow, Viceroy, 29, 264n126
Lohia, Rammanohar, 101
Lothian, Sir Arthur, 58
Lunje, Abdul Karim Ghudabhai, 117

Maa Bhoomi (film), 191
Madigas, 183
Mahboob Ali Khan, 21
Maine, Henry, 17
Majlis-e-Ittehadul Muslimeen, 43–46, 60, 76, 81, 93, 97, 99, 103, 110, 125
Malas, 183
Manchester Guardian, 114
Mandal, Jogendranath, 139–40
Mantena, Rama, 38
Manto, Saadat Hasan, "Toba Tek Singh," 149
Maoism, Indian: continued development of, 242, 243, 250; Telangana revolution and, 7, 8, 184–85, 188, 192, 193, 196–99, 221, 223–24, 249

Marathas, 17, 18
Marx, Karl, 166
Maududi, Maulana, 47
Mazhabi Sikhs, 142, 143, 144, 145
Megh community, 148
Mehta, Asoka, 195
Mehta, Uday, 131
Menon, Rita, 136
Menon, V. P.: land reform and, 218; Police Action against Hyderabad and, 78, 108, 121; sovereignty of Hyderabad and, 12, 63, 65, 66, 68–69, 260n15, 268n242; on Telangana revolution, 126
Military Evacuation Organizations (MEOs), 133–35, 144, 145, 146, 152, 153, 284n24
military units: division of Punjab and proliferation of, 131–32; in Telangana counterinsurgency, 207–10, 298n98, 299n121. *See also* home guards; *specific groups*
Ministry of Relief and Rehabilitation, 143, 146, 152
minorities pact, 139
Mohuiddin, Makhdoom, 193
Moid, M. A., 44
Monckton, Sir Walter, 59, 277n162
Montagu, Edwin, 21–22, 39, 40
Mookerjee, Syama Prasad, 101
Moonje, B. S., 98, 275n117
Moore, R. J., 262n72
Mountbatten, Lord, 62–63, 65–69, 101, 113, 126, 277n162
Mughal Empire, 10, 17, 24, 37, 46, 47
Mullik, B. N., 232
Munshi, K. M., 95, 109–10, 114–15, 125–26, 229; *Report on the Razakars of Hyderabad*, 110
Muslim League: division of Punjab and, 128, 132, 139; Hyderabad and, 29–30, 44, 50–53, 60–62, 64, 69, 75; Indian minority, Muslims as, 119; National Guards, 131; SCF (Scheduled Castes

Federation) and, 139–40; in testimonial narratives from Punjab, 175–76

Namboodiripad, E. M. S., 221
Nanjappa, V., 200–201, 202–3, 207, 209, 211, 213–14, 219, 229, 235, 244, 298n91
Narasimha Rao, P. V., 94, 223
Narayan, J. P., 108
Narendra, Pandit, 106
Nathu Ram, R. B., 285n27
Nehru, Jawaharlal: China and, 249–50; Churchill on, 72; communists and, 182, 194, 197, 204, 220, 222, 250; Constituent Assembly, demand for, 33–34; *The Discovery of India*, 55, 204–5; on division of Punjab, 134–35; evacuees/refugees and, 163, 165; in first universal franchise election, 223; on home guard units, 111–12, 113; on international standing of India as secular state, 282n259; as key thinker and practitioner of sovereignty and democracy, 7; on "land question," 215–16, 218; on Muslim minority, 119–21, 282n263; nation-building projects under, resettled persons recruited for, 130, 136–38; on paramountcy, 63; on Partition, 55, 62, 63, 64, 172–73; Police Action against Hyderabad and, 78–79, 80–81, 83, 101, 103–4, 110–15, 117, 119–25; princely states and republican turn of, 4, 31–34; Scheduled Castes of Punjab and, 146; socialism and, 194; on sovereignty in Hyderabad, 11, 69; Telangana revolution and, 204–6, 208, 211, 222; on transformation of Raj into Republic, 247, 248, 250, 251; on tribal people, 231
Neogy, K. C., 147
Nizam of Hyderabad (Osman Ali Khan): after WWI, 22–24; assassination attempt against, 98; Azad Hyderabad, quest for, 66–70, 71, 73, 93, 115, 117; Azad Hyderabad and, 67–70; Berar, contention over, 19–21, 23–24, 27, 29, 40, 44, 59–60, 67–68; federation, resistance to, 29; forced conversion to Islam under, accusations of, 99, 114, 116, 118; Hindu-Muslim question and, 5, 45–46; under imperial constitution, 17–21; incorporation/dissolution of Hyderabad into India and, 71–73, 75; map of dominions, 20; modernization efforts of, 23, 35–46; Muslim state, regarded as leader of, 56–52, 69, 75; Partition and, 56, 58–60, 63; Police Action against Hyderabad and, 77, 93–94, 98, 99–101, 103, 109; sovereignty, declaration of, 2–3, 10–12, 14, 63, 69, 106; Telangana revolution and, 183, 184, 186, 188–92, 198, 199, 212, 214, 219, 221, 249; tribal people of Telangana and, 229, 230; United Nations, appeal to, 4, 12, 14, 63, 68, 72–73, 76, 77–78
Nizam's Subjects League, 38, 95

Omvedt, Gail, 91
Osman Ali Khan. *See* Nizam of Hyderabad
Osmania University, Hyderabad, 3, 35, 38, 47, 49, 94
"Other Backward Classes," 186, 236, 307n91

Pandey, Gyanendra, 115, 117, 146, 173
Panikkar, K. M., 82
paramountcy, concept of, 3, 12–14, 17–18, 21, 24–26, 28, 32, 37, 56–58, 63, 65–66, 71
Parishath, Andhra Saraswatha, 182
Partition and Hindu-Muslim question: castes and caste system, 130, 134, 138–47; as civil war, 130, 132; Federation of India and, 64–65; fifth columnists and foreign nationals, Muslims regarded

as, 100, 101, 113–14, 120; June 3 Plan (1947), 53–54, 62–66, 67, 128, 132; majoritarianism and, 34, 43; map of Hindu and Muslim majority areas and princely states before Partition, *13*; place of Muslim minority in India and, 115–25, 128, 139; princely states and, 3, 29, 52–66; territory lost to India by, 268n242; violence as constitutive in creation of India and Pakistan, 2, 127–29. *See also* conversion; Hyderabad, Partition, and Hindu-Muslim question; Punjab, division of; testimonial narratives of Partition in Punjab

Patel, Kamla, 154, 178–79

Patel, Sardar Vallabhbhai: communism/ communists and, 125–26, 194, 195, 283n292; death of, 211; as key thinker and practitioner of sovereignty and democracy, 7; on "land question," 217, 218; on Muslim minority, 119; Police Action against Hyderabad and, 78, 80–82, 84–85, 100–106, 110, 113, 114, 121, 123–26, 277n162; on sovereignty claims of Hyderabad, 11–12, 52, 62, 63–66, 259n5, 259n9, 270n288; Telangana revolution and, 126, 206; on transformation of Raj into Republic, 247, 250, 251; *White Paper on Hyderabad,* 79, 99, 121

Patwardhan, Achyut, 108

PBF (Punjab Boundary Force), 132–33, 284n22

People's Democratic Front (PDF), 223

Pickthall, Marmaduke, 48

"Plan Balkan" (1947), 62

Police Action against Hyderabad (1948), 4–5, 76–126; amnesty following, 84–85, 122–24, 273n51; arrests of Muslims preceding, 102; Azad Hyderabad, end of idea of, 70; border camps, 88, 90, 94, 106–7, 280–81n234; civil insurrection campaign preceding, 104–11, *107*; concluding political, criminal, and administrative actions, 121–25, 282n265; creating support for, 99–104; economic blockade preceding, 4, 45, 68, 93, 104, 110, 114–15, 281n237; geopolitics of, 85–93, *86, 91*; home guard units in, 111–15; mobilization of Hindu nationalists for, 93–99; Muslim minority's place in India and, 115–25; Partition and Hindu/Muslim question, 4, 52, 53, 63, 75, 99–104; perpetrators of violence in, 89–92; propaganda relating to, 102–3, 110, 114, 278n175; prosecution of, 76–78; reactions to, 78–80; refugees and, 88, 102, 276n129, 276n132; security concerns as justification for, 99–104; Telangana revolution and, 88, 125–26, 184–86, 188, 191–93, 198–203, 207; Underlain report on, 81, 82–87, 89, 90, 92, 116; United Nations appeal and, 72–73, 76, 77–78; violence in, 79–93, 105, 109, 111, 115–18, 121–24, 271n24

Poona Pact, 139

popular sovereignty: Congress's demand for, 34; in Hyderabad, 4–5, 27, 44, 46, 49, 123–25; Indian Republicanism, as basic ingredient of, 249; in Telangana revolution, 6, 182–84 (*See also* sangham)

population exchanges: in Bengal, 120; Hyderabad, proposals of 1930s in, 100; in Punjab, 120, 128–30, 132–36, 284n24

praja rajyam (people's rule), 6, 183

Prasad, Rajendra, 50, 182, 241

Preventive Detention Act (1950), 205, 211, 226

princely states: Chamber of Princes, 23, 24–25, 56, 66–67; in Constitution of 1950, 13; federation of India and, 24–27, 29–31; under imperial constitution, 15–17; incorporation and

dissolution of, 64–65, 73, 268n242, 268n246; Instruments of Accession confirming sovereignty of, 28; Junadagh, 108, 109; maps of, *13, 16*; paramountcy, concept of, 3, 12–14, 17–18, 21, 24–26, 28, 32, 37, 56–58, 63, 65–66, 71; Partition/Hindu-Muslim question and, 3, 29, 52–66; republican turn of Indian National Congress and, 3–4, 27, 29–34, 53, 75; *satyagrahas* against, 3, 32, 75; Sikh states and Partition, 131. *See also* Hyderabad, sovereignty of
provincial elections of 1937, 28, 29, 33, 34, 39, 48
provincial elections of 1946, 60–61
Punjab, division of, 5–6, 127–58; castes and caste system, 130, 134, 138–50; evacuee, transit, and refugee camps, 130, 135–37; Hyderabad compared, 82, 100, 128; ideal national subjects, Punjabi refugees in India viewed as, 147–48; liaison agencies and officers, 5, 6, 133–35, 143–45, 147, 149, 151–53, 285n30 (*See also* East Punjab Liaison Agency); national status of subaltern groups, 130, 133–35, 138; nation-building projects, resettled persons recruited for, 130, 136–38; natural border between Indian and Pakistani Punjab, lack of, 127; number of persons moved, 284nn24–25; "pocket" clearances, 135, 145, 153, 285n35, 288n81; population exchange in, 120, 128–30, 132–36, 284n24; resettlement of Scheduled Castes, 145–50; social heterogeneity of, 127–28, 129–30; sovereignty of new states and division of, 129, 130–38, 157; violence and, 5–6, 127–33, 157–58. *See also* abducted and recovered women; conversion; testimonial narratives of Partition in Punjab
Punjab Alienation of Land Acts (1901 and 1907), 145

Punjab Boundary Force (PBF), 132–33, 284n22
purna swaraj resolution (1929), 31, 263n98

Qadri, Muhammad Afzal Husain, 51; *The Problem of Indian Muslims and Its Solution* (with Sayyid Zafarul Hassan), 50
Qaid-e-Millat (Bahadur Yar Jung), 44–45, 97, 99, 265n160
Quit India Movement (1942), 55, 108, 194

Radcliffe, Cyril, 128, 132
Rahman, Maulvi Hifzur, 87, 90–91, 122
Rahmat Ali, Choudhry, 48–49
Raj to Republic, 1–9, 247–52. *See also* democracy; Partition; Punjab; sovereignty; Telangana; violence; *specific entries at* Hyderabad
Rajagopalachari, C., 63, 222
Rajah, M. C., 151
Rajeswara Rao, Chandra, 192, 196, 221, 226
Ram, Mangoo, 141
Ram, Mohan, 176, 177
Ramayana, 142
Ranadive, B. T. (BTR), 195–96, 297n64; *Political Thesis*, 195
Ranga, N. G., 195
Rao, Chandrasekhar, 196
Rao, D. V., 184, 186, 190, 192, 196, 198, 221
Rao, Hanumantha, 196
Rao, Narsing, 87, 91, 105
Rashtriya Swayamsevak Sangh (RSS): Police Action against Hyderabad and, 98, 101–2, 109–10, 111, 114, 120, 131, 275n117; Punjab and, 131
Ravidas *(sant)* and Ravidasis, 139, 142
Razakars: Police Action against Hyderabad and, 83–84, 87–94, 99–101, 103, 104, 108, 110, 113, 117, 122–26,

212, 271n3, 278nn175–76; sovereignty of Hyderabad and, 45, 76; Telangana revolution and, 184, 192, 212, 213
Razvi, Qasim, 45, 81, 90, 125
Reading, Viceroy, 21, 23–24, 25
Reddy, A. R., 202
Reddy, Baddam Yella, 190, 199, 223
Reddy, Rapaka Ramachandra, 182, 189
Reddy, Ravi Narayan, 88, 185, 187, 188, 190, 199, 220, 223, 296n43
Reddy castes in Telangana, 186–87, 188
Rehman, Maulvi, 87
Report of the Congress Agrarian Reforms Committee (1949), 217
Robeson, Paul, 213
Round Table Conferences, 26–27, 39, 139
RSS. *See* Rashtriya Swayamsevak Sangh
Russian Revolution, 191, 196

sangham in Telangana: concept, formation, and activities of, 182–83, 184, 187–89, 191–93; elections and, 221, 222; land distribution issues and, 187–89, 215, 218–19; Police Action against Hyderabad/counterinsurgency and, 198–203, 206–8; tribal camps and, 225, 226, 228–30, 235, 238–40
Sanghatana, Stree Shakti, 235
satyagraha: against Hyderabad (1939–39), 3, 33, 37, 43–44, 46, 75, 92, 94–98, 109, 187–88; against princely states, 3, 32, 75; Quit India Movement (1942), 55, 108, 194
Savarkar, V. D., 97
Scheduled Castes and Scheduled Tribes, 130, 134, 139–50, 227, 229, 241–42, 307n91. *See also specific types,* e.g. Dalits
Scheduled Castes Federation (SCF), 139–40
Server-ul-Mulk, 47
Shah, Alpa, 228
Shakir, M. A., 118
Shani, Ornit, 227
Shaukat Ali, 48

Sherwani, H. K., 43
Shukla, Ravi Shankar, 113–14, 120
Sikhs: abducted/recovered women and, 154; Akalis, 142–43; Dalit conversion to Sikhism, 140, 142, 145; Mazhabis, 142–43, 144, 145; princely states and Partition, 131; Punjab, evacuation from, 163, 288n89; Singh Sabha, 140
Simla Conference (1945), 56
Simon, John, 26
Singh, St. Nihal, 36
Singh Sabha, 140
siris, 143
Sitaramayya, Pattabhi, 79–80
Skaria, Ajay, 231–32
social contract, 6, 131, 151, 157, 161–66, 172, 238
socialism: sovereignty of Hyderabad and, 31, 42, 66, 95, 101, 102, 108–9; Telangana revolution and, 184, 187, 194–96, 205–6, 215–17, 223, 249
Socialist Party: Police Action against Hyderabad and, 82, 93, 105, 107, 108, 278n178; sovereignty claims of Hyderabad and, 4, 31, 45, 60
sovereignty: abduction/recovery of women and, 151, 152, 156–57; division of Punjab and, 129, 130–38, 157; majority/minority populations and development of, 115–25; national and non-national conceptions of, 3–4; Nizam of Hyderabad's declaration of, 2–3, 10–12, 14, 63, 69, 106 (*See also* Hyderabad, sovereignty of); paramountcy, concept of, 3, 12–14, 17–18, 21, 24–26, 28, 32, 37, 56–58, 63, 65–66, 71; of princely states, after WWI, 18, 19, 21–27; of princely states, Instruments of Accession confirming, 28; Raj's regime of, 3, 24; social contract and, 6, 131, 151, 157, 161–66, 172, 238; Telangana revolution and, 202–2, 204–5, 208–9, 213; testimonial narratives of Partition in Punjab and,

161–62; tribal camps of Telangana and, 227, 234, 236–42; violence and postcolonial regime of, 1–2, 7, 75, 82, 130–32, 161–62, 181, 185, 227, 238, 248–52; vulnerability and suffering as authorization of, 161–62. *See also* popular sovereignty

"Spring Thunder" (1967), 8, 223
Stalin, Joseph, 191, 221
States Reorganization Act (1956), 49
street sweepers, 143
student activism: in civil insurrection preceding Police Action against Hyderabad, 108–9; in Telangana revolution, 193
subaltern groups: division of Punjab and national status of, 130, 133–35, 138; Scheduled Castes, 130, 134, 139–50 (*See also specific types*, e.g. Dalits); testimonial narratives of, 166. *See also* abducted and recovered women; conversion
Subbarayan, P., 106, 277n166
Sundar, Nandini, 227
Sundarayya, P., 87–88, 182, 185, 192, 196, 218, 221, 226, 298n85
Sunderlal, Pandit, and Sunderlal report, 81, 82–87, 89, 90, 92, 116
Suneetha, A., 44
Swamiji, Mahatma Narayan, 75n116, 98
Swarajyam, Mallu, 188, 295n25
Syed Ahman Khan, 46

Tara Davi (maharana of Jammu and Kashmir), 171
tattooing, ritualized, 116–17
Tebhaga movement in Bengal, 193
Tehsildar, Mohn Akbar Khan, 180
Telangana Praja Naya Mandali, 191
Telangana revolution, 6–8, 182–224, 249; communism and, 7, 85, 125–26, 184–85, 187, 189–200, 203–5, 208–12, 219, 220, 222–23, 238; counterinsurgency in, 7–8, 204–14, 218–19; CPI and, 7, 8, 184–85, 186–88, 192–95, 197–99, 204, 206, 211, 214, 215, 219, 220–23, 226, 230, 235, 240; democracy and, 6–7, 8, 183, 185, 196, 198, 204–6, 215–20, 223–24; first universal franchise election in, 220–23; as Indian Yan'an, 7, 8, 94, 184, 193–98, 223; land distribution issues in, 183, 186–90, 196–97, 208, 215–20, 221–22, 302n177; Maoism in India and, 7, 8, 184–85, 188, 192, 193, 196–99, 221, 223–24, 249; Nizam of Hyderabad and, 183, 184, 186, 188–92, 198, 199, 212, 214, 219, 221, 229, 230, 249; organizations active in, 42, 45; pledge used in, 294n10; Police Action against Hyderabad and, 88, 125–26, 184–86, 188, 191–93, 198–203, 207; popular sovereignty in, 6, 182–84; Razakars in, 94, 103; revolutionary process in, 6–7, 45–46, 60, 71, 182–84, 189–93; socialism and, 184, 187, 194–96, 205–6, 215–17, 223; socioeconomic demographics of, 186–89; sovereignty of Indian state and, 202–2, 204–5, 208–9, 213; unilateral withdrawal of CPI from, 8, 185, 199, 214, 222, 230; violence and, 211–12, 251. *See also* Adivasi communities in Telangana; *sangham* in Telangana; tribal camps of Telangana
Telangana Special Area, 200–201, 206, 210, 211–13, 229, 241
testimonial narratives of Partition in Punjab, 159–81; of abducted and recovered women, 161, 166–67, 169–72, 174–80; documentary evidence of, 159–62; new social contract in, 161–66, 172; sovereignty and citizenship, testimonial statements and, 161; state appropriation and shaping of, 166–73; subaltern groups, narratives of, 166; truth/factuality and subjective character of, 173–80; virtuous victims, narrators always assuming role of,

169–72, 180; vulnerability, suffering, and violence, 161–66, 172–73, 180–81
Thankkar, A. V., 237
Thirumali, Inukonda, 186
Thus Fought Marathwada (Hyderabad State Congress), 108, 278n176
Times of India, 114, 200, 207
Tipu Sultan, 17
Tirtha, Swami Ramananda, 78, 89, 94, 106, 192, 235, 277n166
tribal camps of Telangana, 225–46; "the Cage," 207; civilization/modernization and, 231–32, 244; colonial landscape, tribal reclamation colonies as feature of, 230–31; communism and, 228, 230, 232, 305n33; as counterinsurgency/security tactic, 227, 228–32, 238; development ideology and, 214, 227–28, 232–36; fate of, 242–43; forced relocation to, 225–26; as ideological paradigm, 228, 242–46; land question and, 221–22, 239–41; legal status of, 227, 241–42; paternalistic protectionism and, 228, 231; purpose of, 226–27; resistance of tribal people to, 242–43; *sangham* and, 225, 226, 228–30, 235, 238–40; sovereignty and citizenship, incorporating tribes into, 227, 234, 236–42; "squatters," tribal people viewed as, 239–40; violence and, 228, 235–36, 239
tribal people: as colonial category, 236–37; criminal convicts, tribes, and castes, 134, 148–50, 230–31, 241; development ideology, modern application of, 243–44; forest use by, 221–22, 240–41; national status of, in division of Punjab, 130, 134, 150; racial determinism and, 244; Scheduled Tribes, 227, 229, 241–42, 307n91. *See also specific groups*
Truman, Harry, 72

Umri Bank Affair, 109
"united front" strategy, 191, 194
United Nations: on Hyderabad, 4, 12, 14, 63, 68, 72–73, 76, 77–78, 259n9; on Kashmir, 11
Untouchable castes, 139

Vaidya, Kashinath Rao, 101
Valmiki, 142
Vellodi, M. K., 88, 121, 207, 211, 233, 301n170
Venkatarangayya, M., 43
Venkatswamy, M. P., 108
vetti in Telangana, 183, 187, 190, 191, 201, 209
violence: constitutive of Partition and creation of India and Pakistan, 2, 127–29; democracy in India, shaping historical development of, 1, 2, 7, 185, 223–24; in division of Punjab, 5–6, 127–33, 157–58; in Hyderabad, 4–5, 75; new social contract and, 162–66; in Police Action against Hyderabad, 79–93, 105, 109, 111, 115–18, 121–24, 271n24; sovereignty, postcolonial regime of, 1–2, 7, 75, 82, 130–32, 161–62, 181, 185, 227, 238, 248–52; in Telangana revolution and counterinsurgency, 211–12, 251; tribal camps of Telangana and, 228, 235–36, 239; vulnerability and suffering in Punjab, political significance of, 161–66, 172–73, 180–81

Wavell, Viceroy, 56
White Paper on Hyderabad, 79, 99, 103, 121
Willingdon, Viceroy, 27

Yusuf, S. S., 221

Zamindar, Vazira, 129
zamindari abolition, 216, 217, 219

Also Published in the
SOUTH ASIA IN MOTION SERIES

The Greater India Experiment: Hindutva Becoming and the Northeast
  Arkotong Longkumer (2020)

Nobody's People: Hierarchy as Hope in a Society of Thieves
  Anastasia Piliavsky (2020)

Brand New Nation: Capitalist Dreams and Nationalist Designs in Twenty-First-Century India
  Ravinder Kaur (2020)

Partisan Aesthetics: Modern Art and India's Long Decolonization
  Sanjukta Sunderason (2020)

Dying to Serve: the Pakistan Army
  Maria Rashid (2020)

In the Name of the Nation: India and Its Northeast
  Sanjib Baruah (2020)

Faithful Fighters: Identity and Power in the British Indian Army
  Kate Imy (2019)

Paradoxes of the Popular: Crowd Politics in Bangladesh
  Nusrat Sabina Chowdhury (2019)

The Ethics of Staying: Social Movements and Land Rights Politics in Pakistan
  Mubbashir A. Rizvi (2019)

Mafia Raj: The Rule of Bosses in South Asia
  Lucia Michelutti, Ashraf Hoque, Nicolas Martin, David Picherit, Paul Rollier, Arild Ruud and Clarinda Still (2018)

The authorized representative in the EU for product safety and compliance is:
Mare Nostrum Group
B.V Doelen 72
4831 GR Breda
The Netherlands

www.ingramcontent.com/pod-product-compliance
Lightning Source LLC
Chambersburg PA
CBHW030604230426
43661CB00053B/1840